The Theology
of the Reformed Confessions

COLUMBIA SERIES IN REFORMED THEOLOGY

The Columbia Series in Reformed Theology represents a joint commitment of Columbia Theological Seminary and Westminster John Knox Press to provide theological resources for the church today.

The Reformed tradition has always sought to discern what the living God revealed in scripture is saying and doing in every new time and situation. Volumes in this series examine significant individuals, events, and issues in the development of this tradition and explore their implications for contemporary Christian faith and life.

This series is addressed to scholars, pastors, and laypersons. The Editorial Board hopes that these volumes will contribute to the continuing reformation of the church.

EDITORIAL BOARD

Shirley Guthrie, Columbia Theological Seminary

George Stroup, Columbia Theological Seminary

B. A. Gerrish, University of Chicago and Union Theological Seminary and Presbyterian School of Christian Education

Amy Plantinga Pauw, Loiusville Presbyterian Theological Seminary

Donald K. McKim, Westminster John Knox Press

Columbia Theological Seminary wishes to express its appreciation to the following churches for supporting this joint publishing venture:

First Presbyterian Church, Tupelo, Mississippi

First Presbyterian Church, Nashville, Tennessee

Trinity Presbyterian Church, Atlanta, Georgia

Spring Hill Presbyterian Church, Mobile, Alabama

St. Stephen Presbyterian Church, Fort Worth, Texas

COLUMBIA SERIES IN REFORMED THEOLOGY

The Theology
of the Reformed Confessions

1923

KARL BARTH

TRANSLATED AND ANNOTATED BY
DARRELL L. GUDER AND
JUDITH J. GUDER

Westminster John Knox Press
LOUISVILLE • LONDON

Originally published in the German language as *Die Theologie der reformierten Bekenntnisschriften,* Vorlesung Göttingen Sommersemester 1923, by Theologischer Verlag Zürich.

Book and cover design by Drew Stevens

Published by Westminster John Knox Press
Louisville, Kentucky

This book is printed on acid-free paper that meets the American National Standards Institute Z39.48 standard. ∞

PRINTED IN THE UNITED STATES OF AMERICA

03 04 05 06 07 08 09 10 11 — 10 9 8 7 6 5 4 3 2

Library of Congress Cataloging-in-Publication Data is on file at the Library of Congress, Washington, D.C.

ISBN 0-664-22261-7

CONTENTS

PREFACE

On January 29, 1921, Johann Adam Heilmann, who was pastor of the Reformed congregation in Göttingen, Germany, from 1891 to 1920, wrote to his pastoral colleague Karl Barth in the Swiss village of Safenwil:

> For years I have been striving to establish a Reformed professorate in Göttingen. The Reformed Church had five universities and academies at the beginning of the nineteenth century. All of them were taken away from it, and the result is that its scholarly work has remained underdeveloped to an extent that we should be ashamed of. There is insufficient education of the ministers of the Reformed Church, a confusion, in many cases a deadening effect on the Reformed congregations, and great damage to the entire Protestant church! I do not want to recreate something old and past, nor even less conjure up any confessional narrowness, but what I would like is that the charismata that the Lord has given to the Reformed branch of the church should not remain unused, forgotten, and scorned. Reformed Protestantism has a calling and should fulfill it to the blessing of German Christianity.[1]

With these sentences, Heilmann described the meaning and purpose of the Reformed professorate in the theological faculty at Göttingen that was then founded in October 1921, and he invited Barth to become its first incumbent. Heilmann's ultimately successful plan was clearly related to the confessional renewal of the Reformed movement that had begun toward the end of the nineteenth century. This renewal was a reaction, on the one hand, to the widespread liberalism that disavowed confessionalism, and to the widely lamented danger of "Lutheranization" on the other hand. A movement emerged here which, in its reaction to these trends, articulated with notable zeal the importance of preserving "Reformed concerns."[2] The movement was a counterpart to the German Lutheran renaissance that paralleled it and, in a similar way, had its roots in the confessional revival of the nineteenth century. It too devoted itself industriously to the legacy and confession of the "fathers." It also fit well into the context of that time, particularly in the "Young Reformed Movement" with its pronounced antiliberal and conservative stance, a movement that contributed outstanding leadership to the renewal.[3]

With his move to Göttingen in the fall of 1921, Barth encountered this situation without ever having been a part of this movement until then, and lacking any closer acquaintance with it. He came from the world of the Swiss church, in which "our churches continue to call themselves Christian, Evangelical, and Reformed to this very day," but in which

> since the middle of the last century there is neither in its ordination obligations any mention of a particular Reformed confession (as had earlier been the case with the Helvetic Confession of 1562), nor a particular catechism for its instruction of youth (such as earlier the Heidelberg Catechism), nor any commitment to a particular confessional formula (such as the Apostles' Creed) prescribed at its baptisms. The statutory obligations that were once in place had been quickly 'removed' at approximately the same time and in the same breath as the destruction of many an old gate tower and fortification in our cities as they were found to be superfluous and bothersome.[4]

Barth preferred to call this church situation "confessionally *weak*" but not simply "confession*less*."[5]

He had himself critically engaged such churchly liberalism, especially in his first exposition of the *Epistle to the Romans* (1919), which resulted in his call to Göttingen, and then in its second revised version (1922), which appeared after he arrived in Göttingen. But in his writing he had done this in a way that did not relate directly to the substantive expectations connected to the establishment of the Reformed chair in Göttingen. In 1920 he had prevented the inclusion of even the faintest reference to a "confession" in the formulation of the new constitution of the Church of the Canton Argau.[6] Looking back to his transfer to Göttingen, he remarked, "It was not for me a matter of significance that I was Reformed. . . . I was not a confessional Reformed Christian."[7] Now, however, in his new position and sensing his own need to catch up, he devoted himself to his responsibility to teach *Reformed* theology with intense engagement. In the winter of 1921–22, he gave lectures on the Heidelberg Catechism, in the summer of 1922 on the theology of Calvin,[8] in the winter of 1922–23 on the theology of Zwingli, and finally in the summer of 1923 on the theology of the Reformed confessions, the lectures presented in this volume. He prepared himself for these lectures so thoroughly during the preceding semester holidays that he was able to say during the semester, for the first time in his academic career, "The difficulty of preparation has not been that bad up to now."[9] And when the semester labors were over, he reported that these lectures had been a joy to him, together with the course on 1 Corinthians 15 that he conducted at the same time.[10]

There is no doubt that he had expanded his theological learning in his work on Reformed theology. Without anticipating the assessment to be made by the secondary literature, it can be said that his "theology of the Reformed confessions" represented an advance for him—a movement beyond not only the theology of his *Epistle to the Romans* but also that of his brilliant *Theology of Calvin*. One may describe what is new in this fashion: Adolf Schlatter had criticized the second edition of the *Epistle to the Romans* by saying that Barth overlooked that we are "not isolated" readers of Paul but "that we are members of the church."[11] Barth had immediately accepted the objection "attentively and gratefully."[12] The significance of the 1923 lectures lies chiefly in the fact that he attempts here to do away with the theological deficit that he had himself acknowledged and to begin to develop the dimension of the church itself as he thinks through the confessions. It is not without importance, and moreover it is precisely Reformed, that for him "the church" unfolds itself out of the understanding of the confession. Thus, he develops in these lectures the particular structures of dogmatic thought that persisted in the years that followed.

This can be demonstrated with his lecture at the 20th General Assembly of the Reformed Federation on June 3, 1925, in Duisburg-Meiderich, entitled "The Desirability and Possibility of a Universal Reformed Creed."[13] For one thing, this lecture is in large measure a precise summary of his 1923 university lectures. Later, the lecture was incorporated, up to and including literal quotations, in his exposition of the concept of the church's confession in his *Church Dogmatics*.[14] J. F. G. Goeters correctly remarked, speaking of this lecture, that it was "significant as the very first prelude to the Barmen Declaration of 1934."[15] If he is right, then the same judgment applies all the more to the lectures on the Reformed confessions.

It should, however, also be noted that the concept of churchly confession as formed by Barth in his lectures relates critically to the concept of confession as defined by that so-called confessional movement under the banner of the "preservation of Reformed concerns." This became obvious in the negative response to Barth's lecture on "Reformed Doctrine, Its Essence and Task," which he gave at the 19th General Assembly of the Reformed Federation on September 17, 1923, and in which he drew together in a different way the results of his summer lectures.[16] Barth wrote, "My Emden lecture was the voice of a preacher in the wilderness."[17] This impression was no accident. In the Reformed movement of the twenties there was an unresolved tension between two conceptions of confession that were hardly susceptible to harmonization. This is the tension that led from 1933 on to an actual "split," "which divided the Reformed throughout the Church Struggle." This split was between a position of "preserving Reformed concerns" and a position of a Reformed "office of watchman in the service of the entire church."[18] The latter position was Barth's, to which he apparently came in the labors of the summer of 1923. The significance of this dispute reaches far beyond the Reformed camp, however. As E. Wolf has noted, the Confessing Church during the Third Reich was generally burdened by a similar and profound lack of clarity about whether its task was to confess Christ relevantly or to focus upon the doctrinal maintenance of a confessional status.[19] That may well suggest the situation in which Barth's lectures were written at the time, and also the way in which they engaged this context.

In this volume, we have attempted to reconstruct the library, so to speak, with which Barth, at that time, explored the broad and complex field of confessional formation within the Reformed branch of the Reformation. Regarding the technical aspects of this project, it should be noted that, in accordance with the practice of the general edition of Barth's works, we have carried out a reserved orthographical modernization of Barth's writing style in his manuscript, and we have standardized the way in which he wrote the names cited.[20] In the citation of pages where Barth only entered "ff.," we have added the last page number of the passage cited by him. In citations from Calvin's works, we have given not only the volume number in the Corpus Reformatorum but, where possible, also the corresponding location in the *Ioannis Calvini Opera Selecta* (Munich, 1926–1952). In his lectures, Barth used the version of the Lutheran confessions (as far as they are printed there) edited by J. T. Müller (Gütersloh, 1847), and the Reformed confessions in the edition of E. F. K. Müller (Leipzig, 1903). In this edition, we have noted wherever J. T. Müller's collection is cited (=SBLK), but we have also included the corresponding location in the new edition of the *Bekenntnisschriften der evangelisch-lutherischen Kirche* (=BSLK).[21]

Several people have been involved in the preparation of this manuscript for publication. I would like to thank Uwe Lay for his resourceful decoding of a manuscript that is difficult to read, thereby producing a legible typescript. I wish to thank Antje Donker and Thomas Herwig for their help in producing the text and the annotations, and Margret Lessner for the typing of the final manuscript. I thank Dr. Hinrich and Elisabeth Stoevesandt, who have supported the development of this volume at every stage with their accustomed helpfulness. Above all, my appreciation goes to Margit Ernst, who assumed overall responsibility for the preparation of this volume for publication with great and conscientious care as well as expertise and erudition. Wolfram Ehlenbröker tackled the preparation of the indices, for which we are also grateful.

Göttingen, June 1997   Eberhard Busch

TRANSLATORS' PREFACE

It has been both an honor and a challenge to continue the work of Professor Busch's research team in the Institute for Barth Studies at the University of Göttingen and to render their German edition (1998) of Barth's 1923 lectures on the theology of the Reformed confessions into English. Their scholarly detective work has earned them the appreciation of the theological world. They not only made Barth's lecture transcript available in print but provided the critical annotation that allows us to study his lectures in their context—the turbulent twenties, between the end of the World War I and the onset of the Third Reich and World War II.

Professor Busch's preface further clarifies the context of this semester of lectures at the theology faculty in Göttingen. We recommend that the English language reader also review the section in Busch's biography of Karl Barth that describes his professorate in Göttingen (Eberhard Busch, *Karl Barth: His Life from Letters and Autobiographical Texts*, trans. John Bowden [Philadelphia: Fortress Press, 1976], 126ff.). It is important many decades later for the reader to understand the particular kind of Lutheran confessionalism with which Barth was contending in the twenties, particularly in light of the much more constructive Lutheran-Reformed interactions in North America that we enjoy today.

With this book, the reader is "hearing" Barth's lectures. The work was not intended for publication, and it was obviously never edited for publication by the author. One will not find chapters here, but thematic sections that differ greatly in size. The annotations are provided as endnotes, so that the reader may encounter these lectures initially as did the students who attended this course. It is our hope that one will be able to read the book at two levels: at the level of the students as they listened to Barth expound the Reformed tradition, and at the level of the contemporary scholars who relate the lectures to their context both in Barth's own development and in the theological process with which he was interacting. As one aid to such a reading, we have rendered all the languages used by Barth in his lectures into English.

The distinctive character of this work has required that both the German and English editors adopt some practices that depart from the conventional structure of such scholarly works. The parentheses in the text are Barth's; typically he listed the page number before the comma and the line number after the comma; anything in brackets in the text was placed there either by the German editors or the English translators, unless expressly noted. The Latin or other non-German terms used by Barth without quotation marks in the original are rendered here in English in single quotation marks, with the original wording immediately following in brackets. Similarly, terms quoted by Barth are rendered with double quotation marks both in English and inside the brackets. The longer phrases in Latin and French have been moved to the notes, however, so as not to burden the reader by interrupting the text with long bracketed citations.

The italics in the German and English texts render Barth's underlining of his lecture text, obviously for rhetorical emphasis in delivery.

The German editors have also provided, in the margins, the dates on which each lecture was held, which often helps the reader understand the transitions and repetitions in the text.

In the notes, the German bibliographical citations have been carried over into this edition in their original form, with their italicization. We have translated the terms that an English reader will find useful in searching for a source ("edited by," edition number, etc.), and we have rendered volume numbers and pages in the customary English form (e.g., 2:442–695, without "p." or "pp."). The only exception is cross-references to pages and notes within this edition, which are introduced with "p." or "pp." and "n. or nn."

Wherever possible, we have provided citations from published English translations of the works originally cited in German, Latin, or French. These follow the indication "ET"(=English translation). Where we have not found the source, we have provided our own translation. The non-German texts cited in full by the German editors are also provided in the notes. The bibliographical citations of all published English sources are given in the standard format, including their italicization. Following the page numbers, we have placed in square brackets the number of the section or paragraph cited in the source where that is helpful to find the precise wording.

We have preserved the numbering of the German notes so that citations in the German original can readily be found. Where it has been necessary to annotate further, we have added letters in alphabetical order to the original numbers of the German notes (e.g., 122a, 122b).

All of the bibliographical abbreviations used in the German edition have been carried over, and we have added many abbreviations for the English resources. They are listed together in the list of abbreviations.

Biblical citations in English are taken from the New Standard Revised Version.

It is obviously difficult to apply current canons of inclusive language to older texts, especially those translated from German. Our primary concern has been to render Barth's German into English as accurately and yet as idiomatically as possible. Wherever we could do so and both remain true to the original and produce readable English, we have rendered *Mensch* with "human, person, humanity" and used "one" to translate the German impersonal pronoun *man*. We have followed the German original in the gender of pronouns and in language for deity.

We would like to express our appreciation to the editorial board of the Columbia Series in Reformed Theology for their invitation to prepare this English version of Barth's 1923 lectures. We appreciate the gracious and patient support provided by Dr. Donald McKim of Westminster John Knox Press. The resources of three theological libraries have made the research for this English translation possible: the John Bulow Campbell Library of Columbia Theological Seminary, the Pitt Theological Library of Emory University, and the Speer Theological Library of Princeton Theological Seminary. We would like to express our deep appreciation to their professional staffs for the assistance we received in finding the resources, and especially to Dr. Stephen Crocco of the Speer Library at Princeton for his special courtesies.

We are grateful that Professor Margit Ernst, who guided the German edition through to completion, has been our colleague at Columbia Seminary while we have prepared this edition. She provided translations of the Latin texts and has otherwise been a great help when the dictionaries could bring us no further. As we have worked through the German edition, our admiration for the work done by Margit and her colleagues, under the leadership of our good friend, Eberhard Busch, has grown immensely.

Decatur, Georgia, August 2001 Darrell L. Guder
Judith J. Guder

ABBREVIATIONS OF GERMAN
AND ENGLISH RESOURCES

ARG	Archiv für Reformationsgeschichte. Berlin, u.a.
Aug./Augusti	Corpus librorum symbolicorum, qui in ecclesia reformatorum auctoritatem publicam obtinuerunt, 2d ed. Edited by J. Chr. W. Augusti. Lipsiae, 1846.
BOC	*The Constitution of the Presbyterian Church (U.S.A.): Part I, Book of Confessions.* Louisville, Ky.: Office of the General Assembly, 1999. See BSRK.
Bray	*Documents of the English Reformation.* Edited by Gerald Bray. Minneapolis: Fortress Press, 1994.
BSKO	Bekenntnisschriften und Kirchenordnungen der nach Gottes Wort reformierten Kirchen. Edited by Wilhelm Niesel. Zurich, 1983.
BSLK	Die Bekenntnisschriften der evangelisch-lutherischen Kirche. Edited by the Deutschen Evangelischen Kirchenausschuß. 11th ed., Göttingen, 1992. ET: see K/W.
BSRK	Die Bekenntnisschriften der reformierten Kirche. Edited by E. F. K. Müller. Leipzig, 1903 (reprint, Zurich, 1987). ET: A variety of resources is used.
Bw.Th. I	Karl Barth/E. Thurneysen, Briefwechsel, Band I: 1913–1921. Edited by E. Thurneysen (Gesamtausgabe, section 5). Zurich, 1973.
Bw.Th. II	Karl Barth/E. Thurneysen. Briefwechsel, Band II: 1921–1930. Edited by E. Thurneysen (Gesamtausgabe, section 5). Zurich, 1987.
CD	Karl Barth. *Church Dogmatics.* Trans. G. W. Bromiley (Edinburgh: T. & T. Clark, 1936–1969). See KD.
Chr. Dogm.	K. Barth. Die christliche Dogmatik in Entwurf, Band I: Die Lehre vom Worte Gottes: Prolegomena zur christlichen Dogmatik 1927. Edited by G. Sauter (Gesamtausgabe, section 3). Zurich, 1982.
CO	Ioannis Calvini opera quae supersunt omnia. Edited by G. Braun, E. Cunitz, E. Reuss. Braunschweig,

	1863ff. (=CR 29–87). ET: A variety of resources is used.
Cochrane	*Reformed Confessions of the 16th Century.* Edited by Arthur C. Cochrane. Philadelphia: Westminster Press, 1966.
CSEL	Corpus scriptorum ecclesiasticorum latinorum. Vienna, 1886–.
CR	Corpus Reformatorum. Halle/Braunschweig/ Berlin; Leipzig; Zurich, 1834–1900.
Denziger	H. Denziger. *The Sources of Catholic Dogma.* Translated by R. J. Deferrari from the 30th ed. St. Louis and London: B. Herder Book Co., 1954. See DS.
DS	H. Denziger. Enchiridion symbolorum, definitionum et declarationum de rebus fidei et morum. Edited by P. Hünemann. Barcinone/ Friburgi Brisgovae/Romae/Neo-Eboraci, 1991, 37th edition. ET: Denziger.
EA	M. Luther. Sämtliche Werke. Erlangen, 1826–1857. ET: see LW.
Ebr./Ebrard	Salnar's Harmonia confessionum fidei: Das einhellige Bekenntnis der reformirten Kirche aller Länder neu bearbeitet und auf Wunsch des reformirten Bundes herausgegeben von A. Ebrard. Barmen, 1887.
EG	Evangelisches Gesangbuch (since 1992)
EKG	Evangelisches Kirchengesangbuch (since 1950)
End./Enders	Dr. Martin Luther's Briefwechsel. Revised and with annotations by E. L. Enders. Frankfurt am Main, 1884–1932.
Hinke	*The Latin Works of Huldreich Zwingli.* Edited by William J. Hinke. Philadelphia: Heidelberg Press, 1922. See Zwingli.
HpB	H. Heppe. Die Dogmatik der evangelisch-reformirten Kirche dargestellt und aus den Quellen belegt (1861). Newly revised and edited by E. Bizer. Neukirchen, 1935.
Inst.	J. Calvin. Institutio christiani religionis (1559). ET: *Institutes of the Christian Religion.* Edited by John T. McNeill. Translated by Ford Lewis Battles. Philadelphia: Westminster Press, 1960. Citations are Book (I), chapter (i), section (1), followed by volume number and page in the ET (e.g., 1:1).
Institutes (1536)	John Calvin. *The Institutes of the Christian Religion (1536).* Rev. ed. Translated by Ford Lewis Battles. Grand Rapids: Wm. B. Eerdmans, 1986.

Instruction in Faith	John Calvin. *Instruction in Faith (1537)*. Translated and edited by Paul T. Fuhrmann. Louisville: Westminster/John Knox Press, 1992.
KD	K. Barth. Die Kirchliche Dogmatik. Munich/Zollikon-Zurich, 1932–1970. ET: see CD.
Krüger/Hermelink	H. Hermelink. Reformation und Gegenreformation. Section III of Handbuch der Kirchengeschichte. Edited by G. Krüger. Tübingen, 1911.
K/W	*The Book of Concord: The Confessions of the Evangelical Lutheran Church*. Edited by Robert Kolb and Timothy J. Wengert. Translated by Charles Arand et al. Minneapolis: Fortress Press, 2000. See SBLK.
Lang	A. Lang. Der Heidelberger Katechismus und vier verwandte Katechismen (Leo Juds und Microns kleine Katechismen sowie die zwei Vorarbeiten Ursins). Quellenschriften zur Geschichte des Protestantismus. Vol. 3. Leipzig, 1909.
Leith	*Creeds of the Churches: A Reader in Christian Doctrine from the Bible to the Present*. Rev. ed. Edited by John H. Leith. Richmond: John Knox Press, 1973.
Loofs	F. Loofs. Leitfaden zum Studium der Dogmengeschichte. Halle, 1906, 4th edition.
LW	Martin Luther. *Luther's Works*. Edited by J. Pelikan and H. Lehmann. St. Louis: Concordia, 1955–1976. See WA.
M	(=Müller, see BSRK and SBLK).
Niemeyer	H. A. Niemeyer. Collectio confessionum in ecclesiis reformatis publicatorum. Lipsiae, 1840.
OS	Ioannis Calvini Opera Selecta. Edited by P. Barth et al. Munich, 1926–1952.
Pipkin	*Huldrych Zwingli: Writings*. Vol. 2, *In Search of True Religion: Reformation, Pastoral and Eucharistic Writings*. Translated by H. Wayne Pipkin. Allison Park, Pa.: Pickwick Publications, 1984. See Zwingli.
RE	Realencyklopädie für protestantische Theologie und Kirche. 3d ed. Gotha, 1896–1913. For some ET, see S/H.
Reid	*Calvin: Theological Treatises*. Edited by J. K. S. Reid. London and Philadelphia: Westminster Press, 1954.
RGG	Die Religion in Geschichte und Gegenwart. Tübingen, 1909–1923, 1st ed.; 1927–1932, 2d ed.; 1956–1965, 3d ed.
Romans	Karl Barth. *The Epistle to the Romans*. Translated by E. Hoskyns from the 6th ed. London: Oxford University Press, 1922–1957. See Römerbrief 2.

Römerbrief 1	K. Barth. Der Römerbrief. Edited by H. Schmidt. Bern, 1919. (Gesamtausgabe, section 2), Zurich, 1985.
Römerbrief 2	K. Barth. Der Römerbrief. Munich, 1922, 2d edition (=first reprint of the revision, citations according to the pagination of the editions issued from 1923 onward). See Romans.
Salnar/Hall	[Salnar=Jean-Francois Salvard]. *The Harmony of Protestant Confession: Exhibiting the Faith of the Church in Christ, Reformed after the Pure and Holy Doctrine of the Gospel.* Edited by Peter Hall. Edmonton: Still Waters Books, 1992. Reprint from edition of 1842.
SBLK	Die symbolischen Bücher der evangelisch-lutherischen Kirche, deutsch und lateinisch. Edited by J. T. Müller. Gütersloh, 1847. See K/W.
Schaff	Philip Schaff. *The Creeds of Christendom with a History and Critical Notes.* Vol. 3, *The Evangelical Protestant Creeds with Translations.* New York: Harper & Row, 1877. Reprint, Grand Rapids: Baker Book House, 1969.
Seeberg	R. Seeberg. Lehrbuch der Dogmengeschichte. Vol. 4, Part 2, Die Fortbildung der reformatorischen Lehre und die gegenreformatorische Lehre. Leipzig, 1920, 2d and 3d editions. See Seeberg/Hay.
Seeberg/Hay	R. Seeberg. *Text-Book of the History of Doctrines.* Translated by Charles E. Hay. Grand Rapids: Baker Book House, 1952–1961. See Seeberg; the ET is so strongly abridged that many references cannot be traced.
S/H	*The New Schaff-Herzog Encyclopedia of Religious Knowledge.* Edited by Samuel M. Jackson and Lefferts A. Loetscher. Grand Rapids: Baker Book House, 1977. See RE.
S.th.	Thomas von Aquino. Summa theologica. See Summa.
Summa	Thomas Aquinas. *Summa Theologica.* Translated by Fathers of the English Dominican Province. 3 vols. New York: Benziger Press, 1947–1948. See S.th.
SVRG	Schriften des Vereins für Reformationsgeschichte. Gütersloh.
Th.C.	K. Barth. Die Theologie Calvins. Edited by H. Scholl (Gesamtausgabe, section 2), Zurich, 1993. See *Theology of Calvin.*
Theology of Calvin	Karl Barth. *The Theology of John Calvin.* Translated by Geoffrey W. Bromiley. Grand Rapids: Wm. B. Eerdmans, 1995.

ThExh	Theologische Existenz heute, 1–77, 1933–1941, Munich.
ThExhNF	Theologische Existenz heute, Neue Folge, 1–, 1946–, Munich.
Tracts and Treatises II	John Calvin. *Tracts and Treatises on the Doctrine and Worship of the Church.* Translated by Henry Beveridge. Edinburgh and London: Oliver & Boyd; Grand Rapids: Wm. B. Eerdmans, 1958.
Tracts and Treatises III	John Calvin. *Tracts and Treatises in Defense of the Reformed Faith.* Translated by Henry Beveridge. Grand Rapids: Wm. B. Eerdmans, 1958.
TRE	Theologische Realenzyklopädie. Berlin/New York, 1977–.
Unterricht I	K. Barth. "Unterricht in der christlichen Religion." Bd. I: Prolegomena 1924. Edited by H. Reiffen. Gesamtausgabe, section 2. Zurich, 1990.
Unterricht II	K. Barth. "Unterricht in der christlichen Religion," Bd. II: Die Lehre von Gott, die Lehre vom Menschen 1924/25. Edited by H. Stoevesandt. Gesamtausgabe, section 2. Zurich, 1990.
V.u.kl.A. 1922–1925	K. Barth. Vorträge und kleinere Arbeiten 1922–1925. Edited by H. Finze. Gesamtausgabe, section 3. Zurich, 1990.
WA	M. Luther. Werke: Kritische Gesamtausgabe. Weimar, 1883–. See LW.
WA.B	———Briefwechsel. See LW.
WA.DB	———Deutsche Bibel. See LW.
WA.TR	———Tischreden; See LW.
Zwingli, S	Huldrici Zwingli Opera. Edited by M. Schuler and Io. Schulthess. Turici, 1841. See Hinke and Pipkin.
Zwingli, Z	Huldreich Zwingli. Sämtliche Werke. Berlin and Zurich, 1905–(=CR 88–101). See Hinke and Pipkin.

1.

THE SIGNIFICANCE
OF THE CONFESSION
IN THE REFORMED CHURCH

The significance of the confession in the Reformed church can be clarified for us in the simplest way by first investigating the significance
of confessions in the *Lutheran church*, which is the most immediate
counterpart to the Reformed church. We shall proceed from the Formula of
Concord,[1] in which the Lutheran church has expressed itself not only officially but in a historically decisive way by establishing the foundational significance of the so-called Augsburg Confession.[2] There are five points that,
in my view, are important for the character of the Lutheran confession.

1. The Lutheran confession intends to be an *ecumenical* confession. By that,
I mean that it wants to be seen as having the same dignity and validity as
the confessions of the one ancient imperial church of Europe. The Formula
of Concord does not say this in so many words but certainly implies it when
in its frequent references to the major Lutheran confession, the *Augsburg
Confession*, it constantly emphasizes that this statement was presented by the
Protestant electors and estates to the *emperor* in 1530 (J. T. Müller, 4, 6, 518,
568, 569).[3] It is not a private document, but by virtue of its shared presentation by the churches represented by the electors and estates, it was a "*public
document*" ["*publicum scriptum*"]. That was, according to the Formula of Concord, an essential component of the concept of a valid and authentic ecclesiastical doctrine (568,2).[4] It must necessarily *receive public notice*, even if in the
form of a protest, as in this case. The public intended was the broadest possible audience, which in the time of the Formula of Concord and in the thinking of its authors and protectors was still the empire and the imperial church.
Early Lutheranism *affirmed* this empire and its church. The protesting presentation of *its* faith was meant to be taken as its assertion of the true *catholic*
faith, and thus it *insisted* upon this *visible* form of its catholicity, the public
reading of the document before the emperor and the empire. The broad significance that the Augsburg Confession attained remains incomprehensible
if this dimension is disregarded. That significance was not due to its internal theological aspect but rather to this apparently most external aspect,
which for early Lutheranism was by no means merely external. Under the
fresh impression of the events at the presentation on July 6, 1530, Luther
wrote to Conrad Cordatus that he was "tremendously" ["vehementer"]
pleased to have lived to this moment, since it was the fulfillment of what was
written, "I spoke of your testimonies in the *presence of kings* . . . and I was not

1

put to shame," and, "Whoever will confess me . . . before men, him I also shall confess before my Father who is in heaven" (End. 5,42).[5] In another remark, the decisive aspect of the Diet of Augsburg was characterized in this way: " [F]or we openly and freely confessed the Gospel before the Emperor and the whole empire" (EA, 62,80).[6] One can sense the pathos of this thought reverberating in the preface of the electors, princes, and estates to the Formula of Concord, when they extol the Augsburg Confession because at that time it "was made known publicly to all confessors of the Christian faith, yes, to the entire world, broke through everywhere and came into the mouth and speech of everyone" (M 4).[7]

2. Lutheranism places decisive importance on the *unity* and the *united interpretation* of its confession. The Augustana becomes its *one* confession through its character as a *public* document that secured its claim to ecumenicity. The writers of the Formula of Concord rather anxiously emphasize that it was never their concern "in this document nor in others to depart in the slightest way (unguem discedere) from this highly regarded confession, nor to set up another or a new confession" (566,5).[8] Thus, the Formula of Concord does *not* seek to be a *new* confession but rather a confession of the one old one (568,2).[9] It makes the same claim regarding Melanchthon's Apology,[10] Luther's Smalcaldic Articles,[11] his Small and Large Catechism,[12] all of which are incorporated into the Book of Concord next to the Augustana as confessional documents. They are all related to the common foundation provided by the Augustana. They are intended to be detailed, polemic or popular explanations of the Augustana, written and distributed at a time in which the content of the Augustana was not yet very controversial among its adherents[13] (569–70).[14] One should note how here Luther's writings are reduced to the significance of authentic commentaries on the one official Lutheran doctrine preserved in the Augustana. Even Melanchthon, who wrote the Augustana, is only allowed to interpret himself with his Apology, in accordance with the explanatory and refining repetition that the Formula of Concord, as the third level of the 'body of doctrine' [corpus doctrinae], imposes upon the preceding levels. That is its purpose, and for that reason the various documents, the one confession and its appendages, are drawn together in order to be *interpreted* as a unity and in a unified fashion in one last and concluding step.

3. According to the Formula of Concord, the one public confession of Lutheranism has the character of a *symbol*. It describes the Augustana expressly as "our creed for this age" (4,659,3)[15] and compares it with the Nicene Creed as having emerged under similar circumstances.[16] What does that mean? In his treatise on the councils (1539), Luther had written that "the articles of faith must not grow on earth through the councils, as from a new secret inspiration but must be issued from heaven through the Holy Spirit and revealed openly" (EA 25,267).[17] A council cannot posit new articles (267,

280)[18]; rather, it "falls back on the holy church of God *in former times*" (280).[19] It is "the great servant or judge" (343),[20] assembled by emperor and kings in their character as Christians (351),[21] in order to exercise and to defend the rights of the church of God, God's Word, and the Christian faith (343–44).[22] In these comments, Luther was not thinking of the Diet of Augsburg and the Augustana, nor were the writers of the Formula of Concord thinking of Luther's remarks. They contain, however, all the necessary elements in order to understand the sense in which the Concord writers conceived of the Augustana as symbol. They call their doctrine the *"ancient, united consensus* believed in by the universal, orthodox churches of Christ and fought for and reaffirmed against many heresies and errors."[23] It was as such that it was confessed by the princes in 1530. It proved itself as such by its grounding in the Holy Scriptures—it is "drawn . . . from the Word of God"[24]—and by its agreement with the recognized ancient symbols. Therefore, the Augustana is, according to the Book of Concord, not intended to be a *new* confession, but rather simply the new confessing of the *ancient* confession, the articles of Christ, which are revealed and given from heaven, according to Luther.[25] The issue now was to separate the church "from the papists and other condemned sects and heresies,"[26] as the ancient church was accustomed to do. The Formula of Concord does not fail to mention that the Augustana was delivered "anew . . . by *Dr. Luther* of blessed and holy memory."[27] But it was not the classical aspect of its historical emergence that made it into a symbol—that could only strengthen and emphasize its symbolic character—but rather the fact that it repeated and defended the revealed *faith*, which leads the holy church of God *of former times*, as Luther had written. This is what made the Diet of Augsburg into a council in disguise and the Augustana into a symbol. *That is the reason* for its claim to public status in the empire. *That is then also the reason* for the anxious concern for its unified interpretation.

4. This is also the reason for its claim to *authority*, its claim that it cannot be changed and cannot be replaced. A new and difficult set of problems emerges here that we must examine more closely. The Formula of Concord knows that the Augustana is only the "witness[es] . . . of faith, which show how the Holy Scripture has . . . been understood and interpreted in the church of God by those who lived at the time (a doctoribus, qui tum vixerunt)" (518,26).[28] But one cannot remain at that point anymore. Since this witness is the witness of the true, ancient, universal faith, it must be understood as "the unanimously received doctrine (forma doctrinae) that all our evangelical churches acknowledge and affirm, and in accordance to which, since it is taken from God's Word, all other documents are to be assessed and judged as to whether one should approve or reject them" (571,10).[29] It is to be the "reliable public witness" ["publicum solidumque testimonium"] testifying not only for those now living but "also for following generations" ["ad omnem posteritatem"] what is and should

always remain for our churches the unanimous position and decision in controversial issues ("fuerit esseque perpetuo debeat") (572,16).[30] In view of these statements, I do not contest, as *Seeberg* does (Seeberg IV, 536), that the Formula of Concord ascribes to the confession "judicial authority."[31] It is, on the contrary, quite apparent that it does so in every way. |

To be sure, there are also many statements that appear to assign this judicial authority exclusively to the "pure, clear fountain of Israel" (568,3),[32] the Holy Scripture. This is true of the first statement of the entire book: "We believe, teach, and confess that the only rule and guiding principle according to which all teachings and teachers are to be evaluated and judged are (nullam omnino aliam) the prophetic and apostolic writings of the Old and New Testaments alone."[33] All other writings of old and new teachers are to be subjected to them. They are to be the "touchstone" ["Lydius lapis"][34] on which all teachers are to be examined (517,1–2; 518,7; see 568,3).[35] What is then valid? The position of the Formula of Concord is certainly not clearly expressed, but in spite of that it is not unrecognizable. It does assert that there is between the Holy Scripture and all other writings a "brilliant distinction" ["luculentum discrimen"] (518,7).[36] But whenever the Augustana is questioned, then this distinction gets *blurred*. In its concluding definition, it confronts one more time (571,12–13)[37] the Holy Scripture and the confessional documents and describes the former as *"eternal truth"* [*"immota veritas"*] and *"basis"* [*"fundamentum"*], and the latter as *"testimonies* of the truth" [*"testes* veritatis"].[38] One should note, however, that the restrictive "sole" ["solum"] or "only" ["tantum"] is lacking as a clarification of the latter concept[39] and, further, that the entire statement is intended to support the argument that we "present and cite" ["recte in medium producimus"] these writings because they are testimonies of the truth and they reproduce the unanimous and correct view of our predecessors who firmly stood with the right doctrine (the *"testimony* of the truth" [*"testes* veritatis"] is not intended to *have* any restrictive meaning at all!). Finally and most importantly, when one examines this section more carefully, one sees that the wording deals with the confessional documents *with the exception* of the Augustana, that is with the Apology and the others. They are called upon as witnesses to the "eternal truth" ["immota veritas"], which converges in effect with the "pure teaching" of the ancestors, that is, with the doctrine of the Augustana. The Formula of Concord seeks to ascertain, on the basis of these second-level confessional documents, which positions in the previous doctrinal disputes agreed with *"God's Word and the* Christian *Augsburg Confession"* (567,10).[40] This astonishing combination is repeated later (726,7).[41] Twice it is said that we confess the Augustana *"because it is drawn from the Word of God"* (569,5; 571,10).[42] With that, it moves fundamentally into remarkable proximity to the Holy Scriptures, even though set somewhat apart as merely "drawn from it" [desumpta"]. True Christians, it says, should in this time be guided by it, "*after the Word of God*" (565,4).[43] |

Whoever emphasizes these strong statements about the exclusive and highest normativity of Holy Scripture might place the following question: Is there for the Lutheranism of the Formula of Concord a basic and legitimate freedom to call upon this *highest* authority, the Scripture, *without reference* to or even *against* the Augustana? Is the church itself fundamentally willing to review the question, Whether the understanding of Scripture preserved in the Augustana is the right one?[44] That would be, I think, the persuasive proof that the "brilliant distinction" ["luculentum discrimen"] between the Bible and all other documents is understood to be a fundamentally *qualitative* one and not merely a *quantitative* one. Further, I think that the actual course of events has shown that Lutheranism has sought to *exclude* such freedom and openness toward the Formula of Concord. This leads to a further question. If one affirms a normativity of the Augsburg understanding of Scripture that is at least *similar to that of Scripture*, then what is the situation with the normativity of the *second-level* confessional documents, the Apology and the rest? After all, according to the clear statement of the Formula of Concord, they are to be understood as authentic interpretations of the Augustana.[45] Is there a legitimate possibility to appeal to the Augustana *without reference* to or even *against* the understanding of it in these documents? Is there a basic openness to revisit their interpretation of Augustana? If there is not, then do they not also participate in that dignity which is ascribed to Augustana itself as "drawn from the Word of God" ["e verbo Domini desumpta"], if at a somewhat lower level? We must *then* ask further, What is the situation with the normativity of the *Formula of Concord*, which puts together the Augustana and its interpretations in one document and then provides for them a "Solid Declaration" ["solida declaratio"] as a conclusive explanation of the whole? Should the eight thousand Lutheran church leaders and scholars who after 1580 signed the famous solemn obligation to the Formula of Concord have the freedom to revisit this Concordistic explanation of the confessional documents?[46] Has the Lutheran church itself made this reservation or acted in accordance with it? And if not, is it not then clear that, at a lower level, something of the dignity of the Scripture that has been transferred to the Augustana and from it to the other confessional documents is also delegated to the Formula of Concord? |

I note in this regard that, in fact, these consequences *have been drawn* in *post*-Concordistic Lutheranism, as for example by the well-known dogmatic theologian *Hutterus* (died in Württemberg in 1616, author of a "Malleus calvinistarum" ['hammer of the Calvinists']),[47] who wrote: "As the 'primary Author' [Auctor primarius] of the *Book of Concord* we recognize no human, be it a theologian or a politician, but rather God himself, the *Holy Spirit*, the source and giver of all good things, in the sense that we do not hesitate in the least to regard it as *divinely inspired*, although with the *distinction* which must be maintained between the Holy Scripture and the symbolic or ecclesial documents."[48] Similarly, one hundred years later, David Hollaz (d. 1713) wrote that the symbolic books should be called *"in a broader sense* . . . inspired" [*"sensu latiori* [. . .] θεόπνευστοι"] because they contain and expound the word of God once given by inspiration to the prophets and apostles and because it cannot be doubted that God, through a *"special working"* [*"specialis concursus"*] so influenced, illumined and guided their authors that they thought and wrote "the truest and most salubrious dogmas" ["verissima saluberrimaque dogmata"] (*Hase*, Hutt. Red. 125).[49] I mention these extravagant but not illogical consequences merely to illumine the fundamental situation. I regard it as proven that the difference between Scripture and confession according to the teaching of the Formula of Concord is in fact only a quantitative one and not qualitative. Like stage scenery, one entity stands behind the other: In the foreground we see the *Formula of Concord*, and behind it the *Apology*, the Smalcaldic Articles, and so on, and behind all of these, dominating the center of the scene, the *Augsburg Confession*. Finally, as the ultimate background upon which our vision ultimate rests we see the *Holy Scriptures*. Each level explains the next, referring back to it and to that extent subordinate to it, but everything is on *one* stage or level. Or was it a mere oversight that in the Formula of Concord the Holy Scriptures (568,3)[50] are simply listed as number 1 in the series of "creeds and common confessions,"[51] which are supposed to be acknowledged and put in a stable order by the Formula of Concord: (1) "the pure, clear fountain of Israel," (2) the ecumenical creeds, (3) the Augustana, and so on?[52] No, in Lutheranism the Augustana is really more than a "witness of the faith."[53] To put it another way, *as such* it is simultaneously an *authority* of faith, not mutable, but rather an *immutable* entity.

5. Resulting from this authority of the confession is the *obligation* to it expected of the teachers of the church, which is characteristic for older Lutheranism. In terms of its theory, "Lutheran" now means the confession of the Augsburg explanation of Scripture, while in terms of practice and fact, it means the confession of the Concord's concept of this explanation of Scripture. Upon this *confession* rests, albeit in a subordinate way, the sacredness and necessity of the revealed Word of God itself. Something of that must apparently transfer to the *obligation* to it, the binding character of it. This has decisively shaped the face of Lutheranism. The disadvantage of a certain rigid immutability that emerges out of this kind of obligation for all times is the reverse aspect of the equally indisputably firm formation and closedness of its theological and ecclesial stance, which can never be completely lost or erased even in its most modernizing proponents. The advantage of this stance over against the *Catholic* Church is the fact that it has replaced the apocryphal and flexible authority of the church's teach-

ing office with its confession of Luther's understanding of the Bible, which it has drawn together from the sources and formally enacted once and for all. It also has an advantage over the *Reformed* churches, which certainly want to work from the sources but do so without the criterion of a *guideline* that provides security by virtue of a standing *judgment* over all impulses and innovations. This judgment has been judicially promulgated and, after attempted and rejected appeals, has been affirmed to possess the dignity of law. Another matter entirely is the fact that these advantages have over the course of history lost much of their original splendor, mostly because modern Lutheranism does not know how to take seriously, to use, and to assert the ideology that underlies them. That does not change the fact that they *are* real advantages, still effective in their own way. It was not merely bombastic or pastoral illusion when a North Schleswig theologian in the middle of the nineteenth century wrote a hymn lyric about the Lutheran church, expressly looking back upon the Augsburg Confession:

> *Pure* church, our church! / A precious meal is the Word from God, / it is its sword and its crown against all hostile hosts. / Its chambers are filled, / rich in light, comfort, and power, / in righteousness and peace / and profound knowledge. . . .
> *Secure* church, our church! / Walled about, salvation and defense / Augsburg's victorious confession, / like a fortress all around it! / On the foundation of the holy Bible / stands the secure city of God; / three centuries confess / that it has God as its protector!
> (*Knapp's* Liederschatz, 450–51)[54]

This song and its mood would have been completely impossible in a *Reformed* context. Essential to the *Reformed* church is the fact that in *this* sense it is *not* a pure and *not* a secure church. As far as the *Reformed* confession is concerned, there is *no victorious* confession here like the Augsburg Confession. This needs to be clarified now with reference in detail to the five points we have laid out.

1. The Reformed confessional documents completely lack, above all, the character of *ecumenical publicity* that for the Lutherans was of such importance for the Augsburg Confession Invariata [unchanged] of 1530. To be sure, two Reformed confessions were submitted to the emperor at the time. One of them, however, Zwingli's *Fidei Ratio*,[55] was clearly the work of a private individual,[56] and neither the Zurich church nor any other Reformed church opted to have it officially recognized after the fact, thus seeking a formal connection to the emperor and the empire. The other one, the so-called *Confessio Tetrapolitana*,[57] was dropped by its authors and supporting public groupings in favor of the Augustana a few years after the Diet,[58] rendering it moot for our discussion. Thus, the Reformed churches *failed* to make the connection to the Roman *Empire* and its *imperial* church that

Lutheranism formally attained. Luther once claimed that the Diet of Augsburg was "the last trump before the day of judgment," because there "our doctrine and faith were brought to light" through the Confession (62,82).[59] But the Reformed, who were not part of the music then, could not claim such eschatological significance for *their* doctrine. All of their confessions, even where they were published in the name of entire countries (which happened in very few instances) had *particular* character. This meant that they had to live out of the catholicity that they ascribed to themselves or that was accorded them through the relevance or usefulness of their content, as in the case of the Heidelberg Catechism. For the Holy Roman Empire, from which at that time the general concept of the church could not be separated, they did not exist. As far as the law of the realm was concerned, and up to the Peace of Westphalia of 1648, the Reformed were not schismatics like the Lutherans but simply heretics. When that changed, it was no longer possible to ascribe to their confessions the solemn character of "emperor and empire" that they lacked. In Switzerland, the Netherlands, and Scotland, this deficiency was not that difficult to tolerate. |

One can see how great was the authority of the Augustana as a general Protestant confession even on non-German territory in the fact that the *Waldensians* subscribed to it completely in 1609 and 1655. They did so, to be sure, under the erroneous assumption that this had been the case with all the other Reformed churches of Europe. The clause "as it was explained by the author"[60] apparently implied that what they were affirming was the version of the Augsburg Confession that Melanchthon himself had *altered*.[61] There is also an express concurrence with the Augustana, with an appeal to its general and public character, in the Polish confessions of *Sendomir* (1570)[62] and *Thorn* (1645).[63] The latter document even declares unabashedly that the confessors do not care whether one understands their confession to relate to the Variata or Invariata. Even more remarkable is the fact that, under the regime of Calvin's successor, Theodore Beza, two collections appeared from *Geneva* that will concern us later on, one by *Salnar*[64] and another by *Laurentius*,[65] in which the attempt was made to present a consensus of the contents of the most important Reformed confessions, incorporating not only those documents but also the Augustana (although with the Variata).[66] In all of these endeavors, the appeal could be made to *Calvin* himself, who had signed the Augustana in Regensburg in 1540. He did so, as he later testified, "happily and willingly" ["volens ac libens"], namely, "as it is expounded by its author" (C 16,430).[67] As was made clear in another remark by Calvin (C 9,19),[68] this was also the Variata.[69] In Regensburg, however, Calvin was thinking and acting as a representative of Strassburg and thus as a *German* Protestant. In 1651, he energetically *resisted* the introduction of the Augustana into *France*. This was due not only to his fear of the transplantation of the German theological divisiveness into the French church, which was already seriously threatened by external dangers. Rather, as he stated in a letter to Coligny, he regarded the Augustana's content as "such a meagre composition, so feeble and so obscure" ["maigrement bastie, molle" and "obscure"] (18,733).[69a] This criticism could be compared to Luther's well-known accusation that the Augustana "step[ped] so softly and quietly" (EA 54,145),[70] which is proof enough that he did not regard its *content* as so great and valuable as to be the "last trump before the day of judgment." If, after Calvin's death, there were those in Geneva who thought they could move away from his tactically and materially based reserve, and if the works of Salnar and Laurentius found both interest and acclaim in French Reformed circles for a time, then this shows how strong the foreign sense of dependency could be over against the main German confession with its positive characteristic of ecumenicity. |

For all that, it would be impossible to speak of the Augustana Variata as a Reformed confessional document. It is helpful to remember that the idea of the empire was of great significance in Germany up to the threshold of the nineteenth century. It is thus understandable that the Reformed felt constrained to adapt themselves in their confessions to the Augustana as the only confession having broad public recognition. They might well attempt to claim it *as their own* and to position themselves in its beneficial shadows, competing with the Lutherans of the Formula of Concord. Confessions like that of the *Dillenburg* Synod of 1578[71] or of Margrave Ernst Friedrich von Baden-Durlach (the so-called *Staffort* Book)[72] present themselves as virtual Reformed parallels to the Formula of Concord. The Consensus *Bremensis* of 1595[73] subscribes to the Augustana as the first and oldest evangelical confession, publicly placed in opposition to the papacy by the electors and estates of the German Empire. Thus, it was known to everyone as the hallmark of separation from the papacy, with which the confessions of the non-German Reformed agreed in both foundations and argumentation, as Bremen states with express reference to Salnar's Harmony of the confession.[74] To be sure, they also did it with the reservation that it was "in the right and basic understanding that it agrees with the certain and infallible Word of God, to whom all things are properly subjected."[75] Similarly, the General Synod of *Kassel* in 1576 made its confession of "the Augsburg Confession, explained and proven on the basis of Holy Scripture, and which in the years 40 and 42 was reviewed and extensively improved."[76] The famous convert Elector *Johann Sigismund* of Brandenburg finally documented his own efforts for the ecumenical character of the confession he proposed in 1614[77] by not only expanding the series of the three ancient confessions (as did the Bremen confessors as well[78]) to include Ephesus and Chalcedon,[79] but also by formally acknowledging the "Augsburg Confession as it was presented to Emperor Charles V in the year 30 by the protesting princes and estates, and after it had been reviewed in several points and improved."[80] That restrictive clause reveals the painful gap in the argument advanced by the Germans and with them certain circles of foreign Reformed, who were seeking to prove the ecumenical character of their own confessions. The link they claimed to the Augustana always referred to the *Variata*, or, as they preferred to say, the *Emendata*. Against this, the Lutherans could make the valid historical claim, and did so, that *this version* of the Augustana was certainly *not* the general and evangelical confession delivered to the emperor, even if it did then receive the concurrence of many princely and theological conclaves between 1540 and 1580.[81] |

To confess the *genuine* and publicly received Augustana with its Article 10[82] would, Poland being the somewhat puzzling exception,[83] have been impossible even for those Reformed who most needed to establish such alliances—unless they were willing to dispose of their Reformed identity.[84] The entire endeavor to edit out the well-known deficiencies could *not* really succeed. The Reformed confessions never achieved the formal recognition of the ecumenical public, neither early on when they were quietly placed under the protection of the empire nor after 1648 when they received that protection publicly within their own defined circles.[85] Striving after such recognition *should* not have succeeded, however. In terms of the origins of the Reformed Reformation, the effort can only be described as a "false tendency,"[86] as an alien body that penetrated into the church of Zwingli's and Calvin's successors only through a misunderstanding and under the pressure of custom and the environment. It was *not without reason* that, in this relation as well as others, the Reformed were originally simply called "the Swiss."[87] In a fundamental sense, they had *little* understanding and certainly no *heart* for the idea of the Roman Empire and its united church. Thus, they saw little need for a formal alliance, if even a protesting one, to *this* empire and *this* church. For them, the Reformation, precisely in its human, historical, and organizational aspects, was definitely not the legitimate organic continuation and further development of the medieval world and church but rather virtually a complete *break* with it and a new beginning! |

If you read Zwingli's 67 Farewell Discourses of 1523[88] or Calvin's chapter "On False Sacraments" ["De falsis sacramentis"] in the Institutes of 1536,[89] you will know what I mean when I say that there is a fundamental *lack of piety* in Reformed Christianity compared to Lutheranism. From the beginning onward, Calvin had broken with *historical* Catholicism in a much different way than Luther perhaps ever did inwardly, not to speak of Zwingli.[90] Calvin's stance toward the idea that one could bring about the victory of the Reformation through a general council, which both Luther and Melanchthon long advocated, was never other than cold and skeptical. He wrote in 1541,[91] "What should one expect from such a society where among one hundred there is not one who could and will understand what

May 3

the honor of God and the salvation of the church are? . . . We know what kind of theology reigns in Rome. . . . Its first principle is that there is no God, that Christendom is a bad joke and what remains is what must result from all that" (5,654).[92] For his part, he would rather have stood under the suspicion of atheism than with the adherents of the old church under the suspicion of idolatry (5,274).[93] He judged that, since it was apparently God's will to cleanse the church thoroughly, stained as it was by the pope's deceptions, there could be no better procedure in the future than "by plucking up by the roots, and . . . by one stroke of the pen erasing everything which has proceeded from his hand" (5,252).[94] It was *Beza's* opinion that anyone who expected a proper ecumenical council from these usurpers was as clever as the one who would expect that a general council of prostitutes and pimps would result in the abolition of public houses (Hungarian Confession, M 428,5[-8]).[95] The political plans that Calvin considered, especially during his stay in Germany from 1539 to 1541,[96] were no less bluntly directed against the continuation of the Roman Empire than the better known ones that had preoccupied Zwingli ten years earlier.[97] People of this persuasion could have no interest in the continuity of the millennium that had passed since the ancient church's confessions had emerged. |

The universality of the faith, which these people also strove for, does not lie in the past, or better, it lies only in the qualified and elevated past of the prophetic and apostolic age and at best the immediately following centuries; otherwise, this universality lies in the future. It is not something given but something sought. The Lutheran concept of symbol stands on the shaken but yet not broken belief in the spiritual and worldly unity of Roman-Christian-German Europe. In Calvinism, this belief (one could also call it this hope directed backward) is shattered. That was one of the reasons that its external appearance was so hard and somber. Ecumenical public recognition could be the quiet and distant goal for which one prayed and for which one ultimately worked, but one did not speak about it. The process of confessional formation moves along for now without any visible flinching, oblivious to this ideal. The Reformed approach was that their confessions would have only the particular public recognition of city or national church fellowships or eventually of a coalition of these. As though from one island to another, greetings were exchanged between Geneva and Zurich, Basel and Strassburg, with recurring delight and sometimes disappointment about the possibilities for constructive communication of the thinking going on here or there.[98] Such a *particular confessing church* sought to prove and defend the truth of its confession *solely* through its connection to Holy Scripture and not through its formal connection to a universal church or a normative exposition of Scripture. And it was such churches that, on Reformed ground, were the bearers of hope for an ecumenically recognized confession; the Reformed held to that hope as firmly as they held to the confessions of the first centuries. The legitimate pathway to universality is here the pathway of particularity. Certainly they sought with all urgency to move beyond that particularity—Calvin indeed did that[99]—but they were content in the process to have a Genevan, an Emden, and a Heidelberg Catechism; a Dillenburg and Bentheim Confession; a Zurich, Genevan, and Bremen Consensus; and a Helvetic, Gallican, Belgic, Scots, Bohemian, and Hungarian Confession. This confusing provincialism was noted by the Catholic polemicist Bossuet[100] and has continued to be a source of alienation among Lutherans when they deal with Reformed confessional literature. The Roman Empire no longer exists, and the fall of the European West has begun.[101] The kingdom of Christ is not yet here, except perhaps in the faith of the congregations in diaspora who confess him. That is the situation in which the Reformed confessional writings emerged. *None* of them is a 'public document' [publica scripta] in the strict sense of the term.

2. We have already begun addressing the second issue: Each Reformed confession is really a *singular work*, one next to many others. Its confessors had little or no actual drive, whether out of a sense of duty or even ambition, to compose a confession for *all* the Reformed churches. They had little interest either in giving up their confession for the sake of *another one*, or in allowing their work to flow into a *general* confession of all Reformed churches.[102] A certain self-confident if not defiant assertion of one's own approach is connected here in an unusual way with an equally confident respect for other approaches. "[N]o church shall claim any authority or dominion over any other" (Gallicana, M 229,11).[103] The Reformed movement has developed a very long and strong tendency toward *practical* coalition, or at least cooperation, among its various churches. Calvin's correspondence is witness to that. In the seventeenth century it can be seen working impressively in the actions of all the European Reformed churches to support the persecuted Huguenots in France. It should be noted that we would not be gathered here today were not something of that practical sense of solidarity among the international Reformed family still vital.[104] |

The tendency toward *confessional* unity of these particular Reformed churches is, on the other hand, remarkably weak in its development. We remember that the section of the Formula of Concord already cited begins with the sentence: "Fundamental, enduring unity (concordia) in the church requires above all else (primo . . . necessarium omnino) a clear and binding summary and form (forma et quasi typus) in which a general summary of teaching is drawn together from God's Word, to which the churches that hold the true Christian religion confess their adherence" (M 568).[105] From a Reformed point of view, one can only say *No*; such a formula and pattern of doctrine may well be very nice and desirable, but it is *certainly not* that which is "required above all else" for an accord. That which is "required above all else" is that the doctrine of the church everywhere and constantly be grounded upon Holy Scripture,[106] which defines not the confessional *unity* but the confessional *freedom* of the particular churches in their relationships to each other. That was one of the first things that Luther noticed in his opponents from the Alps: the unconcerned lack of uniformity in their formulations, which was a sign for him that their doctrine was of Satan (End. 5,294).[107] "The Holy Ghost is a God of unity and grants one meaning, foundation, and doctrine" (53,362).[108] In the sixteenth century, the Reformed were scornfully described as "Confessionists" ["Confessionistae"] because of their many personal, local, and national confessions, and they were quite content to be such.[109] How easy it would have been for Calvin to install a normative Reformed confession, possibly written by him, in the circles and countries open to his influence. But he never sought after such a thing. The fact that he imposed the Gallican Confession of 1559 on the French[110] was not an act of the "pope from Geneva," as he was called,[111] but rather a fraternal and friendly form of help from church to church. He wrote a catechism,[112] but we find his most loyal adherents—John Knox,[113] John à Lasco,[114] and Caspar Olevianus[115]— all writing their own confessions and catechisms as a matter of course. |

Related to that was the consistent way they left it to their opponents to use such generalizing terms for Reformed confessions and churches as "*Zwinglian*" or "*Calvinist.*" They did so with more success than Luther had with his protest against the use of his name. It is significant that Luther's name is constantly mentioned in a whole series of German-Reformed confessions (Dillenberg,[116] Bremen,[117] Staffort,[118] Confessio Sigismundi[119]), usually with the purpose of asserting his authority against the promotion of the Formula of Concord, albeit with mixed success. In contrast, *Zwingli's* name is never mentioned in the German-Swiss confessions, and *Calvin's* only once in the entire literature. That was in a Congregationalist gloss to the Westminster Confession (K. Müller 550,21), and there it is mentioned next to Luther's name as an example of a person who, like Cyrus, was an instrument in the hand of God.[120] Luther's name, as perceivable in the Formula of Concord, has itself become a symbol, but the names Zwingli and Calvin did not and could not do so. |

Unity must be sought and tended, then and now, along another, less illuminating path. Obviously there was general delight at the agreement of one Reformed confession with another. It is just as obvious that the authors of a confession gave careful attention to previously composed ones, whenever they were known (although this appears often not to have been the case). In general, they went about their work very thoughtfully. Such agreements, however, did not descend somehow from above, from some kind of central coordinating agency, nor were they an agreement of the letter but of the spirit and matter. In the process, they left each other a great deal of room for movement, so that serious differences were not to be ruled out, as we shall see. Toward the end of 1565, Bullinger[121] sent Elector Friedrich III of the Palatinate a confession of faith that he had personally requested as a private initiative and intended for his private use. This document later came to be called the Second Helvetic Confession. In the accompanying letter, he wrote simply *"agreeing* with" [*"congruit* cum"] all confessors of the true faith "everywhere in all the churches of Germany, France, England, and of other regions and rulers,"[122] without any appeal to any authority other than the Holy Scripture that could have confirmed this "agreeing" ["congruit"]. The *Heidelberg Catechism*, the best known among all Reformed confessional writings, established itself simply because of its dogmatic and pedagogical usefulness, and gained preeminence over Calvin's Catechism and other respectable contenders. Whether it did so rightly or wrongly is not the question here. It happened in the freedom that was always openly or secretly characteristic of the "confessional position" of the entire Reformed church, to the extent that one can even speak of such a thing. It was *only* in this way that a certain confessional universality could and can be achieved on Reformed soil. Calvin coined the phrase "godly compact" ["pia conspiratio"] (5,321) for the fraternal and peaceful agreement linked with respect for one another's freedom among the various allied groups of the Reformed church family.[123] This very term was used again in the Helvetic Formula of Consensus of 1675.[124]

What was not excluded in this process of respect for each other's freedom were (1) *special agreements* among particular Reformed entities such as the general Swiss acceptance in 1566 of the Second Helvetic Confession. The process of acceptance, however, allowed the oldest Swiss university city, Basel, to wait eighty years to declare its agreement with this acceptance, after it had recovered from a temporary period of Lutheranization—that could also happen![125] Also not excluded were (2) *declarations of special mutual acknowledgment* of each other's confessions, such as those exchanged in 1583 between the Dutch and French national synods,[126] and (3) *mutual consultation*. By the latter, I mean the possibility to request help from Reformed sister churches in a particularly difficult and important case of local doctrinal dispute. This could mean the solicitation of a written expertise such as in Geneva during Calvin's time, especially in the cases of Bolsec and Servetus.[127] It could also mean inviting foreign theologians to meet for joint consultation with local leaders with the request that they prepare written findings about the contested matter. This is what happened in Dort in 1618–1619 in response to the Arminian debates about predestination. To describe such a synod as a "Reformed Council"[128] and to view its canons[129] as a counterpart to the Formula of Concord[130] is not permissible, even though they were approved later in all the participating churches. The Synod of Dort was a Dutch synod, assisted by a total of twenty-eight foreign Reformed guests, among whom the French, the Hungarians, the Poles, and the Bohemians were absent. To compare its canons with the Formula of Concord is clearly inappropriate because there was nothing remotely like an Augustana in place as a common foundation for such decisions. Further, these decisions related authoritatively to one point alone and were neither meant as a general confession of faith nor appropriate to serve as one. Not excluded, finally, were (4) *scholarly collections* of different Reformed confessions. We name here the two works that appeared in Geneva: the "Harmonia confessionum Fidei orthodoxarum et reformatarum ecclesiarum" [Harmony of the confessions of faith of ortho-dox and Reformed churches] prepared by the pastor from southern France, *Salnar*[131]; and the "Corpus et Syntagma Confessionum fidei" [Body and arrangement of confessions of faith], written by a certain Caspar *Lauren-tius*[132] in 1612 and often confused with the previous work. The purpose of both was to unite the actual texts of the most important Reformed confes-sional documents in a harmonious whole, including as mentioned above the Augustana Variata and two further confessions by Philip Melanchthon, the Saxon of 1551[133] and the Württemberg of 1552.[134] Salnar's work included a careful parallel listing of the different confessional propositions theme by theme, whereas Laurentius provided a short harmony as a preface to the var-ious texts cited. (A new edition of Salnar's Harmony was published by August Ebrard in Barmen in 1887.)[135] One can understand why such attempts were made. One may venture to say that these represented an imitative and ultimately un-Reformed endeavor, which was much too clearly marked by the desire for the fleshpots of Egypt (see Exod. 16:3). They did not have major or widespread impact in their own century. Salnar's Harmony received in 1583 the approbation of the French National Synod at Vitré together with the Belgic Confession of the Netherlands.[136] It was mentioned in 1595 in the Bre-men Consensus and recommended for reading to the pastors,[137] and it was translated several times into English.[138] Laurentius's "Corpus et Syntagma," in which the characteristic attempt to produce a synoptic survey of the con-fession was given up, was proclaimed as the teaching norm of the theologi-cal faculty at the reestablishment of the Reformed university of Marburg in 1653.[139] |

That is, however, all that was done, and similar attempts to publish such collections of Reformed confessions were *not* made again until the nine-teenth century. Are we in error when we say that the reason for this was that the Reformed, given their basic attitude, had at best a lukewarm if any interest at all in such external literary demonstrations of their doctrinal unity? Even the first *more recent* "Collection of Reformed Symbolic Books" ["Corpus librorum symbolicorum . . . reformatorum"] is *not* the work of a Reformed theologian but rather of the Lutheran Johann Christian Wilhelm Augusti (Elberfeld, 1827).[140] He undertook this assembling of the confes-sions of the old confessional opponent with the intention of making his own contribution to the general battle for confessionalism and against the newer opponent, which was the modern spirit of the age seeking to dissolve and set aside all confessions.[141] Of the newer collections of Reformed confessional documents, we can name that of Hermann Agathon *Niemeyer* (Leipzig, 1840),[142] that of the German-American Philipp *Schaff* (in the third volume of his "Bibliotheca Symbolica Ecclesiae Universalis" [New York, 1877]),[143] and, above all, that of Ernst Friedrich Karl *Müller* ("Die Bekenntnisschriften der Reformierten Kirche" [Leipzig, 1903]).[144] The genesis of all these works is to be sought in the flourishing academic *historicism* of the nineteenth century. They are *not* to be claimed as expressions of a Reformed confessionalism comparable to the well-known "Symbolischen Bücher der evangelisch-lutherischen Kirche" ["Symbolic Books of the Evangelical-Lutheran Church"] by Johann Tobias Müller[145] on the other side. Only the aforementioned new edition of Salnar's Harmony by Ebrard could be taken as such, but it is simply the continuation of the exception to the rule, which is how Salnar's book should be regarded in general. Even the question of what belongs in such a collection and what does not is answered in a variety of ways. In his preface, Karl Müller says that if he had wanted to be comprehensive, he would have had to double the number of documents incorporated into his book, which is already almost a thousand pages in length.[146] This illustrates the fact that the Reformed confession is, to be sure, a very particular house, but a house whose doors and windows are open in all directions. A Reformed theologian or Christian could or can regard, either by free choice or in terms of the origins of one's church, *this* or *that* confession as definitive for oneself. One could and can eclectically affirm *all* of them in order to take from each what is *personally meaningful*. If capable of doing so, one could or can follow the example of Zwingli, Bullinger, Calvin, or Elector Johann Sigismund, and with due respect for the others write *one's own* Reformed confession. The only thing one cannot do is to argue to oneself or to others that *one's own* confession is *the* Reformed confession. Reformed confessions, as long as and to the extent that they are Reformed, will always be *many* and not *one*.

3. We can relate the definition of a third distinctive characteristic

| May 4 |

to the observation that the older Reformed *avoided* calling their confessions "*books of symbols*" ["*libri symbolici*"]. Augusti puts it this way in the title of his book and often elsewhere,[147] but he does so as a Lutheranized habit.[148] The Reformed confessions are precisely *not* symbols. They are called *Confession of Faith* [Confessio fidei] (this is the usual term), or *Consensus* or *Catechism* or *Articles* [Articuli] or *Theses* or *Declaration*. In other words, they do *not* want to be placed at the same level of dignity as the confessions of the first centuries, which belong to a higher order, so to speak. To be sure, they are not quite sure how to deal with the early confessions, although that is due less to their content than to their normative claim. The writers of the Book of Concord did rank the Augustana at the same level as the early confessions. The position of the Reformed in regard to the *ancient church's symbols* was not quite clear from the *beginning*. It was natural that both the concept and the content of such a historical authority interposed between the Scripture and the present day would be fundamentally alien to the Reformed view of the total sufficiency of Holy Scripture. It is expressly formulated in the Second Helvetic Confession (M 199,40): "The catholic faith is not given to us by human laws, but by Holy Scriptures, of which the Apostles' Creed is a compendium."[148a] With the exception of the Apostles' Creed, whose apostolicity as well as its fealty to Scripture were unquestioned, we are dealing here with an *alien element*, an unavoidable *concession*, when the Reformed confessional documents speak at all of a symbol, which they only do with reference to the ancient ecumenical symbols. It is remarkable that *Zwingli never* saw a problem here. |

This question was, however, the subject of the first of Calvin's numerous theological struggles. His view was that a confession is a "*testimony of the inwardly conceived faith.*"[149] When composing such a document, one could not emphasize enough that in both content and mode of expression nothing other should be included than the "most authentic truth of Scripture, devoutly composed of choice and solemn words."[149a] Their sentences should reproduce the sense of Scripture, if not the literal wording, and nothing else. For "we should seek for God nowhere else than in his *word*, think nothing about him except his *word*, and say nothing about him except through his *word*" (7,311–12). As Calvin made very clear from early on in Geneva, based on this principle he found the Athanasian and Nicene Creeds especially, among all the ancient confessions, to be quite simply unappealing and suspect. He gave free rein at that time to the substantive criticism of them that he felt compelled to make. He felt that he was dealing here with "idle speculation" ["otiosa speculatio"] (7,313). He complained about the Nicene Creed's redundant wordiness ("battologia"), which would be more fitting for a song than for a confessional formula, and he doubted whether this confession really resulted from the Synod of Nicea (7,315–16). He refused to sign the Athanasian Creed, for he had pledged faithfulness to God and not to the symbol of Athanasius, which in his view had not been formulated in a legitimate way. Moreover, he was not accustomed to acknowledge as the word of God something that was not substantiated as such (10/II, 83–84, 86).[150] In his Institutes of 1536, he made very clear that although he might not reject the terminology of these confessions as a way to describe the biblical truth, still for his person and use they had nothing more than historical value (1,59–62).[151] His friend and colleague Farel was even more explicit in his rejection of them, for in his writings these confessions are never mentioned, and their typical terms, especially "trinity" ["trinitas"] and "person" ["persona"], are ostentatiously avoided. It was because of this attitude that Dr. Peter Caroli of Lausanne, one of the most ambiguous figures of that period, attacked the two Genevans in 1537. They had to appear before a series of synods and colloquia in order arduously to struggle for their vindication, and for a while, they were seriously suspect of *anti-Trinitarianism* throughout Switzerland and all the way to Wittenberg.[152] Calvin's name was mentioned together with Servetus's in *one* breath (10/II, 103).[153] |

Although Arianism could never really be proven against Calvin, this suspicion and the negative society in which he suddenly found himself forced him, and with him the Reformed churches in general, to adopt what was at least formally a more positive stance toward the symbols. The Reformed irreverence for history had reached its limits. These churches, although fundamentally particular in character, did not want to be forced into the isolated situation of the spiritualists. They certainly desired to have nothing in common with the Arians and other "isms" of the long history of heretics, which this whole controversy made very clear to them. This is how Calvin arrived at the intentional and conscious shift to Trinitarian Orthodoxy that would later cost Servetus his life: Calvin did not want to be confused with him.[154] Similarly, the Reformed confessions made the shift to a modest concession at the cost of the principle of Scripture. This concession meant that honorable mention was given from now on to the old symbols, although it was never quite clear why. It was not so much because one needed them but rather because one did not want to oppose them. They did not want to do that because, in fact, they agreed with the symbols' content without wanting to put great emphasis upon them. |

This crisis of the early years could never be completely forgotten. We find a solemn affirmation of consensus with the ancient church—like that at the beginning of the Augustana[155] the Smalcaldic Articles,[156] and both parts of the Formula of Concord[157]—only in the Confessio Rhaetica of 1552,[158] and in a few German-Reformed confessions, the Dillenburg,[159] the Bremen,[160] and the Confessio Sigismundi.[161] In the Swiss canton of Grisons [Rhaetia; Graubünden], they were engaged in a difficult defensive struggle against the spiritualism spreading north from Italy. In Germany they were affected in this regard as in many others by the powerful magnetic force of Lutheranism. These cases are, however, *not* in any way characteristic. In the *Gallican Confession*, composed by Calvin himself in 1559, the symbols appear at the end of the fifth article, after the scriptural principle has been asserted very emphatically against antiquity, custom, the majority, human wisdom, judgments, decisions, edicts, decrees, councils, visions, and miracles. He does so with one sentence: "And therefore, we confess the three creeds, to wit: the Apostles', the Nicene, and the Athanasian, because they are in accordance with the Word of God."[162] One could translate this *"because they are"* [*"pource qu'ilz sont"*] just as appropriately with *"since"* [*"quatenus"*] or with *"which are"* [*"quia sunt"*], similar to the Irish Articles of Religion of 1615.[163] This was in fact the argument made in the Tetrapolitan Confession of 1530 in its apologetic assertion that the newly introduced biblical preaching did not distance people from true Christian doctrine. They were, rather, *strengthened*, in that this preaching was in agreement with such doctrines, "among [which] is what the Church of Christ has hitherto believed concerning the Holy Trinity" (56,10[–12]).[163a] In Zwingli's *Fidei Ratio*,[164] the *Belgian Confession* of 1561,[165] the *Second Helvetic Confession*,[166] the *Netherlands Confession* of 1566,[167] the *Bohemian* of 1609,[168] the English *Thirty-Nine Articles*,[169] and in the *Staffort Book*,[170] they are appealed to only in the exposition of the doctrines of God, the Trinity, and Christ. The vast majority of the confessions find it sufficient, at some more or less prominent point, to mention, recite, or extensively expound the Apostles' Creed. There is quite a number of confessions (of the older ones I mention the *Bern Synod* of 1528[171] and the *Scots Confession* of 1560[172]) that never refer to any of the ancient symbols, not even the Apostles' Creed. It is not without significance that Calvin finds it necessary and proper, in both of his catechisms, to articulate clearly his doubts about its apostolic origins (C 22,52[173]; M 118,11[174]). We note as a curiosity that in 1562, the Reformed Christians in the Erlau Valley of Hungary made the following selection from the long list of ancient symbols: the Nicene Creed, the Milevitanum of 402, the Second Arausicanum of 529, and, astonishingly enough, the "Canons of Trent, published in 1547 and 1546, on justification, faith, and works." The confident comment is then added, "Also many other councils and decrees which present the truth of scripture."[175] |

We must, moreover, remember that the Reformed confessional documents, whenever they speak of the authority of councils and synods in general (e.g., the *Second Helvetic*,[176] the *Scots*,[177] the *Hungarian*,[178] the *Thirty-Nine Articles*,[179] the *Irish Articles*[180]—the exception being the *Westminster Confession!*[181]) unreservedly emphasize their *humanity* and *capacity for error*. The Thirty-Nine Articles make this emphasis with express regard to matters of faith,[182] but this is the consensus of all the others. Bullinger, in agreement with Calvin's definition of a confession,[183] defines a symbol as a "sincere exposition of the faith" ["sincera fidei explicatio"],[184] to make plain that talk about symbols is an imposed alien thing in Reformed discourse. The concept of the symbol as a solemn repetition of the ancient articles of faith given and revealed by the Holy Spirit, which repetition must itself be elevated essentially to an article of faith, cannot be accepted by the Reformed. The simple reason is that, for the Reformed, that which is given and revealed by the Holy Spirit can only be the Holy Scriptures themselves. As a Reformed Christian, one firmly confesses *one's own* faith, certain that what one confesses is true, and concerned to demonstrate that one's confession is in agreement with the confession of all the faithful of all times. But, with one's confession, one does not claim to restore again the "holy church of God in former times" as it was put in the Luther citation above.[185] What is *given* and *revealed* in Scripture must not be confused with what one subsequently *confesses*, for which it is the eternal *origin*. The "*testimony* of faith" ["*testificatio* fidei"] must orient itself to the "truth of Scripture" ["veritas scripturae"], as surely as it is the "testimony of *faith*" ["testificatio *fidei*"], but it does not become in the process a kind of lower level or further development of Scripture. Scripture remains Scripture, unique, incommensurable, one of a kind. The Reformed confessions *were not able* to claim for the ancient church's symbols that higher level of holiness but, on the contrary, *denied* such a claim. With every acknowledgment of their content, their validity could only be seen in what they truly were, "sincere expositions of the faith" ["sincerae fidei explicationes"] or, more clearly in Calvin's words, "testimonies of inwardly conceived faith" ["conceptae intus fidei testifactiones"]. |

As an illustration, I will remind you once more that on the Reformed side, they always avoided moving their Reformers into that half-mythological radiance in which that man of God, Martin Luther, soon came to be seen by his followers.[186] Zwingli and Calvin were on occasion spoken of in such a way, but their memory was dealt with as a remembrance of *humans* and thus and even more pointedly their confessions were unsentimentally and unambiguously regarded as *human* confessions. I find no reference among the Reformed to "books of our symbols" ["libris symbolicis nostris"] until the much *later* period of epigones, as for instance the Helvetic Formula of Consensus of 1675,[187] then the Doctrinal Articles of the Palatinate Union,[188] which are dubiously Schleiermacherian in their thrust, and finally some more recent French and French-Swiss Confessions.[189] These are all documents for which the ancient confessions are no longer "confessions" ["confessiones"] in the sense of Calvin's definition, but rather appear to them as did the ecumenical confessions for Calvin, as honorable witnesses of the past and to that extent in fact "symbols." The Reformed confessions are and desire to be nothing other than mere human confessional *acts, over against which* the revelation of God in Scripture also stands constantly as a *given*. They position themselves in the bright light of *history*, albeit on occasion with a certain solemnity (Calvin himself had spoken of "choice and solemn words" ["solennibus et exquisitis verbis"][190]). They are measures, significant actions, one might even say solemn gestures, carried out by believers or by those chosen by believers for the sake of the good order and edification of the community of God on *earth*. They are made available for examination, to prove themselves, and for discussion. They bear the marks of the occasional, of relatedness to a specific time and situation, of the unique. Of course, the Augustana has all of these characteristics as well. Among the Reformed confessions there is more than one that, in a very different way from the Augsburg Confession, makes the impression of being well considered, comprehensive, necessary, and timeless. The difference, however, is that this earthly and historical character of the confession on the Reformed side was never romanticized or mythologized, even when it was the most carefully conceived miniature dogmatics. Without placing less emphasis upon the pure and the true, upon orthodox doctrine, they never hesitated to say, This is *our* confession! That was not the same thing that Lutherans meant when they said, This is our *symbol*! The well-known Wittenberg saying, "God's Word and Luther's teaching will not perish now or ever" ("Gottes Wort und Luthers Lehr vergehen nun und nimmermehr!")[191] could never be uttered by a Calvinist. To put Calvin in the first line, pairing it with God's Word, would be impossible for even the most enthusiastic Calvinist. Just as impossible would be the couplet that occurs frequently in the Formula of Concord: "the Word of God and the Augsburg Confession" ["Verbum Dei et Augustana Confessio"] (567,10; 726,7).[192] |

Let us turn to the first of the Reformed confessional statements in Müller's collection, *Zwingli's Sixty-seven Articles* of 1523.[193] What are these sixty-seven propositions? They are nothing other than theses for disputation, independently composed by the People's Priest Zwingli, obviously in great haste as was his style generally, and then successfully defended against the adherents of the old church. The Zurich Council declared that he had won the debate, and then ordered all preachers to preach nothing other "than that which they can prove with the holy Gospel and other divine Scriptures."[194] Now the Sixty-seven Theses became in the Zurich region the standard for scriptural faithfulness, until they were replaced by a further instruction written by Zwingli and sanctioned by the authorities, the "Christian Introduction" or "Short Christian Instruction" (the second document in Müller's collection[195]). As a result, they no longer needed to be taken into consideration. How could a document written and handled in such a way ever seek to be or be capable of attaining the dignity of a "symbol"? It was, at its time, a practical, powerful, broadly visible and influential action, no less and no more than that. Or let us take the *Lausanne Theses of 1536* (M, Nr. 9).[196] They were the basis for the disputation by which the Reformation was introduced into the territory of the Vaux, which had only recently become Bernese. Later, no one would ever remember them. When they had fulfilled their purpose, they became a historical document. One can demonstrate even more instructively the difference between a Reformed 'confession of faith' [Confessio fidei] and an ecclesial symbol by turning to the "Confession of Faith which all the citizens and inhabitants of Geneva and the subjects of the country must promise to keep and hold."[197] It was written in 1536 by *Farel* on the basis of Calvin's Catechism, and in 1537 it was imposed by both of them upon the citizens of Geneva, as the title indicates. We possess an authentic explanation by Calvin (in the preface to the Latin edition of the Catechism of 1538, 5,317–18)[198] regarding his intentions with the imposed recognition of the confession at that time and his own thinking about it.[199] He perceived that, following the renunciation of the papacy and the establishment of evangelical preaching, the Genevan *civil* community must now *constitute* itself as a worthy and virtuous *eucharistic* community. This did not mean that God's baptismal covenant with his people required any kind of confirmation on their part. But they the people needed to make their covenant with God anew. Just as Moses, Josiah, Asa, Ezra, and Nehemiah, in spite of, or better, precisely because of the covenant sealed in circumcision, constantly had to call upon God's people to present themselves to God with a new vow of faithfulness, now the Geneva populace at the inauguration of a new age should carry out a "holy action" ["actio sacra"][200] and give God the honor through the confession of his truth. Calvin's intention and Farel's confession were then criticized and protested not only in Geneva but by Christians elsewhere—probably they were from the Bernese Oberland.[201] How would Calvin respond? He pointed out that under the banner of the one 'Emperor Christ' [Imperator Christus] there are different 'soldiers' [milites] who are to carry out their common task in mutual harmony *next* to each other, each with his own gifts and weaknesses, without depriving each other of their freedom through a "servile conformity . . . in external matters" [servilis . . . conformitas in rebus externis"].[202] Thus, the necessity of a confession, just asserted and demonstrated, is for Calvin a necessity on the level of *freedom*. Freedom is superior to necessity, and superior to freedom is the 'Emperor Christ' [Imperator Christus], whose every command everyone must always be prepared to obey. Calvin believes that he is obeying Him when he now requires of his congregation this "sacred act" ["actio sacra"], the significant event of confession, *this* confession. To do so sends a signal that illumines like a stroke of lightening the seriousness and irrevocability of the situation now established in Geneva by the Reformation. He had no objection when the taking of the churchly oath was connected to the civil oath in the formulation of the new constitution of the city-state of Geneva, finding it entirely compatible with his intention. This meant that both oaths were read out from the pulpit and repeated by the entire population with hands raised to form the traditional sign of oathtaking. He looked upon the entire matter as precisely not a question of "doctrine" ["doctrina"] but of "ceremonies" ["ceremonia"], as an opportunity for "edification" ["aedificatio"].[203] He was aware that the procedure took place in the midst of the ambiguity of the *world* and that one could and might arrive at differing judgments of its rightness or wrongness. He ascribed to it no absolute significance, which might obligate others to emulate it. Rather, he asked of his critics—in this preface Calvin requests, even pleads—that he might take *this* step *now* with *his* church, without being judged by others. Later on, following his recall to Geneva in 1541, he never returned to the Confession of 1537 nor to this requirement of a general oath-taking. For him it was a unique event, a special case, a measure that was deprived of its holiness after it had happened, and thus was not a real symbol, that is, a permanently established one. Similarly, the first Reformed confessional act in what is today Germany, the *Confession of the East Friesian Preachers* of 1528,[204] written in Dutch, described itself expressly as the product of a particular occasion, namely, as an apology that those evangelical preachers, Zwinglians all of the first water, found necessary over against the accusation leveled at them that they despised God's Word and the sacraments. Aportanus,[205] who was an ally of the Honius who had such a decisive influence on the formulation of Zwingli's Communion doctrine in 1523,[206] was the author of this strange confession. It is a document that reminds one of a basalt stone crag piercing the sky, bordering on Schwenckfeldian spiritualism, and certainly a confession that in no way seeks to be a symbol. I

The continuation of the process of Reformed confession formulation corresponds completely to these early stages. Viewed from a distance, the first wave of impressive and strong personalities, motivated by their somewhat uncontrollable initiative, was followed *later* by the synods, governments, and princes with their more transparent consultations and decisions. But the results always had the character of the relative and unique, of earthly rather than the heavenly decisions—even if all the bells did sound at the proclamation of the Canons of Dort.[207] Of course, neither they nor Luther and the Lutherans ever thought that they were capable of positing new articles of faith; they did not even see themselves as positing the old in a new way. In each particular statement they were saying, *we, here, now, and for the time being*, want to understand in this particular way, not the articles of faith, but the Word of God given alone in Scripture.[208] "Testimony of the inwardly conceived faith" ["conceptae intus fidei testifactio"][209]—as a matter of principle, a Reformed confession cannot base its dignity on any other kind of argumentation. The Reformed church is genuinely horrified by "church-power, properly so called," as stated in a Congregationalist Declaration of 1658.[210] The fact that Zwingli's Fidei Ratio and later the Erlauthal Confession of Hungary and that of the Bohemian Brotherhood were presented to the *emperor* in 1609[211] did not enhance the qualified authority of these confessions at all in their respective geographical regions. Even *authorship* by a Zwingli, Farel, Calvin, or Bullinger could not guarantee such respect. The most excellent *content* of a document could not transform it into a symbol, although the Germans occasionally tried to make that claim for their Heidelberg Catechism.[212] A Reformed confession always stands under an ultimate, articulated or nonarticulated reservation because it is always located at a completely *different* level from *Scripture*. It essentially always thinks and speaks from *below*, and is not a revelation from *above*. It is not the "last trump before the day of judgment."[213] I need not explicate further how the offensive multiplicity of Reformed confessions, which we have already discussed, relates to this deficiency (if it is one).

4. A fourth distinctive characteristic consists of the fact that, | May 8

regardless of how seriously they were meant, how powerfully and resistant to all contradictions their propositions were, and how widespread the general acknowledgment of their content might be, these confessions were fundamentally intended as merely *provisional*, improvable and replaceable *offerings*, never as an authority, as the "form and rule" ["forma et regula"] that the Formula of Concord found in the Augsburg Confession.[214] This is expressly stated in the oldest documents by Zwingli or from his circle. One of the earliest objections raised by Luther against the Reformed was that they were not certain about their cause. "For the spirit is not so timid and does not argue as they do" (End. 5,264–65).[215] A genuine Lutheran today can only shake his head when he beholds the picture that now is to be unrolled. In presenting his Sixty-seven Theses for discussion, Zwingli wrote, "And where I have not now correctly understood the said Scripture, I am ready *to be instructed and corrected* from the aforesaid Scripture."[216] In the mandate that the Zurich Council attached to the second confession, Zwingli's Christian Introduction, which followed immediately, we read:

> Once again, we desire that whoever is able *advise us better or differently* by the true divine Scriptures. We *shall gladly receive* such advice from them with particular gratitude and joy. Hereby we also once again ask each and everyone, that whoever finds us in some way to have *erred* against God and his word of the holy gospel, or *to be wrong*, to *point it out* in a friendly way out of the true word of God and of the gospel for the sake of the honor of God, of truth, and Christian love. We shall receive and welcome such with the highest gratitude. (Z 1,543)[217]

In a similar way, the Bernese authorities concluded their introduction to the Bern Consensus of 1532 with these words:

> If anything were presented to us by our pastors or others which might *lead us closer to Christ* and in the power of God's Word be more supportive of common friendship and Christian love than the views presented here, we *will gladly accept it and not block the course of the Holy Spirit*. For it is not directed backwards to the flesh but always forwards towards the image of Christ Jesus our Lord.[218]

This same grateful willingness to be corrected at any time from Scripture is found in the conclusion of the *First Basel Confession of 1534*[219] and in the *Preface*[220] to the *Second Helvetic Confession*.[221] The old Reformed consciousness *combined* a sense of the perfectability of its dogma with a confidence and certainty with which it still affirmed its dogma. An instructive instance of this combination is found in the *Preface to the Scots Confession of 1560*, in which the vow is made that they will be willing to be corrected from Scripture, followed by the second vow that they "intend to endure to the end in

the confession of our faith as in the following chapters" (Beck II, 238).[222]
The Duisburg General Synod of 1610 stated,

> If there be anyone who, in the future, should feel doubtful in his con-
> science or have difficulty with one or the other point of the Catechism,
> and who believes that he could express this in God's Word more clearly
> and plainly, then he should not bring this directly into the pulpit and crit-
> icize the catechism but rather speak fraternally and in a friendly way
> with his classis.[222a] If this should not suffice for him, then the matter
> should be brought before the Synod where it will be dealt with, so that
> the two extremes may be avoided, namely, 'license of novelty' [licentia
> novitatum] and 'enslavement of the conscience' [servitus conscien-
> tiarum]. (*Bredt*, Kirchenrecht II, 742)[223]

In a weaker although still clearly recognizable way, this view of the perfectability of churchly doctrine is reflected in the synodal oath used in the
church of *Zurich* in the seventeenth and eighteenth centuries, in which the
participants had to swear that they would

> teach and preach the Word of God according to the correct Christian
> understanding, both the Old and New Testaments as able to do so, in
> light of the mandate issued by my lords of Zurich to improve teaching
> and the faith, and thereby to refrain from introducing any dogma or doc-
> trine which is doubtful and not yet accepted and preserved, *unless* it is
> *presented* beforehand to a general and regular assembly, which meets
> twice a year, and is *endorsed* by it. (Finsler, Statistik, 41–42, 584)[224]

The conclusion of every synod consisted of a general inquiry into whether
anyone would have something to present regarding doctrine, the method
of teaching, or the practice of worship.[225] It is thus still the case, even in the
age of Dort and the Helvetic Formula of Consensus, that the church's
dogma is subject to *discussion*. |

Most of the confessional documents, to be sure, did not articulate this
reservation so expressly, and some of them seem to exclude it all together.
The *Rhaetic Confession* of 1552, for example, while confirming that we are
humans and thus easily err, are ignorant, and can be deceived,[226] restricts
its openness to further teaching to the paragraphs relating to ecclesiastical
orders, while declaring that its actual doctrinal articles are "lasting and
fixed divine oracles" ["divina oracula stabilita et fixa"].[227] The Helvetic Formula of Consensus of 1675, which is to be sure a most unusual phenome-
non among the Reformed confessional documents, virtually prohibits
either now or in the future the proposal of a "doubtful dogma, a new one,
or one unheard of in our churches."[228] This certainly means that, in *this*
regard, the concept of the confession in the sense of the *Formula of Concord*
had been *attained*. This prohibition, comparable with the Zurich Synodal

Order of the same period, was nothing other than the strained attempt to hold on to the faith of the fathers at a period in which the "unheard of dogmas" ["dogmata inaudita"] rightly or wrongly stood threateningly at the gates of the church. It was an attempt that was non-Reformed in its very essence, and it generated no historical impact. The Formula of Consensus had become obsolete in all the participating churches within a few decades.[229] The majority of the confessions from about 1540 on *remain silent* about the fundamental question of the perfectability of the doctrine they contain. To deduce from this silence that the old Reformed view of this question was never totally forgotten, or in any event was never basically set aside, is just as probable as the contradictory conclusion. |

The facts themselves shape the conclusion that the Reformed confessions essentially could not have the character of final words, as did the Lutheran. To be sure, there was a rigid orthodox theology on Reformed soil just as there was a Lutheran. But the source of knowledge of this orthodoxy was the Holy Scripture, interpreted through the internal witness of the Holy Spirit, which from about 1600 on could be replaced by reason illumined either by the Aristotelian or Cartesian tradition. It could never, however, become a symbol. What was lacking for the formation of a genuinely Reformed confessionalism, in spite of the pointed way in which the doctrinal differences were sensed and debated, was the one unchangeable confession like the one to which the Lutherans could always relate. No pious reverence for the original historical documents could prevent the fact that *Zwingli's Sixty-Seven Theses* were replaced by another formulation within a year, the theses of the *Bern Disputation* after four years, the *First Basel Confession* after two years, the *First Helvetic Confession* after twenty-six years, and the *Erlauthal Confession* within the same year. The *Belgic Confession* was constantly revised from 1561 until 1619.[230] After standing as authority for 130 years, the *Scots Confession* was set aside in 1690 in favor of the Westminster Confession, which has in turn been constantly edited and worked on up to the modern day.[231] We need scarcely speak of the recklessness of the English Congregationalists (Independents), who have elevated to the level of principle the idea of freedom over against one's own ecclesial past.[232] Any concern for the external continuity of his own proclamation certainly did not prevent Calvin from replacing his own Catechism of 1536[233] with another one in 1545.[234] His Institutes, which in their original intent and form were really a confessional document, an apology for the evangelical Christians of France, were subjected to constant revision during his lifetime.[235] This was done in the good and certainly justifiable confidence, especially in Calvin's case, that no harm would be done to the continuity of the content in this constant process of revision, improvement, and expansion. *Luther* is supposed to have said to *Melanchthon* once (J. T. Müller, LXIX),[236] "Philippe, Philippe, it is a wrong thing that you are constantly altering the Augsburg Confession, for it is not your book, it is the church's book." If the anecdote is true, then one can say about the Reformed that they did this wrong thing with great ease and the easiest of consciences. For there *was no such thing* as a "book of the church" here in Luther's sense. "For what would be the point of living," Calvin once asked in his writing against Pighius (1543), "if neither age nor practice nor constant exercise nor reading nor meditation were *of any benefit* to us? And what would be the point of making progress if it did not result in some profit reaching others also? On the contrary, if Pighius does not know it, I should like it to be absolutely clear to him that we strive night and day to shape our faithfully transmitted teachings into a form which we also judge will be the best" (6,250).[237] That theologians in times of doctrinal disputes should consult together and arrive at unifying decisions about the right form of the confessions was for Calvin both a necessity and a command. "But I *deny* it to be *always the case* that an interpretation of Scripture adopted by vote of a council is true and certain" (Inst. IV, 9,13).[238] The Reformed formation of confessions is, seen as a whole, not a *frozen* river like the Lutheran, on which one could *walk* ("Secure Church, Our Church" [239] can therefore *not* be sung here!). It is rather a freely flowing river, in which one can only *swim*, despite the bulky bodies it carries along. Looking backward to a normative past is *not* the Reformed way, even though on occasion it has been done with great style (e.g., by Abraham Kuyper[240] and his followers in Holland). |

Several things must be said about the consequences that ensued. The confessional flexibility of the Reformed tradition can be seen especially well in the obviously much greater *open-mindedness* with which it has continually learned from Lutheranism. It was seen at the beginning of the nineteenth century in its overt willingness, which at times degenerated into a spineless servility, to be absorbed into the so-called *Union*.[240a] This passage perhaps did more damage to the German Reformed Church both externally and inwardly than one is likely to know today, where one has become used to its very small size. The *Reformed*-United began immediately to allow their worship, doctrine, and constitution to be Lutheranized, whereas the *Lutheran*-United almost universally made certain that they did not respond in kind. The particular consequence was that the specifically Reformed *theology* in Germany in the nineteenth century remained significantly *underdeveloped* in contrast with the Lutheran, which had no intention of climbing down from its confessional throne. There would certainly be some things to say about the relationship between *Zwingli* and *Schleiermacher*.[241] It is in any event certainly not the Reformed confession that relates these two to each other. We have as little reason to turn to *Alexander Schweizer* and *Biedermann*[242] as Reformed as we do to Lipsius and Pfleiderer as Lutherans.[243] *Fréderic Godet* and *Schlatter* are to a much greater extent free biblicists than they are Reformed.[244] Of the more well-known names there remain only Max

Goebel and Heinrich Heppe, who made their name primarily as historians.[245] Of the systematically productive theologians one can name only *August Ebrard* and especially *Hermann Friedrich Kohlbrügge*.[246] Of all those named, I discern in him the strongest and most important Reformed instincts, but he was as much an outsider over against the official German Reformed establishment as was August Vilmar for his part over against official Lutheranism.[247] And what could be the importance of these occasional "swimmers in the vast abyss"[248] over against the series of more or less genuine Lutherans from Klaus Harms to Scheibel, Friedrich Julius Stahl, Löhe, Rudelbach, Harless, Thomasius, Schmid, von Zezschwitz, von Hofmann, Martensen, Kahnis, Luthardt, Philippi, Frank to Ritschl,[249] whom Harnack has rightly or wrongly designated the last Lutheran church father?[250] We have yet to mention the great host of older and more recent, positive and liberal United theologians of Lutheran origins, all of whom have been far less unfaithful to their roots than have been their Reformed counterparts in the Union. One can derive some comfort from the fact that the Lutheran persistence was as much a genuine and necessary consequence of a profoundly unspiritual secularization, as was the Reformed a betrayal of its tradition. It is certainly justifiable to ask whether it is that much better to appear to hold high the Reformed banner but in reality to pursue in the name of Calvin the worst kinds of historicism and psychologism, as appears to be the case in America according to reliable reports.[251] In any event, this *is* the way that this secularization, by virtue of Reformed flexibility, has had its impact on the *Reformed Christians in Germany*. A further demonstration of it can be seen in the Reformed territorial churches in *Switzerland*, where the relations between the church and the common life of the people and the state have always been more intense than elsewhere. These churches have found it relatively easy to open themselves officially to the worldview and dogmatics of enlightened and modern man. It is a profoundly disturbing experience to trace in the doctrinal decisions of the various Swiss church constitutions and ecclesiastical orders of the nineteenth century just how the church's doctrine in its emptiness and lack of credibility has steadily retreated over against the assertive sentimentality of the middle classes. |

I will mention two extraordinary horrors so that you will know what I mean. The church constitution of *Zurich* of 1850 begins with the following sentences (General Regulations, par. 2):

> The Zurich church as part of the entire Christian church has as its purpose the education of its members to a religious way of thinking and a moral life according to the teaching and example of Christ and *seeks ever to proceed forward on its way to its infinite goals*. In accordance with the foundational principles of Protestantism and in agreement with the freedom of religion guaranteed in Article 4 of the Constitution, it seeks to attain this goal solely along the way of spiritual and moral influence and

rejects all forms of coercion. It recognizes scientific and theological academic freedom. (Finsler 45)[252]

The oath of office of Reformed pastors of the canton of *Baselland* [the region surrounding the city of Basel—Trans.] was formulated as follows in the regulations of 1838: "I pledge *to honor the Christian religion and virtue, faithful to the people of the Canton of Baselland*, to administer the constitution in all its parts, if circumstances require to commit body and life, property and blood for its maintenance, and to repudiate promptly every violation of the constitution and every danger which threatens it." It continues,

> I pledge to proclaim the Gospel of Jesus Christ, as it is contained in the Holy Scriptures, *solely in accordance with the principles of Biblical study which strive for evangelical truth*, solely and only to acknowledge the constitutional and legal agencies of the Canton Baselland as *my superior authority in churchly affairs as well*, and to receive from no agency outside the Canton Baselland any direction relating to the fulfillment of my official duties.(Finsler 199)[253]

I need not analyze further the political dalliance[254] that is the actual explanation of the terms of this wondrous symbol. You can see how far things could go. And yet the Reformed churches of Switzerland were not, to my knowledge, more godless and unbelieving than the others. They were rather more democratic, so that they demonstrated externally much more plainly what was really driving the spiritual life of so-called Christian society at the time.[255] Elsewhere, people were able to conceal the true state of things with lovely illusions. Who would want to doubt that the formulations just cited would have been the "testimony of the inwardly conceived faith" ["conceptae intus fidei testificationes"][256] of the majority of the Reformed church population (and not only the Reformed!) in all the enlightened parts of Germany, if one had given them the opportunity to express themselves so unapologetically loudly and officially. |

The confessional frailty of the Reformed in response to the movements emerging from the *revival* of the first half of the nineteenth century is especially instructive and *somewhat* encouraging. In Lutheran territories they almost automatically triggered an energetic recourse to the Augsburg Confession and the Formula of Concord.[257] In Reformed areas as well, Pietism immediately emerged as ecclesial orthodoxy. When it could not formally establish itself in the official Reformed churches, then this orthodoxy moved bravely on to the formation of *free churches* (with no concern for the historical continuity that was so important to its forefathers three hundred years earlier). This was especially the case in French Switzerland, France, England, and America.[258] But it never occurred to these orthodox free churches to restore the old confessions. Rather, while making a deep and respectful bow in their direction, these churches regard them as having become obsolete. Nowhere do they repeat them in their founding documents, nor is a new obligation to them introduced. In their place, *new* confessions are formulated, reflecting what people considered to be orthodox at the time. I will cite as exemplary for many the introduction to the "Profession of Faith of the Evangelical Church of Geneva" of 1847 (regrettably omitted in K. Müller, 905).[259] It states:

> Although no confession of faith written by humans, regardless of how excellent it may be, can be put in the place of Holy Scripture, and although everything which is necessary for salvation is clearly taught in this divine Word, it still appears to us that we live in an age in which the churches are called upon to confess their faith in more definite articulations. Therefore, while we are pleased to accept the confessional documents of the sixteenth century (especially the Catechism of the old Genevan church) in their opposition to Pelagianism, Arianism, and Papism, and in their confession of the teaching of salvation in Jesus Christ our Redeemer, we unanimously make the following confession. (Finsler 568)[260]

The position of these nineteenth-century Reformed Orthodox on the *Reformation* confessions resembles that of the old Reformed to *the ancient church symbols* as one egg does another. They know that no confession can replace Scripture; they must have and need, in spite of that, a confession. They acknowledge respectfully that the old books were the right word in their time and as such should always be "accepted" in the present situation, but then they move beyond them as they sit down to formulate their own modern confession. It is perfectly obvious that the old confessions were, by all comparison, much more substantive and valuable than these modern ones (cited in K. Müller under 46–54)[261] with their open and concealed concessions to the same spirit of the age to which the Pietists also paid their tribute (although somewhat more ashamedly than did the radicals of the Canton Baselland). One cannot fail to recognize the internal legalism that influenced in this process, nor to acknowledge what was at least formally the solidly Reformed way in which the Genevan Mômmiers [hypocrites][262] solved the problem. I

As far as the future is concerned, it can be said with relative certainty that any movement of the spirits on Reformed soil, if it were to happen again (if possible in a somewhat more serious way than a century ago) and were to refloat the ships that are stranded on the sand everywhere, would even less now than then pursue the repristination of the old confessions, but would necessarily emphasize the formulation of new confessions. Meanwhile, perhaps all of the churchly infirmities and emergency measures cited above are to be understood and borne as just that. These include the honorable burial in the *German United Church* that the German Reformed largely brought upon themselves, the virtually complete disappearance of the Reformed confession from the German *theological* arena which, speaking humanly, is still the most promising arena, the "freedom" of the Reformed mother churches of Switzerland, which borders on confessionlessness,[263] though the modest contemporary confessional formulas have become again somewhat more Christian and palatable than before,[264] and finally the deficiencies in the modern Reformed confessions that are available to us today. One can speak of a field of dry bones [see Ezek. 37:1]. Coming from a Reformed perspective, one must add that this is the normal scene 'things being as they are' [rebus sic stantibus]. The confession and the confessor are not to be separated from each other, according to the Reformed view. The so-called confessional stance must, if things are proceeding properly, stand here or fall with the stance of its confessor. And so it stands where it stands, testifying as eloquently for, or rather, against the church of our day as the Geneva Catechism today testifies for the church of the sixteenth century. *Without Calvin or without Calvinists there is no Calvinist confession.* The best we can do is to be profoundly ashamed of the poverty in which we find ourselves and anxiously avoid all attempts to act as though we were rich. The current situation has not changed what has been the final wisdom in the Reformed church, which, as classically expressed by the Bern Synod, is not to obstruct the work of the Holy Spirit who does not press back to the *flesh* but always *forward* toward the image of Christ.[265] The current situation does make it especially advisable that the Reformed church should set its only hope (truly its only hope) on the prayer, 'Come, creator Spirit' [Veni creator spiritus]![266]

5. In conclusion, we consider the character of the *commitment*[266a] that was to be made to the confessions in the Reformed churches. It is clear that it must be defined by the distinctive aspects of these confessions discussed up to now. The stringency with which they were acknowledged in the earliest years, and the unquestioned and universal acceptance with which they were immediately received, were based upon the *seriousness* with which, at decisive times, Reformed Christians determined that they must confess, and upon the *vitality* of the knowledge out of which the confession emerged. "This is the true and apostolic authority . . . which is not built upon place or persons, but upon pure doctrine that is derived from sacred scripture" (Bohemian Confession 1609, M 475,38[–40]).[267] Both were clearly remembered by the successive generations up to the threshold of the eighteenth century, and as long as this memory was *more* than historical and antiquarian, it was certain that the confession of the church, once made, would be preserved for both the shepherds and the flocks in an inwardly appropriate and necessary way. Next to this internal connection with the living act of knowledge and confession going back to the earliest period, the commitment to the confession as a binding *juridical* act was, in terms of its substance, a secondary matter of merely external order. It was a pillar that stood there, for the sake of completeness, but it did *not* actually support the roof. "It is not possible that the true authority, wherever it is passed on and demonstrated, is personally presented and defended in vain" (Bohemian

Confession 1609, M 475,45[–46]).[268] If this connection were to fall, then of necessity this pillar, the juridical bond, would also fall, and with it the roof that made the Reformed church recognizable as a confessional church, unless new artificial supports were brought in. The great third support that the Lutheran church possesses in the symbolic character of its confession was *not* foreseen in the Reformed structure from the beginning.

The seriousness and the ready acceptance with which the confessional *commitment* could become authoritative in the earliest period were based on the fact that in this period one still knew that faith is an *objective* thing, not an arbitrary act at the individual's discretion, and thus it is a *public* affair. With all seriousness it counts on the fact that the center of the religious question lies in the counsels of *God*, the Lord of the world and of history, and not in the sentiment, the heart, or the conscience of the *person* who believes in God. This commitment, as an act of inward integrity and uprightness, was still able to assert a *demand* of faith and to carry out the *obedience* of faith. We can neither understand nor do this any more. Religion had to be properly defined as a private matter from the moment[269] it became clear that it was understood solely as a sentimentalized thing inside us. This was the so-called religious experience, which Pietism and the Enlightenment, not without antecedents, moved to the center, and Schleiermacher made into the holy of holies of official Protestantism. The Reformed repudiation of the European and public character of the Christian confession did not fundamentally alter the concept of faith as an objective thing and a public matter. The break with the imperial church was for Zwingli and Calvin not a loss but a major gain, a move toward a method that was newer, better, and more appropriate to the matter. The various Reformed churches, although they were not bound together by a symbol, did not understand themselves as "religious fellowships,"[270] as later usage would put it, but rather as the nuclei of a new and emerging objectivity and public character of faith, following upon the defeat of the old lie. The Calvinist definition of the confession as "testimony of the inwardly conceived faith" ["conceptae intus fidei testificatio"][271] cannot be understood as the prelude to the establishment of the tyranny of religious subjectivism. We have seen and will see that this was meant not as a restriction but rather as a sharpening of the objectivity and universality of faith. This was true to the extent that, for Calvin, "faith" ["fides"] was indissolubly linked to the standard of the highly objective, highly universal given of the "most authentic truth of Scripture" ["ipsissima scripturae veritas"].[272] Defined in such a distinctive way, faith was not affirmed by the subject as a mood or a movement of the human subject, but rather as its relation to this 'truth of truths' [veritas veritatum] "inwardly conceived" ["intus conceptae"], which should then be testified to in the confession.

The thought of the individual citizen's, or even the preacher's, so-called "freedom of faith and conscience"[273] *within* the church was at least as strange and unnatural to Zwingli and Calvin as it was to Luther and Melanchthon.

May 11

I have already reported how Calvin managed to require of the entire citizenry of *Geneva* that they subscribe to Farel's Confession of Faith in 1537. Even earlier, the *First Basel Confession of 1534* was solemnly pledged by all citizens, and up to 1821 was at least read annually in the church during Holy Week.[274] Similarly, in John Laski's London congregation and later in[275] his "*Foreigners Church*" that moved to Frankfurt am Main, the membership of *all* members was bound to one's signing the confession (quoted in M, Nr. 33).[276] In 1581, the so-called *Covenant* in Scotland, in which the king (not entirely voluntarily![277]) and people made their mutual commitment to the Scots Confession of 1560, concludes with a formal oath that has two emphatic thrusts.[278] Such commitments were all the more binding for theologians. The participants in the Bern Disputation of 1528, for example, signed a statement to the effect that they "recognize the articles as Christian and desire in eternity not to oppose them but to prove them obediently with body and possessions" (M, XIX,48[–49]). The authorities' preface to the Bern Synod of 1532, the one that has the phrase about the Holy Spirit's finding freedom to move, ordains that the text of the Confession shall be dutifully read, explained, expounded, and renewed every year in synod. It stipulates further that at no point shall there be any substantive alteration of it.[279] Moreover, as late as the beginning of the eighteenth century the council provided a durably bound edition as a permanent piece of the inventory of every Bernese manse, with the expectation that it should be adhered to.[280] The *Confessio Rhaetica* [Rhaetian Confession] of 1552 excludes summarily from the practice of the preaching office in the Church of the Grisons anyone who does not know or want to acknowledge the content of its doctrinal articles.[281] The preface to the *Heidelberg Catechism* by Elector Friedrich III of the Palatinate emphasizes that the book is intended and is to be used not only as a teaching tool; it also should ensure, as it abrogates the dominant "incorrectness and imbalance," that "preachers and school-masters should have a certain and lasting form and measure which describes how they should conduct themselves in the instruction of youth and not undertake daily alterations after their own fancy nor introduce contradictory doctrine."[282] The most formal and positive commitment to the confession is found in the canons of the Polish *Synod of Thorn* of 1595, according to which the superintendents and seniors were required to maintain a permanent chronicle in which the signatures of the pastors of their districts were to be entered.[283] I

More than one of these regulations reveals, however, clear indications that the perspective of the "*godly compact*" ["*pia conspiratio*"],[284] from which Calvin in 1538 had initially viewed the unity of the different Reformed churches among themselves, was of importance for the internal church situation and for our understanding of the actual meaning of Reformed confessional commitment. That curious requirement that the citizens of Geneva take an oath (1537) also certainly makes clear that for Calvin the *congregation*, not as something invisible but as the completely visible community of citizens who documented with their concurrence with the Reformation that they wanted to be constituted as a eucharistic community,[285] was the actual subject of the confession. The Bern Theses of 1528, which contained the oldest formula of commitment, like Zwingli's Theses of 1523, had to pass through the fire of a general *disputation* in order to become the object of such an act of commitment; in both instances the *laity* were invited to and participated in these disputations. The Bern Synod of 1532, as implied by its name, was a freely adopted agreement arrived at by the assembly of all Bernese clergy, working with Capito of Strassburg, which was only then approved and enacted by the authorities.[286] The Rhaetian Confession and the Heidelberg Catechism were discussed in great detail at synods, after having been initially drafted by individuals, and it was only on the basis of such consultations and on nothing else that they were then introduced as confessions.[287] This is also true of all the subsequent Reformed confessions, with the exception of the two royal confessions in Reformed Germany (Confessio Sigismundi and the Staffort Book). When considering this matter of confessional *commitment*, we should give thought to the following sentence from the invitation to the Bern Disputation of 1528 issued by the city authorities: "Whatever at such a disputation is tested and proven by divine Biblical scriptures, is preserved, agreed to, accepted, decided, and deemed worthy of observance hereafter, should then be *empowered* without contradiction and have *eternal validity*" (M, XIX,27[–30]).[288] The commitment to confessions formed in this way was, in spite of this "eternal," as well as the substantive seriousness and legal stringency with which it was demanded, in its *essence* very different from the commitment to the Augsburg Confession. In the latter's formulation and proclamation, neither the affected congregations nor the great majority of the German theologians had anything to do other than to give their subsequent agreement with it. The Reformed confessions were as a matter of simple fact never such given entities but rather clearly the *work* of the participating churches. This prevented the formation of the ideology that emerged around the Augustana. This, in turn, had its bearing on the character of the commitment to be made to it. "What hands can make needs only hands to break."[289] Taken together with the other distinctive characteristics of the Reformed confessions in general, the memory of the *emergence* of this commitment must have indelibly marked it with the character of 'human law' [jus humanum]. This did not make it any less serious, but together with the confession itself, the commitment was *not* removed from the sphere of the discussable. There is proof enough in that Zurich regulation according to which the doctrine to which one was committed was made into the object of an annual and general review.[290] What the Reformed confessional commitment lacked was that consecration to a *higher* necessity, with which the Lutheran confession was later enveloped, and which on Reformed soil was reserved exclusively for the Holy Scriptures. |

This was demonstrated as the modern age emerged in which the Reformed church, together with Christendom in general, could with integrity only confess much less than its founders did, as the certainty of its convictions diminished. The Lutheran church, inwardly emaciated by neology, was firmly held in the iron armor of the fathers and continued to be externally and purportedly the confessional church, the church of the Augsburg Confession, which it started out to be. The Reformed, by contrast, were basically capable of submitting their earlier agreements to a process of revision, and to relegate parts or even all of their armor to the museum, or more respectfully, to the armory, without being conscious of rebelling against a *higher* order. They were able to weaken the relevance of their *commitment*, first of all morally and then with time legally, so that finally they could declare that the commitment was set aside. The idea of a confession that was foundational for the church did remain alive, together with the concept of a commitment to it, at least for the theologians of the church. But it became plain that they did *not* feel themselves to be committed in principle to a historically given confession *as such*. If some of the old confessions such as the Heidelberg retained their normative prestige, then that was an affair of individual churches or church circles. The decisive thing is that it was just as possible for them *not* to retain these confessions.[291] We have already seen that even the orthodox Reformed free churches of the nineteenth century did not stand or fall because of their teachers' commitment to the old confessions, whereas official Lutheranism asserts such a commitment until today, regardless of how modernized it might be.

The ways in which the Reformed chose to *relinquish* their old confessional commitments in favor of new ones were diverse. As we have noted, one could move toward the composition of new confessions that were *modestly* orthodox while making *modest* concessions to the spirit of the age. With regard to whether their obligatory character could be acknowledged or would persist, they had the same experience after a few decades that the state church had had after centuries. Another option was demonstrated by the remarkable declaration of the English *Congregationalists* of 1833. They propounded a new and orthodox confession as the contemporary expression of faith *as such* of the denomination, combining it simultaneously with a sharp protest against the authority and normativity of various other doctrinal formulae. At the same time, they affirmed total freedom of conscience for all church members, and did away with every *external* doctrinal commitment—while making a strong confession of the witness to which they wanted to commit themselves.[292] Perhaps one would have to be an Englishman to be able to appreciate fully the value of this very unprincipled solution, which was in its way quite respectable. In similar fashion, *the Chiesa Evangelica* (Evangelical Church of Italy) stated in 1870 that they regarded their articles as "the expression of biblical Christianity" ["l'espressione del Cristianesimo biblico"] and as the bond of unity and the banner (bandiera) of the church, but not the cause and foundation of salvation, for immutability and infallibility could be ascribed solely to the Word of God.[293] Further, one could work with the general assertion of one's "connection" to the churches of the Reformation, as did the *Free Church of the Canton Vaux* when it declared in 1847: "It has connected itself . . . to the evangelical churches that in the sixteenth century expressed their faith with an admirable agreement among their symbolic books, in particular in the Helvetic Confession of Faith."[294] There is a similar formulation in the *Constitution of the Free French Churches of 1849*,[295] while the General Synod of *Église réformee de France* [Reformed Church of France] declared in 1872 that it stood in confessional solidarity not only with the fathers and martyrs of the Confession de la Rochelle (Confessio Gallicana) but with all "Reformation churches in their various symbols," and thus also with the Lutherans.[296] It should be noted that the "connection" asserted in all these instances was only the transition to the publication of one's own more or less detailed new confession. One could appeal to the *"fundamental principles"* of the Evangelical-Reformed (as did the regional churches of the Cantons *Baselstadt, Graubünden, Schaffhausen, Aargau,* and *Glarus*), or join the more expressive *St. Gall* church as it called upon the "spirit" of this church, or with *Zurich* and *Bern* merely *mention* the historical "Evangelical-Reformed" without making any express commitment *to it.*[297] As an example of how the German Swiss solve the problem today, I will cite for you the formula with which I took my vows in *Bern* at the time of my ordination:[298]

> I vow as a servant of the divine Word to teach and to preach the gospel of Jesus Christ faithfully and purely on the basis of Holy Scripture, to the best of my knowledge and belief, to give witness through my unimpeachable conduct to the doctrine of salvation in all its parts, to fulfill conscientiously all the obligations of my calling and office, and in the official duties that may be entrusted to me to work for the welfare of the fatherland, the Evangelical-Reformed Church and the Christian community. (Stuckert, 67–68)

Or one could say with the words of the Church Order of the *Confederated Congregations* of the Evangelical-Reformed Confession in Lower Saxony: "Although the Confederation regards the Holy Scripture as the sole guideline for the faith and life of its members and also for the doctrine taught in our churches, it also subscribes in general(!) to the various(!) confessional documents of the Evangelical-Reformed Church."[299] One could reverse the emphasis with the wording of the Unifying Charter of the Palatinate Union of 1818: "The Protestant-Evangelical-Christian(!) Church respects appropriately(!) the [general symbols and] the symbolic books used in the separate Protestant confessions but acknowledges no other foundation of faith nor teaching norm than the Holy Scripture alone."[300] Obviously, one could declare the old confessions or various ones of them, with varying degrees of emphasis, as *still being in force*. The case in point today would be the still authoritative status of the Heidelberg Catechism in the Reformed church of North America, the Second Helvetic Confession in Austria, Bohemia, and Hungary, and the Westminster Confession in the Presbyterian churches of England, North America, and the regions that belong to them. We will not pursue the inquiry into the integrity or relevance of their authority in actual practice today.[301] |

I repeat that this apparently normal situation on Reformed soil is still only *one* possibility next to others. There is *no* standard Reformed resolution for the problem of confessional commitment that has arisen through the general spiritual vacuity of modern Protestantism. Rather, we see a whole series of attempts to resolve the problem, which as a whole can only document the absence of a normative Reformed resolution. They are all emergency measures, temporary bridges upon which one can proceed, necessitated by the 'rationale of the times' [temporum ratione], without really being certain whether or not they will end in thin air. I scarcely need to note that this is perhaps even truer of the Lutheran attempts to resolve the problem of commitments. But let us cease looking sideways. If the Calvinist *'godly compact'* [*pia conspiratio*] of genuine confessors, genuine because they truly know what they are confessing, is lacking, then on Reformed soil everything is left to chance, and it is really not all that important whether a church has an old confession or a new one, a good or less adequate one, or none at all. Nor does it matter whether this commitment to it is, as a whole or in part, really a noncommitment. If Calvinist *'faith'* [*fides*] with its strict connection to "most authentic very truth of Scripture" ["ipsissima scripturae veritas"][302] is lacking, then there is no 'godly compact' [pia conspiratio] in the Calvinist sense but only machinations that should just as well be avoided. Certainly no romantically antiquarian gaze into the past can restore to the Reformed churches the seriousness and truth with which their fathers confessed in the sixteenth century and made their commitment to their confession joyfully and consistently. Further, it is certain that for every single Reformed church that has openly or (what is much worse) secretly lost its confession, the way to serious, true, and thus committed confessing will have to be a *new* synod and the formulation of a *new* confession. It is, thirdly, also certain that such an act, if it is not to be a game, will require a 'power' [ἐξουσία] [power], and by virtue of this 'power,' a 'courage' [παρρησία] that no one can *reach out and take*, but that, if all the evidence is not deceptive, is also not *given* to anyone today. In the meantime, we have the emergency measures and next to them the will at least not to forget and to waste the heritage of that faith which we have *not* earned and thus do not *possess*.[303] May these lectures serve the awakening of that will.

2

THE PRINCIPLE OF
SCRIPTURE AND ITS GROUNDS

Discerning the significance of the confession in the Reformed church has presented us with a puzzling and paradoxical picture. Putting it all together, one is tempted to formulate an answer along these lines: The significance of the confession in the Reformed church consists in its essential *non*significance, its obvious relativity, humanity, multiplicity, mutability, and transitoriness. One could describe the Reformed confession in its totality the way Schiller spoke of the bell: "And as the mighty sound it gives / *Dies gently* on the listening ear / We feel how quickly *all* that lives / *Must change, and fade, and disappear.*"[1] In point of fact, the Reformed confession is a *fading* bell stroke, a *falling, streaming* cascade, or, as we said, a *disappearing* shadow. The one who knows that this is a *positive* statement about the confession should say it loudly and confidently. Yes, the bell stroke fades and says as it does so that the time is fulfilled [see Gal. 4:4], unrepeatable, but also irrevocable, and the hour has come to arise from sleep [see Rom. 13:11] once and for all. *Yes*, the waters stream and fall, *'everything flows'* (πάντα ῥεῖ),[2] inexorable, turbulent at all points, and speak with their falling and cascading of the majesty of the mountain heights from which they flow. *Yes*, the shadow disappears and must disappear, and in the very fact of its disappearance it witnesses to the rising light of the sun, an involuntary, vanquished, beaten, teeth-grinding witness perhaps, but still a *witness*. That is the essence of the Reformed confession, the obvious riddle of its history. It never was the light, and it never wanted to be, because it knows that it cannot and may not be the light, but rather *testifies* to the light like the Baptist of the New Testament [see John 1:8], in whom the Reformed church has had of necessity to recognize its most profound and most authentic being, in this as well as in other aspects. Whoever understands that will not be very amazed at the great 'decreasing' (ἐλαττοῦσθαι, John 3:30), which in our survey up to now we have perceived in its causes and effects at every point.

The Reformed confession points *beyond* itself. Its center of gravity, if not in fact its very content, is not in itself but rather *beyond* itself. *Faith* confesses. But it does not confess itself, but what is *written*. In the Reformed church, confession is in its entirety 'testimony' [testificatio],[3] a pointing toward. The object itself is and remains something other, a second thing, something encountered outside oneself. This other issues a demand toward the person, which is a *power*, a power that is a *demand*, a humiliation that is a *knowing*, and a knowing that is a *humiliation*. One has called the Reformed church the church of the *formal* principle of the Reformation, the principle of Scripture; in contrast, the Lutheran church has been called the church of the material principle, the doctrine of justification.[4] We would like to understand this in the following way. The principle of the Reformed confession consists in the fact that it is form and vessel. It is the form and vessel of the same content that the Lutheran confession claims to take as its own, as its material. The Reformed confession stresses that it is *only* form and vessel of this content, and does *not* claim as its own the content itself. The content is written, written by God's finger on the paper of the Bible *and* by God's finger in our hearts, truly and inviolably, completely and sufficiently, neither to be repeated nor to be continued. God has *said* what we must know. We can and should only *respond* that we have *heard* it.[5] That is the confession. God's word about the justification of the sinner through his grace is not repeated in the Reformed confession, not even at reduced level; it is not historically reproduced, nor placed in our time as "our symbol for this time"[6] but quite simply *witnessed* to not as the truth in our mouth but as the truth in God's mouth.[7] The witness of the Reformed confession is a confirmation of reception. The witness [as person] speaks, and his witness [as content] says that *God* has witnessed to himself.[7a] The witness [as person] stutters, and the witness [as content] is confused, but 'the Word of God will stand forever' [Verbum Dei manet in aeternum] [see Isa. 40:8]. There is fundamentally nothing other to witness to, to confess here, whether eloquently or with stammering. |

From this perspective, all of the "deficiencies" of the Reformed confession we have treated in lecture 1 are clarified to be fundamental necessities. There was that lack of *ecumenical* character—but what does the witness of *God's* Word have to do with the universality of the European empire and its church?! There were deficient *unity* and uniformity—but was not in fact the Holy Scripture, which the people in Scotland as in Bohemia, in Bremen as in Zurich, all wanted to confess in the same objective, rigorous sense, the sufficient bond of unity, and must not this unifying bond necessarily sunder every other artificial bond?! There was the inadequate sacredness of the *symbol*—but could the unique sacredness of the origin be transferred and delegated to something derived and secondary (the Scripture principle is the death of the concept of symbol)?! There were these remarkable and often so fateful qualities of *variability* and adaptability—but were they not the necessary witness to the fact that there is and can only be *one* Invariata, even if that should be at the cost of the shame of the church of the formal principle? There was the strangely elastic commitment to the confession—but can faith obligate itself to itself with absolute earnestness, as though the Word of God that alone and absolutely obligates must not secretly explode all these other obligations? Ultimately, the Reformed *principle of Scripture* forces the Reformed *confession* against the wall and renders it so fragmented, so desecrated, so human and temporal, so minimally binding. Woe is me, I am lost [Isa. 6:5], it says, and as by a devouring fire [see Isa. 30:27], the truth of *Scripture* that is confessed attacks the truth of the *confession*, puts it in question, destroys it to the extent that it does not glow with the same fire that consumes it. Reformed confession is confession of the truth of Scripture; as long as and to the extent that it is this, it has not ceased to exist. |

What we earlier reported should now be amended by saying that the situation is still truly and in every form the same today, no matter how impoverished and dubious might be the perspective that it otherwise presents. The Second Helvetic Confession and also the Heidelberg Catechism have largely *disappeared* from the scene, or they remain on the scene in such a way that it would be preferable for them to disappear. What has *not* disappeared, as though by some general secret agreement, is the reference, in all of the named and unnamed church constitutions and ordination formulae in which the Reformed confession continues its modest existence, to the foundational and obligatory significance of Holy Scripture. Even the questionable symbol of the Canton Baselland of 1838[8] did not forget this 'article upon which the church stands and falls' [articulus stantis et cadentis ecclesiae].[9] When it then adds that the gospel contained in the Scripture should be proclaimed "solely according to the principles of a Biblical study striving for the evangelical truth," one could see this as an intensification of the Reformed principle and, properly understood, be content with it—even if it was meant as an homage to the newer theology that was much discussed at the time in Switzerland because of David Friedrich Strauss's influence.[10] The church constitutions of Glarus and Graubünden add to "in accordance with Holy Scripture" rather redundantly, "especially the New Testament."[11] With this antic they showed that they found it necessary to sacrifice at least a lock of hair to the gods of the age.[12] Similarly, the English Congregationalists in 1833 were content with the mentioning of the New Testament (M 902,8).[13] But the principle itself is not invalidated by any of this. It will not be invalidated. As long as Reformed *pastors* by virtue of their office must focus upon the Bible, indeed as *Reformed* pastors, dispensing with all liturgical pleasures, must focus on the Bible alone in the worship service, we can be certain that the material connection to the confession of the founding period, as narrow and frail as it may have become, has not completely broken off. We can be certain that a new flow from the springs at which once the old confessions were framed is not ruled out. —Let us now attempt to arrive at an understanding of the essence of the Reformed principle of Scripture with the use of two simple questions: (1) What is meant by it? and (2) how is it grounded?

Our first task is simply to formulate the *thesis* more precisely and to explain it. *The church recognizes the rule of its proclamation solely in the Word of God and finds the Word of God solely in Holy Scripture.* Pay May 15 attention first of all to the expression "the rule of its proclamation." This contains both an assertion and a restriction. The *assertion*: The church's proclamation is to be dependent upon the Word of God, grounded upon it, oriented to it, and indeed to it *alone*. The *restriction*: Proclamation is not the Word of God itself but rather human word ruled by the Word of God, dependent upon it, grounded upon it, oriented to it. Both must be kept clearly in view if one wants to understand correctly the stipulations in the Reformed confessional writings. I said above that the Scripture principle was the 'article upon which the church stands and falls' [articulus stantis et cadentis ecclesiae]. This is, to be sure, true. In the Reformed confession, this is not one statement among many, but rather the statement that generates the entire confession. That the church is to recognize in the Word of God articulated in Scripture the sole rule of its proclamation was a firm principle *before* the confession was formulated. Note the public announcement of the *First Zurich Disputation* issued by the Council of Zurich (M 1[–2]). They specify there, as though it were completely obvious, that in the pending discussion about the question of the "faithful and total" preaching of the gospel, which at Zwingli's emergence had become controversial, both Zwingli and his critics should make their cases *"with the divine Scriptures"* (*"mit göttlicher geschrifft"*). Whoever could argue his case in accordance with *"divine Scriptures"* would be vindicated by the Council, which thereafter would no longer tolerate "that any should continue to preach from the pulpit whatever seems good to him, without foundation in the true *divine Scriptures.*"[14] Zwingli concludes his theses with a similar challenge (M 6,30[–34]): "Let no one attempt to contend with sophistry or trifles, but let him come having *Scripture* as judge, in order that the truth *be found*, or when it *is* found, as I hope it would be, that it be kept. Amen. May God grant it."[15] In like manner, the invitation to the *Bern Disputation* of 1528 states that it had been decided "that in this discussion no other scriptures than those of both the *Old* and *New* Testaments, called Biblical, [. . .] shall have place and authority. The Bible alone shall explain the Bible, shall expound, compare and illumine the dark places with the bright ones. No one other than divine scripture shall judge what is the level, guide, foundation, and sole judge of the true Christian faith" (M, XIX,18[–27]).[16] The Catholics ought to have been content to stay away from these disputations under protest, as did the bishops of Constance and Lausanne, although they had in fact been politely invited.[17] They *could* not have joined in a disputation with such a basis. According to the view of the ancient church (soon to be formulated in Trent, Session IV), the official view was to receive and venerate with the *same* pious love and respect both the Scriptures of the Old and New Testaments *and* the unwritten "traditions . . . preserved in the Catholic Church by a continuous succession."[18] The Reformed Scripture principle, which excluded the 'traditions' [traditiones], signified a complete break with the 'continuous succession' [continua successio], the splitting apart of the "pious love and respect" from bottom to top. This radical principle was declared victorious in the *rules of debate* established for this disputation, which was so basic for Reformed doctrinal development. "For, in short, when Almighty God reveals his word, then people must see that they comply with it, or they will invite the wrath of God on themselves," says Zwingli at the end of the Christian Introduction (M 29,29[-31]).[18a] With that he expressed the basic rationale of the Reformed Reformation. The new was already there long before one sentence of the later "confessional documents" was composed, not to speak of demonstrated or acknowledged. The new was there as axiom, as obvious assumption, as original recognition: *Thy* Word is truth [John 17:17]! |

It did not fall from heaven; it had its retrospective history. This is not the place to pursue that theme. We would need here to consider that reemerging classic insight that was latent in the great theological systems of the Middle Ages although more or less dormant everywhere. It began then to bestir itself in the fourteenth and fifteenth centuries, showing itself in a Wycliffe, a Peter of Ailli, a John of Wesel. In the course of the Renaissance, it awakened that remarkable longing for and movement toward the sources, not only to the *Bible* but also to Plato. The longing was certainly not only for the old *books* but for the ancient times and their insights and works. It was not just a longing for the *ancient* but for the simple, the great, the true, the natural, the originally human. It was a search for that human's undistorted rationality as well as his sensuality, to the clearly perceived riddle of his existence—and beyond that to its authentic, lost and yet unlosable answer.[19] The 'continuous succession' [continua successio] was jeopardized at many points, and "pious love and respect" divided itself then at many points between that which was a given here and what were the origins over there. One piece of the history of that longing and movement is doubtless also the emergence of the Reformed Scripture principle.[20] Zwingli *and* Calvin were enthusiastic students of *Erasmus*.[21] |

And then it came to pass that in Wittenberg *something very particular* was discovered: the justification of the sinner through God. Zwingli and Calvin, following in Luther's steps, also discovered this very particular truth. The way it happened with Zwingli was that he, as a humanist friend of the Bible for many years under Luther's influence, which was more decisive than he knew and admitted, learned to understand what he had long since found in the Bible.[22] The probable process with Calvin was that he encountered both Erasmus's edition of the New Testament and Luther's sermons at the same time, and that he never seriously read the Bible in any other light than that of this particular discovery of Luther's.[23] But *neither* became what they were through following Erasmus or Luther. That happened as they came to know the Bible that had been excavated by humanism and as Luther discovered in that Bible the doctrine which exploded in them both with a penetrating new knowledge: The Bible is the word of truth, the Word of God that the world urgently needs and that must be the criterion for the proclamation of the church in the world. Especially Zwingli was a man of the world, even as a Christian and a theologian. He was most actively involved in the intellectual and political movements of the day. He had compassion for the world [see Matt. 15:32]. He was driven by the desire to discover how to help that century bleeding from a thousand wounds. But Calvin as well was a Renaissance man[24] from head to toe, both before and after his "sudden conversion,"[25] which in my view has received too much attention.[26] He was, however, more concentrated, more circumspect, maturer than Zwingli from the very beginning. His question as well was, What should happen now? |

The answer given by both, illumined by Luther's discovery, was that a revolution needed to happen and not one of those apparent shallow revolutions imagined by others awakened by Luther's word: a Karlstadt, a Münzer, and many other overly hasty ones of their ilk. They sought a foundational, quiet, comprehensive revolution that would take place in that the norm of the church would become the Bible, the Bible alone. One has understood the fathers of the Reformed church correctly when one understands their biblicism as a very sober, practical, almost homespun *rule*. It is really a *formal* principle that is grasped here. Zwingli commenced his ministry in Zurich in 1519 with a preaching series on Matthew,[27] and Calvin began his ministry in Geneva in 1536 with a lecture series on Romans,[28] beginnings as clear and transparent as any conceivable. If only the Bible is heard again, then the necessary consequences will follow: the necessary debate with the ancient church, its dogma and worship, the raising up of the new church, the tasks and possibilities relating to how one should live, and finally, the confession. But *first of all*, the Bible, the Bible as the rule of faith *and* life— for it is obvious that life cannot be ignored if the Bible is the word of truth!— and then everything that must be carried out according to this rule. The methodical, revolutionary but not tumultuous process of establishing the authority of the Bible in the midst of life, although, or better, precisely because it is the Word of God, is the *new thing* that Zwingli and Calvin learned neither from *Erasmus* nor *Luther*. In contrast to Erasmus, they were bound to the Bible; once having discovered it, they were transformed from *observer* theologians to *witness* theologians. They were not so bound to the one particular theme that Luther had discovered in the Bible. To be sure, they *also* put it at the heart of their proclamation. But one will always find that it was developed in Luther more profoundly and more powerfully.

Thus, they were freer to let the Bible speak in its fullness, the entire Bible, freer to avoid reducing the Word of God to the doctrine of the forgiveness of sins. They let the Bible simply *speak* for itself as the form that best handles the question of its content *itself*. There was, moreover, not some kind of theory along these lines that was first of all developed. Rather, four long years before the Zurich Disputation, Zwingli simply *held* these views, together with his friend Berthold Haller[29] among others, who was devoted to the new doctrine in his post in Bern. When, then, the hour of fundamental consideration and decision arrived for the churches, they simply had to draw the conclusion, articulate the necessary consequences and results whose foundations and origins had long since firmly stood for the Reformers themselves *and* for the broadest circles surrounding them. Based on the *preaching* that they had already been risking as they moved along this path, they were now *persuaded* of the rightness of *this path*, whatever its further implications might prove to be. The publication of the invitation to the Disputations was itself a foundational confessional act of a persuaded Reformed *congregation*. The first confessions were then generated by these Disputations with their rules of debate characterized by a remarkable and unjust 'begging of the principle' [petitio principii] over against the ancient church. Similarly, when Calvin came to Geneva in 1536 under the influence of lesser spirits such as Farel, Froment, Viret,[30] and others, it was already clearly decided that they wanted to 'live according to the gospel' [vivre selon l'évangile] or 'live according to the Word of God' [vivre selon la parole de Dieu].[31] The Reformed confession was already contained in that '*according to*' [*selon*]. That was already the declaration of obedience whose subsequent interpretation was a necessary and constantly astonishing thing for those courageous and unsuspecting confessors. Not even Calvin's catechism would fundamentally surpass it. The Genevans were and remained persuaded of its obligatory authority, even when they at times, in the "blossoms of [their] sin,"[32] preferred to have absolutely nothing to do with its much too rigorous interpreter. |

The specific content of the Reformed confession lies in its relation to the Word of God spoken in the Scriptures. It does not stand independently next to this relation—that is the *assertion* contained in the Reformed thesis about Scripture. Nor does it merge with the absolute but remains in relation to it—that is the *limitation* contained in the thesis. It is important always to understand in this double light what the *First Bern Disputation* expresses in this succinct formulation: "The holy Christian church, whose only Head is Christ, is born out of the Word of God, and abides in the same, and listens not to the voice of a stranger" (M 30,9[–11])[32a] or the *Tetrapolitan Confession* of 1530 with its characteristic expression: "For it seemed to us not improper *to resort* in such a crisis whither of old and always not only the most holy fathers, bishops and princes, but also the children of God everywhere, have always *resorted*—viz. to the authority of the Holy Scriptures" (M 55,27[–30]).[33] Calvin says in his *Catechism* of 1545 that the holy Word of God is given to us as the way to eternal life, that is, to the knowledge of God as our Lord and Father: "for spiritual doctrine is a door by which we enter his heavenly kingdom" (M 145,33[–35]).[33a] *Bullinger* states in the Second Helvetic Confession that true 'wisdom' [sapientia] and 'godliness' [pietas] are to be learned from Scripture, as well as the 'reformation' [reformatio] and 'governance' [gubernatio] of the churches (M 170,35[–36]),[33b] while the *Rhaetian Confession* says that the true faith is passed on and taught in the Holy Scriptures (165,35[–37]). The most frequent term for this normative character of the biblical Word of God is the word that I also used in my definition, *rule*, with the addition, rule of *faith*, or of *truth*, or (as modern confessions like to emphasize especially, although the Waldensians said it in 1571 [XLI,21])[34] of faith and *of life* or *of obedience*,[35] or similar. The word 'rule' first occurs in Farel's Geneva Confession (III,13).[36] The French and English were usually content with that much.[37] The Germans like to add *'guideline,'* or *'foundation'* [*fundamentum*], or *ground*, terms no longer unambiguously pure.[38] Next to these, there are concepts such as *'method'* [ratio], *'authority'* [autorité], *standard*, *'norm'* [norma].[39] What I have not encountered, on the other hand, are terms such as "fountain" (which the Formula of Concord applies to the Scriptures at a decisive point)[40] or "source," "root," "beginning," "origin," or the like. I do not think that is an accident. According to the Reformed view, there is no continuity between the Word of God and the faith that is nourished by it. The Word of God always stands in *another* book from the one that we believe, confess, and proclaim, in obedience to this rule. It penetrates most visibly and audibly into this world, but it does not enter into an organic relationship with it; it does not become a component of the world. It is and remains its *rule*. To that extent I described the terms "foundation" ("fundamentum") or "ground" as not purely Reformed, because inadvertently they create the idea of a continuing relationship between this ground and what is built upon it. According to the Reformed view, the Word of God is the plan of the entire house and not merely its lowest floor. The Formula of Concord also speaks of the Scripture as "rule" ["regula"] (517),[41] but then goes on to designate it the "fountain" ["fons"] and "basis" ["fundamentum"] (568, 571),[42] and conversely applies the term "rule" ["regula"] to the church's confession as well,[43] in both instances without noticing the 'transformation into another genre' [μετάβασις εἰς ἄλλο γένος]. It is properly Reformed to do without such combinations and to remain with the distinction. It should not be forgotten that behind Reformed theology, as especially clear in *Calvin*, stands *Plato's* philosophy.[44] This is no mystical Neoplatonism but rather rigorous and critical classic Platonism with the hard and inexorable lines of his doctrine of distance and relations, which in the Reformed world has entered into an unusual connection with the spirit of the *Old Testament*, which in this regard is oriented similarly. We shall often stumble upon this unmentioned background. There can be no doubt that the relation between Scripture and confession is both positively and negatively the same formally as Plato's relation between the idea and the things. The strictest and most indissoluble *relation* between here and there is simultaneously the impassable polar region that *divides* here from there once and for all. This is fundamentally different from the catholic "continuous succession" ["continua successio"],[45] as well as from the stairstep or background relation in which Scripture and confession are, in the Lutheran view, oriented to each other.

It is, of course, completely unplatonic when then in Reformed theology the regulative *idea* is replaced by the regulative *codex* of the Old and New Testaments. The feeling is quite justified that this is not just an erratic stone that lies on the field but rather a meteoric rock. The Word of God is not the general truth of the relation between time and eternity, human and deity, nor is it the human's indelible character of being in the image of God and in fellowship with God, nor the law of nature written at creation in the human heart, although these were all concepts well known and much discussed by the early Reformed. All of that must be actualized by the Word of God, must be enacted by it. The Word of God is the witness of the *revelation* of God, of the *new* relation with humans created by God, special, direct, unique, actual, conquering the chasm of the fall. It is not the revelation of the *relationship to infinity* of *human* consciousness but of *God's thoughts become finite*, of Jesus Christ. The Word of God to us who are neither prophets nor apostles is the witness of the old and new covenant of this Jesus Christ, the Holy Scriptures. In this form, as prophetic and apostolic word, the eternal Word of God penetrates into our world. From the beginning, Reformed Christianity had a strong sense of the *paradox* of what it confessed. It did not make the move to this exclusive conception with theological haste and certainty. I already said that the Reformed Reformers were Renaissance people, people of the world. For them it was by no means self-evident that there was a holy book that contains the whole truth, the Word of God, and indeed, *alone* contains it. Rather, this was for them a *discovery*, a step of knowing that they took hesitatingly and consciously. But they *took* it. |

I am thinking especially of *Calvin*. You will know that the first book of his Institutes in the definitive version has the title, "The Knowledge of *God the Creator*," and the second book, "The Knowledge of God *the Redeemer*." This differentiation is often blurred and ignored in the content. For instance, Calvin speaks at length of the doctrine of the Trinity in the first book.[46] Together with many hints from the content of the first book, this doctrine is an indication that Calvin counts on the possibility that God can be known aside from biblical revelation—to be sure, a possibility that is set aside and de facto is not there. It must be understood that he never posits this possibility as real, nor does he ever develop something like a natural theology as a preliminary stage to revealed theology, as later on many liked to do.[47] It is no coincidence but rather a matter of principled importance that the "Creator God" ["Deus creator"] is described as the triune God in the light of the "knowledge of God the Redeemer" ["cognitio Dei redemptoris"]. What is asserted as a *hypothesis*, so to speak, as a pure possibility[48] that is only realized in Christ,[49] what is asserted is that we know God, even as the Creator, in his *works*.[50] *Calvin* developed this in especially clear fashion in the original French version of the Catechism of 1537 (C, XXII,35[-36]).[50a] He says there that, in order to develop, nourish, and maintain truly profound godliness and a faith bound to the fear of God's majesty, it is useful to know that all things in heaven and on earth are "representations of invisible things" ["spectacles des choses invisibles"], portrayals of the Lord who is not accessible to our understanding. In the "universality of things" ["université des choses"], we behold the "immortality" ["immortalité"] of God, from which the beginning and origin of all things derives—his power, wisdom, goodness, righteousness, and mercy. In this way, we ought really to know *everything* about God that we need to know about him. In this "we ought" is the turning point, the elimination of this possibility, and its limitation to a *mere* hypothesis. In fact, Calvin thinks that we do *not* know it in this way. Not only our blindness is to blame for that, but also our "perversity" ["perversité"] is so great that there is nothing which it does not grasp wrongly in its view of the works of God, "so that it turns upside down all the heavenly wisdom which otherwise shines so clearly in those works."[50b] Therefore, we must hold to the *Word*, where we find the works of God viewed according to the rule of eternal truth and where through the action of divine life, wisdom, and power at work in us we first learn to understand the language of heaven and earth. This is the Calvinist *step* of knowledge from the mere hypothetical *possibility* to the exclusive *reality* of revelation. What lies between here and there is the chasm of the fall and of grace. |

In the *Gallican Confession* of 1559, Calvin also implied, although not without misleading brevity, that the issue involves taking this step: God reveals himself in this way, firstly through the creation and preservation of his works, "secondly, and more clearly, in his Word" (M 221,38[-222,1]).[50c] The *Belgic Confession* of 1561 follows the Gallican, but with the remark that the recognition of God from creation suffices only to convict and make man inexcusable, while to His honor and our salvation He can be recognized "more clearly and fully" in his *Word* (233,13[-21]).[50d] We hear similar thoughts in the *Waldensian Confession* of 1655 (M 500,31[-34]).[51] More plainly in agreement with the original Calvinist expositions are the Erlauthal Confession ("The knowledge of God comes about through the communication of creatures, but this knowledge does not save.

May 17

In a special way and inwardly through the revealed Word it is recognized from the Sacraments in the Son through the work and revelation of the Holy Spirit in salvation through faith" (M 267,14[–17])[52] and the beginning of the *Westminster Confession*. Here, for the first time, the concept of the 'Light of Nature' [Lumen naturae] occurs next to the works of God. It refers to the inner light of the inborn image of God in the human. The light of nature appears as a source of knowledge, but immediately is placed beneath scripture as ineffective and incapable of revealing to us the will of God.[53] There is a similar stipulation in the *Larger Westminster Catechism* (M 612, 31[–33]).[54] On the other hand, it is typical modern bungling when the *Revision of the Westminster Confession* of the American Presbyterians (1902) changes it to read that God reveals himself in nature, in history, and in the hearts of men, graciously and more clearly through the men of God inspired by the Holy Spirit, and then finally as the incarnate Word in Christ.[55] Along the same lines, *the Confession of the American Congregationalists* of 1883[56] says that God reveals himself through his works, through the course of providence, through the conscience of people, through supernatural revelations to his people, and finally through Christ. What is totally *lost* here is the awareness of the necessity of critical-dialectical *differentiation*, without which such formulae should not be cited.

The sharp line of the old Reformed view runs, *on the one hand*, toward the clear exposition of the possibility that there could be a general knowledge of God that can be derived from things and then abstracted. Here Reformed theology momentarily brushes up against philosophical realism! *On the other hand*, the line moves toward the equally clear reversal that insists that the things can only speak when the Word out of which all things are made is given to us. The knowledge of God is not mediated but is only unmediated, that is, God is known through God himself. The expression for that immediacy, for the absolute *facticity*, for the paradox of revelation is the scriptural principle, precisely *by virtue of* its offensiveness. The scandal of revelation is unavoidable and *necessary* in a world that lies under the power of evil [see 1 John 5:19]. It was the knowledge of the goodness of God toward the *fallen* world that in Reformed theology *shattered* the Platonic system at this decisive point. One must see both here: how Reformed thought intentionally based itself on an element that was absolutely superior and alien to the world and humanity. For the Reformed, the word "God" was a concept of superiority, majesty, and freedom, which was very alien to the preceding Middle Ages. Lutheranism, and perhaps Luther himself, did not have such a sharp sense of this concept and certainly did not express it with this emphasis and pointedness. This concept, which characterized their entire theology, comprehended for them both God's revelation and the *witness* to God's revelation. For them, the isolatedness of God generates the isolatedness of his revelation. *Revelation* is not this and that, not everything and anything, but rather this definitive, incomparable one thing. Therefore, legitimate witness to revelation cannot be any random human word about God but rather this definite human word about God, which the prophets and apostles were called by God and equipped to say. It is the word of Scripture. The *Bremen Consensus* begins with these decisive words: "God neither can be nor desires to be known and honored by us humans in any other way than as he has *revealed* himself to his churches in his holy Word in inexpressible goodness from the beginning, and has let it be written in a certain Scripture through the prophets and apostles" (M 739,24[–27]).[57] I am saying that one must see what kind of breakthrough, what kind of arbitrary act this foundation represents, viewed from normal, synthetic thought. One must also see how normally, how practically, how concretely this foundation, laid with the help of this daring hypothesis, is then carried out, and how the other, earthly side of the great paradox—this is God's Word!—is a robust wisdom for life that knows what it can depend on, namely, the "Scriptures," what they spoke of in Bern and Zurich as the "Gschrift."[57a] Standing immediately over against the mystery that seems so irrational there is a principle of knowledge that the simplest person could understand and apply in its logical consistency. When Zwingli began the first Zurich Disputation, they put him in the middle of the chamber alone at a table upon which the Bible in four languages lay like the lawbook on a judge's bench.[58] He needed only to open it, to quote it, to verify with it, to apply it almost like a soldier using his weapon! That was the fundamental position of early Reformed theology in general. One must always keep in mind the primary point, the *grounds* of this argumentation: Here and only here one heard the voice of the one true *God*. By virtue of this marvelous *hearing*, the regulative codex of Scripture took the place of the regulative idea.

It becomes understandable in this context why a number of Reformed confessional documents take such an unusual interest in the concept of the biblical *canon*. This was an interest Lutheranism could not have because, as we saw, the Bible, councils, and the current church situation all lay basically on the same level. In this it was more historically sensitive in the modern sense, because it did not place such emphasis upon the isolated normativity of the Bible. For the Reformed, it is precisely the Bible's *isolated* normativity that is important as an image of the isolated authority of God—and thus it is the only allowable and required earthly image! To express *where* they concretely heard God's voice and to *what* they concretely will subscribe is for them an integrating component of their confession. For this reason, we find in a series of confessions (Zurich Confession of 1549,[59] Gallican,[60] Belgic,[61] Waldensian of 1655,[62] the Irish Articles,[63] the Anglican Articles,[64] the Westminster Confession,[65] and several modern ones[66]) the formal and complete listing of all the books of the Bible regarded as canonical. These catalogues never diverge, of course, from the traditional canon. But with these lists, they wanted to document their fundamental right to reject what nonbiblical history and even the church might prescribe as canonical, and to make such decisions themselves as the ancient church had done. This express or silent confirmation of the biblical canon may perhaps be called the fundamental act of Reformed confessing. In the Second Helvetic Confession,[67] in the Belgic,[68] in the Westminster Confession,[69] in the Anglican[70] and Thorn Articles,[71] we then find the express formulation that the well-known Old Testament apocryphal books *cannot* lay claim to the normative character of 'scripture' [scriptura]. In the *Zurich Confession* of 1545 there is an amusing little polemic against *Luther's* dismissive opinion of the Epistle of James and the Apocalypse:[72]

> In all of the books of the New Testament there is no hard knot to confuse us, nor do we hold that there might be some *useless straw* in them or that they mix up *one thing in another in a disorderly way*. And if the *human spirit cannot make its sense of the Revelation* or other books, then we pay no regard to its problem. For we know well that we humans should be guided by the Scripture, not the Scripture by us. (M 155,19[–25])[73] I

Moreover, the negative assertion is important, that aside from and next to and even over against Scripture, no other authority for faith can come under consideration. It is understandable that the trumpet here produces a much clearer tone [see 1 Cor. 14:8] than in the Formula of Concord. "Therefore all who regard another doctrine as equal to or higher than the Gospel err and do not know what the Gospel is" (M 2,28[–29]),[73a] asserted Zwingli energetically as early as 1523. "The Church of Christ makes no laws or commandments without God's Word. Hence all human traditions, which are called ecclesiastical commandments, are binding upon us only in so far as they are based on and commanded by God's Word" (*Bern Theses* of 1528, M 30,12[–15]).[73b] According to the Geneva Confession of 1536 (111,14[–18]),[74] one should not add any human invention to the Scriptures as the rule of faith; one should neither take away anything nor add anything. Continually from then on, the councils, the church fathers, and the church's traditions are with more or less respect set aside as not normative. "A peasant who presents the 'truth of Scripture' [veritas scripturae] merits more credence than an entire council," was a Hungarian affirmation in 1562 (M 341,36[–37]).[75] The long list of excluded factors that the Gallican Confession offers has been already cited.[76] The Belgic Confession declares that we should not let an apostle or even an angel from heaven teach us anything other than what Scripture contains. The writings of the holiest of men, custom, age, the "succession of times or persons" ["successio temporum et personarum"], all of them can be compared as little with the authority of Scripture as can be the decisions of councils. "For all men are of themselves liars, and more vain than vanity itself," it continues bluntly (M 234,39[−235,5).[76a] When the *Gallican Confession* includes among its list of excluded authorities "visions" and "miracles" (222,39),[76b] and when the *Thorn Declaration* warns against granting judicial authority to the "private spirit" ["spiritus privatus"] of believers (Aug. 415),[77] then we are reminded that the Reformed principle of Scripture also formed a front against Enthusiasm with its appeal to subjective inspiration. "There is today no word of God, nor can one be shown with certainty, . . . that was not written or founded in Scripture" (this last phrase is not Reformed!), says the Thorn Declaration,[78] aiming both right and left. *Bullinger* had written, somewhat more reserved in his critique of the left wing than were the Poles, that the direct internal illumination of a person without the ministry of the preached scriptural Word was a possibility but certainly not the rule today (171,10[−38]). The reverse formulation and positive expansion of all of this is the assertion that the Scripture is the judge over all other authorities, meaning that it determines their value and truth. That the endeavor of judging this or that authority according to Scripture was not a simple and unambiguous task in practice can be seen in *Zwingli's* rule in Fidei Ratio (1530) according to which there are two judges, Scripture and the church, but the latter only to the extent that it judges according to Scripture and "by virtue of the Spirit" ["ex spiritu"].[79]

Taken together, all these documents emphasize as the first admonition, often expressly incorporated into the confession: One should *read the holy Scripture*. Theologians especially should do this "night and day" ["noctes diesque"], as the *Bohemian Confession* demands (M 454,32). Zwingli, speaking of his Short Instruction, says that it would be in vain if those who teach it do not firstly petition God "that he give them grace, and afterwards *search in the Scriptures* diligently, *remaining therein day and night*, and as well finally when they do not show a disposition to build the true Jerusalem" (23,11 [−13]).[80] In its thirty-seventh and thirty-eighth chapters, the *Berner Synodus* gives its pastors weighty instruction, still valuable today, regarding how they should do this. Above all, they should *pray*:

> [I]t is abundantly plain that prayer is an emptying and preparing of the heart, so that a person might grasp and retain the *meaning and counsel of God that is concealed in the letters*. Otherwise, lacking devotion one will read the Scripture like a worldly history and apply only one's reason to it. Such a reading produces nothing more than inflated carnal wisdom, which is subsequently imposed upon the poor congregation as though from God and the Word of God. . . . If the prayer is made from a repentant, thirsty heart, then the *book should be opened and carefully read as God's Word*, which it truly is, and *not as human word*. While doing so, one should persist in that intensive prayer until a little divine understanding flows down from above. The reader is obligated to accept this and to consider immediately that the Holy Spirit speaks in it for his chastising and his improving. That is, the reader should freely engage *with God*

alone, excluding all other creatures, with a simple and committed spirit. He should *not consider what he should tell the people but rather how he himself might receive from God further light and knowledge.*

In addition, he should consider his own faith experience up to now, as well as other writings that might contradict his present understanding, and "pray for more insight while he continues with determination in such practice until the truth of the scripture completely illumines his heart, producing a composed gratitude and zealous consideration of the knowledge he has received" (M 54,10[–33]).[81] Moreover, he should certainly make use of old and new books and commentaries. "May they be properly read 'judiciously' [cum judicio], with understanding and improvement. What a joy it is when one discovers that God has given him something with which the gifts of other people agree or that perhaps others have not yet attained. He should not be proud of this, since he has requested it from God and knows very well what will follow if he should fall into rampant arrogance" (B. Syn. 101).[82] Finally, the pastors should "together compare the Scriptures," confer, conduct "conversations" about the gospel, "each one with his neighbor, who is also God-fearing and desires to gain further knowledge of our Lord Jesus Christ." They should be not "biting, angry, stubborn," and insistent upon their own opinion already formed, but thankful for the smallest thing "of Christ and his gifts that one might find in another person" (B. Syn. 102[–3]).[83] This is how the Reformed principle of Scripture should take shape in living theological *practice.* |

Not only theologians but also the *laity* are to read the Bible, which means that it should be translated into the native languages, as strongly emphasized in *Ireland,*[84] *Bohemia,*[85] *Hungary,*[86] *Poland,*[87] and in the *Larger Westminster Catechism.*[88] The *laity* should submit to the *Bible's* teaching. "Moreover, it is wrong that the pictures teach us. We should be taught solely by the Word of God." It was the lazy priests who, instead of teaching us, painted doctrine on the walls and seduced us to idolatry, as *Zwingli* puts it in his *Short Instruction (1523)* (M 24,41[–45]).[88a] If we seek pictures to assist in understanding the Word of God, then we should stick to God's creatures, heaven and earth and all that is in them, rather than to human "imaginings" that can only lead us away from the Creator. This view in the *Tetrapolitana* 1530 (M,76,45[–77,17]) is also energetically emphasized in *Bullinger's Second Helvetic Confession* (M 174,26[–42]).[88b] The *Heidelberg Catechism* is especially pithy in Question 98: "But may not pictures be tolerated in churches in place of books for unlearned people?" Answer: "No, for we must not try to be wiser than God who does not want his people to be taught by means of lifeless idols, but through the living preaching of his Word" (M 710,22[–27]).[88c] Calvin gives the following instruction to the Bible reader in his Catechism of 1545: How should one use the Holy Scriptures so that it might be fruitful? Answer: We are to grasp the Word of God in it with the total conviction of our heart, as "certain truth come down from heaven" ["certa veritas e coelo profecta"]. We are to submit to it. We are to put our wills and sense in its service. We are to love it with all our hearts. Planted in our hearts, it must put down deep roots. We must let ourselves be formed according to its rule (M 145,37[–44]). All this sounds curiously naive and matter-of-fact, and it should. The next question shows that Calvin knows very well what he is saying: Do we have the power to do all these things? Answer: By no means, rather God alone has the power to effect all of this in us through the grace of his Spirit (M 145,45[–146,2]). In a similar fashion, the *Larger Westminster Catechism* requires as the presupposition to reading the Bible usefully the "firm persuasion" ["persuasio firma"] that the Scriptures "are the very Word of God" ["ipsissimum verbum Dei"] and that God alone can "enable us to understand them"—"with desire to know, believe, and obey, . . . with diligence, . . . meditation, . . . application, self-denial, prayer" (M 636,7[–12]).[88d] One senses in these theses the struggle of a spirit that calls for *praxis*, methodical praxis, yet with the very impractical, very unmethodical, very alien *presupposition* that both *confronts* him and that he is *seeking*, the speech of God in this book to which he wants to *point* and to which he can do *no more* than point, in spite of all the prescriptions he might provide. The positivist style of the Western European peoples in particular collides here with an unheard of supranaturalism, and merges with it into a unique totality; for the extremes touch each other.[89] |

The requirement of Bible *reading* is then often and expressly joined with a second requirement, biblical *preaching*. To provide its norms is the next practical purpose of the entire confession. Preaching regulated by the Bible is the central function of the church, according to the Reformed view. One can risk saying that it is the actual Reformed sacrament, around which those actions normally so named cluster as significant gestures for explanation. *Zwingli's Account of the Faith* (M 92,1[–2] describes the "work of prophesying or preaching" as "*most sacred*" and "a work most necessary *above all others*."[89a] Consider also how, in Article 17 of Bullinger's *Second Helvetic Confession* (the parallel to Augustana, Article 7[90]), in the discussion of the "notes of the church" ["notae ecclesiae"], the participation in the *sacraments*, understood and administered in accordance with Scripture, *recedes* over against the all-powerful "sign" ["signum"] of the *preaching* of the Word of God and the unity of the Spirit, of faith, and of worship that is founded *upon that preaching* (M 198,2[–12]).[91] Similarly, Article 23 of the same confession, dealing with public worship, states that most of the customary liturgical prayers should make way for "evangelical teaching" ["doctrina evangelica"] so that the congregation should be not wearied and wish that the service might already end when they reach the end of the liturgical section! (M

214,25[–30]).[91a] The title of one of the first sections of the Second Helvetic Confession is *"The preaching of the Word of God is the Word of God."*[92] It is obvious that this "is" ["est"] must be understood as "signifies" ["significat"] in analogy to the words of the institution of the Lord's Supper. Bullinger knows, as the paragraph itself shows, that in the sermon we are dealing only with the "announcement" ["annunciatio"][92a] of the Word of God. What he intends to stress is that the churchly proclamation regulated by the Bible corresponds appropriately to the *dignity* of the Word of God in a way not to be underestimated by any individual student of the Bible, whether self-taught or illuminated. "Outward preaching" ["externa praedicatio"], the churchly sermon, is the public and general announcement of the Word of God recorded in Scripture from which no individual can without jeopardy withdraw himself by claiming direct spiritual communication (although this is not to discredit the private study of the Bible) (M 171,10[–18]). One should not focus upon the proclaimer but upon what is being proclaimed. The minister may be "evil and a sinner" ["malus et peccator"], "nevertheless the Word of God remains still true and good."[92b] This is what *Calvin's* Catechism had argued: One should adhere to the "holy and inviolable rule" ["sancta et inviolabilis regula"] that no one should think that he knows better than the teacher. In the command to "Go and proclaim," the issue at stake is the ordering of the building up and maintainance of the church. Whoever despises the "pastors" ["pastores"] despises Christ, for it is their function to teach us in his name. The argument that this should be accomplished at one point to last forever is not valid. For "it is little to have begun, unless you persevere. We must be the disciples of Christ to the end, or rather without end" (M 146,5[–26].[92c] |

This high estimation of churchly preaching is obviously inseparable from its biblical *regulation*. The statement, "the preaching of the Word is the Word of God" ["praedicatio verbi est verbum Dei"], refers solely to preaching *in accordance with Scripture*. This biblical regulation is guaranteed, on the one hand, through instructions for the personal Bible reading of the pastor, like those cited from the Bern Synod,[93] and on the other hand by the principle that the essence of preaching is *exposition*, exposition of the *entire* Bible. The Reformed church has no concept of ecclesial pericopes [lectionary texts assigned for preaching, —Trans.]. In the *Dillenburg Confession* of 1578, they are referred to as "widely" used, but with the remark that, as circumstances allow, preachers should be given the freedom not to use them (M 734,2 [–7]).[94] As early as the *Anhalt Articles* of 1597, they are suspect in Germany as a "papist innovation" (Ebr., 29).[95] Zwingli, Calvin, and Bullinger almost always preached serially through entire books and attempted to preach through all the books of the Bible. By exposition, they meant expounding Scripture through Scripture, the difficult passages through the understandable ones, as was already foreseen in the invitations to the disputations.[96]

The principle of interpreting Scripture by Scripture is found in the First Helvetic Confession[97] and the Second,[98] in the Scots Confession[99] and in the Westminster Confession.[100] On occasion, the supplement is added that faith and love[101] (and uniquely in the Scots Confession, the church's confession[102]) should also serve as controls. The further stipulation is variously made that the highest authority can only be the original biblical text,[103] and in agreement with the Symbol of the Canton Baselland,[104] the Declaration of the English Congregationalists of 1833 states that the meaning of the text is to be determined "by the aid of sound criticism."[105] Standing behind this expository principle is the fundamental view, to be discussed presently, that the actual expositor of the text can only be its author, that is, the Holy Spirit.

2. After having addressed the principle of Scripture and its practical application, we turn now to the question of its *grounding*, that is, the ground upon which this principle is established.[106] The axiomatic character of this principle has so unambiguously encountered us in our discussion up to now that we could easily opt to proceed with great reserve and only ask why the principle is asserted without any argumentation to ground it. With this inquiry, however, we would *anticipate* the answer that must in fact ultimately emerge. We want to attempt to *find* it. What the Reformed confessional statements say about the grounding of the scriptural principle I will initially summarize in three very simple statements: *Holy Scripture is the perfect revelation; or, it is the work of the Holy Spirit. This judgment about Scripture is itself a work of the Holy Spirit.*

The most obvious answer given by the early Reformed to the question about the reason for the extraordinary authority they ascribed to the Bible was always the simple assertion of its perfection. With a great variety of terms, the confessions center upon this concept. The *First Helvetic Confession* states that this is the "most ancient, most perfect, and loftiest teaching" (M 101,11[-12]), and it is not without interest that the Latin rendered as "teaching" is *"philosophia"* (Aug. 94).[107] We find virtually the same wording in the *Zurich Confession of 1545*.[108] We note that the term *"most ancient"* is linked with "most perfect," apparently as a way of describing the same fact. We think naturally of the way that the Renaissance returned to the sources, to the period of the origins. As a description of *the* source, of *the* original history[109] that they wanted to speak of *here*, the superlative "most ancient" ["antiquissima"] is apparently no more than a parable, a makeshift. "Most ancient" ["antiquissima"] is intended to clarify "most perfect" ["perfectissima"] as the very first, the most original—that which is God! *Bullinger's Second Helvetic Confession* explains this "most ancient" ["antiquissima"] with the statement, "For God from all eternity foreordained" to save the world through Christ, and he has revealed his eternal decree and plan to the world through the gospel (M 188,29[-31]).[109a] The predicates "sufficiency" or "completeness" ["sufficientia"] and "understandability" or "clarity" ["perspicuitas"] are clearly another way of saying what was meant by perfection; we find them singly or grouped in the Irish[110] and Anglican Articles,[111] in the Westminster Confession,[112] in the Confessio Sigismundi,[113] in the Scots Confession,[114] the Hungarian,[115] the Thorn Declaration,[116] the Confession of the Calvinist Methodists of Wales (1823),[117] the Declaration of the English Congregationalists of 1833,[118] and the Confession of the Cumberland Presbyterian Church of 1883.[119] What is meant by the perfection of Scripture is the perfection of the *revelation* that it contains, to which it testifies, and that it communicates. Teaching, doctrine [doctrina], philosophy [philosophia], and similar terms all refer to the subject to which all of these predicates belong. There are some, especially *English* confessions, that make some explicit restrictions in relation to the *'sufficiency'* [sufficientia] of Holy Scripture, although clearly only where this does not affect the doctrine of and testimony to revelation. The Westminster Confession (M 545,24[–32]),[119a] for example, makes the reservation that certain things relating to public worship and church government should be arranged according to the "light of nature" ["lumen naturae"] and "Christian prudence" ["prudentia christiana"], although guided by the general rule of the Word of God. The Bible contains "all things necessary to salvation," state the *Anglican Articles* (M 506,33) somewhat reservedly.[119b] The *Erlauthal Confession* (M 342,13 [–15]) also stipulated that certain "free actions" ["liberae actiones"] were to be exempted from the sufficiency of Scripture, that is, from its authority. The *'perspicuity'* [perspicuitas] of Scripture is limited by the Westminster Confession (M 545, 37[–546.2])[119c] to that which is necessary for salvation. Beyond that, not everything in Scripture was equally clear and accessible for all people. This emphasizes that the intentional predicates relate to the revelatory character of Scripture; we shall not examine further the question of how much or how little justification there was for establishing such exceptions and reservations. |

Highest revelation, *oldest* revelation, *fully sufficient, fully clear, perfect revelation*—all of this really says the same thing in many ways, namely, *God's* revelation. *God* speaks—and as we say this, we must always hear God in his superiority, his majesty and freedom, in his isolatedness as God—that is what all these praise predicates intend to say, even though in their superlative character and absolutism they completely lose any perspicuity. They intend to say that here the highest word is being spoken, the most ancient, the totally sufficient, the ineluctably clear, the perfect word, that is, *God's* Word. It becomes clear when we draw all this together that the attempt to ground the principle of Scripture in the reference to its perfection brings us no further. This reference is a tautology, to be sure not a useless and spiritless one, but still a tautology. To say, "The Scriptures are perfect!" means nothing other than to say that they are *God's* Word!—and that is what we set out to establish. With the statement, "It is God's Word!" we have arrived apparently at the point where the scriptural principle seems to be grounded on its groundlessness, or better, it is grounded in God alone. For *only* in God, and on no other grounds, can it be established that there is Word of God, and that this or that word is a Word of God. What *Zwingli's Account of the Faith* says about the certainty of *grace* is even more valid for the certainty of the *revelation* of grace: "For none but God himself can give it [the fainting soul] the assurance of God's grace" (M 81, 47).[119d] Of the various predicates of perfection ascribed to Scripture, the decisive one is that of the *authority* that it bears *in itself* or that it has *from God alone*. The Word "receives its authority from him alone, and not from men," as the *Gallican Confession* puts it (M 222,33[–34])[120]; the canonical Scriptures have "sufficient authority of themselves, not of men" in the words of the Second Helvetic Confession[120a]; they "carry the evidence in themselves," according to the Belgic Confession (M 234,20[–21]).[120b] The classic formulation is in the Westminster Confession (M 544,20[–27]): "The authority of the holy Scriptures . . . dependeth . . . wholly upon God (who is truth itself), the Author thereof; and therefore it is to be received, because it is the Word of God."[120c] Here it is very clear: The entire doctrine of the perfection of Scripture is only another expression of the doctrine of its *inspiration*. To say that the Holy Scripture is the *perfect* revelation is the same thing as to say that it is the work of the *Holy Spirit*.[121] This must be supplemented immediately by a third statement: The knowledge of this is itself the work of the Holy Spirit, for the Spirit can only be recognized through the Spirit, God only through God.[122] This is the genuine answer of the Reformed church to the question of the grounding of its Scripture principle. It is an answer that, when examined in terms of synthetic thought, does in fact lead into emptiness, to nowhere. For it is nothing other than the repetition of the thesis for which grounds were sought, the acknowledgement that this thesis is an axiom whose content is established, or better, *pre*established by God. We saw that this conviction was unapologetically proclaimed in the instructions for fruitful Bible reading. The point of the understanding of the Bible is that one reads it as "certain truth come down from heaven,"[123] which means that the Holy Spirit here (in the reader) connects to the Holy Spirit there (in the Scriptures).

There is a series of places in the Reformed confession that reveal how the authors with more or less success and strength struggled with themselves to acknowledge this fact. They did so in an age that was progressively losing its capacity to deal with an objective intrinsic truth, so that this basic fact had to become more and more alien and disturbing, just as it had become alien and disturbing for most of the Middle Ages, in spite of many subcurrents. It would have been truly wonderful if they could have presented *other reasons* for the authority of Scripture than just the one that God is speaking here, or if they could have been able at least to substantiate it with arguments! Thus, the *Belgic Confession* (M 234, 21[–22])[123a] was the first one to refer, next to the testimony of the Holy Spirit, to the fulfillment of biblical prophecies, which even the blind could grasp with their hands. The Waldensian Confession of 1655 (M 501,13[–17])[123b] lists as reasons for the divinity of the Bible these factors: (1) the witness of the church, (2) the eternal and indubitable truth of the doctrine it contains, (3) the "excellency, sublimity, and majesty" with which the divine appears in it, *and* (4) the effect of the Holy Spirit upon us, without noting that the first argument was Catholic, the second and third were meaningless without the fourth, so that only the fourth remains as the real reason. The English proved to be especially inventive in the finding of supportive reasons. The *Westminster Confession* (M 544, 30[–545, 8])[123c] and the *Larger Westminster Catechism* (M 613,2[–8])[123d] produce the following arguments: the testimony of the church at least to the particular dignity of the Bible (as the Word of God it demonstrates the heavenly character of its contents), the effectiveness of its doctrine, the majesty of its style, the agreement of all its parts, its intention to give God the glory, its capacity to demonstrate the road to salvation; of course, as "the very Word of God" ["ipsissimum Dei verbum"], the Holy Spirit alone testifies in it and in us with "full persuasion" ["plena persuasio"] and "infallible truth" ["infallibilis veritas"]. The person who is not satisfied with the special dignity of the Bible or with its character as the Word of God in the broad sense will persistently continue to ask why it is the "very Word of God" ["ipsissimum Dei verbum"], and he will ultimately have to hold to the reason last named. The *Erlauthal Confession* is also very naive in this regard (M 341,40[–45]) when it simply asserts that the true Church endorses the Bible as Christ did the Old Testament and Peter the writings of Paul. The confession of the *Calvinist Methodists* of Wales of 1823 (M 872,14[–42]) develops the following apologetic: The knowledge of God and his nature that the Bible proves is so broad and deep that it can only come from the one who knows himself in this way, that is, from God himself. Then there is added the virtue and self-denial of the biblical authors; the purity and holiness of biblical doctrines; the agreement of all its parts; its capacity to withstand against so many enemies and critics; its influence on the hearts of people; the moral, scientific and humanitarian superiority of those nations that possess the Bible over others; the impossibility of imagining that either evil people or angels could have written the Bible against their very own self-interest. There is further demonstration of the leveling of modern Christianity in that here, while talking about grounding of Scripture, its one truly decisive ground is completely *forgotten* in the plethora of arguments!

As the basis of my presentation of this only possible grounding, that is, of the *doctrine of inspiration*, I turn to Calvin's classical argument (Inst. I,7).[124] That we place faith in the Bible[125] is for Calvin a matter of "common sense" ["sensus communis"] and "humanity" ["humanitas"]. Totally different from that is its "full authority among believers" ["plena autoritas apud fideles"]. It attains this only to the degree that they recognize the Holy Scriptures "*as if having sprung from heaven as if there the living words of God were heard.*" It is not the church that gives it its authority, as though the "truth of God" ["veritas Dei"] could be grounded on the judgment of humans, an impossibility even for those anxious souls that are longing for the certainty of eternal life. The opposite is the case: The church with *its* authority can indeed prepare people for faith in the gospel, but without the authority of the Bible the church would not have been able to emerge. But[126] whence then comes the authority of the Bible? Calvin poses the opposing question: How do we know to differentiate light and darkness, white and black, sweet and bitter? The knowledge of the authority of the Bible merges with the knowledge that God is its author[127]: " *[T]he highest proof of Scripture derives, in general, from the fact that God in person speaks in it.*" The prophets and apostles do not boast of their perspicacity, they claim no credibility for themselves, they do not argue using reasons,"but they bring forward God's holy name."[127a] |

The confessional documents have specified and explained this relatively simple, first, basic thought—God speaks!—in a certain direction, namely, in his relationship to the given literal *text* of the Bible, without accomplishing much more than to make abundantly clear the irresolvable and necessary paradox of this basic thought. If they had done this conscious of what they were doing and in a vital relationship with the original conception, then one could only call it commendable. Apparently, however, they did it out of that scholastic need for completeness and exactness that counts on miracles the way one works with the unknown in an equation, which can be made into a known by methodical rearrangement. Most important, the context in which Calvin had developed this basic concept was disappearing rapidly, and *that* is what made the attempt to refine it, the so-called *doctrine of verbal inspiration*, into a very questionable accomplishment, in the form in which it became both famous and notorious. In Bullinger's *Second Helvetic Confession* (M 170,29[–30]), we first find the conceptual distinction between God's speech *then* (to the fathers, the prophets, and the apostles), and his speech *now* (to us through their Scriptures): "God has spoken . . . and speaks now."[127b] Although this distinction is logically correct, it clearly divides the Bible, valued *in and of itself* as the impression and result of revelation, from the Bible that is intended to be the witness of revelation *to us,* who are isolated by the reminder of the *time* that has passed between then and now. The distinction posits something objective versus something subjective, and thereby jeopardizes the *simultaneity* between the biblical authors and us. Only in this simultaneity, however, can the consequence of the revelation they experienced, their 'writing' [scriptum], become witness for us, become the Word of God, the "very Word of God" ["ipsissimum Dei verbum"]. The *Belgic Confession* goes further in the direction initiated by

Bullinger by stipulating that the holy men of God spoke as they were driven by the divine Spirit. *"Afterward"* [*"postea vero"*] God, out of particular concern for us, commissioned his servants, his prophets and apostles, to record in writing his words (M 233,24[–27]).[127c] It is in the *Hungarian Confession* (M 405, 14) that, as far as I can see, we find the first usage of the unfortunate image that the canonical books were dictated to the biblical authors. The *Bohemian Confession* of 1609 distinguishes three different acts of God toward the biblical authors: inspiration, dictation, and the actual preservation of his words in the documents, in which process they only cooperated as "most faithful amanuenses" ["fidelissimi amanuenses"] (M 453, 33[–35]). In the *Westminster Confession* (546, 4[–14]), neither the original recipients of revelation nor inspiration as a living relationship between God and them are mentioned at all. The "Old Testament in Hebrew" and the "new Greek" are simply givens, both "inspired by God," through God's care and providence preserved pure and unblemished through all the centuries and thus authentic.[127d] |

The process had advanced far enough that now the peak could be climbed. This happened in the Helvetic Consensus Formula of 1675 (Can. I–III, M 862, 33[–863, 17]).[127e] Canon I: The Word entrusted by God to Moses, the prophets and apostles, protected by him against all the tricks of Satan, must be preserved in the church, without the smallest letter or dot being lost. Canon II: In a special sense (*Capellus* contested this at the time[128]), the *Hebrew Codex of the Old Testament*, which we have received through the tradition of the *Jewish church*, to which according to Romans 3:2 the sayings of God were entrusted, and which we possess today (as it has been passed on), is 'inspired' [θεό-πνευστος], both in respect of the *consonants* as of the *vowels*, whether considering the *vowel points themselves* or only their "power" ["potestas"], in respect of both the *matter* and the *words*, and according to this norm (using the official text of the synagogue) all the oriental and occidental translations are to be assessed and where needed improved. Canon III: This official "Hebrew reading" ["lectio Hebraica"] is not based upon human whim and may not be corrected on the basis of the Septuagint or other Greek translations, nor according to the Samaritan Codex nor the Chaldean Targumim, nor mere reason. Especially scorned is the attempt to produce an allegedly authentic text using critical methods ("critical power of human judgment" ["humani judicii κρίσει"]) on the basis of other than the official Hebrew codices, derived from old expositions. Especially because of these stipulations, the Helvetic Formula of Consensus has received much negative and contemptuous commentary.[129] In general, nothing can be done to redeem it. |

In spite of all that, I would like to say a good word for it. Its error is not at the point at which for 150 years every schoolboy has been able, without much effort of mind, to criticize it roundly. The scandal of the attempt to keep modern textual criticism separated from theology is so great because it has not succeeded. This is because the age that was then beginning could not resist eating of this tree of knowledge [see Gen. 2:17], which these tablets of prohibitions, forged in Zurich, could not prevent happening.[130] After a war is lost, the loser tends to be seen by the public as having been in the wrong, and there is usually some justification for this. But the public voice is *not yet* thereby God's voice! The statement that the authors were striving to make was this: If we assume that we possess a holy text, then it cannot be a historical science that decides on its authentic form, especially because such a science by its very nature has no sensitivity for the holy, as does the theological decision making of the church. The normative originality of a text is certainly not the same thing as its age in a temporal sense. The judgment of the synagogue interests us as Christians more than the judgment of this or that professor of philology! It is not foolish to assert that a text becomes holy, canonical, when it is recognized and declared as such by a church, when it is canonized. Over against that process the existence of historically older forms of this text is a completely meaningless fact. This was a clear position that the eighteenth and nineteenth centuries wrongly ignored and forgot, rather than to pursue it further and to support it with new arguments. The especially offensive matter of the Hebrew vowel pointing or their "power" ["potestates"] is merely the consequence of the assumption that we have a holy text, an assumption that is perhaps somewhat bureaucratic but not methodologically impossible. The general tumult that arose about it is more a sign of the fact that the concept of a "holy text" is rapidly disappearing in this age.[131] The actual difficulty with the Helvetic Consensus Formula is precisely *not* what one usually criticizes today—its stubborn insistence upon a "holy text." That makes it all the more respectable and remarkable in its way. Rather, the difficulty rests in the fact that its authors themselves no longer really knew what a holy text was, and with that they involuntarily had to become pacesetters of the progress that they were quite rightly trying to impede. What is completely forgotten and neglected in the Helvetic Consensus Formula is the third and decisive statement of the definition given above, that is, that the judgment that "this text is holy, a work of the Holy Spirit," is itself a work of the Holy Spirit in us and can only be understood as such. For them, the holiness and inspiredness of the text became an intrinsically given and objectively present factuality. The error already presaged in Bullinger's distinction now gained its revenge. In a murky and unbelievable way, they announced to thin air: 'At that time God spoke' [Deus olim loquutus est], and therefore this text with consonants and vowels as preserved in the 'Hebrew reading' [lectio Hebraica] of the synagogue is holy *in and of itself*. They claimed this without thinking of an answer to the question, to what degree it might then be holy *for us*. The simultaneity with the prophets and apostles, within which alone this *for us* as well as the *in and of itself* can be expressed, was lost. The divine wonder of inspiration became the worldly wonder of inspiredness. To put it differently, the wonder [Wunder] became a miracle [Mirakel] that then as such quite rightly had to evoke reservations, criticism, and laughter.

Let us now return to Calvin's doctrine of inspiration. It differs *negatively* from the later confessions, as we just discussed, in that it lacks this special interest in the literal text of the Bible and the difficult distinctions and investigations that must occur as soon as the inspired text as such is the object of our consideration. It differs *positively* through the relationship of the text's inspiredness to the actual process of inspiration as a timeless, or better, simultaneous act of God, by seeing as inextricably linked the then and the now, the there and the here, the biblical *author* and the biblical *reader*, objective and subjective truth. Seen in this context, the idea of a holy text was not only a possibility but rather a vital necessity, not a mere miracle but rather a recognition of the wonder of God. That they no longer understood this and thus no longer knew how to assert it properly is the reason for the criticism that must be directed toward the originators of the doctrine of verbal inspiration that emerged later. Let us listen to *Calvin* as he develops the *second* basic thought in his doctrine of inspiration, the *subjective* side that cannot be separated from the objective. He says that the "proof" ["persuasio"] of the divine authority of the Scripture must be grounded at some other place than in human reasons and judgments, namely, in the "*secret testimony of the Spirit*" ["arcanum testimonium spiritus"].[132] Calvin then claimed that he could cite such reasons—and he does in fact do it for a whole chapter[133]—but knows before starting that they will not suffice as a grounding for a "firm credibility of Scripture" ["solida scripturae fides"].[134] It is profane thinking to assert that Moses' and the prophets' speaking in the name of God could and must be proven rationally. The "testimony of the Spirit" ["testimonium spiritus"] is higher than all reason. Just as God himself is the only fitting witness who can speak to us in his Word, this Word cannot encounter faith in human hearts until it is confirmed to us by the witness of the Spirit. Now comes the decisive statement: "*The same spirit, therefore, who has spoken through the mouths of the prophets, must penetrate into our hearts to persuade us that they faithfully proclaimed what had been divinely commanded*" (I,7,4).[134a] The Scripture is 'self-authenticating' [αὐτόπιστος] and cannot be certified by human proofs and reasons.[135] If we find it worthy of faith, then that is not the judgment of others or our own judgment but rather the submission of our judgment under that of God himself. This has, for Calvin, *nothing* to do with a shudder at the mystical unknown or the superstitious capitulation of reason (in modern terms, irrationalism!). Rather, he states the grounds for our recognition, the "*best reason*" ["optima ratio"] that needs no other "reasons" ["rationes," plural], the "*truth*" ["veritas"] that needs no other "marks of genuineness" ["verisimilitudines"], the *"feeling"* ["sensus"] that cannot emerge in us apart from revelation.[136] In Article IV of the Gallican Confession (M 222,26[–29]), Calvin says expressly that the acknowledgment of these particular Scriptures as canonical rests upon the "testimony" ["témoignage"] and the "inward illumination of the Holy Spirit, which enables us to distinguish them from other ecclesiastical books." [136a] |

The meaning of this old doctrine of inspiration is as follows: Inspiration or revelation is conceived of as one single timeless, or better, simultaneous act of God upon the biblical authors *and* upon us. What appears to be questioning and answering between us and the biblical authors, as though they were standing inside and we outside, so to speak, is in reality a monologue of the Holy Spirit in them and in us. What *cannot* be differentiated with relation to the holiness of Scripture is the real grounds and the cognitive grounds; what *cannot* be differentiated is the fact that there are canonical books and the fact that we acknowledge them as such; what *cannot* be differentiated is the light that shines from the Bible and the eye that perceives this light. This is true whether we are speaking of the "autopistia" ["self-authenticating character"] of the Scriptures or of the witness of the Spirit in us. Historical questions that must arise in view of the fact that the Scripture is a historical and contingent entity are not answered in one or another sense by the assertion that Scripture is revelation. They belong at that very different level of "reasons" ["rationes"] and "marks of genuineness" ["verisimilitudines"], where the decision about the divinity or nondivinity of Scripture cannot be made. Here, where the human in terms of Romans 8[:14–17] stands as a child before its father and hears his voice, these questions cannot be raised at all. Whether one speaks of the *autopistia* of Scripture or of the *Spirit's witness* in us, this implies (1) *not* the presence or the recognition of a historical fact as such, and (2) *not* a subjective inward experience as asserted by the Enthusiasts back then and by the Romantics today, and (3) *not* the self-evident character of a mathematical or other rational axiom. To be sure, this thesis has logically the character of an axiom; to be sure, there is a meeting here of Reformed theology and philosophical rationalism. *But* only one thing can be meant when we speak of autopistia and the Spirit's witness: the *revelation of God* as a *sovereign act*, grounded solely in God, and emerging from God in freedom. At this point the dogma of *inspiration* flows into that of *predestination*. Calvin, of course, was well aware of the fact that innumerable people knew nothing of revelation nor wanted to. But he did not then make use of generally enlightening reasons for its truth in order to prove it. He did *not* become an apologist. Instead, he interpreted this fact through his reference to the eternal twofold decision of God who saves and damns whom *he* will.[137] The 'secret testimony of the Spirit' [arcanum testimonium spiritus] is for him nothing other than an outworking of the 'secret decree of God' [arcanum decretum Dei],[138] over against which it would be foolishness to ask for reasons. The Heidelberg Catechism follows Calvin appropriately when in Question 31 the means by which Christ carries out his royal office (M 691,4[–5]), and in Question 54 the means by which he gathers his elect community together from the entire human race (M 696, 32[–35]), is defined as *Word* and *Spirit*.[138a] If only the strict correlation and secret identity of these two things had not been lost from sight as subsequently happened! When they began to transform this single and unique ground into a ground that can and must have other grounds next to it; when, forgetting that the issue here is the Word and the Spirit of *God*, they began to look for arguments to make the historical word plausible to the human spirit, or conversely, to subordinate the historical word to the human spirit; as the recognition disappeared that we are known by God before we know him [see Gal. 4:9; 1 Cor. 13:12]; then, in spite of all faithful reiteration of the confessions of the fathers, Lessing's ugly ditch between eternal rational truth and contingent historical truth[139] had to open up, and then the Reformed formal principle had to become as opaque and unbelievable as the Lutheran material principle had become.

I said to you at the beginning of this section that the Scripture principle is the only article of faith that has persisted up to today in the doctrinal statements of all Reformed churches. I acknowledge the comforting fact that the spring has not been completely filled in. But there is little evidence of its still flowing. All respectful genuflections before the "Holy Scriptures of the Old and New Testaments," whether orthodox or liberal, do not change the fact that the grounding of this principle, upon which *everything* related to its application depends, its radical and paradoxical grounding through non-grounding, through faith in revelation as it was once taught in Zurich and Bern with intuitive certainty and as it was classically formulated by Calvin, is regarded today as a risk that simply evokes anxiety. Any other grounding than this has *not* emerged through two centuries of historical biblical study. We know better than Calvin that there are no "reasons" ["rationes"] for the divinity of Scripture, there is no God in history[140] and no God in us.[141] Whether we will again come to know as well as Calvin did that God desires to be and is his own witness in history and in us, and whether we will then risk his prescription, which is not just a prescription but health itself: to read the Bible "as if the living words of God were heard"[142]—that it is the fateful question whose answer will decide the future of Reformed (and not only Reformed) Protestantism.

3.

REFORMED DOCTRINE AS A WHOLE

We saw in lecture 1 what the confessional documents as such signify, or rather, do not signify in the Reformed church. Then in lecture 2 we learned the principle upon which they are based, the principle of Scripture, which necessarily puts them at a subordinate level, as we saw in lecture 1. This principle, as we have just heard, has the logical character of an axiom and yet is not meant as an axiom but rather as the expression of the insight that at the beginning of all knowledge of God stands not human self-knowledge but God's own knowing, man's being known by God, that is, revelation. The distinctive character of Reformed theology, of Reformed thinking and speaking about God, has clearly confronted us in these introductory considerations. On the one hand, the human is understood in a sober and rational way, seen in a critically reserved fashion with the possibilities given to him, but then affirmed practically and reasonably in these very possibilities. On the other hand, God as the absolute wonder, God who is God solely in and through himself, especially and most of all when he reveals himself to humanity, is then most to be respected in his deity when the unheard of is to be heard, the unspeakable is to be said: that the human stands in relationship to him. These are the two extreme poles of Reformed thought. Both have their analogies and connections to the view of God and the world of medieval scholastics, mystics, and reforming theologians.[1] Both stand, above all, in the tightest relation to the intellectual world of the Renaissance, on the one hand, and on the other hand, to the Reformation thinking of Luther. On both sides, Reformed doctrine has to cope with the fatal proximity of enthusiastic, gnostic, rationalistic, and naturalistic ideas. In the distinctive way in which it relates these two poles to each other, in Zwingli as in Calvin, in Basel as in Heidelberg, in Hungary as in Scotland, it represents something special, unique, and wholistic, in spite of all its connections, dependencies, and relationships, as well as all its internal inconsistencies. It is not Catholicism, not Lutheranism, not Enthusiasm, and not rationalism, but *Reformed* doctrine of God and Christianity. We are reminded by lecture 1 that relatively little has been done in an external and organizational sense to generate and preserve this distinctiveness for the unity of Reformed doctrine. It persisted and maintained itself as long and as far as the original knowledge remained vital. The fact that it has faded with time and disintegrated and become a historical entity is not because *it* was lacking in power —we can still detect that power today at least historically—but because its heirs, including ourselves, have not been and are not adequate to its power.

Let us turn now to the actual *content* of these documents, whose external character and internal grounding we have sought to clarify up until now on the basis of their own statements. Before we address the details, we shall attempt in this section to gain an overview of the *entirety* of this doctrine. What are they all saying, these people such as Zwingli, Calvin, Bullinger, Beza, Leo Jud, John à Lasco, Ursinus, the fathers of Dort, and all the rest, not as individuals but *together*? What are they saying, not about this and that, not in the arrangement of their many sentences, not in many but in a *few words*, even if it is probably impossible to put it in one word? What were they seeking to *emphasize*, what was their *basic intention* when, instead of simply repeating the Apostles' Creed, instead of acknowledging the Augsburg Confession (as many of them did do),[2] they set out to compose their own confessions, to express the great commonality of Christian thought in a Reformed formulation by making very definite selections, intentional deletions, delimitations, clarifications, and even blurrings? To ask the question from the perspective of the principle of Scripture: What was the faithful *echo* that these confessional documents intentionally sought to give to the voice of God heard in the Bible? We can only attempt here to give a general orientation as we look at the *material* dealt with in the confessions. We shall examine the actual or implied *titles* of the various chapters and sections, consider the *arrangement* and *outline* in which the thoughts of the various confessions confront us, ponder the authors' varying attempts to bring them into a *system* under a dominant *perspective*, attempts that may be strong or weak, articulate or implied. Whoever has surveyed the ocean of Reformed confessions even superficially knows how difficult and tricky it is to answer our question, if only in the most general way. It is of course easy and rewarding to lay out one's course by simply 'begging the question' [petitio principii], that is, by calling on a preconceived slogan to describe the entirety of Reformed doctrine as whatever one wants it to be, whether friendly or polemical in intent. There is much truth in seeking the essential and characteristic center of Reformed doctrine in the concept of the honor of God, or in its decisive ethical intentionality, or, in what appears to be the converse, in its decided orientation toward that which is beyond the grave, or in a certain powerful implementation of the Lutheran doctrine of faith and justification,[3] or in a less positive way in its determinism, its legalism, or its spiritualism.[4] I will certainly not begin with such a statement, and I would like to ask that one not understand my discussion above of the polarity between man and God in that way but rather as the provisional result of our introductory observations. When one reads through the confessions one after another, one is constantly amazed by the many exceptions to these rules, by the lines pointing in completely different directions, by the questionable character of any attempt to arrange everything into what we call a system. Perhaps we need to make very clear to ourselves from the outset that the system— the "unification" of the theological statements in these confessions—simply cannot be demonstrated, but, like the intersection of parallel lines, lies in infinity. This would certainly correspond to the Reformed understanding of the relation between confession and the Word of God. Regardless of that, the issue here is to begin with careful *questions* and not with *answers*.

This process of questioning is, however, not all that easy. K. Müller (947)[5] differentiates in his index into the following types of Reformed doctrine: the Zwinglian Type, the Middle Type (designated by the four Bs: Basel, Bern, Butzer, and Bullinger), the Calvinist Type, and the distinctive confessions from the east—Anglican, Congregational, German, Modern. This is illuminating as a historical outline. It makes clear in an elegant way that the two first groupings, the Zwinglian and the Zwinglianizing B-Type, form *preliminary stages*, Calvinism the dominant *center*, while Anglicanism and the German Reformed are *subordinate branches* of the great Reformed complex. For our purposes, it would not satisfy me to lay so much weight upon this kind of outline, because the question that concerns us—What did this people think and intend?—is different from the questions, Who were they? What were they called? and To what group did they belong? The entirety of Reformed doctrine, when dealt with in this way, would be separated into its historical components, but it would not be grasped in its vital tendencies that were the same both here and there although linked and nuanced differently. We would still have to look, within the various historical groupings, for a creative interpretive principle in order to get at the content.

A very different option would be to sort out the confessions according to the logic or lack of logic in their approaches. There would be (1) those that treat one single dogmatic point, such as the Lord's Supper in the *Consensus Tigurinus*, predestination in the *Lambeth Articles*, and the church in the *Declaration of Savoy*. Then there would be (2) those that systematically emphasize and explicate a certain interrelated cluster of points such as the *Canons of Dort*, working out the problem of soteriology while centered on belief in the idea of predestination. Then there would be (3) those that consist of a terrifying and riotous chaos of points, as is the case in the *Erlauthal Confession*. We would then group (4)[6] those that begin with a shorter or longer organizing concept and then lose their thread and become a listing of all kinds of points, such as *Zwingli's Theses* of 1523 and, generally, most of the confessions from the initial phases of the various churches. The next group would consist of (5) those that carry through one systematic perspective or thread from the beginning to the end, such as Beza's *Hungarian Confession* of 1562 or the *Westminster Confession*. In the next group we would put (6) those that arrange the content, in more or less appropriate ways, under one perspective derived from the tradition, such as *Zwingli's Exposition of the Faith* addressed to Francis I in 1531, which builds on the three articles of the Apostles' Creed, or the catechisms of *Leo Jud, Emden, Hesse, Micronius*, the *Westminster Cathechisms*, and the *Anglican Catechism*, which, following Luther's schematic or their own arrangement, treat the main themes already found in the Roman Catechism, that is, the faith, the Ten Commandments, the sacraments, and the Lord's Prayer. Finally, there would be (7) those confessions that successfully connect the traditional point of view with a systematic approach, seen above all in *Calvin's* Catechism of 1545, which masterfully addresses the four sections under the theme of the way in which man should honor God. The *Heidelberg Catechism* takes a similar approach as it queries the three major themes one must know in order to live and die in blessed comfort: human misery, redemption, and thankfulness. The procedure for the investigation of the entirety of Reformed doctrine, in this arrangement, would consist of reviewing everywhere the more or less clearly and consequently executed systematic points of view, then attempting to isolate them as much as possible from the contents, and finally comparing them to each other and where possible capturing them in a formula. |

I would regard this as permissible and instructive but fear that the resulting picture would be one-sided. The pedagogical documents, as important as they are for determining the entire body of doctrine, would attain an inappropriate normativity. It is remarkable to see here how the *system* has emerged from the need for *instruction*. Precisely this insight will prevent us from identifying too quickly the system, the pedagogically apt arrangement, with the meaning and content of the doctrinal statements. The entirety of Reformed doctrine is not only to be found where the authors themselves saw or constructed such an entirety, but just as much and perhaps even more so in the unsystematic confessions, or in those that are constructed in a traditional fashion, or in those that contain only a fragment of the doctrine. Conversely, the plan according to which the people worked rendered only in very few instances (perhaps only in Calvin's Catechism of 1545 or in the Heidelberg) something even close to a picture of what they thought and intended. |

As a third possibility, I would like to suggest that this question, what the people thought and intended, should simply be asked *historically*. What was their intention in the composition of their confessions? Then, by observing how they carried out their intention, one can use the contents to determine what was truly important to them beyond the historical report—that is, one can determine the essence and character of the Reformed confession. When this historical question is asked in this fashion, four major answers emerge that can be used to group the Reformed confessions. Enumerating them now in accordance with the typical historical course of things, they intend, first of all, to document the discussion with the ancient church[7] and to ascertain its most important findings. Then they intend to create order in their own newly built house, to provide direction for the new preaching and teaching of the church. Thirdly, they seek to draw the lines and define their defenses toward their nearest evangelical neighbor, that is, Lutheranism, which after a decade of vacillation was staking out its exclusivist claims. And fourthly, as documents of the intellectual movement in their own camp, they seek to push certain thoughts into the foreground, others into the background, and thereby correct the original conceptions, or make them more precise, or assert them. As a historical outline, Müller's order is, of course, better than these, for I need scarcely to say that in most cases it is impossible to carry out strictly the differentiation of the confessions into group one, two, three, or four. Those confessions that are primarily anti-Roman are usually simultaneously meant to be constitutive, while the constitutive ones are generally not lacking a concealed or obvious polemic against Lutheranism. Such subdivisions and differentiations are not our chief concern now, for we are more interested in discovering the *types* that can be deduced from the history, not read into it, and that in contrast to Müller's approach are capable of leading us to substantive conclusions. Let us then use the four aforementioned answers as the basic structure of our approach, and then let us see whether or not it will be possible to draw the results together in a summarizing and general overview in a fifth section.

1. THE DEBATE WITH THE OLD CHURCH

In the nature of things, all of the earliest confessions, with a few important exceptions, belong to this group. It includes, above all, *Zwingli's* confessions[8] (with the exception of the Short Instruction of 1523), the *Bernese Theses* of 1528 (the Bern Synod belongs together with Zwingli's Instruction in the second group), the Confession of the *East Friesian Preachers* of 1528, the *Tetrapolitan* Confession, the *First Basel* Confession, the *Lausanne* Theses, and the *Geneva* Confession of 1536. We note already in this list that the Swiss confessions are preponderant, which is no accident. The sharply anti-Roman aspect of the countenance of Reformed Christianity is a specifically Swiss legacy. We encounter it in almost all the Reformed confessions of all countries. In the bitterness and disgust with which they speak of the pope and the mass, there is scarcely any notable difference between the Swiss and German, the Eastern and the Western confessions. In the Lutheran Reformation, the anti-Roman polemic is more accidental, a defensive act inserted after the fact and not without a certain melancholy, whereas it is of the substance of the Reformed Reformation. It is fundamental. These confessors have burned their ships behind them and are beginning church history all over again—one can understand and interpret the process either prophetically *or* humanistically. This setting out and beginning anew (we have seen the particular role the Bible plays in this) took place most characteristically in *Switzerland*. That remarkable figure *Zwingli* is particularly significant here. The same spirit is documented at the same time in certain individuals in East Friesia. Müller calls this confession "a distant product of pure Zwinglianism" (XXII).[9] The names Aportanus, Rhode, and Reese, which stand behind this confession,[10] remind us of those circles of Dutch spiritualists from which conversely a certain influence reaches down to Zurich from afar.[11] I would like to concede their independence to the East Friesians, or rather their independent connection with Holland, which in those centuries was generally a remarkable center of religious turbulence. The identity of the anti-Roman spirit that surfaces both here and there is all the more interesting. Somewhat later in the first Institutes of the young Calvin a third independent source of that spirit became visible. |

What is characteristic of this spirit? What were the Reformed objections to Rome? It is not very fruitful to consider *particular* complaints such as the mass, the saints, dietary prohibitions, monastic vows, and so on, which are mentioned in more or less detail in the oldest confessions and continue to fill innumerable paragraphs in the later ones reaching into the seventeenth century. Obviously, it was these various factors that ignited the fire of anger at that time. For us, who know Catholicism almost entirely from the outside, this polemic and the objects against which it was directed are virtually incomprehensible. In addition, it is also found in almost complete agreement in the Lutheran confessions, and for that reason it is not helpful for our understanding of the Reformed. It should be noted, however, that the Augsburg Confession, in contrast to Zwingli's Theses of 1523,[12] does *not* allude to the consecration of priests, the pope, or purgatory, and on the other hand expressly acknowledges private confession in Article 11 and, above all, priestly absolution in Article 25.[13] In and of themselves, however, these things do not reveal what was distinctive in the Reformed resistance to Rome compared to the Lutheran, even though they were much regarded and discussed at the time. We must ask about the *center* and *point of departure* of this anti-Roman polemic. There is no doubt about where to find it in the *Lutheran* confessions: In Augustana it is in Articles 2–4 dealing with original sin, the Son of God, and justification,[14] and in the Smalcaldic Articles it is brilliantly summarized by Luther himself in the "first and chief article" of the second section, of which he himself says, "Nothing in this article can be given up or compromised, even if heaven and earth and things temporal should be destroyed. . . . On this article rests all that we teach and practice against the pope, the devil, and the world" (M 300).[15] The issue is the justification of the sinful person before God through Christ alone through *faith*. The emphasis is upon "through *faith*." The righteousness of the sinner before God is the righteousness of *faith*. That was the discovery that Luther made in Romans.[16] That was the banner of the Reformation carried out under his name. It opposed the old church because it tortured the conscience on the one hand and on the other hand made the conscience careless through its demand for a righteousness of works. Luther's dispute against Rome is at its root the dispute about the proper care of souls. How a person gets a gracious God[17] —that is what in his view Roman doctrine and practice appear to make hopelessly dark. "Nowhere can our opponents say how the Holy Spirit is given," writes *Melanchthon* in the Apology, Article 4 (M 98,63).[18] But he *knows* what to say: The Holy Spirit is given in that the 'terrified conscience' [perterrefacta conscientia] receives in faith the promise of the forgiveness of sins for Christ's sake. "This consolation is a new and spiritual life."[19] Another question would be whether in Luther's beginnings and in his later statements—I am thinking here precisely of the Smalcaldic Articles—an offensive front can be seen that differs entirely from this explicitly pastoral one. Be that as it may, the pastoral front became, under Melanchthon's influence, decisive for the historical shape of Lutheranism. |

If we compare Article 3 of the *Tetrapolitana* (M 57,1–2),[20] *that* Reformed confession which for tactical reasons was conformed to the Augsburg Confession as much as possible, then we note that, in spite of the apparently complete agreement of the factual results of the thoughts and conclusions on both sides, not only the tone but also the content, not only the nerve but also the movement of thought are totally different.

We receive the forgiveness of sins and are made just before God not through works and satisfaction but out of grace and through May 31 faith—that is what the *Augsburg Confession* says. The *Tetrapolitana* says that becoming pious and just is to be solely ascribed to divine goodness and the merit of Christ and is received by us through faith. Piety and eternal life rest on the knowledge of God and of Christ, but this knowing is not a work of flesh and blood, but requires a new birth, the *Father's* drawing us to the Son [see John 6:44]. The beginning must come from the mercy of God. To be sure, this is not a contradiction, and in its consequences over against Roman doctrine it arrives at the same place, but clearly it is another, new, distinctive direction of attack against this doctrine. The passage in the *Augsburg Confession* concludes with the words, "For God will regard and reckon this *faith* as righteousness" (M 39),[21] referring to Romans 3 and 4, while the *Tetrapolitana* concludes with the statement, "Everyone who calls upon the name of the *Lord* shall be saved,"[22] from Romans 10[:13]. The *Augustana* asks about the right relationship between the human and God, and the *Tetrapolitana* asks what is the decisive thing in the right relationship between the human and God. The *Augustana* says that there is no other way out of the despairing situation of humanity than faith in forgiveness; the *Tetrapolitana* says that God alone can make this way out in that he gives to the human this faith. The *Augustana's* question is about proper pastoral care. The *Tetrapolitana* appears to evade this question with the admonition, Cast all your cares, even your care of souls, especially your care of souls on the Lord, for he cares for you [see 1 Peter 5:7]. The *Augustana* asks, How shall I be saved? The *Tetrapolitana* asks, Who saves me? In the *Augustana*, the article "On Justification" ["De justificatione"] deals straightforwardly with the justification of the human before God, whereas in the *Tetrapolitana* something very different glows dialectically through what appears to be the very same basic theme: the justification of God over against the human. |

It is clear that the complaint against Catholicism that results from the different understanding found in the central Lutheran article must then also differ from the Reformed approach. If in the *Augustana* the terrified and comforted conscience protests, then in the *Tetrapolitana* it is simply the *alert* conscience that protests. If there the devil is the deceiver and seducer of humanity, here he is the one who insults and blasphemes God. If the *Augustana* warns against false trust, the *Tetrapolitana* warns against false gods. The direction in which the polemical interest of the Reformed confession is to be sought is plain: It battles Catholicism as an attempt at self-help, and it sees in this desire to help oneself an arrogance and presumption that do not lead to the goal but rather are an insult to God and thus make genuine help impossible. For God desires to help. But he helps as the one who alone helps. To believe means to affirm that God alone is our helper. The decisive thing to be said about faith is not that faith makes just, but that faith is given, awakened, made by God. It is only this faith, or, in other words, it is only God himself who makes just.

Thus, at its core, the anti-Roman polemic is presented in a confession that, as I said, moves in the direction of the Lutheran confession as much as possible and whose first question and answer are dictated by the Lutheran (although, to be sure, this follows the formulation of a very un-Lutheran principle of Scripture[23]). This is how the first question, and initially its answer, are understood in Reformed thinking. In the other documents, which in their own logic are not affected by any particular concern for the Lutheran confession, it obviously becomes much clearer that the Reformed issue with the Roman Church was really not the problem of pastoral care as it is expressed in the well-known conceptual sequence of sin–Christ–faith. |

Let us begin with *Zwingli's theses* 1–16, the fundamental part of his Sixty-seven Theses of 1523.[24] At first glance, one notes that the terms "righteousness," "sin," and "forgiveness of sins" never occur in this foundational manifesto of the Zurich Reformation, and the term "faith" occurs only once in the conclusion. The basic thrust of Zwingli's polemic is that it is an error and offense against God to think that the gospel should require the church's approbation. The content of the gospel is the declaration of God's will toward us that has taken place in Christ and our reconciliation with God that has been completed in Christ. Therefore, Christ is the only way to salvation for all who have ever lived, do live, and ever will live. Anyone who seeks or points to another door is a murderer of souls and a robber [see John 10:1]. Anyone who regards other teachings as equal to or higher than the gospel, *does not know* what the gospel is. For all humanity, Christ is the one who shows the way, the captain, eternal salvation. He is the head—and the believers are his body, which is dead and powerless without him. The church without Christ is "demented,"[25] and wounds itself with foolish laws. Such Christlessness is the activity of the so-called clergy. That is the reason for their passionate resistance now. To listen to the head of the church would lead back to the will of God and to fellowship with him in the Spirit. *For this reason the gospel of Christ* must be preached. Salvation rests in believing in him, and in disbelief there is damnation. This gospel teaches us that human doctrines and traditions are of no use for salvation. (This is where the details commence, theses 17–63, beginning with an unambiguous attack against the "high priest.") This is how the Reformed confession does its polemics when it is standing on its own feet. What Zwingli intends is very clear: He wants the *exclusivity* of salvation in Christ to be acknowledged again. It is that salvation in Christ that is *for* the church of the faithful, the 'catholic church' [ecclesia catholica], the "bride of Christ,"[26] just as it is also *over against* the church that without him can do nothing, is necessarily against him, and thus against its own salvation. These sixteen theses cannot be explained in terms of the logical necessity of an abstract monotheism. The conviction expressed here is that the only salvation that is divine and real is the salvation that is exclusive over against everything else. Christ is to be acknowledged again as this exclusive salvation. Belief in *this* Christ is salvation; unbelief in *this* Christ is damnation. |

In the confessions addressed to Charles V and Francis I in 1530 and 1531, and in contrast to 1523, Zwingli attempted to place this anti-Catholic fundamental thought in the context of a comprehensive presentation of all the other Christian truths. The 'Account of the Faith' [Fidei Ratio] of 1530[27] begins with the presentation of Zwingli's doctrine of the Trinity and Christology, in which he states (M 81,5[–8]),[27a] without betraying his own nuances, that he is following the path of the tradition. The split in the road and its signpost become clear in the second article (M 81,9[–82, 2]),[27b] in which Zwingli develops the decisive lines of his distinctive understanding of God. I know, he begins, that the highest being, "which is my God,"[28] determines *freely* all things so that his counsel "*does not depend* upon the contingency of any human creature."[29] God, who from eternity and for all time surveys everything with a single and simple look, does not need to consider anything nor to wait upon anything. For, as one who is equally wise, prudent, good, and so forth, he *freely* disposes and determines all things, for whatever *is*, is his. It is this same free goodness of God that, according to Zwingli, shows itself to be truly at work, both as the establishment of the law in the *fall* of man as well as the sending of the Son and Mediator in the *redemption* of man. It is justice *and* mercy, but always *God's* justice, *God's* mercy. This is where we find ourselves when we ask about God's grace: Nothing other than God can make us certain of it. No other pledge (Art. 3)[30] of his mercy than God himself ("nothing is as certain as *God*"[31]), God who is identical with the 'victim' [hostia] Christ who is given for our sin. *For this reason,* neither justification nor satisfaction based on our own works nor reconciliation and intercession of all the saints in heaven or on earth is of any avail. For Zwingli, this then opens the path to the concept of election and to the doctrines of original sin and the church that are dominated by this concept. This 'Account of the Faith' [Fidei Ratio] that is the Zwinglian parallel to the Augsburg Confession never develops a doctrine of the justification of the sinner through faith! The contradiction to Rome, which of course also plays a part in this controversy (but with emphasis on *also*!), is oriented primarily toward that other concern that is expressed here in the thesis of God's unconditional and sovereign *freedom.* |

The argument is similar in the posthumously published '*Exposition of the Christian Faith*' [Fidei christianae expositio] of 1531 (Zw. Op. IV, 45–78).[32] Here the specifically Zwinglian doctrine of God with its polemical thrust is placed at the head of the entire argument, in sequence before the doctrines of the Trinity and of Christ, an order which reoccurs later on in many Reformed confessions.[33] The article 'Regarding God' [De Deo], which appears to be so general and scholastic with its many superlatives and other attempts to say what is most inexpressible, contains here a very definite and consistently emphasized point. Here is how Zwingli develops this point: God distinguishes himself from all other things as the Uncreated One. To be uncreated is the same thing as to be eternal or infinite. But there is only One who can be uncreated, eternal, and infinite. Zwingli describes this "*one only Creator*" ["*unus solus creator*"][34] as the origin, source, and foundation of the first article of faith. Faith in God is confident faith so long as it is faith in *this* God. Whatever is creaturely, whatever has begun and will end in time, can be neither the object nor the basis (both are merged for Zwingli) of a confident faith. Any possibility of placing trust in a creature, even if it were the most sacred one, or upon a sacrament, even if it were the holiest one, "falls to the ground."[34a] They are not God, and thus they are not worthy of faith. "This is the fountainhead of my religion, to recognize God as the uncreated Creator of all things, who solely and alone has all things in His power and freely giveth us all things. They, therefore, overthrow this first foundation of faith, who attribute to the creature what is the creator's alone."[35] It is clear that with this thinking Zwingli is expressing in a third way what he already expressed in 1523 as the exclusivity of salvation in Christ and in 1530 as the freedom of the divine decree. Here it emerges as a jealous *monotheism*, as a battle against the divinization of the creature. But it is not meant speculatively, as though it were an attack upon a metaphysical intrinsic truth. Rather, it is grounded on the claim that one cannot believe in any other than the One God. The attack on the old church in the 'Exposition of Faith' [Fidei Expositio] is carried out under the doctrine of the forgiveness of sins solely through faith, but it is done (1) in a very concealed place in the third section *after* the treatment of the problems of church and hierarchy, (2) with remarkable succinctness, and (3) in such a way that the contrast is not between forgiveness based upon works or upon faith but rather between forgiveness from the mouth of the priest or from the mouth of Christ *himself* and Christ *alone* (1. c. [op. cit.] 60–61). Obviously, Zwingli's deepest concern is *not this* set of problems, or better, this interests him only in the context of his own, distinctive set of problems. |

Let us turn now to the other documents from that initial period of struggle, those not derived directly from Zwingli. In 1528, in the city of Bern, the *Ten Theses* of Berchtold Haller and Franz Kolb[36] were successfully defended (M 30–31). They begin with a statement that we have already cited: "The holy, Christian Church, whose only Head is Christ, is born of the Word of God, abides in the same, and does not listen to the voice of a stranger."[37] This statement and the second one, which rejects "human traditions," are intended first to establish the principle of Scripture. But one can already hear the tone that I have described above as jealousy: Why should the church listen to "strangers" instead of to the word of its head! In the third thesis this tone sounds forth openly: "Christ is our *only* wisdom, righteousness, redemption, and payment for the sins of the *whole* world. Hence it is a *denial* of Christ when we acknowledge another merit for salvation and satisfaction for sin."[38] There is no further mention in these theses of the *human's way* of salvation. The Reformed confession is interested in the *beginning* and the *end* of this way. One cannot fail to see the line here that connects Bern with Zurich! |

In the same year (1528), the *preachers from East Friesia* drew up their confession as a defense against the accusation that they were scorning God's Word and the sacraments.[39] Clearly their defense is directed not only against Rome but also, as was also the case in Zwingli's last confession, against Luther as well, who from this perspective can easily be seen as on Rome's line, providing one no longer understood his particular concern. The East Friesian confession is one of most extreme and radical products of this polemical way of thinking. It virtually outstrips the urgency with which Zwingli pressed his concern. Throughout the entire thirty-three articles and the concluding section[40] one tone is maintained and worked on with remarkable persistence, with no trace of ambivalence or concession toward the side that it apparently intends to confront. God knows his own and has prepared his kingdom for them. But this is a *concealed* truth; its revelation consists solely of the *incarnation* and the *Word* as its proclamation, and inwardly the *Holy Spirit* and *faith*. As Christ *alone* is the mediator, God's self-revelation, so faith, baptism with the Holy Spirit, new birth are God's gift and work *alone*. *His* action alone, which is *not* bound to our action, *nor* to our preaching, baptizing, or eucharistic celebration, decides our salvation. Faith is complete in itself. It has no need of any means or supports that are located outside of it. Just as eternal things cannot create it, they cannot create certainty about it. Preaching and sacrament are an issue only as witnesses to a faith already present, witnesses from human to human, but in no sense a mediation between God and man. As such witnesses they have their right and honor, but only as such. Where the claim is made that they are a means to justification or merely to certainty about justification, then it is allowable, if not required, to abstain from them for a while as a sign of protest: "in order to testify and demonstrate the freedom and purity of faith in Christ."[41] To summarize, we believe "alone" ["alleen"] in God, we receive forgiveness of sins "alone" from God the Father, "alone" through God the Son, "alone" through God the Holy Spirit's assurance. In this sense we reject everything "that God himself is not and does not" (M 930[–35]).[42] It is no coincidence that this confession never received lasting ecclesial acknowledgement, not even in its land of origin.[43] One is unmistakably moved into the vicinity of a spiritualism in whose stiff breeze one can perhaps think and live as a Christian but probably cannot build a church. But we must emphasize that it is only the vicinity. The East Friesians are noticeably reserved in their use of the concept of the "Spirit." As they say in their conclusion,[44] they are free of any sectarian exclusivity over against others who may think more mildly than they. They, for their part, want to be left unopposed in the knowledge they have gained from Scripture. They are certainly very far away from the psychic-mystical sentimentalities of Karlstadt.[45] Nor can one speak here of an Enlightened rationalism along the lines of the Socinians. It is sober enthusiasm or an enthusiastic sobriety, focused completely on the one point: the immediacy not of man to God but of God to man. This is what these men claim as "the freedom and purity of faith" ["vrijheit ende purheit des geloofs"] in contrast both to Catholic and also Lutheran teaching. Something other than the Zwinglian exclusivity, jealousy or freedom is evidently not intended. The problem of pastoral care, of the 'order of salvation' [ordo salutis], is *very far* away for the East Friesians as well.

It is a milder breeze that we encounter in the confession with which the church of Basel finally declared itself to be a Reformed church in 1534.[46] It might be better not to group this confession with those from the earlier polemical period. Oswald Myconius,[47] the gentle friend of Zwingli and later of Calvin, is its author. It contains virtually no expressly polemical edges, except perhaps in the doctrine of the Lord's Supper. At the same time, it does show how Zwingli's front had gained broad and general acceptance. The doctrine of God with which it begins reaches its high point with the concept of election, and is followed by teaching concerning: humanity made in the image of God and fallen; "God's concern for us," that is, the still valid promise of God over humanity; Christ; the church; the Lord's Supper; church discipline; government; and (not until this point in the argument!) the human's way through faith to forgiveness of sins, to righteousness, to works of love; and finally, the last days, human traditions, and the errors of the Anabaptists (M 95–100). If one questions this confession about what its objections to the old church are and what it seeks to say regarding them, there can be no doubt about the answer it will give.

The Ten Theses of the *Lausanne Religious Discussion* in the fall of 1536[48] speak a clearer language; this was the first of these events in which the young Calvin took part, although in a subordinate position.[49] To be sure, these theses begin with the question of the "way of justification" ["via justificandi"], but then the characteristic language follows immediately. Whoever teaches another way than that of faith is "a destroyer of all the virtue of Christ."[50] *This* is what the theses protest against—surely influenced but not inspired by the Bernese theology. It continues accordingly: Christ the chief, the true priest, the mediator and advocate of his church. This church is "known to the eyes of *God alone,*"[51] and thus its sacraments are *symbols* and *signs* of grace. There is no other priesthood than that of the administration of Word and sacrament, no other confession of sins than that to God, no other absolution than that from God himself, no other service of God than the spiritual that consists of love to one's neighbor, no other governance than the worldly ordained by God for that purpose. This subordination of governance in the shadow of exclusive monotheism is certainly to be regarded as specifically Bernese theology.[52] But it demonstrates the direction in which this thinking is moving (M 110). |

Finally, we turn to the *Geneva Confession* by G. Farel (M 111[–16]),[52a] written in the same year (1536). On the first page, we encounter the titles, "The Word of God" ("La Parolle de Dieu"), "One Only God" ("Ung seul Dieu"), "The Law of God Alike for All" ("Loy de Dieu, seulle pour toutes"). And the content of these articles is just as unambiguous. The formation of the principle of Scripture expresses that jealousy: We want to follow the Scriptures "without mixing with it any other thing which might be devised by the opinion of men [. . .] without addition or diminution."[53] Then, in the practical exposition of the thought of God's unity, it is an "abomination"[54] to place trust and hope in any creature, to worship anything other than God, to acknowledge another lord of the soul next to him, to distort the service owed to him into ceremonies and observances as though he were to delight in *such things,* to make images that represent the divine. Therefore—and here a new point of view emerges that leads us further—because he is the sole lord and master of our conscience, we must confess that our *entire* life must be subjected to his commandments, to his law, in that we recognize the perfect and sufficient righteousness next to which there is no other. The continuation shows that the Geneva Confession was drafted in the shadow of Calvin's Institutes.[55]

In Calvin, Luther's problem of the human path to salvation no longer stands in isolation but is worked into the problem of the concept of God. The uniqueness, superiority, and freedom of God and of faith, which Zwingli emphasizes in such a radically one-sided way, are set in *relationship* to the life of the human person, to one's distress and hope. This is done without giving up the original point of approach but in such a way that more can be and must be said than the terrifying and yet bitterly necessary "alone" of the courageous East Friesians. Farel begins to make this plain. In his natural state, the human is damned, say Articles 4 and 5. Then follow in Articles 6 to 9: "*Salvation* in Jesus" ("*Salut* en Jésus"), "*Righteousness* in Jesus" ("*Justice* en Jésus"), "*Regeneration* in Jesus" ("*Régénération* in Jésus"), "Remission of Sins" ("Remission des péchéz") that is always necessary for the faithful since "we always remain poor and wretched sinners in the presence of God."[56] This is indubitably the Lutheran way to salvation together with the deeply pastoral and *more* than pastoral insight of Luther that the *entire* Christian life is an act of repentance and is dependent upon forgiveness, upon forgiveness alone.[57] But here, similar to the Tetrapolitan, one must pay attention to the sense and tone with which Farel engages the entire series of problems in contrast to Zwingli and his circle. Farel says that salvation, righteousness, renewal, and constantly sought forgiveness are all to be found "*in Jesus.*" He does not say, "*in faith* in Jesus." The word "faith" occurs only once in all these articles, namely, in the Apostles' Creed, which is inserted in Article 6. Article 10 has the title, "All Our Good in the Grace of God,"[58] and is a reference to the mercy of God, to whom alone glory and praise are due for the salvation attained in this way. Not until Article 11 does faith finally appear briefly and without emphasis as our "entrance" ("entrée")[59] to the treasures and riches that have been described. Immediately thereafter, Article 12 returns to the main line: "Invocation of God Only and Intercession of Christ,"[60] with a sharp polemic against all other agents of mediation. The remainder of the confession need not be considered for our discussion of the question of the direction of the Reformed *struggle*. As a document of that *struggle*, the Geneva Confession stands fundamentally in the same line as that of Zwingli and his adherents as well as that of the East Friesians.

As a test of the correctness of our findings thus far, it would be instructive to look briefly at the index of alleged errors, appended to the end of the *Waldensian Confession* of 1655 (M 504, 26[–505,81]),[61] of which the confessors "and all the Reformed churches" were accused by "doctors of Rome."[62] The Waldensians stood in an especially exposed point along the frontline of the Reformed struggle, and they were required to defend themselves against the old church at a time in which this polemic was no longer a burning issue for the other Reformed churches. The confession's conclusion states that its confessors find the 'Syllabus of errors' [Syllabus errorum][63] no less heretical and damnable than do those who accuse them of such.[64] But this syllabus shows how Reformed doctrine as a whole was regarded from the *other* side of the chasm. I cite from these statements, imputed by the Catholics to the Reformed, the following: (1) God is the author of sin. (2) God is not omnipotent (=bound to his eternal decree!). (4) In the good works to which the Holy Spirit moves one, the human person is no more active than a piece of wood or a stone. (5) With regard to predestination it is a matter of no consequence whether one does good or evil. (7) Confession of sins and repentance are to be rejected. (9) Each person can explain the Holy Scriptures as he pleases, according to the imagination of his own mind. (10) The church can err and completely "be destroyed" ("être anneantie"[65]). (11) Baptism is not necessary. (12) In Communion, no real fellowship with Christ takes place but rather only a reflection of it. (14)[66] One should not invoke Mary and the saints because they are despised. I have cited these statements, which, in my view, can obviously only be explained as misunderstandings of the Reformed doctrine of God and its direct consequences. But this is ten of fourteen propositions.[67] I think that one can see here *where* the Reformed attacked the old church and where it really felt itself to be attacked and provoked. I scarcely need to add that these same controversial points are the source of the recent accusations of determinism and spiritualism leveled at Reformed doctrine.[68] It is entirely appropriate that the Semi-Pelagians and romantics of all ages should find this provocative.

Let us summarize. The concern of the Reformed in their controversy with the old church consists of a passionate interest in the *theme* of Christian doctrine as such. They are preoccupied not so much with the new formulation of its contents but with the fact that this doctrine deals with *God*. Or better, according to the Reformed, Christendom must be taught anew *because* it must become clear again that the issue in this doctrine is *God*. This insight, God is *God*,[69] has burst upon them like an armed warrior [see Prov. 6:11], as something totally new, alien, and surprising. *This* is what has drawn them into an irreconcilable contradiction to the old church. And it is certainly no accident that this explosion came *first and most strongly* among the Germanic tribes at the foot of the *Alps* and along the *North Sea coast*. One can say that the Reformed fathers were unjust toward the old church when, in confronting it with these insights, they claimed that they were completely new and alien. In history, including the history of thought, injustice is constantly done, and most often precisely where the most justice is done. It was a necessary injustice that happened here to the old church. One can say[70] that the *scholastic* theologians of the Middle Ages had also seen that light about God's uniqueness, rule, and freedom, which had struck the early Reformed like lightning, just as they also knew the Lutheran doctrine of justification and faith. The 'pure act' [actus purus] of the deity, the divine aseity, the 'fearful mystery' [mysterium tremendum] of the 'hidden God' [deus absconditus], 'creation from nothingness' [creatio ex nihilo], the divine providence that defines all things, and double predestination—these concepts were certainly well-known in their fundamental significance by an Anselm of Canterbury, a Peter Lombard, an Alexander of Hales, a Bonaventure, or a Thomas Aquinas. But why were these concepts so harmless in their thinking, so lacking in relevance, so very much in the background? How did it happen that in their thinking these themes could become the foundation of a great theological-ecclesial system of harmoniously arranged mediation of grace, the peaceful alignment of nature *and* grace, immanence *and* transcendence, human *and* divine freedom? How did it happen that at the beginning of medieval doctrinal history there was the barbaric silencing of the *one* man who, as the only one in a broad landscape, drew the consequences from these concepts and spoke out about them: the unfortunate *Gottschalk*?[71] Can one recognize the fundamental significance of these concepts, or rather, of the reality that struggles awkwardly for expression in these concepts, without drawing the consequences, without uttering them aloud, regardless of what then results? Was it not true that the church at the end of the Middle Ages had virtually forgotten the *theme* of its proclamation? Was it not then urgently necessary that it be firmly and bluntly reminded of it again, even at the cost of its unity and its peace (which was not really any peace at all)? Was not the painful disintegration of the European imperial church an unavoidable historical demonstration of the all-shattering truth of the "one only creator" ["unus solus creator"], this truth that it knew so well and yet did not know at all?

This is not the place to draw the lines connecting the major concerns of the Reformed fathers with the thinking of those medieval theologians who were in the *opposition*.[72] One could speak of *Augustinian renewalists* such as Thomas Bradwardine[73] and Gregory of Rimini, and of the great Nominalists from Duns Scotus to William of Occam, and not least of the *mystics* of the school of Eckhardt. God as the "immediate cause" ["causa immediata"] of *all* acts, who gives faith to whomever he will (Gregory of Rimini),[74] God's "absolute power" ["potentia absoluta"], for which all possibilities are open and by virtue of which his "acceptance" ["acceptatio"], his unconditional will, speaks the only and all-decisive word (William of Occam),[75] God as the beginning and ending of all becoming, a "circular ring" whose center is everywhere and whose periphery is nowhere (Seuse)[76]—these were all theological endeavors that had long disturbed the peace of the ecclesiastical Middle Ages both secretly and openly. |

In the Reformation, more strongly in the Reformed Reformation than in the Lutheran, these very lines surfaced again. What was for Luther the question of *salvation* was for them the question of *truth*. The one question cannot be separated from the other, but it matters greatly whether the one or the other is more acutely pressed. Luther, primarily shaped by the interests of a serious monasticism, asked the question about salvation, or better, about the truth of *salvation*, and so the anti-Roman banner of his theology was the doctrine of *justification* and *faith*, which says *how* the human is saved in truth. The Reformed, primarily shaped by the interests of a serious humanism, asked the question about the truth, or better, about the *truth* of salvation, and thus the anti-Catholic thrust of their doctrine was the transcendence of their concept of God, which was the answer to the question of *who* saves the human in truth. One might perhaps, with a certain necessary reservation, express it in this way: The common Reformation knowledge over against the old church was that God and faith "belong together" ["zuhauf gehören"] (Luther, first commandment in the Larger Catechism),[77] that in the relationship of God understood in a Christian way the subject and the object are one. In Luther, however, the major emphasis in this line of thought is that the object is one with the *subject*, that *faith* and God belong together, that "to have a god is nothing else than to *trust* and *believe* in that one with your whole heart."[78] It is the Reformed concern to emphasize that it is the *object* that in this relationship is one with the subject, that faith and *God* belong together, that all trusting and believing of the human heart must stand on the fact that we have a *God*. Their critique of the trusting and believing of the old church was that they had forgotten this. It is no accident that the *doctrine of predestination*, which is the issue at stake, is upheld so firmly in all the Reformed confessions in some way, that it constantly becomes visible in some form in the foreground or background. We have seen how it asserts itself at the most important place, in the grounding of the principle of Scripture, when we spoke of the "inward testimony of the Holy Spirit" ["testimonium spiritus sancti internum"].[79] To the degree that Reformed doctrine is polemical, this doctrine is indeed its essential core. Wherever the situation of the sixteenth century reoccurs—necessitating protest against the forgetting of the *theme* of Christian theology and in response to the neglect of this known and yet unknown Christian *presupposition* requiring the reminder that God is not in *our* hand but we are in *his*— there, the concept of predestination will have to be reasserted in some way and, if it is to have its proper force in this situation, as the *core* and the *entirety* of Reformed theology. The claim may be made that the fathers of Reformed theology have left her a weapon for the task of this struggle that *is* to be used, providing one not only *knows* it but also, 'making the necessary adjustment' [mutatis mutandis], *understands* how to use it.

2. THE POSITIVE DOCTRINE OF CHRISTIANITY

As characteristic of all of Reformed doctrine, we will chiefly cite[1] *Zwingli's Instruction* of 1523 and the *Bern Synod* of 1532. Neither of these is a polemical document; rather, they are ministry instructions for the *pastors* of both

German-Swiss regions. These pastors had been Catholic clergy, and suddenly now—the situation must have been shattering for many as well as
grotesque—they were to be transformed into preachers of the pure Word,
into 'ministers of the divine Word' [verbi divini ministri]. They were
expected not only to understand the Bible laid before them as their radical
norm and rule, but they were also to teach the people to understand it as
such. These two documents may be compared in their purpose with
Luther's Large Catechism, which was also basically conceived of as instruction for new Protestant pastors.[2] In addition, there were the differing confessions of the *national churches*, including the two *Helvetic Confessions*, the
Gallican, the confession of the *Frankfurt Foreigners Community* of 1554, the
Scots Confession, the *Dutch* of 1561 and 1566, the two *Hungarian* of 1562
(Erlauthal and Beza), the two *English* (the Thirty-Nine Articles and the Westminster Confession), the *Polish* of 1570 and 1645, and finally the *Irish* of 1615.
When speaking of confessions in the narrowest sense, that is, of official rep-
resentations of the Christian doctrine of particular churches, then one
should think primarily of these doctrinal statements that, without an
addressee, were simply drawn up as documentation of the state of affairs
for internal and external use. One can add to the list immediately all of the
catechisms, which, as a rule, had the same public character as did the actual
confessions or 'articles' [articuli]. It is clear that, by the very nature of things,
we are dealing here with the actual majority of Reformed confessions.

"The positive *doctrine of Christianity*": The title sounds intentionally mundane and rational. As much as the early Reformed emphasized the transcendence, wonder, the incomprehensibility of the decrees and good pleasure of
God, the depths of his judgment and of his mercy, they were just as persuaded
that, having the 'norm and rule' [norma, regula] of Scripture, they had to
speak of him in a simple, human, matter-of-fact way. They shared the very
unsentimental scholastic view that virtue, or in this instance, religion, Christianity, were *teachable*.[3] Not God himself, obviously: there, everything is election, grace, spirit, faith, God's own work—but what we can know on the basis
of revelation, Christianity, the refraction of the divine light in the prism of
human consciousness, which is not itself the light but can perhaps witness to
that light [see John 1:8]. Once this great critical presupposition was established, it was possible to consider Christianity as Christianity, as religion, as
a humanly comprehensible, discussable, teachable entity, not as revelation
but as the reflective response to revelation. A dangerous endeavor! One could
mistake the variation for the basic theme, inflate the pious self-consciousness
and change it from the reason for to the object of Christian doctrine. This was
not yet a danger for the early Reformed. They were pervasively shaped by
their awareness of the infinite *distance* between God and human, grace and
nature, revelation and reason, by the clear *distinction* between Scripture and
the confession of Scripture, between God's Word and their own Christian

human word. This gave them the serene ability to take very seriously the latter within its assigned limits and possibilities, and to place great emphasis
upon preaching and instruction, in a word, upon *doctrine*. To a certain extent,
all of this was a commonly held evangelical view, but from a certain point on
it was decisively *not* so. A book by Luther with the tutorial title, "Institutes of
the Christian Religion" ["Institutio religionis christianae"], would have been
completely impossible. But obviously this had to be the title of Calvin's book.
His sermons also reason, moralize, and historicize; they are not without the
occasional powerful outbreak of pathos, but the reader who primarily wants
to hear something for "real life" will soon put them aside in disappointment.
That reader will gain a completely different satisfaction from Luther's sermons, in which certainly there is much "teaching" but whose first and most
direct impact is simply to overpower one with the dynamic of the word and
the forcefulness of the personality behind it. "According to the Spirit" or
"according to the flesh" (κατὰ πνεῦμα; κατὰ σάρκα)[see Rom. 8:4]? The latter
is certainly possible. Both are possible: the primarily intuitive style of
Lutheran communication with *its* dangers, and next to it, the primarily doctrinaire style of Calvinist communication, whose special danger is so obvious
that one scarcely needs to mention it. |

To understand Calvin's intention, one must pay attention not only to the
firmly didactic tone with which he shapes his text, constantly adjuring the
reader to "Note this!" ["Notons donc!"] and "Let us learn here!" ["Apprenons
ici!"], but also to the solemn formula with which he often introduced the
Lord's Prayer at the end of his remarks:

> But now let us fall down before the (holy) Majesty of our good God with
> acknowledgement of our faults, praying him to make us perceive them
> more and more, and that we may be so touched with them, as it may
> bring us to true repentance, and that we may seek all our wants in our
> Lord, Jesus Christ, and that there may be such humility in us, that being
> *utterly* brought down, and having put away *all* false presumptuousness
> wherewith we may be deceived, we may not tend to any other end than
> to be received through the *mere* mercy of our God, so as we may come to
> the everlasting inheritance, and in the meanwhile endeavor to walk in
> such wise in his commandments, as it may please him to bear with our
> frailty, till he have quit and clean rid us of it. And so let us all say
> Almighty God heavenly father. . . . (50,683–84)[4]

Perhaps we can grasp that, next to the shattering seriousness of this *adoration*, the place of the sermon could *only* be as doctrine, with virtually no place
for the sermon as experience. In *this* sense, the Reformed chose the doctrinaire possibility 'as the better part' [a parte potiori]. The concept of the
church as school and of the sermon as "instruction" ["enseignement"][5] is not
a later degeneration but the actual and legitimate one from the outset. |

We must at this point be reminded that "doctrine" in Reformed usage is not the presentation of dogmatics, of theological loci, but rather the exposition of Scripture. Reformed teaching has, of course, consolidated itself into dogmatics, and Calvin himself set the first example. But fundamentally it never should seek to be anything other than the explication of the content of Scripture; it can only move very short distances away from its point of departure, the biblical text; it is a moored balloon, not a free-flying one. This is undoubtedly the reason that this somewhat problematic science could never flourish on Reformed soil as much as it did upon Lutheran.

What then does the positive doctrine of Christianity *consist of,* which the Reformed churches desire to proclaim? In the case of Lutheranism, we stand before the remarkable fact that its polemical doctrine and its actual churchly doctrine are basically one and the same thing. We could only refer again here to the interconnected Lutheran doctrine of sin–forgiveness of sin–faith–justification–good works. Well-known is the way that Luther was always able, regardless of the theme or the text, somehow to focus everything on this concept, which for him was clearly identical with "the gospel." His path from a child of the world to monk to child of God to husband to simple bearer of the earthly but God-intended office of a doctor of theology, as he later came to see it, became for him the 'way of salvation' [via salutis] in a definitive sense. The negative component, the separation from the old church that became necessary for him on his pathway, was so powerful for him that it became a positive component, the basis of his proclamation, next to which anything else was impossible for his church. This path, which was not only a matter of biography but also of church history, and not only that but also of salvation history, and which profoundly illuminated the decisive passages of the Old and New Testaments, justified its being established permanently as the only way. This church with its theology is rightly called "Lutheran," because its doctrine can really not be separated from the person of its founder. Its dogmatics is at its core the somewhat mythologized and then canonized 'life of Luther' [Vita Lutheri]. |

If things had proceeded in an analogous way on Reformed soil, then the resulting positive Reformed church doctrine would be for us certainly the doctrine of predestination. It has often been maintained that this is the case, but this opinion is based upon an optical illusion. The doctrine of predestination can, to be sure, not be separated from the positive Reformed church doctrine. One must always remember that *this*, this particular view of God, is in the background. But it is not *the* doctrine in the sense that justification is *the* Lutheran doctrine. Polemical dogma and the actual church dogma are *two different things* in the Reformed church. It is not as though zealous attention were not given to the purity of polemical dogma, especially in Switzerland and the Netherlands. This was the experience of the naive Bolsec[6] in Geneva and later the Remonstrants in Holland.[7] But the Reformed in Ger-

June 5

many, for example, were able to treat the theme of predestination very, very gently in their confessions.[8] Of course, this polemical dogma was openly presented as the doctrine of the church and was preached from the pulpits. That certainly took place at least as long as one understood the meaning of the polemic conducted by the fathers. It continued to happen as long as the critical-polemical importance of their concept of God was not dulled and petrified into a meaningless, monstrous, theological conceptuality. It was also sufficient on occasion merely to touch on predestination without mentioning it; sermon and instruction could be carried out from completely different points of view. Whoever did not like to hear this doctrine for whatever reason could certainly listen for a long time to a Reformed preacher without finding offense, although certainly not without a certain latent discomfort, until at some point he did experience the electrical shock, or perhaps did *not*. It was not inevitable that the term had to be uttered. It sufficed that one knew it, that one thought about it, and that all other terms were secretly filled with it. Based upon what we can conclude from their confessional documents, the early Reformed used their polemical dogma with *self-discipline*. They were aware that they were working with a dangerous instrument, which could not be used by everyone at any time. Calvin presumably had his reasons when in his second catechism he no longer presented the doctrine of election in its own special section but rather alluded to it throughout the document. He could present it in a milder form than implied by his original intention, as seen in Article 12 of the Gallican Confession.[9] In the Heidelberg Catechism,[10] one must use a magnifying glass to find the passages where it is clearly stated. Clearly, a mature striving for a synthetic concept of Christian truth, as well as a self-indulgent evasion of the scandal of the cross of Christ, a justifiable concern for the weak, as well as a cowardly fear of human opinion, could all converge in ways much more dangerous than the dangers that one was seeking to avoid.

Now we shall inquire about the central understanding of Christianity that is basic to all the confessions, *beyond* the concept of God's superiority, freedom, and incomprehensibility, which like the principle of Scripture is presupposed once and for all.

If the contents of *Zwingli's Instruction* (M 7[–29]), with which we are beginning, are surveyed superficially according to the sequence of the title subjects, then one is astonished to see that a very different Zwingli is speaking here from the one whose pen produced the three confessions already discussed. This appears to be a Zwingli who has converted to Luther's approach! "Sin," "Gospel," and "Abolition of the Law" are the titular themes of the first three foundational sections (we will not address the last two about images and the mass).[10a] The human's way to God appears to be the theme of the document. Has Zwingli in the three-quarters of a year since the Conclusions been instructed by Melanchthon's Loci[11] on what the positive doctrine of Christianity might be? A more careful reading of the contents reveals immediately that this is not the case and that Zwingli has his own view of these matters. The system is indeed Pauline but not Lutheran, for Zwingli has filled the Pauline system with a completely *different* content. The task that Zwingli sets his pastors requires of them that they follow the example at the beginning of *Christ's* preaching and "cry in this sinful world: *'Mend your ways!'* "[12] This is what 'repent' [μετανοεῖτε] means for Zwingli; this is *his* theme. For this *mending* to happen, man must confess his sin and in despair commit himself to the mercy of God. Sin is *egocentricity* in flagrant contradiction to the "law of nature" ["Gsatz der Natur"][13] and to the positive biblical command of God, which is identical with it, that hopelessly defines us "so long as we wear the skin of Adam."[14] Over against this stands the gospel, the eternal and incomprehensible *wisdom of God* in Christ, who is so completely different from us and who as such has become flesh and died for us as our savior and doctor. What results from this gift offered in God's Word to our hopelessness? One would expect that the discourse would now turn to faith, but Zwingli uses the word here one time only and is already at Romans 6—the theme is the mending of man— and at the inseparable relation between grace and new life. In Lutheranism this relation is *also* a truth, but for Zwingli it is *the* truth toward which all his thinking strives. "Since I am happy that I have been lifted out of the mire and have been washed, why would I want to throw myself therein again? [. . .] For if we have trusted in Christ then this has come to pass with God's *power*. Where God is, there all *work* is directed as to how one departs *from* sin!"[15] This *work* that flows out of grace, and not *faith* in this grace, is apparently the point that occupies Zwingli's interest, and his actual problem then is the relation of this work to the temptation with which the evil one, the corpse, disquiets us as long we live. And *now* Zwingli speaks of faith and of its righteousness that *consists* in man's constantly running to God, saying "O Lord, how wickedly I live in your eyes,"[16] and throwing himself into the arms of his *mercy*. This righteousness, because it is imputed by *God*, cannot remain *mere* imputed righteousness. It is to *God* that man flees with his confession and pleading, before *him* man capitulates, to *him* man submits as a captive and lost one, and to no one else! What can faith be, if this is all true, other than the true watchman who summons man to struggle, to keep watch, to crucify the flesh? Nothing could protect man more safely from foolishness and lethargy than faith itself. "The believer is faithful through the Spirit of *God*. Now where God is, there the goodness is always increased and grows."[17] For this reason and in this sense, it is true that "no one should let himself be misled so as to seek grace from anyone but God himself."[18] Grace sought from someone else, in Zwingli's view, would not be the grace that inevitably makes a person into a worker and fighter. It should be clear at this point how the anti-Roman polemics relate to Zwingli's positive view of Christianity. The third section, "The Abolition of the Law,"[19] is, in contradiction to what the title might lead one to expect, a sharp polemic against those who forget that only the Jewish ceremonial law and the curse of the unfulfillability of the law have been set aside in Christ, but not the will of God that speaks through his commandments. The "abolition" of the law coincides with the establishment of "the law of the living spirit of life" (Rom. 8:2).[20] One is not prematurely to pass oneself off as free in Christ; one is not to confuse the struggle against the abuses of the old church with the attainment of this freedom, and one is above all not to think that one is confirming that freedom by disobedience to worldly authority. The conclusion consists of a very drastic appeal to the preacher to ensure through serious emphasis upon the remaining law that both good and evil persons "*may know how to come to God*,"[21] as Zwingli dares to say, unconcerned about dogmatic niceties. They are to work both gently and strictly to end the excesses of gaming, drinking, clothing, cursing, fighting, quarreling, and avarice.[22]

This then is the positive doctrine of Christianity that Zwingli recommended for preaching, and one would have to read very inattentively to confuse it with the doctrine of the 'way of Luther' [via Lutheri]. Zwingli will be correctly understood, in a biographical sense as well in view of his roots in humanism, when the doctrine that he presents here and in his other writings is understood as the attempt *to ground ethics upon grace* (and not upon the law). It should be clear that his exposition of *Romans 6,* precisely at the point where one expects the Lutheran hymn of faith, forms the virtual center of the entire document. It is more than likely that this attempt moves in the direction of the most original motives in *Luther's* theology (K. Holl),[23] and to that extent Reformed theology is nothing other than the strong development of a Lutheran line that later faded. The official doctrine of Lutheranism, already effective during Luther's lifetime and continuing without decisive objection, is formulated in Articles 2–4 of the Augustana, expanded by Article 6 on the new obedience and Article 20 on faith and good works.[24] One can*not*, with any seriousness, describe the sense of *this* doctrine as the founding of ethics upon grace. Its sense is the assertion of the all-sufficiency of faith with the appended reference that this faith cannot persist without new obedience and good works. Augsburg's doctrine can, if pressed and needful, be *interpreted* in the sense of the Reformed intention, as the German Reformed did indeed do.[25] But that does not change the fact that, in its essence, it is *another* doctrine.

The *Bern Synod* (M 31)[26] reveals a face completely different from Zwingli's Instruction. Unmistakable is the pneumatic thrust of Bucer, mediated by Capito.[27] The formulations in their details are often unclear and contradictory. A psychic-emotional tone can be heard that gives the entire document an agreeable warmth not found in Reformed confessions generally. At points, one senses the greenhouse warmth of Pietism, which justifiably honors Bucer as its Reformation ancestor.[28] It is no wonder that *Zinzendorf*[29] particularly liked this confession, incorporated it into the Büding Collections,[30] and even composed a longer hymn based on its contents and using the sequence of its articles[31] (Bern. S., 8). On the title page appears, under the crest with the imperial crown and eagle and the Bern bear, the decisive Pauline citation as a confession of Reformed polemical doctrine: "Even though we once knew Christ from a human point of view, we know him no longer in that way" (2 Cor. 5:16).[32] As Christocentric as this motto sounds, however, the doctrine that this confession develops is pneumato-Christocentric. Saving doctrine, it begins, is nothing other than the one eternal Word of God, his fatherly goodness and kindness, communicated to us through Christ, that is, nothing other than Christ himself. Christian preachers are messengers of Christ and witnesses of his suffering. Through him, the Son, the Father speaks to us in the Holy Spirit and in no other way. For that reason, there should be no talk about the natural, almighty God without Christ. God has always spoken through certain symbols and events, if at times unclearly. There, in Christ, God wills that we find him in the new symbol that is God himself. But—and now comes the characteristic emphasis—it is not enough that pastors often use the words, "Jesus is our Savior,"[33] and drum them into the people. For the gospel of the kingdom does not consist of an empty voice and mere words but of the true power of God. The death and *resurrection* of Christ must be preached, that is, *repentance* in the sense that the preaching of repentance emerges from the resurrection in the name of him who suffered and died. Resurrection is the entire "course of Christ" ["Lauf Christi"],[34] including ascension and the pouring out of the Spirit in the conscience of the believers. The *content of all preaching is to be pointed* in this direction, so that *in the future all error will be rejected, morals improved, and the good fostered* (M 37, 22 [-25]). The birth, entire life, and teaching of Jesus are a preparation for his death. The Holy Spirit in us cannot seek anything else from Christ than the word of the cross. Now through his death, Christ takes the burden of sin from us and makes it abhorrent and hateful to us. It is the power of the resurrection that brings about in us this effect of his death. Not through the law but through grace we recognize our damned nature, our sin. Through the living Christ alone, preaching evokes repentance, that is, our displeasure with our sin, and our forgiveness. Through faith and the gift of God that is Christ in the Spirit, *forgiveness impregnates the elect hearts with divine seed and gives birth to heavenly people* for the kingdom of heaven, that is, those whose hearts move them to *turn away* from sin and to *practice* righteousness and piety with the experience of the love of God in faith (M 43,28[-33]). The Holy Spirit carries out two works in us: (1) Through his grace he makes believers righteous and into new people. (2) He helps us to become heirs. This happens in that we persist in the struggle of faith, die daily to the flesh, and are spiritually and heavenly minded (M 41,26[-31]). This is what the Synod calls "the walk of grace"[35] or "the walk of Christ"[36]: from repentance that condemns sin and grasps forgiveness, to justifying faith through the power of forgiveness, to the refining of silver by fire, but all this, as constantly emphasized, *without* the law as the grace proclaimed to *Gentiles*. I

Where the central thrust, the point of the confession is to be sought, cannot be doubted. The issue for the Bernese, inspired by Strassburg[37] and guided by the central insight that the Lord is *Spirit* and the Spirit is *the Lord*, is the focus upon *life*, upon the *rebirth* that is not to be separated from faith, and thus the problem of *ethics*. We do not have to decide here whether the way in which they dealt with this concern was very fortunate. It is reminiscent of the way in which *Osiander* later would deal with the same concerns in the Lutheran church, where he too went back to Luther's *original* approach in which justification and sanctification were still understood as a unity.[38] In terms of its general *direction*, the Bern Synod should certainly be placed at the side of the Zwinglian Instruction in spite of all its differences.

The *First Helvetic Confession* of 1536 (*Confessio Helvetic Prior* or Second Basel Confession)[39] is more difficult to perceive clearly. It was a work of compromise, written by Bullinger, Megander,[40] and Jud, all from Zurich, and by Myconius and Grynaeus,[41] both of Basel, with (unsought) assistance from Bucer and Capito of Strassburg. It was formulated for the Council of Mantua[42] announced for 1537 (parallel to the Smalcaldic Articles) and was secondarily intended for the pending negotiations of a concord with Luther.[43] One should not expect sharply defined contours here but rather a minimum of Reformed distinctiveness. What is decisive for our investigation is found in Article 5 (the purpose of *Holy Scripture*), Articles 10–13 containing the *soteriology*, and Article 4 with foundational material on the *church*. The Bible seeks to represent and prove publicly God's kindness and goodwill toward humanity. Accordingly, the most sublime and principal article of Protestant teaching, which must be energetically set forth in all sermons and be impressed upon the hearts of men, is that we are "preserved"[44] and saved alone through the unique mercy of God and through the merit of Christ. To awaken the knowledge of sin, the law and the death of Christ are needed. God's benevolence is received and appropriated through *faith*, which is expressed, demonstrated, and proven by *love* for one's neighbor. This is an act *of God* in the most miraculous contrast to the nature, constitution, and reason of man. As the *Resurrected One*, Christ becomes for us the pledge of the hope and the trust of our immortal lives, and as the Resurrected One at the right hand of God, he is our pioneer, leader, and head, our high priest and advocate, who "always defends and promotes our cause, *until He brings us back and restores us to the image in which we were created, and leads us into the fellowship of His divine nature*" (M 103,33[–35]).[45] Faith in him effects "innumerable" good works increasingly,[46] but they are not the source of our comfort, which is, rather, the mercy of God. The church is built up out of the faithful as living stones, upon this living rock, as bride and spouse of Christ, which he desires to cleanse through his blood, in order finally to present it to his Father without spot and blemish. This church of Christ, or rather those who belong to it, are known only to the eyes of God, but it makes itself known through the signs established by Christ and through the Word of God as *orderly discipline*, by which it distinguishes itself from the world (M 104,31[–38]). It has the power to prescribe one *pattern for life* to all people, be they of high or low station. In its doctrine of justification, faith, and good works, the First Helvetic comes very close to the Augsburg Confession. What it lacks is the iron clasp that holds them together, which is in Zwingli the application of Romans 6, while in the Bern Synod it is its doctrine of rebirth. One should note how the emphasis of the doctrine of justification here as in the Tetrapolitana lies in the reference to the mercy of *God*, not on faith. On the other hand, one notes how the connection between life now and hereafter and the new foundation of life through Christ *are emphasized* in the idea of the living fellowship of the risen Christ with his invisible church, for whose visibility "orderly discipline" is not to be lacking, and in which we are formed and restored to the image of God. This is no incidental consideration, for, even though it is not developed strongly and dominantly in the First Helvetic, it is a new and important formulation of basic Reformed thinking. While the Swiss and Strasburgian theologians were writing this confession in the Augustinian monastery in Basel, the young Calvin was working on his first Institutes in the St. Alban suburb of that same Basel.[47] We shall yet see how that basic concept is fully developed by him in the very formulation that emerges here.

Before we turn to the Calvinist and Calvinizing documents, we must pursue the line emerging from Zwingli to its conclusion. You will find in August Lang's edition of the Heidelberg Catechism (54[–116]) a *Catechism* by Zwingli's coworker *Leo Jud*, written in 1535,[48] which should be mentioned here as a predecessor of the Heidelberg. Following Luther's procedure, Jud discussed in four articles the Decalogue, the Apostles' Creed, the Lord's Prayer, and the sacraments. But by means of a more or less detailed introduction, he related each of these four pieces to the context of a methodological whole that is quite valuable as a further contribution to our question.

God has created man from nothingness out of pure goodness, so that he might share in God's own abundance, namely, as a living *image of Himself*.[49] This image of God in man, which has been destroyed by the devil, is restored in Christ. For this, the human should be *thankful* to God through obedience to him and through the will to share with his fellow creatures the treasures given to humanity. God, the source of all good, has concluded a *covenant* with Abraham that consists of two articles: He wills to be his God and the God of his children, and Abraham and his children should be committed to walk before him. This is the eternal covenant of grace that is renewed and sealed in Christ. "As I believe, so am I Israel,"[50] a participant in this covenant. Faithfulness on God's side

June 7

requires faithfulness on our side, that is, faith in his promise and the doing of his *commandments*. But the law in and of itself would not save us but would rather only lead us to recognize our sin and condemnation if Christ were not to write the law in our *hearts*. Through Christ we are made *free*, not from temptation but from the rule and power of the devil, free to enter into the service of Christ to our neighbor. Thus, the law is not removed from man, but rather, on the one hand it has become through God's grace his own joy, and on the other hand, it compels him still to flee to the mercy of God because of the sinfulness[51] that still adheres to him. If it is faith in Christ alone that saves, then it cannot be separated from works but is rather their proper source. One can, after all, not behold Christ as savior and redeemer without seeing his life and his teaching at the same time. There is no merit that results from good works, of course, but God is certainly *praised* and *honored* through them. If we fulfill through them our indebted *duty*, even if they had no usefulness but simply because they are commanded, then with them we both *testify* to and *practice* our faith, give a good example and reassure ourselves through action that our election, calling, faith, and salvation are no illusion. We can leave Jud's further remarks for the moment. His central view of Christianity has been covered in these remarks. The creation of man as the image of God, Christ as its restoration, the covenant of grace with its mutual obligation, the law of freedom inscribed in the heart of the believers, good works tied to faith with a sevenfold necessity—all of this points unambiguously in one direction: to a Christianity rooted in the acknowledgment of the *demand* directed toward humanity that is based on gratitude for God's inexpressible *goodness*.

It is remarkable that Bullinger's great work, the *Second Helvetic Confession* of 1562,[52] is less fruitful for our question about the methodological distinctiveness of the Reformed understanding of Christianity. One of the reasons for this was the author's intention, made obvious by his conscious *underemphasis* of everything distinctive, to proceed down a middle line as far as possible, especially between Zwingli and Calvin. This was his intention as well over against Lutheranism, so that wherever he could, he emphasized their common ground, using if possible the language of Lutheranism. He deliberately emphasized the consensus with the old church in all the questions where that was appropriate[53] (e.g., Bullinger completely omitted the concept of the *covenant*[54] between God and man, even though it was personally of great importance to him). This intention lent this confession an extraordinarily mature, serene, and peacemaking tone without denying or giving up anything. Another reason was the fact that Bullinger clearly wanted to provide a kind of *compendium* of Reformed theology, a formulation of his views on every possible problem, a small reference work in which one could find a short but balanced and wholesome answer on virtually anything and everything. This intention is what gives his work the well-rounded and consistent quality that characterizes it. In spite of the fact that it is to this very day one of the most famous and broadly used confessions (next to the Westminster Confession and the Heidelberg Catechism it is the best-known),[55] it is precisely these characteristics that, taken together, make it very difficult to sense in all this content what *mattered most* to the author as he set about confessing his Christianity. Let us with great care attempt to find what is distinctive and see if some particular lines emerge. |

In Article 9,[56] which deals with free will and natural man's incapacity for good, we find in Bullinger a rather extended doctrine about the *new equipping of the regenerate* with Spirit and power. "So if the Son make you free, you will be free indeed" [John 8:36].[57] The regenerate are not only passive but active in the doing of good. "For they are moved of God that themselves may do that which they do."[58] To be sure, their weakness remains in them until the end, but not to the extent that the powers of the flesh and the old man could eliminate the effectiveness of the Holy Spirit. They will not boast of their 'free will' [liberum arbitrium], however. There are several things to be said about this approach, but we shall restrict ourselves to ascertaining this intention, that the human person should know that through grace he has really been put on his feet in order to *walk*. In Article 12, "Of the Law of God" ["De lege Dei"],[59] the vitally positive *valuing of the law* that we saw in Zwingli and L. Jud, here, in a way similar to the Bern Synod, recedes behind the well-known Pauline concept that the law serves our knowledge of sin [Rom. 3:20]. To be sure, Bullinger also refers to Matthew 5:17 (" . . . not to destroy . . . but to fulfill").[60] For him, the majesty and authority of the law are certain; just as certain and especially important is the identity of the Mosaic law inscribed on the tablets with the 'law of nature,' as Zwingli had already taught: this "law is, by the finger of God, written in the hearts of men, and so is called the law of nature."[61] This is unambiguously the humanist-ethical approach of Reformed theology, which, without diminishing its strict understanding of the absolute character of the wonder of God, still soberly and straightforwardly finds in it the answer to the problem of *man*. This same interest is asserted again when in Article 13 (the doctrine of *promise*)[62] the point is made that even the fathers *before* the law and *under* the law were not without the gospel in that they participated in the divine promises, not only the earthly ones but the spiritual promises in Christ, as we do. The gospel, in contrast with the teaching of the Pharisees, only appeared to be new, just as now it only appears to be a novelty over against the papists. In reality, it is the oldest and most universal truth. In Article 14 (on *repentance*),[63] next to the knowledge of sin, contrition, and confession (not to humans but to God), it is strongly and extensively emphasized that the issue now is to practice repentance "in the endeavor of a *new life*,"[64] a *practice* that is to fill all the days remaining for the converted person. For "*true* repentance is conversion to God."[65] In the doctrine of *justification* (Article 15),[66] "justified only by faith" recedes behind "justified on account of Christ"[67]—we saw in the first paragraph of this section what this means. Faith is the gift of God. But, on the other hand, faith means to receive Christ, 'to believe' [credere] = 'to eat' [manducare; John 6], to "partake of Christ" ("participare").[68] Here there is *no* contradiction between Paul and James—this is the unanimous Reformed view. A faith that were not a "lively and quickening faith" ["fides viva et vivificans"] would be a "feigned faith" ["fides ficta"], really no faith at all.[69] Article 16[70] on *faith and good works* corresponds to and continues this line of argument. Finally we turn to Article 17[71] *on the church*, in which the 'communion of saints' [communio sanctorum] in this confession of faith is understood as the 'city' [civitas] of those who live under the same Lord, under the same laws, sharing the same goods, the "house of the living God."[72] Its signs are, of course, the preaching of the pure *Word* and (for Bullinger, as I already remarked, with measured *distance*) the *sacraments* instituted by Christ. But, picking up on a specifically Zurich theological emphasis going back to Zwingli,[73] it is an open house in that God has had at all times his friends "not of the commonwealth of Israel" ["extra Israelis rempublicam"],[74] outside the visible church and among the alleged unbelievers. On the other hand, not all those who belong to it are truly members of the church of God. These most noticeable points in Bullinger's confession certainly show, when they are placed next to each other, the direction in which his argument is going: What God does for man *does not tolerate* any form of passivity, nonparticipation, spectatorship on the part of man. Without 'true' conversion' [*vera* conversio] there is no true repentance. Or, to put it in the terminology of the article on the church: God is also the God of the *Gentiles* [see Rom. 3:29]. |

Let us turn now to Calvin, whose *catechisms*[75] and *Gallican Confession* we shall treat together[76] for the sake of brevity (Catechism of 1536 *French* vol. 22, pp. 33[–74]!; 1545, M 117[–153][77]; Gallican, M 221[–32]).[78] In view of the approach in *both* of his catechisms and especially in view of the basic thinking of the revised *second* one, there can be no doubt that Calvin comprehended Christianity as a whole as the well understood answer to the ancient question, 'Say, why are you here' [Dic cur hic]?[79] *For what purpose* is the human created (A 33)?[80] What is the "chief *end*" ["praecipuus *finis*"] of human life (B 117,7)?[81] For what purpose? 'What... the end' [Quis... finis]? It is clear with these words that the decisive issue is already assumed, that life here is supposed to be understood as a *task*; it is about this task that *questions* are raised, and Calvin sees Christianity challenging humanity with this task as the great claim that seeks to fulfill and occupy human life completely. This is not to say, of course, that Calvin found Christianity to be only a task placed before man. As man moves nearer to Christianity as task, he immediately presses on to the insight that there is much more here, that this is an infinite *gift*.[81a] But according to Calvin, one can only comprehend this gift in that one engages it as *task*. For him, Christianity is the *answer* to the *ethical problem*. The *answer* (and to that extent totally a gift) to the *ethical* problem that is placed afresh at every moment in time, and to that extent totally a *task*. Calvin takes as his point of departure this moment in time in which the gift presents itself as task. As remarkable as it may sound when I say this about Calvin, he thinks initially not from God but from the human person and his situation. Yet the situation of *humanity* cannot be considered with any seriousness at all without thinking immediately of *God*. For what purpose is the human created? We have already encountered this question in Leo Jud. But the systematic track that opens up there is almost immediately lost again. In Calvin, this question receives fundamental and dominant significance. Let us attempt to follow it through the texts themselves! I

So the human is then to understand himself as *created*? Is that the meaning of his situation: a *created* being? And he is supposed to ask about the *'end'* [*finis*] of this his *created* life? What other kind of an answer is possible, what else, if this question is a serious one, stands before him in shattering reality and majesty than—the Creator? But the human is not asking about the purpose and direction of life as a spectator. 'For it is your own concern' [Sua res agitur]![82] *His* life is in question. *He* is the created being whose problem finds its answer in the Creator. *He* has placed the question, and just as it is *his* most specifically existential question, so then the answer is directed to him specifically and existentially. It is not merely the case that the creature is here and the Creator is there, but rather that the creature sees himself confronted *there where he is* by the Creator *there where he is*. Is there basically any other answer to the question of purpose, of 'to what end' [quis finis], than this: *to see* what is to be seen when this *question* is posed? If the question is understood as the question about the human's *task*, is there any other answer for the human than *knowing*?[82a] Only *one* kind of knowledge comes under consideration when the questioner has grasped his createdness and asks seriously about the purpose of *his* life: the knowing of the *Creator*. And such *knowing* only comes under consideration when this question leads to *this* answer, seeing the confrontation of creature and Creator. Therefore, we are created (A 33) "that we may *know* the *majesty* of our Creator."[83] Or (B 117,8), this is "the chief end of human life," "to know *God [himself]* by whom men were created."[84] Note that the issue in the first definition is the knowing of the *majesty* of God! And note the *"himself"* [*"ipsi"*] in the second definition! The human himself here, God himself there—that is what is at stake in this knowing. In A, Calvin clarified this with the following thought: Whoever has not stifled this proper knowing as the heathen have done knows that this mortal and frail human life can be nothing other than "a meditation of immortality" ["une méditation d'immortalité"].[85] Eternity and immortality are in God alone. Therefore, to live means to seek God. In

B, this thought that betrays the Platonist Calvin is replaced by the following: The one who has *created* us desires this unheard of thing, to be glorified through us[86]: He "created us ... to be glorified in us."[87] We, for our part, can only by rights put our life, which has its beginning in him, in a purposeful relationship to his glory: "our life ... should be devoted to his glory."[88] That this happens is the 'greatest good' [summum bonum] of humanity, that which makes one truly into a *human* and distinguished from the animal. There could be nothing more disastrous than that this distinction not be made! It is clear that both considerations are only varying definitions of the one fundamental insight: The creature fulfills the purpose of its existence when it knows itself to be a frail and mortal creature created for the glory of God (both are contained in the concept of createdness), and thus knows God, who alone possesses eternity [1 Tim. 6:16] and has the sole claim to receive glory in and through this created life. |

We can refine our understanding of what is meant here by 'knowing' [Erkenntnis] by noting that in Article 1 of the Gallican Confession, the normal series of divine predicates is expanded with the terms "incomprehensible" and "ineffable" (M 221,34).[88a] It cannot be otherwise. What does knowing mean if man is the subject and God is the object? The issue here is the knowing of the *unknown* God [see Acts 17:23]. The task placed before man is stamped "impossible" from the outset. But *this* task is the one *that has been given*. In A, Calvin sought to show how a false religion results when man, relying upon himself and upon his totally inadequate insight into God's revelation seen in his works, fluctuates uncertainly between foolishness and fear and fails because of the impossibility of the task. On the other hand, *true religion*, which seeks the knowing of God in God himself, understands him as he has revealed himself in his Word, and thus comprehends him as Father *and* as Lord. In B he takes a somewhat *less direct way*. He asks, What is the *"true and right knowledge* of God"?[89] He is asking about the more precise definition of that task, and in doing so the question of its answerability is left open. Or, rather, it is presupposed that that task is put to man in the totality of the Christianity that is now to be discussed, so that it is in fact not impossible but truly possible. Now it must only be defined more precisely. Apparently Calvin did not intend to resolve quickly the dialectical tension that arises in the placing of that task but to move through his argument accompanied by that tension. The fact that God must speak the decisive word first, that in reality the discourse should not be primarily about human knowing but about God's revelation, should be *shown* in the course of the discussion. He answers then initially in a simple and direct way: There is the true and correct knowing of God where the glory due to God is rendered to him. As we have seen, this is not a thought that leads us further, for to know God and to give God the glory have been expressly established to be one and the same thing from the very outset. But here, at the decisive point where the question is *true* knowing, where what is apparently a *given*, know-ing itself, should now be understood as *task*, this analytical sentence serves as a reminder that the 'knowing' [cognitio] we are discussing is a human *deed*, not merely a relation between man and God, but an event, the estab-lishment of something new. The issue is not that God *might have* his glory but rather that the human who asks what the purpose of his creation is *might give* God his glory. The possibility of his doing that is, as we said, *presupposed*, anticipated in what will be presented as Christianity, and what will be seen to be the right way to know God. This *right* way to glorify God, which is the goal toward which Calvin is moving, is then the *possible* way to do it. When we remember that the entire discourse is about the *human person*, this per-son, then it is very paradoxical when the question is asked about "the method of honouring him duly,"[90] which is then answered with the famous fourfold statement that is in fact a systematic of Catechism B, lacking in A. God is 'duly' [rite] honored when (1) we place our entire trust in him (the Apostles' Creed!); (2) when we earnestly seek to serve him with all our lives and willingly to obey him (the Ten Commandments); (3) when we turn to him in prayer for every need, whether a matter of our own salvation or some-thing else (the Lord's Prayer); (4) when we present to him our praise and thanks as the "sole Author" ["solus auctor"] (Word of God and sacra-ments).[91] Believing, obeying, praying, thanking[92]—everything focused upon God, the historical traditions of the Christian religion all understood under the *one* perspective that the issue is God, God alone, God himself at work; under this perspective *understood*, appropriated, confirmed, all the substantives transformed into verbs: "to place in him, to study, to call upon him, to acknowledge him"[93]—*this* is duly to honor God, *this* is to know him aright, and *for this* we are created. That is the task: Christianity.

Whether or not Christianity is really something other than the task

June 8

set before us, whether or not these human actions, signified by these encouraging verbs that call us to action, should intend something other than to present the actions of God to our view, all of this can only be shown in that the task is tackled and the way of those human actions is resolutely walked. That is enough now about the framework within which Calvin fun-damentally viewed Christianity, one might say, about his Dogmatics I.

It is certainly not unimportant to ascertain that in Calvin there even *is* such a framework, such a human consideration of Christianity, under the per-spective of ethics. As we have just seen, this is only possible under the pre-supposition of Christianity itself[94] that moves as the possible task, possible in God, into the place of the *impossible* task that is really *given* to man in his situation between heaven and earth. Based on Christianity, especially upon Reformation Christianity, Calvin saw it as possible and necessary to view the great Renaissance problem, 'human life' [humana vita] or the problem of humanity (in Luther this human problem had dropped by the wayside in order then to be taken up again much later), a priori together with the problem of God.[95] The issue is not primarily the *religious* person with his special problematic, with his "terrified conscience" ["perterrefacta conscientia"].[96] Nor is it the person who wants to be saved through good works, or, when he has seen that this does not work, then through faith. Rather, it is simply the person as such in his createdness, with the inescapable question of his *existence*, with his question—What is my purpose as a *human being*?—and the equally inescapable, unheard of, and burdensome answer that must follow. It is the human person in the problematic of his real actions. Calvin dares to take this person seriously, to see him in *relation* to the Christianity whose content is entirely *God's* action, and to relate that Christianity to this question. He does so at the risk that Christianity as God's action might disintegrate when it is placed in *this* context. The further danger is that the human question might explode when it receives this answer. Calvin accepted both of these dangers. He trusts that neither will happen in the reality of the knowing that should take place between *this* question and *this* answer. Whatever he is discussing, be it the Ten Commandments or Christ's descent into hell and ascent into heaven, he will always have in view the *totality* of God and the *totality* of the human, obviously with differing consequences and varying success and failure. He will always function according to the canon that he expressed in the first sentence of the Institutes: "Nearly the whole of sacred doctrine consists in these two parts: the knowledge of God and of ourselves."[97] This implies, to be sure, what one has called the dialectical character of Calvin's theology, which is regarded by its most recent interpreter (H. Bauke)[98] as its very essence. Yet it is only its formal distinctiveness that is objectively grounded in this methodological approach. I scarcely need to say that what is found on the first pages of Calvin's catechisms and later in the entire first book of the Institutes is nothing other than the concern that, as we saw, has occupied Reformed theologians from the beginning, now finally understood by a systematic thinker of the first rank and worthily addressed. This concern may be put as a question: Given the Lutheran answer to the specifically religious Lutheran question, what happens then to the human person understood not as a religious person but as the natural person? What is his relationship to that answer, and the relationship of that answer to him? Can the belated assertion suffice that faith does not remain without good works? Should not Christianity from the very *beginning*, in its very *essence*, be understood as the truth of *life* and the power of *life*?

Let us now attempt to clarify the overall character of Calvinist Christianity by examining its most definitive *substantive* statement! It is correct to say that the theology of *Luther* made a *deeper* impression on Calvin than it did on Zwingli and his adherents.[99] To be sure, one should not appeal to the fact that Calvin took over the Lutheran catechetical outline in his Institutes,[100] because, firstly, the Zwinglian Leo Jud did that as well, and secondly, Calvin dropped it in B and in the later editions of the Institutes. It is, however, proper to point out that Calvin better understood Luther's driving concern to deal with the concept of *faith* in his well-known and strangely isolated way than did his German-Swiss predecessors. For Luther, it is doubtless true that faith is somewhat hypostatic; it functions in some ways like a mythological intermediary, gifted with distinctive characteristics, that moves between God, man, and the world like the Alexandrian logos. Zwingli and the Zwinglians pass by this wondrous thing shaking their heads. For them, the issue is God alone, and then thereafter man as such. Calvin agrees with them on this, but perhaps because he thinks through this concept, with its remarkable connection of rational and revelational reflection, in such a fundamental way, he has the freedom and serenity to hear thoroughly what Luther wants to say about faith. In A (45), after explaining that the knowledge of sin follows from the law, he does not continue, as do the Tetrapolitana and then Zwingli, with the statement that man is thus made just through God's mercy in Christ. Rather, he proceeds almost exactly as Luther does, saying, "The Lord, therefore, after reminding us (by means of the law) of our weakness and impurity, comforts us with the *assurance* of his power and mercy."[101] There then follows an entire article under the title, "That we appropriate Christ through *faith*," which begins with the words, "As the merciful father offers us his son through the word of the gospel—so we *embrace him* through faith and acknowledge him as given *to us*" (A 46).[102] Calvin understood Luther's desire to show how the human becomes *certain* of the salvation created in Christ. He says expressly in B (117, 31[–41]) that it does not suffice to comprehend God's almighty power and goodness. That is not the casting of one's entire trust upon God that he had described as the first element of the true knowledge of God. It is, rather, necessary, "that *each of us* should set it down *in his mind*" ["ut *cum animo suo quisque nostrum* statuat"[103]; French: "que nous sayons certains"[104]] that we are loved by God and that he wants to be our Father and the ground of our salvation. Or as the Gallican Confession says in Article 20: Faith is "*to appropriate to our use* the promises of life which are given to us through him" (M 226,24–25).[105] All of this simply means for Calvin that he should extend a line of thought that is somewhat abbreviated in his highland colleagues. What must be fully expressed is that trusting *God*, as his honor demands, is real and personal *trust*, fiducia. Then, however, comes the sharp corner that certainly is frequently found in Luther *as well*[106] but that is *not* in Augsburg, Articles 2, 3, 4, 6, and 20.[107] The decisive definition of faith, Calvin says in A (47),[108] arises out of the substance of the *promise* that it grasps. Because it is *God's* promise in Christ that is given us in the gospel, faith is *therefore* that most personal and most certain trust. As faith in *God's* promise in all its incomprehensibility, it is itself a gift of God, "a light of the Holy Spirit" (48),[109] resting upon eternal predestination (46).[110] The Augsburg Confession puts it in the exact reverse way: " [T]he Holy Spirit is received through faith" (M 46,29).[111] The *righteousness* of faith is not the righteousness *of faith* but the righteousness *of God* or *of Christ*. It lies in the "perpetual *object* of faith."[112] Calvin is an adherent of a strictly imputative doctrine of justification. We are justified through faith "not in the sense, however, that we receive within us any righteousness, but because the righteousness of Christ is credited to us" ([A]49).[113] It is not by virtue of faith but by virtue of the Holy Spirit, who gives us faith and in faith our justification before God, that we are justified, because the substance of the promise, *God*, can only be grasped through *God's* working in us. |

But the selfsame Lord, the selfsame Holy Spirit, who *justifies* us in *faith*, now *sanctifies* us in repentance. That righteousness, because it is *God's* righteousness, *cannot* be separated at all from good works, "so as not to divide Christ from himself" (B 128,37–38)![113a] "Repentance is *always* joined with the faith of Christ" (A 50).[114] "The whole doctrine of the gospel is comprehended under the two branches, faith and repentance" ([B] 128,41–42).[114a] Calvin certainly distinguishes between the two, the righteousness of faith and the good works of repentance. But just as certainly, he relates the two to each other in precise correspondence. One might compare the relationship with that of two connecting pipes, except that here the point where they meet is infinite. The Holy Spirit, who is the Spirit of 'illumination' [illuminatio] *and* 'regeneration' [regeneratio] (B 125,16[–20]),[114b] thus of justification *and* of sanctification, is the 'third factor' [tertium], in which both are one, while in us they are always *two*, yet never one without the other. There is no faith that could replace repentance, nor repentance that could replace faith.[115] Thus, Calvin comes from firmly demanded *faith* to equally firmly demanded *obedience* via the simple and yet unfathomable route through the one who is the *object* and the *ground* of faith. That same one is also the object and the ground of *obedience*. In this clarity, the *ethical* approach of Calvin's proclamation of God is rewarding. It makes it possible for Calvin to ascribe to faith all that it is due. In so doing, he unavoidably confronts the object of faith and is immediately driven by *this* to a new ethical approach, to a new questioning of the "true and legitimate rule" ["vera ac legitima regula"],[116] namely, *of the will*. For the human who asks himself why he exists and receives the answer, to the glory of God, cannot and should not only *trust* but also *will*, not only expect something from God but also *do* something for God. For Calvin, faith, fiducia, does not absorb all other action. |

That faith for him was, from the other side, both limited and inadequate act, is seen in an instructive way in the discussion of *hope* that is attached to his explanation of the Apostles' Creed in A (A 59).[117] He relates hope as patient *waiting upon fulfillment* to faith as claiming the promise. It constantly repeats, *"faith believes"* ["*la foi croit*"]; it believes in the truthfulness of God that he is our Father, that we are receiving eternal life. In contrast, *"hope expects"* ["*esperance attend*"] that all this will be shown and will happen. One cannot hope and wait upon God without believing, but the "weakness of our faith" ["imbécillité de notre foi"] must be supported and preserved through patient hoping and waiting. In B, Calvin deleted this section. But here as well, faith stands next to other action. Next to believing there must be obeying, praying, and thanking. Faith is not a god that tolerates nothing next to it, as often appears to be the case in Luther. In this reserve and modesty, which is actually the energy of the highest objectivity, Calvinist faith leads beyond itself to the other, which is *also from* God and toward God, to life, to the world, to one's fellow human, and it becomes obedience. This is the sense in which Article 22 of the Gallican Confession says, "This faith not only doth not hinder us from holy living, or turn us from the love of righteousness, but *of necessity* begetteth in us all good works."[118] Merit and justification, "active righteousness" ["iustitia activa"] as Luther put it,[119] are not to be expected from such good works, but certainly God's free beneficence and the reward of grace, which cannot be lacking in whatever his Spirit has caused to happen in us, are. And since God's beneficence and grace can only be found in *faith*, this final goal of *obedience* for its part confronts us again with the task of *faith* (B 128).

Building on all of this, it is entirely understandable that the *Decalogue*, which makes up the second part of B, and the law in general have a very different position than in the Lutheran conception of Christianity. The external evidence for this is seen in the way that Calvin in B no longer begins along the lines of Luther's model but rather with the Apostles' Creed in order to move from there to the Decalogue—we have just seen the context in which this happens. The law for Calvin is *more* than the great means to the knowledge of sin and as such the springboard to the knowledge of grace. That is how things were in A, but a glance at the Institutes at that time instructs us that Calvin by then saw beyond that scheme.[120] In neither of the catechisms did he ever speak of the abrogation of the law. Instead, he concludes that one should live according to its prescriptions (the conversation here is about what the human should will to do) (B 136, 42–43). In it, God "prescribes to us what is the service of his majesty which pleases him" (A 38).[121] The silhouettes of the ceremonies of Mosaic law have collapsed with the appearance of Christ, but their substance and truth have remained for us in the person in whom all things are fulfilled. The law and the prophets are necessary for us in order to give order to our lives and to strengthen us in view of the promises of the gospel, says Article 23 of the Gallican Confession.[122] The impossibility of fulfilling it does not change the fact that it was given to us to be fulfilled (B 136, 49–50).[122a] The fulfillment itself can only be the work of the Holy Spirit. The law is indeed the lamp that illumines the path of believers (A 50).[123] It keeps them humble; it urges them to seek the Lord; it is the reins by which they are kept in the fear of the Lord. It shows the goal of this "earthly pilgrimage" ["terrena peregrinatio"].[124] Our distance from that goal is pardoned as long as we are moving along the way. The law is and remains the "perfect rule of righteousness" ["perfecta regula omnis justitae"].[125] God accepts no other sacrifice than obedience (B 136–37). That is what is commonly called Calvinist *legalism*.[126] One may call it that, but it must be very clear that this *works* legalism has nothing to do with justification through the law, that is, with what Luther called the 'righteousness of the law' [iustitia legis].[127] Whoever accuses Calvin and Reformed theology in general of *that* only proves that he has not noticed the dialectical curve. Calvin is asking about what the human should will, and he arrived at this question at the very moment in which he found the right answer to the question about what one may believe. He who gave the gospel also gave the law; as seriously as the gospel is to be taken in faith, so seriously is the law to be taken for the will. Here, to be sure, ethics is established not directly upon faith, as Luther attempted to do, but upon grace. The law does not establish obedience, as little as the gospel itself establishes faith. Rather, both obedience and faith are established through the grace of the Holy Spirit, and as the gospel sets the direction there, now the law does so here. Corresponding to the way in which Christianity, according to Calvin, addresses the problem of human life in its *totality*, not merely in the narrowly drawn specifically religious sphere, is his emphasis that the Bible binds the will to faith. Fundamentally, Calvin's "legalism" is not greater than Luther's, but it is more obvious because the entire question of God is placed by him in a much more *universal* way.

One detail should be noted in passing, having to do with what is often described as typically Calvinist, namely, the rigorous Sabbath observance of the English on the basis of the Fourth Commandment.[128] This is precisely *not* Calvinist.[129] To be sure, in his Catechisms[130] and in the Institutes[131] he treated this commandment thoroughly and lovingly. But he reckoned the unconditional prohibition of labor and even the fixing of the seventh day on this or that particular day as part of the rejected ceremonial regulations of the Mosaic law.[132] His major emphasis was, first, upon the social dimension—the relief of those who are "under the power of others" ["sub aliena potestate sunt"],[133] that is, the wage laborers. Secondly, and most importantly, he emphasized public worship, for which space must be made on Sunday because it could not take place every day due to the "weakness" ["infirmité"] of our flesh.[134] Thirdly, and a favorite concept of Calvin's, he refers to the "perpetuel sabbath" ["perpetual sabbath"] given by this day of rest,[135] "the spiritual rest, whereby believers must cease from their own works in order to let the Lord work in them."[136] This is, incidentally, one of those passages, and not the only one, that show that Calvin's broad spirit could occasionally move along the well-known paths of mysticism, even if one does not expect to find this in him. I am telling you this also as an example of the way that Calvin concretely understood this second path, that of obedience to the law of the Lord.[137]

From the last two sections of Catechism B, I mention the following as germane for our theme. *Prayer* is initially treated by Calvin very soberly as one of the series of human activities. Calvin simply assumes that humans will always seek help. They will seek it from other humans, from angels, saints, or by means of mere words, possibly in other languages, without having their heart in it.[138] Now, as an answer to the question, "to what end?" ["quis finis?"],[139] he speaks of "the manner of prayer" ["de orandi ratione"].[140] Here again, he pushes through to the actual issue. To pray is to lay before God our faults and despair and to seek grace from him. Can we do that? No, we are too "stupid"[141] for that, in Calvin's own words. The true prayer is solely the Holy Spirit in us with its inexpressible sighs. Should we then idly wait around for the Holy Spirit? Never, but precisely when we feel ourselves to be sluggish and unprepared for praying, we should seek refuge in prayer, but then remembering that prayer means to pray in the name of Jesus. That means that everything we ask for must ultimately have to do with the 'glory of God' [gloria Dei] and nothing else, as the Lord's Prayer shows us. In A 67[142] there is a very strong paragraph about "perseverance in prayer" that is lacking in B. To pray means, above all, not to impose law upon God but rather to say to him, "Thy will be done!" to *submit* oneself to the benevolence of providence, to learn to *wait* patiently on the Lord, to learn to understand that God is present with us even if the hour of his help has not yet come, and if it should never come still to believe that this too is good, and thus to be rich in humility and comforted in testing. "And he alone will be sufficient unto us for all things, inasmuch as he contains in himself all goods, which in the time to come he will fully reveal to us."[142a] He will ultimately not permit the waiting of his own to be in vain. It almost appears that this beautiful section, like the other one about waiting in hope, was a victim of the tendency to avoid bringing anything that could be mistaken for quietism into this presentation of Christianity as the deed that is to be done to the glory of God. Thus, this doing is also related to what God does and is then drawn again into the series of answers to the question, "What should we do?" which for Calvin is a given in Christianity.

In the fourth section, Calvin wants to understand the *Word of God*

June 12

and the *sacraments* as subsumed under the concept "Praise and Thanksgiving." Here again the dialectic is clear. How can we worthily praise God? Answer: according to the rule of Scripture, that is, through the proclamation of the Word and the administration of the sacraments. But Word and sacrament are no less than the offering of God's beneficence to us. For that reason, it is important to understand them correctly and to use them zealously and worthily.[143] |

One detail from the first section[144] must be emphasized in our conclusion, and that is the doctrine of the *church*, because it establishes the criterion for the way in which Christianity, understood as Calvin does, is to function within the arena of history. Calvin understood "I believe in one holy catholic church"[145] as a special fourth article of the confession of faith, and in particular he places the subsequent "remission of sins" ["remissionem peccatorum"] in the *context* of the 'church' [ecclesia] (B 126, 24–27).[145a] That is to say, the central promise that faith claims and upon which everything stands is no more to be found outside the church than faith and repentance are to be found outside the Holy Spirit! Now the church, like the entire content of the Apostles' Creed, is primarily the object of proper 'trust' [fiducia], that is, the work of God. It is "the body and society of believers whom God hath predestined to eternal life."[146] The very fact that the church exists is the actual *effect* of the entire work of Christ. The holiness of the church is based upon the "justifying and reforming" ["justificare et reformare"][147] that God carries out upon his elect. "Catholic" means that there can only be *one* church of Christ. "Communion of saints" ["communio sanctorum"] means that everything that God gives to the whole church or to individuals (A 57)[148] is given to all. So much then about the invisible church, only visible to God. Calvin never speaks of any other church in the catechism; one must see the entire fourth part[149] as the substitution for that. We may supplement, however, using the following content from the Gallican Confession, Articles 25–33[150]: One can believe, in the sense of 'trust' [fiducia], only in the "one holy" ["una sancta"] of the Apostles' Creed, that is, in the "company of the chosen" ["coetus electorum"],[151] which is the body of Christ. Such believing must apply also to the *order* of the externally visible earthly church as such, that is, believing in the general sense as revealed truth (in the same sense that one must believe in the Decalogue or the Lord's Prayer as the necessary rule of life and of prayer). The order, not the church(!), is based on the authority of Christ and is "sacred and inviolable" ["sacre et inviolable"].[152] Calvin held the ecclesial offices of *'pastor'* (pasteur, for the sermon), of *elder* (for the supervision of moral life) and of *deacon* (for the care of the poor) to be ordinances of Jesus himself[153] (later he added the 'docteur' [docteur], the theologian in the more limited sense!).[154] For Calvin, all pastors have the same standing; no hierarchy is foreseen. Whenever possible, pastoral appointments should be made by *election*, as Calvin prescribed for the French Reformed, who were independent from the state. The purity of the congregation assembled around the Lord's Table was the concern of *church discipline* that was to be practiced by the elders. These ordinances were not to be binding upon the conscience. In particular, the practice of church discipline stood according to Calvin not only under the reservation that those who were punished would better themselves and be capable of readmission, but more importantly, that in the final analysis only God sees through and judges humans. What is meant are actions that *"conduce to concord and hold all in obedience, from the greatest to the least"* (Gall. 33).[155] As such, they are divinely commanded and are *confessed* in Calvin's church with "we *believe*" ["nous *croyons*"]. Even the proposition that "outside the church there is no salvation" ["extra ecclesiam nulla salus"],[156] which in the strict sense only applies to the invisible church *of God*, has its practical and earthly converse side: One should *listen* respectfully to the pastors, to the extent that they are properly called and practice their office faithfully. This is not to say that God is restricted to them, *"but because it pleaseth him to govern us by such restraints"* (Gall. 25).[157] One should *be faithful to* the church, wherever there is one, "even if the magistrates and their edicts are contrary to it" (Gall. 26).[158] To be sure, there are hypocrites and reprobates among the allegedly faithful, but in spite of that, the true church is recognized in the presence of Word and sacrament *and* (this is the significant Calvinist addition over against Article 7 of the Augsburg Confession![159]) in that its members *"agree to follow his Word, and the pure religion which it teaches; who advance in it (that which they confess) all their lives, growing and becoming more confirmed in the fear of God according as they feel the want of growing and pressing onward"* (Gall. 27).[160] The papal church is *not* church because "the pure Word of God" ["pure vérité de Dieu"][161] is suppressed in it. Whoever participates in it and its worship *separates oneself* from the body of Christ. The only concession is that Roman Catholic baptism is not invalid, implying that there is "some trace of the Church left in the papacy," which does not however change the fact that it is a sin to have one's child baptized a Catholic (Gall. 28).[162] |

One has spoken here of the legalist, humanist, pre-Reformational, even medieval character of the doctrine of Calvin (Seeberg).[163] This can either be very right or very wrong. It would be wrong if one were to think that this concept of the church differed from or repressed in any way the specifically religious fundamental thought of the Lutheran Reformation regarding the church of the Word and of faith, especially if that alleged difference implied the formation of a community of saints along the lines pursued by the Anabaptists. It would be right if one means by this that Calvin's Reformation, his way of posing the question of God and of finding its answer in revelation, does not limit itself to the specifically religious territory but confronts humanity in the totality of its possibilities, each one of which he understood in a certain independence. That there is no law for faith does not rule out the fact that for obedience the law is not removed but affirmed. That obedience must be spiritual does not change the fact that Christ's ordinances for the proper service of God are literally to be taken seriously. The differing norms for the former and the latter have varying character among themselves. The Apostles' Creed, for example, is neither a law nor an ordinance for faith but rather the summarized biblical *gospel*. The Ten Commandments are not gospel and not ordinance but *law*. The fundamentals relating to the church are virtually *ordinance*. What all have in common is that they are the valid *Word of God* that is authoritative here in one sense and there in another. With this manifold normativity of the *one* Word of God, which corresponds to the manifold character of human life, Calvin did in fact, in contrast to Luther, receive and dignify the concerns of humanism, the concerns of the pre-Reformation reformers, and even the concerns of the high Middle Ages. All of this, of course, was in terms of his own understanding and under the presupposition of the decisive Reformation concern. |

His ideas about the visible church must, especially, be understood as the energetic attempt to make Protestantism *historically functional*, that is, to give to this fellowship in Christ that is based radically upon election and faith an earthly form that takes into account as much as possible human "infirmity" ["infirmité"] and "weakness" ["imbécillité"].[164] These ideas express perhaps in the most distinctive way the substance of Calvin's Christianity. One can arguably view Calvin from two sides. One approach is that of the Catechism (but one dare not forget that in the Catechism Calvin speaks as the man of the church and as the ethicist). Here we have the picture of man shattered by the problem of his existence, fleeing to God only to discover that he has been found by God before he ever sought him. The other option is to proceed from what is, after all, the goal and the meaning of this self-representation, and then we see the incomprehensibly and ineffably majestic God in Christ, through the daily new wonder of his Spirit, electing man, calling him, justifying him, saving him, and unavoidably driving man to ask the question, "What is the end of human life?" ["quis finis humanae vitae?"]. The answer: "our life devoted to his glory" ["vitam nostram in eius gloriam referri"].[165] What is, in both instances, first, and what is second? Which formulation of the question is the primary one? It is my view that one may not question Calvin in this way. The one exists completely in the other; it may not and cannot be isolated from the other. It may well be (this is yet to be considered in detail) that in this unity he is completely the disciple of Martin Luther.[166] In this unity of the one with the other, in this possibility of being a *Reformer* as a humanist, and a *humanist* as a Reformer—or, to put it differently, to be a *prophet* as an ethicist and an *ethicist* as a prophet—he is *not* a disciple of Luther. Here, in every way, Calvin is the vertex of that Reformation movement that we see emerging in German Switzerland with all kinds of one-sidedness, limitations, and discouraging prospects. Calvin took it up and brought it to its classical expression, so that it became *the* Reformation movement for the larger part of Europe and for the New World across the oceans.

The confessions that we now must consult for our question are without exception variations on the theme formulated by Calvin. One can, however, treat very few of them as expressly Calvinist confessions; the reason for that, as we discussed in lecture 1, lies in the *essence* of Reformed theology.

The next group of documents to which we now turn, the confession of the *Frankfurt Refugees Congregation* of 1554 (M 657[–66]), the *Emden Catechism* of 1554 (M 666[–82]), and the *Catechism of Marten Micron* of 1559

(Lang 118[–149]), all emerge from the Odysseus among the Reformed fathers, John à Lasco.[167] He should probably be regarded as the actual author of the first two. There are many details that make clear that we are dealing with the Calvinist school [e.g. "He created man . . . in order that only He may be worshiped and glorified by him"[167a] (Frankfurt, M 660,4[–5]), the interpretation of the "communion of saints" ["communio sanctorum"] as the possession of the gracious work of God *common to all* (Frankfurt, 663,37[–45]; Emden, 674, 36[–40]), the view of the Sabbath commandment (Micron, Lang 123), the fourfold division of the Apostles' Creed].[168] What is more important and more characteristic here is the great weight placed upon the visible church and upon church discipline. In the calling to membership in the true church, the individual should virtually have a "most certain sign" ["signum certissimum"][169] of his election that must be linked to the proper obedience of the gospel. Lasco proposes four signs of the true church: (1) pure preaching, (2) worship of the one God in Christ alone, (3) the sacraments ordained by God, and (4) church discipline (Frankfurt, M 664). These four things taken together form the "vital . . . ministry" ("vivax [. . .] ministerium"),[170] the "certain service,"[171] which God has ordained for his church, which the church itself is to maintain and through which it distinguishes itself from all godless assemblies (Emden, M 675,17ff.). The presence and authority of this service is an "article of faith" ["credendum"] (Frankfurt, M 664, 9), that is, it is based upon revelation. Of course, here too behind the visible church there stands the invisible church of God to which one belongs through the "inward breathing of the Holy Ghost" as Micron ([Lang] 134) puts it, the "church of the faithful and elect" ["ecclesia fidelium et electorum"],[172] whose head is Christ. The emphasis that "the right and true church of Christ" may "be outwardly known" in spite of its scattering throughout the world (M 675, 17), the weight placed upon the emergence of the *hidden* church into the earthly public arena of *history,* is unmistakable here. It is possibly stressed even more zealously than Calvin himself does. Here, in the doctrine of the *church,* is where I would see the decisively and characteristically Reformed aspects of the Lasco statements, especially in the context of our discussion. |

It must then be immediately noted, of course, that Lasco did not succeed in making this doctrine so clear and credible in the context of the whole as was the case with the master of Geneva. Generally, Lasco tends to *blur* the fact that there is both trust *and* obedience, both a 'passive righteousness' [iustitia passiva] that is imputed to us by God *and* a 'pilgrimage' [peregrinatio] in time that submits to the divine law, not confusing or intermingling both but also not dividing them from each other, rather both next to each other, united in their common *grounding* in revelation and through their common *realization* by the Holy Spirit from above. Occasionally he implies something of this, for example, in Article 3 of the Emden Catechism,[173] where it states that one is certain of his faith through the Holy Spirit who testifies to us through faith in Christ that we are God's children, but also through the will and desire to serve God, which we sense in the inward person through the Spirit. This is, however, *not* a very positive application of Calvinist thought, for basing the *certainty of salvation* upon the feeling of our desire and will to serve God is certainly questionable. The question, "Why are you created?" and the answer, "To know, love, and to serve God," with which both catechisms start in apparently very Calvinist fashion, have no systematic power in Lasco. Instead of maintaining the ethical perspective and answering with Calvin, "To know, love, and serve God means, in particular, to believe, obey, pray, praise and thank him in this church" (or however this might be formulated in detail), he stumbles over the question of how the natural man could fulfill and do what he is created for. This leads him necessarily into the customary Lutheran, or better, *Melanchthonian*-Lutheran scheme of law–sin–Christ–faith, within which the obligatory weight of obedience simply cannot be made clear. The refrain, faith of course never without works, always comes across here as something awkwardly tacked or pasted on. Consider, for example, Articles 60 and 68 in the Emden Catechism with their assurance that Baptism and the Lord's Supper *in addition* (that is, beyond their character as the seal of promise) must serve as an admonition to gratitude. It is immediately obvious that Lasco did not understand Calvin here, when both in the Emden Catechism and in that of Micronius Calvin's carefully structured sequence 'confession of faith–law–Lord's Prayer–sacraments' is set aside and the law is put at the beginning. In this process, it loses necessarily its independent significance and becomes as in Luther and Melanchthon effectively and exclusively the dark backdrop against which faith is to be contrasted, regardless of all the good things they say. This faith is then defined in strictly Lutheran terms, and rightly, as "the most certain persuasion" ["certissima persuasio"],[174] as the confidence and trust that God is gracious to us in Christ, that we are his children in Christ. In his introduction to the Frankfurt Confession, Lasco declared that this faith was the essence of Christianity. |

We shall not examine further the extent to which this obvious conformity to Melanchthonianism can be explained by church politics, thinking especially of the survival problems of the Lasco congregations that were under Lutheran attack.[175] What is both a finding and a fact is that Lasco's line begins on one track with the narrowly religious question of Luther and ends on a dual track with Calvin's concept of the church. What lies between concretely, the way from fiduciary faith correctly and purely defined to the demand for church discipline, remains in the dark. At one point, in the third article of the Frankfurt Confession, dealing with the Holy Spirit, the answer appears to be very near. The Holy Spirit is described there in strong terms (1) as the Spirit of personal, individual cleansing and sanctification, (2) as the Spirit that rules over the invisible church of God, and (3) as the Spirit that makes the 'ministry' [ministerium] of the visible church 'vital' and 'effective' [vivum, efficax].[176] But what is missing here, remarkably, is what must be first and foundational, which is that the Spirit is the one who makes the elect certain of their justification in faith. A few pages earlier, Lasco had also said this in passing,[177] but that he did *not* say it here proves that he did *not* see the bracket that holds together justification faith, obedience to the law, and the visible church. This deficiency in his exposition does not change the fact that his documents, viewed in terms of their intention, expressed the typically Reformed concerns and belong in the group we are discussing.

We now turn to the most famous of all Reformed confessions, the Palatine Catechism, better known as the *Heidelberg Catechism*,[178] written in 1563 as a commission of Elector Friedrich III of the Palatinate by Zacharias Ursinus and Kaspar Olevianus,[179] the first of whom was primarily a student of Melanchthon, and the latter chiefly a student of Calvin! |

In treating the Heidelberg Catechism, one must avoid the temptation to base one's interpretation on the wording of the well-known first question— "What is your only comfort, in life and in death?"[180]—and upon its equally well-known outline of human misery, redemption, and thankfulness. Whoever knew only this much about the Heidelberg would be justified in assuming that the central view of Christianity presented here should be regarded as essentially Melanchthonian-Lutheran,[181] over against which the mildly Reformed deviations[182] in the doctrine of the sacraments, Calvinist Christology, the not very emphatic doctrine of church discipline, and so on, would not mean much. The question of comfort placed at the beginning seems to be identical with the narrowly religious question of salvation, and that outline appears to concide with the well-known schematic of the classic 'way of Luther' [Via Lutheri].[183] Closer acquaintance with the content of the catechism will show in contradiction to that assumption that, in this instance, the hands are Esau's but the voice is Jacob's voice [see Gen. 27:22]. It cannot be disputed that, for many reasons, the Heidelberg theologians began with the Lutheran question. These include considerations of church politics and an astuteness with regard to religious pedagogy, more importantly, a certain inevitability in the German spirit, and not least significant, the objective truth of the 'way of Luther' [via Lutheri] that Calvin always respected. The answer that they gave to this question, however, is indubitably a Reformed answer. |

What is described as "comfort" in Question 1, belonging to Jesus with body and soul and in life and in death, sounds so comprehensive that one might well ask whether the question, "What is your comfort?" can be so narrowly meant as it appears to be at first glance, especially when the discussion of the *Holy Spirit*, given to us by Christ, continues by stating that he "assures me of eternal life, *and makes me wholeheartedy willing and ready from now on to live for him.*"[184] This is quite unambiguously the typical Calvinist duality of salvation certainty and readiness for obedience bound into a unity in the source out of which both flow, namely, the Holy Spirit. If that is the "comfort" of which the Heidelberg wants to speak, then it cannot be very different from what Calvin has described as the "end of human life" ["finis vitae humanae"].[185] This impression is confirmed when we then note that the Heidelberg, in distinction from Lasco's documents, adopted the new approach introduced by Calvin in 1545, placing the treatment of the Apostles' Creed at the beginning of the four sections of the catechism.[186] This means that it does not use the law as the stirrup to faith but rather acknowledges its distinctive significance. Question 115 makes the fundamental statement:

> Why, then, does God have the ten commandments preached so strictly since no one can keep them in this life? First, that all our life long we may become increasingly aware of our sinfulness, and therefore more eagerly seek forgiveness of sins and righteousness in Christ. *Second, that we may constantly and diligently pray to God for the grace of the Holy Spirit, so that more and more we may be renewed in the image of God, until we attain the goal of full perfection after this life.*[187]

This double meaning of the law for justification *and* for sanctification is expressed in the Heidelberg in the following ways. In the first section, "Of Man's Misery,"[188] Question 4 articulates the "law" only in the form of the "summary" taken from Matthew 22:34[–39], love of God and of neighbor,[189] in order then to surpass it in Question 5, "Can you keep all this perfectly?"[190] which leads to the fall, original sin, and 'the captivity of the will' [servum arbitrium]. Then in the third section, "Of Thankfulness,"[191] under the perspective of *conversion* and especially the resurrection of the new person that consists of his joy in doing God's will, Question 91 speaks of *good works* "which are done out of true faith *in accordance with the Law of God, and for his glory,* and not those based on our own opinion or on the traditions of men."[192] This grants an independent origin and legal foundation to the unfolding of the law in the exposition of the Decalogue. |

This dual argumentation is anticipated with obvious zeal in the Heidelberg's second section, "Of Redemption,"[193] where it defines the content of faith. Question 31 ("Why is he called *Christ*, the Anointed One?")[194] is followed by Question 32 ("But why are *you* called *a Christian?*"): *"Because through faith I share in Christ and thus in his anointing, so that I may confess his name, offer myself a living sacrifice of gratitude to him, and fight against sin and the devil with a free and good conscience throughout this life and hereafter rule with him in eternity over all creatures."*[195] Questions 37–42, which describe 'vicarious satisfaction' [satisfactio vicaria] as the result of the death of Christ, are followed by Question 43 ("What *further benefit* do we receive from the *sacrifice and death of Christ* on the cross?"): "That *by his power our old self is crucified, put to death, and buried with him, so that the evil passions of our mortal bodies may reign in us no more, but that we may offer ourselves to him as a sacrifice of thanksgiving.*"[196] Continuing this line of exposition, Question 45 describes the further "benefit" of the *resurrection*, next to that which is understood in a narrower sense as primarily religious, "we too are now raised by his power to a new life."[197] Similarly, Question 49 describes the benefit of the *ascension*, "that he *sends us his Spirit as a counterpledge by whose power we seek what is above, where Christ is, sitting at the right hand of God,* and not things that are on earth."[198] The *'communion of the saints'* [*communio sanctorum*] in the Third Article, Question 55, has the significance, next to its being a divine gift, "*that each one ought to know that he is obliged to use his gifts freely and with joy for the benefit and welfare of other members.*"[199] In the doctrine of *baptism* (in the Heidelberg the sacraments are in the second section), it says in Question 70 that "to be washed with the blood and Spirit of Christ" means "to have the forgiveness of sins [...] through grace ... *and also to be renewed by the Holy Spirit and sanctified as members of Christ, so that we may more and more die unto sin and live in a consecrated and blameless way.*"[200] And in the doctrine of *the Holy Supper* in Question 76, to eat the body and blood of Christ means "not only to embrace with a trusting heart the whole passion and death of Christ," but also "*it is to be so united more and more to his blessed body by the Holy Spirit dwelling both in Christ and in us that, although he is in heaven and we are on earth, we are nevertheless flesh of his flesh and bone of his bone, always living and being governed by one Spirit.*"[201] Thus (Question 81), the contrite and those seeking forgiveness should come to the Lord's Table as those who "desire more and more to strengthen their faith and *improve their life,*"[202] to which then in Questions 82–85 the doctrine of the keys, that is, of church discipline, is appropriately developed. Throughout the catechism, the *task* [*Aufgabe*] is incorporated into the presentation of the *gift* [*Gabe*] and at the same time clarified in its necessity from above. This is an undertaking that lies completely along Calvin's line and for most of its points has even direct analogies in the Genevan Catechism, although it is not so significant there for the character of the whole as it is here. Here, working in the structure of the Lutheran schematic, and lacking Calvin's comprehensive concept of God that guarantees their unity, this undertaking was indispensable to ensure that the Reformed emphasis, this both/and, the indivisibility of faith and obedience was appropriately upheld. |

The Heidelberg Catechism also attempts to ground the unity of the two perspectives from below, to make them understandable psychologically. It does this with the help of the term *thankfulness*, which we have already encountered in L. Jud[203] and Lasco.[204] Question 64 responds to the objection that the doctrine of justification through faith alone might make people "careless and sinful" with the statement, "No, for it is impossible for those who are ingrafted into Christ by true faith not to bring forth *the fruit of grat-itude.*"[205] And Question 86 resolves the apparent paradox that we are redeemed without merit and still ought to do good works by answering the question "Why?" with these words: "Because just as Christ has redeemed us with his blood so he also renews us through his Holy Spirit according to his own image, so that with our whole life we may show ourselves grateful to God for his goodness and that he may be glorified through us."[206] Question 87 responds even more pointedly that those who do not forsake their ungrateful and impenitent lives and convert to God can never be saved, while Questions 88–90 expound the fact that conversion consists of the dying of the old and the resurrecting of the new person, followed by Question 91 with the transition to God's *law* that has already been described. This psychological motivation was superfluous in Calvin as well. The unity of faith and obedience are given from the very beginning in the unity of God, who lays claim to the entire human person. Within the Lutheran schematic adopted by the Heidelberg Catechism, that unity was presented as well. It really should have been valued by Lutheran dogmatics as a desirable supplement of its own thinking that in this point was deficient. For what is merely asserted in the Augsburg Confession is actually *demonstrated* here— that and why there can be no faith without good works. |

In situations where for pedagogical reasons Calvin's more comprehensive approach is held to be unacceptable, or for national or other pious reasons Christianity needs to be understood in terms of the 'way of Luther' [Via Lutheri], the Heidelberg Catechism is the prime example of how it must be done if one still wants to uphold pure Reformed doctrine. It is precisely the right textbook on Reformed Christianity for Germany, assuming of course that its Calvinist presuppositions, without which its intentionality is fully un-understandable, are thoroughly known and made clear. If our findings thus far are more or less correct, then it should never have been claimed that it was not typically Reformed. |

The *Hessian Catechism* (M 822[–833]) is, by contrast, a more modest theological achievement; it was adopted for Reformed Hesse by the General Synod of Kassel in 1607.[207] It shows in a very instructive way how far one could go on the Reformed side when located out on the margins in a region especially subject to Lutheran influence. They were able to accept the entire Small Lutheran Catechism by incorporating a series of deletions, additions, and amendments that in their way bravely assert the Reformed points of view, but in relation to Luther's succinct sentences appear to be hopelessly pasted on. (If I were a Lutheran and inclined to be mean, I would say that they were like no-parking signs or election posters on the walls of a Gothic cathedral, or the multicolored illumination of the Rhine Falls.) If one were *so* much under the fascinating influence of Luther that one really wanted to speak with his very words, then it would have been

better to do this without abbreviation and alteration. Luther's Small Catechism is, as far as I am concerned, beyond confessional differences and
could be used without alteration as the basis for good Reformed instruction,
with an occasional appeal 'to the better informing of Luther' [ad Lutherum
melius informandum].[208] It is *much* better than the Augsburg Confession
that, from a Reformed perspective, reflects an *inferior* Lutheranism. A
Reformed plagiarization and variation of the Small Catechism was, on the
other hand, an endeavor that was destined from the outset to bear the mark
of the irrelevant and unappetizing. |

Still, it is interesting to observe how here the Reformed view of the positive essence of Christianity seeks to assert itself. I shall set aside the anti-
Lutheran polemics (it is almost touching to see how, for example, the
Lutheran explanation of the First Commandment is enriched by Calvinist
sentiments: "We are to *acknowledge God above all things*, fear, trust, and fear
him alone"[209]; further, in Hesse they conducted a life and death struggle over
the dispute about the correct numbering of the Ten Commandments[210]) and
focus upon the following. After listing the five numbered major sections,
using Luther's approach (the sacraments are divided into two), Question 5
proceeds: "What is the purpose of all of these together? Answer: *That we
might, firstly, recognize who we are and how we stand with our Lord God; secondly,
who our Lord God is and how we might be reconciled and united with him.*"[211] This
is clearly Calvin's "knowledge of God and of ourselves" ["cognitio Dei et
nostri"],[212] in which, as we saw, the unity of faith and obedience is embed-
ded like a seed. The Lutheran exposition of the Ten Commandments, with
its admirable formulation repeated at the beginning of each explanation,
"We are to fear and love God,"[213] fits well within this perspective. But when
Question 24, at which point the plagiarizing stops, asks about the benefit of
the Ten Commandments and then responds, firstly, for the knowledge of sin,
and so forth, and secondly, "*they teach what are the good works which believers
and the regenerate are obligated to do, to show their obedience and thankfulness to
their gracious Father in heaven*,[214] then it is clear that this Reformed "secondly"
is completely incomprehensible in the Lutheran arrangement of the catechism and hangs there in the air lacking all credibility. Where do these believers and regenerate come from so suddenly? Then follows the Lutheran
explanation of the Apostles' Creed, about which it would have been better to
remain respectfully silent if one did not have something truly decisive to add
for its Reformed interpretation. Instead, the Hessian Catechism states in
three superfluous questions that the purpose of the Apostles' Creed is to
teach us to know the being and the will of God,[215] and then in three further
questions,[216] that one is saved through faith, that faith is a heartfelt trust and
that it comes from the Holy Spirit—all of which is unhelpful repetition of
what Luther has already said much better. But no word is found to establish
somehow the double-sidedness of the Reformed-Christian view over against

the overpowering monism of Lutheranism. It is clear that this will not be possible in the Lord's Prayer discussion, where Luther's wording (fortunately) is respected. The Reformed corrections, which are somewhat livelier and more extensive in the treatment of the sacraments, impress more as trivial than necessary over against that larger deficiency. There is no mention of church discipline or of the visible church in any form. The best aspects of this catechism are, even from a Reformed standpoint, the sections taken over from Luther. The Reformed additions are like the helpless hand-waving of a drowning person who was about to say something when his mouth sank into the water. Still, one can *recognize* what he wanted to *say* and could not. The fact that he really *wanted* to say it is evidence of the extraordinary persistence and bitterness with which this harmless little trace of Reformed tradition struggled for its survival and was opposed up to the days of Vilmar.[217] Our concern here has been to ascertain the Reformed *intention*.

There is little of distinctive interest for our question in the two *Netherlands Confessions* contained in Müller, that of 1561 (the Belgic, 233[–49])[218] and of 1566 (935[–40]). The Belgic Confession is an expanded paraphrase of the Gallican, but omits, for example, in Article 22[219] (which corresponds to Articles 20–21 of the Gallican) the idea that God not only sets us in faith upon a pathway but also enables us to pursue it to the end. Also, in Article 22 (on faith and good works, corresponding to Gallican 22), the decisive thought is left out that the good works "proceed from the Holy Spirit"[220] and come about through the "grace to live holily and in the fear of God"[221] received by faith. The result is that the relationship between faith and good works remains as unclear as in the Augsburg Confession. Article 6 of the Confession of 1566, dealing with justification through faith, makes the minimal statement that a vital faith, strong in works, is meant.[222] The distinctively Reformed component of both confessions is to be sought in the doctrine of the church, churchly office, and church discipline,[223] where well-known content from Calvin is repeated. Their view of the positive essence of Christianity, measured against Calvin, is to be ranked at about the level of the documents by Lasco.

More distinctive and productive are the two confessions of Calvinist Hungary, both from the year 1562, which we must discuss separately because of their very different origins and character. The first one is called in Müller the *Erlauthal Confession*[224] and is an apology sent by the pugnacious Reformed Christians of the Eger Valley to the Emperor Ferdinand and his son, King Maximilian of Bohemia.[225] These Reformed confessors were both spiritually and militarily ready to do battle and were accused of being both arsonists and rebels. Their confession has more than one highly unusual characteristic. First, it is incredibly long—110 pages in Müller in spite of the deletion of citations. Second, as a whole it lacks a clear sense of thematic organization. Consider, for example, the titles of the sections in just the last twenty pages: "On

Adultery"; "The Resurrection Body"; "The Varying Degrees of Salvation"; "The Moral Justification of War and the Making of Alliances"; "On the Difference between the 'Remission of Guilt' [remissio culpae] and 'Remission of Punishment' [remissio poenae]"; "Whether One Should Re-baptize the Heretical Baptized?"; "Whether the Church Can Err?" "On the Kingdom of God"; "On the Resurrection"; "On the Condition of Man before the Fall"; "On Usury, the Charging of Interest, and Property"; "On Church Visitations"; "Prayer"; "Whether One May Break a Military Alliance?"; "On the War with the Turks"; "On Church Weddings"; "The Elect's Certainty of Salvation"; "Whether One May Participate in Catholic Worship"; "Exposition of the Ten Commandments"; "Whether Illegitimate Children Can Be Saved?"; "That the Children of the Elect Are Also to Be Regarded as Such"; "On Eternal Life"; "On the Unity of the Old and New Testaments"; "On Nightmares." Third, it has a very unusual relationship to Catholic dogma that at many points is straightforwardly affirmed, so that we have in this Reformed confession an article 'On merits' [de meritis], 'on indulgences' [de indulgentiis], 'on purgatory' [de purgatorio], 'on fasting' [de ieiunio), 'on the mass and oblation' [de missa et oblatione], 'on sacrifice' [de sacrificio], 'on vows' [de votis], and so on.[226] In the exposition, each of these themes is first of all very seriously affirmed, whereupon each one is immediately reoriented and reinterpreted in a Calvinist fashion, with mixed success. Fourth, the confession naively and openly affirms all kinds of dubious religiosity,[227] such as magic and witchcraft, demons, ghosts, and nightmares, although to be sure it was in this instance simply putting on paper what not only Luther but also Calvin energetically believed.[228] |

All that having been said, this monster of a confession is still very instructive about the way in which Calvinism at the time influenced people who were theologically naive and untamed, people who never gave a thought to the theology of other people, such as Luther, but frankly and bluntly confessed just how they understood things, with no holds barred. Setting aside much that is truly peripheral, and making the effort to sort out the decisive points of view in this chaotic mass, one must then affirm that among "all the cavalry and infantry" ["universus exercitus equitum et peditum"], the 'nobility and citizens' [nobiles et incolae] of the Eger Valley, as these confessors described themselves on the title page,[229] there must have been people who had read their Institutes and their Geneva Catechism with open eyes and a good sense for the essentials. They were certainly more alert to the central issues of the Genevan master than certain Western colleagues who could not resist peeking at the Augsburg Confession now and again. What they particularly understood well was Calvin's method of deriving and grounding each Christian truth, whenever possible, not from or on one another, but each severally and directly from its origin in God, in revelation, grace, and the Spirit. Almost every one of the articles of the Erlauthal Confession begins at the beginning,[230] with the 'only God' [solus Deus] who must always have the first word. This is an approach that bluntly challenges every dogmatic method but has perhaps for that very reason a certain relevance. |

I will select a few details that are important for our question. Speaking of the *law*, it says, "Christ is the fulfillment of the law."[231] Outside of him there are only 'death,' 'foolishness,' and 'scandal' [mors, stultitia, scandalum].[232] Through his grace alone, the Holy Spirit and faith create in the elect 'life' [vita], 'power' [potentia], law *and* gospel, fulfillment of the commandments, firstly through the imputation of the righteousness of Christ, secondly through the rebirth based therein, and thirdly through the new covenant that he writes in our hearts (M 272). |

It says with regard to *free will* (apparently following Bullinger),[233] that by virtue of new birth there is a free will in the elect, based on | June 15 | God's mercy, created by the Holy Spirit. God drives and leads it, but it "does good works freely, willingly, obediently, . . . assenting, spontaneously" M 274–75)![233a] It teaches about *good works* that we are justified only "passively" ["passive"],[234] that all causes of our justification are solely in God. But that does not exclude but includes that God "alone works actively"[235] in our rebirth and that our reason and our will then become obedient to him. Thus, not with regard to the cause of our justification but with regard to its effects before the eyes of men, one can say with James that the human is justified through his good works [see Jas. 2:24], to the extent that they are visible "signs and demonstrations" ["signa," "demonstrationes"] of what the human experiences of God in justification (M 282, see 285). Regarding *justification and sanctification*, the two are not to be separated. They are the one work of God in us, "moving towards one goal."[236] We should be holy, righteous, and free, and we should truly live. But they are to be distinguished as different and yet equal acts in the 'process' [processus] of the Holy Spirit. Christ himself justifies us in that he makes us into a new creation, and he makes us into a new creation in that he justifies us (M 331). Both taken together constitute our *perfection*, the "perfection of the members" [perfectio [. . .] membrorum] of Christ,[237] which is clearly to be differentiated from the "perfection of Christ" ["perfectio Christi"][238] that we do not attain. Yet, with regard to his perfection, the 'elect' [electi] *are* also 'perfect' [perfecti]. The entry into this state is then *repentance*, the "true conversion" ["vera [. . .] conversio"][239] to the knowing of God, so that the glory of his grace might be honored through us. Its "efficient cause" [causa [. . .] efficiens"][240] is grace, working through the Holy Spirit. Its instrument is faith with the Word. Its goal is the new obedience (M 289). Regarding the church, the Erlauthal confessors taught that it is identical with its salvation, its foundation is grace, Christ, and his merit. But then it becomes more Calvinist than Calvin when it states that "the true church is the *visible* assembly of the elect,"[241] those gathered around the Scriptures and the sacraments, the contenders against human doctrine, the antichrist, sin and the world, who preserve the faith and the conscience, whose head is Christ. They are 'visible' [visibilis], although there are hypocrites among them like wolves among sheep. They are at times also 'invisible' [invisibilis] (the reservation of "eternal predestination" ["aeterna praedestinatio"] remains!)[242], and there are at times also 'elect' [electi] outside the 'visible assembly' [coetus visibilis] (M 289–90). It must be acknowledged that this is all extraordinarily healthy and powerful and speaks to the core of things, and that the coherent clarity with which Calvinistically understood Christianity is comprehended and affirmed could stand up well against many a more famous, more concentrated, better arranged and dogmatically more correct confession.

Given the formal deficiencies of the Erlauthal Confession, we can understand why it did not persist as a document of the church. As early as 1562 there was a synod at Tarczal and then in 1563 one in Torda, the first of which drew up a new confession and the second of which acknowledged it,[243] the so-called 'Tarczal-Torda Confession' [Confessio Tarcza-Tordaensis], which was basically the adaptation to the Hungarian situation of a confession written by *Theodore Beza*, Calvin's coworker in Geneva, in 1560.[244] We shall now turn to this document (M 376–448). Next to the Second Helvetic Confession, by which incidentally it was replaced in Hungary within a relatively short period of time,[245] this may be grouped with Calvin's Catechism and the Heidelberg Confession as the most detailed, the most carefully thought out and systematic of the Reformed confessions, and next to the Erlauthal the largest, taking seventy pages in Müller. It arranges its contents after the classical Calvinist division into four parts modeled on the Apostles' Creed: Father, Son, Holy Spirit, church. It begins with a short chapter "On the Trinity" ["De trinitate"][246] and concludes with a short statement "On the Last Judgment" ["de ultimo iudicio"].[247] The actual center of the work is in chapters 4 and 5, "On the Holy Spirit" ["De spiritu sancto"][248] and "On the Church" ["De ecclesia"],[249] which will be the sections we examine for our question. |

Here is Beza's view of Christianity. The Holy Spirit as the third person of the deity creates faith in the elect through the means of Word proclamation and the sacraments. Such faith is the sole means by which we can be saved, yet we can no more produce it in ourselves than a corpse can fly. Faith is a "certain knowledge" ["certa scientia'],[250] which 'embraces' [amplectitur] Jesus Christ, and to that extent it is the certainty of our salvation. As certainly as Christ is presented to us through the Word of God, so certainly does the one who in faith possesses him possess *everything*.

Therefore, it is faith, not as 'virtue' [virtus] ("for it would be to substitute faith in the place of Jesus Christ," 387,5),[250a] but formulated in terms of its object, faith *alone* that justifies us before God. To be sure of one's salvation in faith is thus nothing less than arrogance and Pharisaism; rather, in this process all arrogance is rejected and God is glorified. The certainty we truly do have is there where we seek every 'remedy' [remedia] for our weakness in the one Christ. That, however, must be understood to mean that nothing else is ours except Christ and what belongs to Christ, when we enter into fellowship with him through believing, into the "spiritual marriage" ["spirituale conjugium"],[251] in which our misery becomes his and his wealth becomes ours (Beza likes to cite Bernard of Clairvaux,[252] whom Calvin also esteemed highly[253]). |

Everything then, according to Beza, that relates to the attainment of salvation works itself out remarkably enough in the form of a broad depiction of the struggle in which this certainty must assert itself against the 'testing' [tentationes] that "Satan and our conscience"(!) ["Satanas et conscientia nostra"][254] cause us. The *first form of testing* concerns the *objective* side of our relationship to God. Three assaults (insultus[255]) of the enemy are to be beaten back here. He reproaches us with *God's eternal righteousness* in relation to our unrighteousness. The response to that is then that God's righteousness works according to the legal principle, "not twice for the same thing"[256]; he has punished our unrighteousness in Christ, so that it no longer burdens us. The enemy then reproaches us with the necessity of *perfect fulfillment of the law*. The response to that is that this has been done in Christ and that through faith we are the brothers and coheirs of Christ. He reproaches us with our *"depraved nature"* [*"natura depravata"*],[257] the hopelessness of our human existence with which we cannot appear before the majesty of God. The response to that is that, through the incarnation of Christ from the very moment of his conception in the body of the Virgin Mary, our nature has been sanctified and restored, more perfect than the purity in which Adam was created, and that this sanctification of human nature benefits us through faith in Christ. The *second testing* addresses the *subjective* side of the relationship. We have said that faith saves us from perishing. But *do we have this faith*? is Satan's objection. There are two responses to this.[258] Firstly, we have the *'testimony of the Holy Spirit'* [*testimonium spiritus sancti*] (the principle of Scripture), which continually enables us to cry out undauntedly, "Abba, Father!" Secondly, faith as the 'application of Christ' [applicatio Christi] is not without *'effect and power'* [*effectus et vires*], not without his bringing about the 'regeneration' [regeneratio] or 'sanctification' [sanctificatio] of the person. Beza understands this to comprise three things.[259] He speaks, first, of the *'mortification'* [*mortificatio*] of the old person, the fundamental and effective setting aside of his existence. Then he describes its *'burial'* [*sepultura*], the 'continuation' [continuatio] and the 'increase' [progressus] of 'mortification' [mortificatio]. This is understood as the factual decaying and decomposition of the dead old person, which happens in the afflictions that come to us, in the 'exercises' [exercitationes] that we must undergo to tame our rebellious flesh, and finally in our bodily death, which ends the battle between flesh and spirit. The third moment of sanctification or rebirth is the 'resurrection of the new person' [resurrectio novi hominis], the illumination, strengthening and tutoring of our intelligence, of our will, and of all our capacities through grace. The subjective presupposition to which we shall cling over against such testing is that we shall believe the testimony of the Holy Spirit, and practice, each of us on the basis of our calling, the use of the 'gift of regeneration' ["donum regenerationis"],[260] which is inseparable from faith as the 'application of Christ' [applicatio Christi]. |

At this point, Beza inserted an eight-page-long excursus on *good works* (M 393[–401]). As the light is to the sun and warmth to fire, so they are bound to faith. It is a despicable lie, he says, to call oneself a Christian and not to seek after the good and flee the evil. But what are then good and evil? Not what humans designate such but that which is so designated by God's "most holy law" ["sacrosancta Lex"][261] and which we have come to recognize as pleasing to God or abhorrent to God. Among all that is good, that which is the first thing that God commands and which is pleasing to him is *worship*, carried out in agreement with God's Word, directed solely toward him and turning to him alone, for otherwise it is 'sin' [peccatum]. The second thing is *love* for one's neighbor, even for one's enemy, based on the love of God who is reconciled to us in Christ, for otherwise it is a lie. What can be said about the *origin of good works* is that our reason and will are certainly involved in them, but only to the extent that God draws us, who resist him with all our power, to himself and makes us into new people. We have nothing that we have not received, received "not from being born but from being re-born, not from nature but from the grace of regeneration,"[262] which works freely in us every day. There is no predisposition in us toward the reception of grace. Decaying and dead stalks must become living fruit trees, and stony hearts must become hearts of flesh! Without God's grace even our most excellent works would merit nothing other than eternal punishment. Thus, we can say about the *goal of good works* that they cannot be the 'causa' [causa] of the righteousness that we have from God (this righteousness is and remains the righteousness *of Christ*) but certainly its 'witnesses' [testes], which compel others to give God the honor and which strengthen the certainty of salvation in us. Not for their own sake but because of their source they look forward to their temporal and eternal divine reward in spite of their total imperfection. |

The *third* and heaviest *testing* is directed against the certainty of our *election*,[263] in which the objective and the subjective aspects of the relationship apparently merge, that is, the possibility and the reality of our fellowship with Christ. Can 'vocation' [vocatio], in which 'eternal election' [aeterna electio] is realized within temporality, not sometimes be delayed until "the very point of death?"[264] Cannot God's dearest friends have the experience that they sense little or nothing of that 'effect' [effectus] of faith, of the 'testimony of the Holy Spirit' [testimonium spiritus sancti] and of 'sanctificatio' [sanctification], and thus stray into doubt? Answer: If it should really happen that *both* of these anchors give way, then one should remember that what is required for fellowship with Christ is not a "perfect faith" ["fides perfecta"] but a "true faith" ["fides vera"],[265] of which only a spark is needed, since its healing power rests not in us but in Christ. Let us keep before our eyes the model of all true saints who, even when "immersed in the deepest depths,"[266] did not cease calling upon God! Let us with David remember the days gone by, when we were certain of our election, if even for no more than a moment, and then let us consider these three axioms: (1) God does not change his intentions. (2) What he has once decided he necessarily brings to its conclusion. (3) Faith is a gift of God that only the elect have. If we have *once* believed, then we *are* elect, for with the "gift of faith" ["donum fidei"] we are also given "the gift of perseverance" ["donum perseverantiae"].[267] Just as an infant or a drunkard *has* reason although it does not help him, just as a sick person can be regarded by the doctors as apparently dead and can even have lost his own consciousness of being alive without really having lost the "vital faculties" ["facultas vitalis"],[268] so also the doubting believer continues to stand in his election; it persists because it persists in God. Let no one then say that a believer could think that he might sin without punishment! Justified by faith, he is also sanctified by the Spirit and struggles against sin even if at times it might seem to him that God had forsaken him or, even worse, that he might have forsaken God. Rather, he will always understand (IV 19, at the end[269]) his sanctification as the first step to new certainty about his election. The assault of the enemy is also overcome here, if we only remain persuaded that "it is entirely necessary that our salvation is deposited with God, who is much more able to guard it than we are" (404[,45–47]).[270] I

From here, Beza goes on to the doctrine of the means by which the Holy Spirit makes faith in the hearts of the elect—Word and sacrament. From this conclusion of the chapter on the Holy Spirit, I will mention the doctrine of the *law* that Beza develops in this context. For Beza as well, the law was originally one with the 'law of nature' [lex naturae], with which man came into the world. Only in its explicated form (the Decalogue) is it authentic revelation, in distinction from the gospel, which is essentially "disclosed from heaven" ["e coelo patefacta"],[271] "transcending nature itself" ["naturam ipsam transcendens"][272] (not a very happy solution to this problem!).

The law reveals to us the same righteousness and majesty of God as does the gospel but "as though naked" ["veluti nudam"][273] and thus terrifying and deadening, whereas in the gospel they appear as reconciled through God's mercy in Christ. The law's one significance is to show us how things stand for us with God, as though to compare black and white (405–8). Its other meaning is to show us the way to good works, after our hearts have been renewed (411–12). The chapter concludes with the pointed reference to the fact that Christ called the Holy Spirit the Paraclete, the *'comforter'* [*consolator*].[274] What Beza means by that is that the Spirit makes Christ our own through faith and thus gives peace to our conscience so that we are able to boast even in distress. But it also means that the Spirit guides us to hate sin, to hold the world in contempt, to call to the Father with inexpressible sighs, to forget ourselves and to become ever firmer. "For God takes pleasure in us that we are a drama before the entire world to show what is the power and working of his Spirit in such fragile vessels, to the eternal glory of his name."[275] |

Let us finally note several things from the detailed chapter *"On the Church"* [*"De ecclesia"*].[276] Obviously, for Beza the church is the "assembly and multitude of elect persons,"[277] in which the "saving power" ["virtus [. . .] salvifica"][278] of Christ is effective, spread across the entire world. It is at the same time the church of "citizens of one and the same city,"[279] united under the one head Christ, recognized by its preaching, sacraments, and church discipline, and its members by the fact that they *fight* the battle of the Spirit against the flesh. The 'power' [potestas] and 'authority' [auctoritas] of the church stand and fall with its obedience to Christ. It can practice this authority in a general *council*, convened and presided over by the emperor, but also in *synods* whose business cannot be to formulate new articles of faith but rather to affirm the pure doctrine contained in the Word of God over against heretics and to make decisions about the church's order. The *order* of the church must primarily pay attention to pure doctrine, to the prevention of all idolatry, and to the scriptural appropriateness of all institutional forms. Regarding the churchly *offices*, Beza in agreement with Calvin only wants to recognize for our time the offices of doctor, pastor, 'deacon' [diaconus], and presbyter.[280] Ecclesiastical jurisdiction is to be strictly separated from worldly authority, and one should remember that God alone can bind the conscience through his law. One should also bear in mind in practicing church discipline that in the proper attempt to avoid Epicureanism, one can end up in Pharisaism and Monasticism and cause wounds where the intention of the law is to heal wounds. What is decided on earth "unjustly" ["inique"][281] will not be confirmed in heaven, even if the decision is made by an ecclesiastical agency. The "pure church" ["ecclesia pura"][282] must be the purpose of ecclesiastical punishment, especially with regard to the sacraments, the improvement of the fallen, and the warning of others. |

If one surveys the entirety of Beza's thought as it is formulated in this most important and largest part of his confession, one is surprised at how faithfully he has taken up and continued the intention of his theological *master* at almost every point. But one is also surprised to see how Calvinist Christianity under his hands has become something *different*, and then how this different form enters as a further independent voice into the *series* of formulations we have been discussing. There can be no doubt that Beza has adopted with profound understanding the decisive emphases of Calvinist doctrine. How genuinely Calvinist and yet distinctively understood is, for example, the central place that he assigns to the *Holy Spirit* as the one God who turns himself to his elect in a creative, preserving, protecting, and guiding way. How genuinely Calvinist is the mysticism of his *doctrine of justification*, which reminds us strongly of Luther's doctrine and his Galatians commentary,[283] which may have perhaps directly influenced Beza. How genuinely Calvinist is the strict correlation of *justification* and *sanctification*, unmixed and yet not separated like the two natures of Christ in Chalcedon, so that it links an imputative doctrine of justification with an emphatic and strongly conceived sanctification that is often otherwise easily underdeveloped and poorly argued. How genuinely Calvinist is the representation of the *Christian person* as the struggler who spends his life engaged in the battle between spirit and flesh, but whom God then uses, uses in his total frailty as the instrument of his glory. How genuinely Calvinist is his view of the *church,* whose visible side is possibly emphasized more strongly by Beza than Calvin. Beza is markedly more Calvinist in the specific sense than are the authors of the Heidelberg Catechism. There is less trace in him of outside influences and elements—except for the *one* element that Beza contributed to Calvinist doctrine and by virtue of which his entire system, in spite of all its Calvinism, becomes something very different and very original. It was an original idea, not taken over from Calvin, to project the entire doctrine of the appropriation of salvation on the one point: the struggle of the Christian resulting from his being tested by doubt in the certainty of his salvation, faith, and election. In this struggle, he focuses on the reasons and arguments that he can use against his own conscience and the devil when they try to persuade him, "You are not a Christian!" It is the concentration on this point that gives Beza's statement its color and that accounts for its quite distinctive, profoundly edifying, apologetic power. But with that I have mentioned the fatal word. In Beza, Christianity is in a defensive posture. It is not yet a defense focused outward, against reason and the experience of a world estranged from God. It is a defense against certain fatal conclusions that could result from his own logic. The point is that he is *defending* himself. Beza focused his view on the person, on the Christian as such, and in so doing revealed a certain relationship to Melanchthon's Lutheranism. More strongly than

Calvin, Beza thinks when dealing with the "elect" ["electi") of particular persons with particular names. He directs his interest toward what is going on inside them, their questioning and receiving answers, their unsettledness followed by quiet resolution and then more unsettledness in their souls, the entire process of strange ups and downs, backs and forths, which constantly goes on there. |

Yet Beza is a Reformed Christian, which means, as we should gradually begin to see, that he was a dialectic theologian. He cannot find resolution on the straight path of the Augsburg Confession, where man finds his justification in faith and that is good. For faith is not without works. He must consider the fact that faith comes from God and only for that reason justifies, but the requirement of *obedience* also comes from God, introducing an element of extreme disquiet and insecurity that cannot be removed by some kind of theoretical or emotional appeasement. What has often been said of Reformed theology(!) appears to be true of him, which is that it does not provide an authentic certainty of salvation.[284] "For the Spirit is not so timid," as Luther had said.[285] However, this only appears to be the case for Beza, for repeatedly he finds the way out of the pietistic inferno of doubt and objections[286] back to the giver of all good things, who as the true subject, Lord and victor over all the controversial concepts such as justification, sanctification, faith, repentance, gospel, law, spirit, and flesh, is also their peace and gives this peace to the Anthony who is being plagued by demons.[287] Beza constantly finds splendidly clear and convincing statements when he makes this 'recourse to God' [regressus ad Deum]. And yet certainly *one* of the total impressions derived from his confession is of a certain darkness, melancholy, distortedness, if not morbidity. A Reformed Christian *is not to direct* his interest toward the psychological subject of religion in this way. Otherwise the certainty of salvation is *really* jeopardized, because in fact there is in principle no resting in faith. This danger becomes *obvious* in Beza, while in the Heidelberg Catechism it is happily avoided (although perhaps it is more concealed there than truly overcome). I will not say more than that. He fought in the strongest fashion against that danger, and in his way he won. The enthusiasm of that struggle and defense indicates, however, that something is not in order. Classic Reformed thought looks at these human matters, including those that take place in the Christian soul (most particularly those), from God's perspective. From God's perspective, all these matters become necessarily dialectic in Reformed thought. There is nothing wrong with that; it has to be that way. God stands over all these matters. The soul's life with God cannot and may not become a theme for Reformed thought. Otherwise the theme itself will become the dialectic. To seek the certainty of salvation in me rather than in God is to produce of necessity the uncertainty of salvation. That is the result at which Beza constantly arrives. Calvin was greater in this, because he *began* with this result! |

We must note further that there is another option that must be avoided—and Beza did not quite manage to do so—in which the concept of election would be the last dropping of the anchor by that person who is concerned about *his own* salvation. If this concept becomes that, then it ceases to be the theological expression of our knowledge of God's majesty and freedom regardless of what happens to us, and it unavoidably gains a certain narrowness, mustiness, sectarian feel, a whiff of a highly human religiosity.[288] The defensiveness that characterizes Beza's Christianity must necessarily follow. Christianity seen from the perspective of the glory of God does not need to defend itself. It knows these questions, including the question of the certainty of salvation, but it works on them and resolves them in passing, so to speak, so that they do not become the theme of Christianity. Where that does happen, Christianity cannot help but land on the 'escalator' [trottoir roulant] of emotional experiences, up into that "sky high exulting,"[289] before which the soul that *loves* God is not protected and must therefore be defended. As far as I can see, this is the decisive factor that separates Beza from Calvin and that makes him into an extremely respectable, noteworthy, but unmistakable epigone. He guided the entire Calvinist material into a channel that had to end in Pietism and the Enlightenment. For, when the question of the certainty of salvation receives this independent significance, why not then the related question of the certainty of truth? When the human person once has begun to seek *his salvation* in Christianity as his chief priority, then the hour is not far off when he will demand that it must also be *his truth* as his chief priority. One might risk the statement that the 'cavalry' [equites] and 'infantry' [pedites] of the Eger Valley, whose theological superior Beza doubtlessly was, understood Calvin and perhaps even the gospel itself better than did this most famous of Calvin's disciples. Unless you become like children . . . [Matt. 18:3]! But I am only saying all this in order to make the species of Reformed theology, which are our concern here, more understandable. The genre itself has not changed. Given the strong variations that we see here, one can see how indomitably the basic type as such persists with all its hallmarks.

So that we do not completely neglect the Reformed believers in *Poland*, we will mention here the most detailed of their different official doctrinal statements, namely, the Reformed declaration prepared for the Religious Consultation among Reformed, Lutherans, and Catholics at *Thorn* in 1645—which, incidentally, produced no results (*Declaratio Thoruniensis*, Augusti, 411–22).[290] Outside of Poland it was also acknowledged by the Reformed Church in Brandenburg as a confession of faith (next to the Confessio Sigismundi).[291] This declaration is not without interest because it demonstrates how far the Reformed side could go in a real emergency, when

June 19

the challenge was to move toward the *Catholic* Church in the formulation of the positive foundational concepts.[292] In Article 4, "On Grace" ["De Gratia"], justification and sanctification are both distinguished and inextricably connected with "at the same time" ["simulque"],[293] looking backward together to vocation and forward to perfection of the blessed. On that basis, there is the express *contesting* of the idea that the human is justified "solely externally . . . through the imputation" ("sola externa . . . imputatione"),[294] which is at first a puzzling statement. But the "solely" ["sola"] refers here to an *exclusively* external imputation without inward renewal. There is no such thing as isolated imputation. The true 'imputation of the righteousness of Christ' [imputatio justitiae Christi] happens only to those who repent and believe in Christ "with a vital faith" ["viva fide"].[295] There is an immediate formation of the heart by the Holy Spirit on the basis of which a person loves Christ and devotes himself to a new obedience. To that extent, one can speak of an *'inherent* righteousness' [justitia *inhaerens*] of the person, except that this will always be an imperfect righteousness with which one cannot face God; it does not justify one. Rather, that happens *"solely* through and on account of . . . the righteousness of Christ,"[296] whereby "solely" ["sola"] here is to be understood as through the righteousness of Christ *alone*. They can even speak of *"being justified* by *infused* charity and other virtues" except that "being justified" ["justificari"] is then to be understood as "being made just and holy" ["justi et sancti fieri"].[297] This refers in turn to imperfect righteousness, not to that righteousness that justifies before God, the rigorous concept of which is strongly maintained 'in its forensic sense' [sensu forensi]. In a similar way, 'faith alone' [*sola fide*] appears to be contested, since the human is incapable of receiving forgiveness "without any contrition," persisting in his sin.[298] What is again meant here is faith *that stands alone* in order then to be reintegrated quite properly; the "solely" ["sola"] refers then to 'being justified in the heart of God' [justificari coram Deo], which only comes about through faith in God's promise.[299] Therefore, *good works are necessary for salvation*, not as "causes of justification" ["causae justificationis"] but because justifying faith and justification itself cannot exist without them.[300] Christ's commands may not be defined as unfulfillable, and their fulfillability may not be restricted to wish and intention. Rather, they should and can be fulfilled by the reborn "doing the works themselves" ["ipso opere"], although this does not mean that the laws of God can be fully conformed to in this life.[301] There is *no certainty* of salvation that cannot be lost. The reborn who fall back into sin against their conscience and then persist in it *lose* not only "living faith" ["viva fides"] and justifying grace but also the certainty of it and the Holy Spirit as well. They stand anew under the judgment of wrath and of eternal death; they lack "the special grace of God" ["specialis gratia Dei"], which the elect cannot be without and which calls them to repentance, and they are without doubt *damned*.[302] One certainly can and should strive for the certainty of salvation, but it is never merely given in such a way that one could thoughtlessly and self-confidently count upon the grace of God.[303]

It would be difficult to describe this doctrine as a propitious version of basic Reformed views. The dialectical game with the terms "solely" ["sola"] and "to be justified" ["justificari"], even though carried out precisely and correctly, has a game-playing feel to it in comparison with the seriousness with which Zwingli and Calvin insisted on the singular clarity of these words. In doing so, they were no less certain and emphatic about the other aspect, that is, that the same Spirit who makes us certain of our justification also confronts us with the requirement of sanctification. The drive that the Reformed Poles seem to have felt to merge these two lines (although the dialectical turning still always comes at the last minute) points to the fact that the process whose beginnings we have already observed in Beza has advanced here. One was no longer quite sure of the point of departure of these two lines, of their original unity in God. And so, with growing zeal they had to seek them in the believing individual, because they certainly were necessary. Because they were Reformed, they could not easily get rid of their remembrance of the second line, that is, of the ethic that must be grounded on grace, as could the Lutherans with their doctrine of the primacy of faith. Since the picture of a free and autonomous act of God as the common source of both faith *and* obedience began to fade, grace merged into faith along Lutheran lines, in order there to be entangled as a Reformed necessity in a dialectic between believing and obeying that is now really unavoidable. It was *bound* to *obedience*. That 'justifying *faith*' [*fides* justificans] is bound to obedience goes without saying in Reformed thought. But that 'justification' [justificatio] here was bound to 'repentance' [resipiscentia] went too far, revealing even more clearly than we saw in Beza the corruption that had to surface on the Reformed side when one no longer really knew how to speak of *God* in Christianity when speaking of the religious *relationships*. When this was no longer known, then all these relationships necessarily had to collapse like so many bowling pins stood on their heads. This is made fatefully clear in the dreadful way in which the Thorn Declaration develops its doctrine of the certainty of salvation. What was still crystal clear for Calvin, and was still at least an open door through which Beza would constantly enter (and also constantly *exit*), appears here to be completely concealed. Like salvation itself, the *certainty* of salvation rests in *God*, who is the source of justification and sanctification. And, since it rests in *God*, it is truly the certainty of salvation, regardless of all the wanderings of our faith *and* our obedience. Since they no

longer dared to think this thought, since they now reckoned only with faith
and obedience—to put it sharply, since the atheism of modern piety was
already at the door—they taught a certainty of salvation that was in fact
the *un*certainty of salvation and that differs only terminologically from the
well-known views of the Roman Church on this matter. One could take the
Catholic approach and teach that no one could be certain of one's salvation
apart from "special revelation" ["specialis revelatio"].[304] Or one could take
the Polish-Reformed approach and teach that even the elect, should they
fall into sin against their conscience, are dependent upon a 'special grace
of God' [specialis Dei gratia].[305] One could say with the Catholics that all
must constantly doubt their gracious pardoning,[306] or one could say with
the Polish-Reformed that we can and must *strive* for the certainty of our
gracious pardoning our life long.[307] Regardless of which approach one
takes, there is no *decisive* difference here. Then one need only remember the
reassurance that Catholicism can place on the other side of the scale, the
constant availability of the church to administer its means of grace. Against
this option, the Reformed reference to our possible election really carries
no weight. Thus, this little excerpt reveals the disastrous and grave impoverishment of Protestantism over against the Roman Church, which sets in
at the very moment that it begins to lose sight of the 'salient point' [punc-
tum saliens] of its doctrine, which is not the immediacy of humans to God
but of God to humans. Obviously this impoverishment is neither typically
Polish-Reformed nor typically *Reformed* in general. Just as clear is the fact
that the presumptuous and artificial certainty of salvation claimed on the
other side, where one would not engage the dialectic of the concept of faith,
was no better than the *un*certainty of salvation openly admitted here. This
was how things had to proceed on the Reformed side, once they had got-
ten this far.

We turn now, in the conclusion of this section, to the confessions of what
is today *Great Britain*. They are of special interest for the question we are
pursuing because we are dealing here, at least initially, with an indigenous
form not only of the Reformed movement but of the Reformation in general. The inglorious initiator of the English Reformation was, as is well-
known, the cruel *Henry VIII*, who had made a name for himself as, among
other things, a literary opponent of Luther.[308] Under his successor *Edward
VI* and, following the Catholic interlude under bloody Mary, under *Elizabeth*, the English submitted themselves eclectically to all kinds of Conti-
nental influences: the Augsburg Confession, Calvin, Bucer, John a Lasco,[309]
all of which did not prevent them from going their own way. The results
of this first phase of development are found in the 42, later 39, *Articles* of
1552 and 1562. In the meantime, an articulate *Calvinism* had gained a hold
in Scotland and Ireland, documented for us by the *Scots Confession (Con-*

fessio Scotica) of 1562 and the *Irish Articles* of 1615. In a process influenced primarily by Scotland but supported and welcomed by the Christian party in England known as the Puritans, Calvinism triumphed in England and produced in the *Westminster Confession* of 1647 its own confession, in favor of which then the Scots and Irish set aside their own older documents.[310]

We shall begin with the pre-Calvinist *English Articles of 1552 and 1562*.[311] The first thing that claims our attention, after the articles on the Trinity, Christology, and the authority of Scripture, is Article 6 (=7),[312] entitled *"The Old Testament not rejected,"*[313] because, as the text explains, in both testaments eternal life through Christ is offered to humanity, and because it is an error to think that the Old Testament only contained temporal but no eternal promises. We shall see how the Scots Confession also took up from Calvin's Institutes and emphasized this conception that those who lived under the law are declared to be in essence Christians.[314] This appears to be a typical theme of the Anglo-Saxon Reformation. The consequence drawn from this insight by the English Articles is very categorical: No Christian is freed from obedience to the moral commandments of the Mosaic law.[315] Thus, just as our faith was already in force for those under the old covenant, their obedience is still in force for us. Article 9 (=10) supplements its denial of 'free will *after* the fall' [liberum arbitrium *post* lapsum] with the declaration that there is through Christ a 'preventing grace' [gratia praeveniens] "that we may have a good will" ["ut velimus"], and a 'cooperating grace' [gratia cooperans] "when we have that good will" ("dum volumus"), on the basis of which "good works" ["opera pietatis"] that are pleasing to God are possible.[316] Article 10 in the 1552 version was apparently written under the influence of Bucer[317]: The grace of Christ or the Holy Spirit takes away the stony heart and gives a heart of flesh, making us willing to do good and unwilling to do evil, without doing violence to our will. Thus, no one has an excuse if he sins, as though he were forced to do so and were not responsible for it. The 1562 version removed this article and put in its place Article 12 on good works. Good works are called the fruits of faith, having no reconciling power and not capable of enduring God's judgment but still pleasing to God and necessarily the result of a living faith, so that faith is discerned in them as is a tree in its fruit. Articles 14 and 15 (=15 and 16) reject a perfectionism that thinks that to be reborn is the same thing as to be without sin, and that wishes to see in a mortal sin committed after baptism the unforgivable sin against the Holy Spirit. No, it states, after receiving the Holy Spirit one can fall from grace and be received again into grace. What all of this might mean for the question of the certainty of salvation was as of yet no concern here. Especially characteristic of the certainty with which the English sought to walk along the edge of the abyss was Article 17 on predestination. The 1552 version specifically states, "The decrees of predestination are unknown to us."[318] The same mystery that serves the one as comfort and salvation is for the other the cause of despair or a carnal security. One should adhere then to that which is known and clear, God's promises and obedience to the will of God made known to us in Scripture. Article 18 then condemns those who assert that the only important thing in religion is that one should live according to the law and the "light of nature" ["lumen naturae"].[319] |

In contrast with the main teaching, which is expressly ethical and rather lightly evades any confrontation with the more complicated problems, the Anglican view of the *church* is remarkably isolated. It is essentially an *institution* whose hallmarks are described[320] with wording almost literally that of the Augsburg Confession,[321] while the unsettling reference back to predestination is carefully avoided. The church is "a witness and a keeper of holy writ,"[322] that is, bound to Holy Scripture but still having the right to establish its rites and to make decisions in faith controversies. 'Legitimate calling' [legitima vocatio] is necessary for ecclesial office, and this must take place through "men who have public authority given unto them."[323] In other words, ecclesial office only comes about through cooptation, practiced by a bishop who must himself have attained his office through legitimate means. There is no express reference in the Anglican Articles to the *apostolic succession* that this requires, but the Articles were interpreted in that way in the Acts of Uniformity of 1662.[324] The difference between the High Church and evangelical movements within the Church of England emerges at this point together with the issue of the significance of the *laying on of hands* in ordination (When one says "receive the Holy Spirit . . . !" is this an intercessory prayer or the actual mediation of the grace of the office?).[325] Article 33 [=34] expressly defends ecclesial traditions and ceremonies as long as they do *not contradict* the Word of God and are publicly instituted and acknowledged. Article 34 [=35] officially mandates a Book of Homilies, and Article 35 [=36] authorizes the famous Book of Common Prayer of 1550,[326] which contains the instructions for proper ordination. Whoever is ordained according to this book is a legitimate preacher. Worthy of mention is the proudly caesaro-papist Article 36 [=37]: "The King of England is the supreme head on earth, under Christ, of the Anglican and Irish Church."[327] We also note the solemn declaration in Article 37 [=38] that there is nothing to the idea that Christians hold their property in common, at least as far as the "right, title, and possession" of the same is concerned ("quoad ius et possessionem").[328]

The Anglican *Catechism* (M 522–525; 1549/1622)[328a] begins in this fashion: "What is your name?" "N. or M." "Who gave you this name?" "My Godfathers and Godmothers in my Baptism; wherein I was made a member of Christ, the child of God, and an inheritor of the kingdom of heaven." "What did your Godfathers and Godmothers then for you?" "They did promise and vow three things in my name. First, that I should renounce the devil and all his works. . . . Secondly, that I should believe all the Articles of the Christian Faith. And thirdly, that I should keep God's holy will and commandments."[328b] The four sections that then follow are in the sequence characteristic for Calvin: faith, law, the Lord's Prayer, and the sacraments. It would be difficult to sort out whether the High Church hierarchical tendency in Anglicanism should be regarded as original and essential or secondary. It is my impression that it is a matter of necessary compensation at the institutional level for a certain noticeable flatness of doctrine. In any event, the Calvinism that led later to more complicated and deeper doctrinal concepts automatically sets aside what one tends to regard as the Catholicizing tendency in the Anglican concept of the church.[329] It will suffice here to state that the problem of Anglican doctrine, which can be cleanly separated from its concept of the church, is the *ethical* issue, the unity of faith and obedience that is pursued in a process of uncertain groping between scholastic and spiritualistic concepts.

We now come to the *Scots Confession* of 1560.[331] Here another spirit, which is radical and aggressive, is blowing. It closes with the words, "Arise, O Lord, and let Thine enemies be confounded; | June 21[330] | let them flee from Thy presence that hate Thy godly Name. Give Thy servants strength to speak Thy word with boldness, and let all nations cleave to the true knowledge of Thee. Amen."[332] Bristly *John Knox*[333] and his friends are speaking here. But let us turn to the matter at hand. I have already noted that the Scots Confession, after the introductory articles about God, creation, original sin, and so on, immediately moves in Articles 4–5 to its view of the unity of the Old and New Testament revelation.[334] It begins at the point that God looks for Adam in the garden, continues in the promise given to him about the seed of the woman that will destroy the serpent's head, which has been believed by all the faithful from thence to Noah, Abraham, David, and up to the incarnation. All of these saw the day of Jesus Christ and rejoiced. Thus, God has at all times preserved, taught, increased, honored, and adorned his church, calling it from death to life, this church that as "the holy city,"[335] even though God has had to chastise it for its sin, has awaited the coming of the Messiah against all the deceptions and assaults of Satan. One can immediately see that the idea of the unity of Israel and Christendom, whose practical significance in the Anglican Articles was to assert the enduring validity of the Mosaic moral law, serves here the more heroic purpose of understanding Christendom as the direct continuation of the elect people, the "holy city" ["sancta civitas"] that cannot perish, led by God victoriously through the storms of history. *Predestination* is linked in an unusual way in Articles 7–8 of the Scots Confession with the *incarnation of Christ* grounded in God's eternal decree. It was because of God's *righteousness* that Christ had to be true *man*, and because of his *mercy* that he had to be true *God*. This is the only election that is spoken of here. The *Christology* (Articles 9–11) reaches its climax by looking toward the Lord's return to judge. The remembrance of him is the bridle with which we govern our passions, but also the "inestimable comfort" ["inaestimabilis [. . .] confirmatio"][336] that strengthens us to resist the threats of earthly princes, the terrors of mortality, and all other dangers that seek to separate us from fellowship with our Head and Mediator, who is none other than the Messiah promised to the fathers under the law. "To which honors and offices, if man or angel presume to intrude themselves, we utterly detest and abhor them, as blasphemous to our sovereign and supreme Governor, Christ Jesus."[337] |

The Scots Confession places emphatically at the center its view of the free and autonomous action of God over against which everything that happens in and through humanity appears as derivative and secondary. We are *created* by God the Father, *redeemed* by Jesus Christ, *reborn* and *sanctified* by the Holy Spirit. *Faith* (Article 12) and the *assurance* of faith do not arise from flesh and blood, not from a potential that is in us, not from "natural powers" ["potentia naturalis"],[338] but from the inspiration of the Holy Spirit. Without that we would remain eternal enemies of God and would not know Jesus Christ. By nature we are dead, blind, insensitive, so that even if one were to prick us with needles we would not notice it, nor would we see a light held before our eyes, and we would not agree to the will of God if it were directly revealed to us. The formation of faith within us through the Holy Spirit is nothing more or less than an awakening from the dead. God relates in the same creative and original way to the *sanctification* that follows after our faith. "Not even the smallest part" may be ascribed here to our merit,[339] either before or after regeneration. "[B]y ourselves we are not capable of thinking one good thought."[340] Rather, *he* who has *begun* the good work in us (in faith) will complete it (in sanctification), "to the glory and praise of *his* name."[341] It is remarkable that the doctrine of *justification* is never discussed in the Scots Confession (as far as I can see, the term "justification" ["justificatio"] never appears). The pronounced development of the typically Reformed concept of *faith*, where all the emphasis falls upon the *object* of faith so that what appears to be the object virtually becomes the *subject*—God and God alone creates faith through the Spirit—provides here a completely valid alternative for that which is lacking. Given its extraordinarily precise application of the Reformed method, it is impossible to speak here either of a separation of justification and sanctification or of a confusion of these two perspectives. The unity and distinctiveness of the religious and the ethical problems are as solid and certain as that of the second and third persons of the Trinity, whose works are recognized in them. One sees how independently and necessarily the grounding of *ethics* proceeds from the one overarching principle in

Article 13, "*Of the cause of good works.*" They have a "cause in us,"[342] it says, but this is not based in our freedom of the will but in the Spirit of Christ, who lives in our hearts through true faith, and to that extent faith gives good works. Persistent unworthiness can *therefore* not prove anything against true faith because it is simply the sign that such faith and the Holy Spirit are simply not present in such a person, not even a trace of them! Over against that, the presence of the Spirit and faith manifests itself in that the human is drawn into the conflict with himself, into the war between the Spirit and the flesh [see Gal. 5:16–17]. There, the serious fall of a Christian can only lead to a new arising in true repentance, not out of one's own power, of course, but in the power of Christ. It is the truest sign of the absence of the Spirit and of God when one does *not* stand in this conflict and does not need repentance. |

What then does *good* mean when we are speaking of good works? That is the question of Article 4, and its answer is, that which "in his law" ["lege lata"][343] God himself has commanded with respect to our stance *toward him* and our *neighbor.* True of both classes of commandments is that "both have the revealed will of God as their assurance."[344] There are no other grounds than revelation for that willing of the good, understood from the perspective of that which we ought to do. It is good because it wills what God wills. The evil is not only that which clearly battles against God's Word but also that which (especially in reference to piety and the service of God) has no other grounds than what humans think to be best. From the beginning, God has rejected and abhorred such works. Here we are dealing with one of the points that necessarily lead Anglo-Saxon Calvinism into conflict with Anglicanism. In Article 15, the *law* is defined as just, perfect, and capable of leading us to eternal salvation if we were to fulfill it. But our nature is depraved and weak, and it remains so after regeneration, so that it continues to be necessary for Christ to intervene for us as the one who fulfills the law. Whoever places his trust in his own works should know that he is boasting of something that is in fact nothing and that promotes idolatry. One should note that the problem of the *assurance of salvation* is resolved here by simply never posing it. The reason it is *not* raised is rooted in the matter itself. The question about what God desires and does dominates the foreground here, so that the other question about how the human attains salvation attains no independent significance. The third, insipid, question about how one can come to *know* with assurance that one is saved is completely deflated, so that it never finds utterance. |

Articles 16 and 18 on the *church* are just as assertive: Just as "firmly" ["firmissime"] as we believe in one God, Father, Son, and Holy Spirit, we believe in one *church,* which was, is, and will be until the end of the world, the "company of the chosen" ["coetus [. . .] electorum"],[345] which comprehends all the faithful of all times, peoples, and languages, founded by the

Father, the Son, and the Spirit in one person, "the communion, not of *profane* persons, but of *saints*,"[346] that is, of those who are citizens of the heavenly Jerusalem. Outside of it there is no life and no salvation. "Wholly and utterly" ["plane ex diametro"][347] are those renounced who say that one could be saved in every religion if one's life is right—this is a polemic that occurs in all the Anglo-Saxon confessions.[348] No, the Father's movement to the Son [see John 6:44] is decisive for salvation, and this constitutes the invisible church known only to God (for he alone knows whom he has elected), which comprehends *at once* those who have already died, those who live now and are struggling with Satan and sin, *and* the future elect. One should note how the religious relativism germinating from below, which first asserted itself strongly in England, is rebutted by a relativism from above. There is a criterion for salvation, the Scots Confessions avers, which cuts as a dividing line through all humanly visible distinctions. This criterion, however, is not human good behavior but divine election. |

But precisely *because* it is *God's* church, one cannot remain at its *mere* invisibility. In the world, God stands over against Satan, who since the very beginning (the names of Cain, Ishmael, Esau, the "priesthood of the Jews"[349] are given in a kind of sweeping summary) has attempted to pass off his pestilential synagogue as the church of God and to persecute and confuse the members of the *true* church of God. Therefore, it is necessary to make an external differentiation through visible signs between the church and the synagogue of the devil. Neither age nor majority is one of these signs. Cain was older than Abel, and the Pharisees had more disciples than Jesus Christ, but instead—and here the Calvinism of the Scots Confession becomes very concrete—the emphasis is on *"true* preaching" ["*vera* [. . .] praedicatio"], *"right* administration of the sacraments" ["*legitima* sacramentorum [. . .] administratio"), *"severe* observation" ["*severa* [. . .] observatio"] of church discipline.[350] Pay attention to the adjectives upon which everything depends: It is not the existence of the institution as such that is decisive, but that *what happens* in it is done 'truly' [vere], 'rightly' [legitime], and 'strictly' [severe]. The express emphasis here is not upon the universal church but upon the *particular* church, the Corinthian, the Galatian, the Ephesian, or then the Scottish. As long as the world lasts, the focus must be upon the particular church, and it must be ascertainable "beyond any doubt" ["procul dubio"] that "there . . . is the true Kirk of Christ,"[351] and 'there it is *not*' (ibi *non* est). Then Article 25 reminds us expressly that it is not the fact that one belongs to *this* visible 'company' [coetus] that thus makes one an elect member of Jesus Christ. Weeds and wheat grow up together there [see Matt. 13:24–30, 36–43]. One should not be surprised if many fall away, are hypocritical, or otherwise evidence a lack of steadfastness. The final judgment will bring the last decision.

It is truly regrettable that in the seventeenth century the Scots Confession became obsolete and today only has historical significance.[352] It receded as a result of the absorption of Scottish Calvinism into English Presbyterianism. The situation in regard to it is comparable to that of the Erlauthal Confession, although the Scotica is far superior by virtue of its unity and clarity. It allows one to study how Calvinist doctrine made its impact where it was reflected in a relatively coherent way in an independent and yet healthy national character. Here there was a certain naive and willing openness toward this doctrine's superiority; the necessary courage and defiance were there to make an unflinching confession to it, without the distortions caused by political maneuvering and, above all, without the distortions of theological subtlety and sickliness. The Reformed dialectic asserts itself here with clarity and consequence and yet with an undogmatic vitality. It is encountered in a variety of ways: God and the human, faith and repentance, invisible body of Christ and the combative Church of Scotland, ultimate decision and penultimate ambiguity (although not opaque in spite of its provisional character). Special attention should be given to the clear way in which an iron bracket holds together the gift of God and the task of life, without eventuating either into a mystical spiritualism or a rational moralism. Moreover, we note how clearly the meaning of the doctrine of predestination is handled: This doctrine treats of what God does, not what happens to the human person. Whoever notes and grasps this does not need to be warned about the danger of losing oneself in its mystery. And yet another point: We see how the unclassical problem of the assurance of salvation, this problem whose very *emergence* is an indicator of confusion and wrong questions, never commands any attention in this context. That is certainly the best thing that can happen to it. It is my opinion that, because of all of this, the Scots Confession, like few others, may speak to us as a normative and model confession for our pursuit of the question of the positive doctrine of Christianity. Zwingli's *Instruction*, Calvin's *Catechism of 1545*, the *Gallican Confession*, the *Heidelberg Catechism* with a few gentle reservations, and the *Scots Confession*—whoever knows these five can form an accurate picture of what the early Reformed intended. All the rest are repetitions and variations, and when variations, often departures from the main tradition that then easily lead astray.

Before we turn in conclusion to the great document of English Presbyterianism, the Westminster Confession, we shall consider briefly a second British document of a relatively pure Calvinism, the *Irish Articles* of 1615, written by Archbishop Ussher (M 526–39).[353] Its placement of the doctrine of predestination toward the beginning puts it at a later time with its more systematic theological thinking, which is not necessarily an advance in meaningful knowledge. This is an approach that, as logical as it appears, is completely opposed by Calvin's model. This critical principle overarching all of doctrine becomes here a first truth in and of itself, which understandably attracts all attention and evokes questions that cannot promote the understanding of the whole. Ussher thinks of the making of the divine decree of salvation, following the model of Bullinger and Jud, in the form of a double covenant between God and humans, the two *"covenants"*[354] of law and grace, the first made with Adam in paradise and the second made in Christ with humanity. Note that although Ussher will later emphasize in Articles 81–84 the unity of the Old and New Testaments, we see here how Calvin's view of the *one* church of God from the beginning of the world on, which we just encountered in the Scots Confession, begins to disintegrate. Cocceius developed this differentiation even further, making it into the basic perspective of his doctrine, and thus earned the dubious credit for having introduced the idea of a *temporal history of salvation* into theology.[355] Aside from this, the Irish Articles offer a rather correct Calvinism and in their own way provide an overview of Reformed intention. Articles 31–33 speak in general of the *communicating of the grace of Christ*. The elect are in an inseparable unity with Christ through the real and vital "influence"[356] of the Holy Spirit, which proceeds from him into all the proper members of his mysterious body and makes them into participants in all his benefits. This view—we encountered it also in Beza[357]—is more strongly emphasized in Calvin's Institutes and in his sermons[358] than is generally known. The mystical drive, which was very strong in Calvin but could not find expression in his concept of faith, was satisfied here at a higher level, the superior level of grace itself, flowing out of justification and sanctification. In these statements, Ussher proves himself to be a good student of Calvin. |

Articles 34–38 develop the doctrine of *justification and faith*. It is rigorously forensic. Righteousness is Christ's righteousness. Faith grasps it. Faith alone. To be sure, it will never be alone, never without contrition, hope, and love. However, that we have contrition, hope, love, or even faith does not justify us, for faith is given to us by God and is based upon the mercies of God. Ussher emphasizes that faith is not the affirmation of the articles of the Christian religion or a general persuasion of the truth of the Word of God. Instead, it is a special and individual appropriation of the promises of the gospel, a serious trusting in God. Thus, Ussher thinks, the believer is *assured* with the *assurance* of his faith, of the forgiveness of sins, and of eternal salvation. There is a particular emphasis then in Article 38: A truly vital justification faith and the Spirit of sanctification cannot be erased and reduced to nothing in a reborn person, either finally or completely. Thus, the question of assurance is answered, but not very persuasively, in the context of a presentation of what is true faith, which is actually a rather lovely and edifying psychological argument. To couple this assurance with the condition that these elements of the beautiful and edifying should be present is precisely what ought not to have happened. But if the questions are asked in this way, then these answers are unavoidable. Articles 39–45 treat of *sanctification and good works*. "All that are justified are likewise sanctified."[359] Faith is necessarily accompanied by repentance and good works. Repentance is a gift of God, good works are in the same sense the fruit of faith that cannot assure us of our right before God but do find God's free pleasure, just as they proceed necessarily from a living faith. Their rule is the Word of God. Even if the reborn person cannot perfectly fulfill the law of God, he may never regard his sin as the unforgivable sin against the Holy Spirit. There is always room reserved for his repentance. Good works aside from God's commandment are nothing more than arrogance and godlessness. Articles 68–74 unfold the doctrine of the *church*, in which the proximity of Anglicanism is felt in the strong emphasis upon the ecclesial office of the "minister." Aside from this last point, the dominant role played by Calvinist thought in this confession reveals the intellectual force that strictly Reformed thought had accumulated before the Revolution in the island kingdom. The Puritans in England were moving in this direction, and thus the Anglican position was becoming ripe for attack.

The *Westminster Confession* (Confessio Westmonasteriensis), together with the *Larger* and *Shorter Westminster Catechisms*[361]—all from 1647[362]—is not only important as the documentation of the establishment of Calvinism in England. It is, with certain changes, not only still standard for all of the so-called Presbyterian English-speaking churches on both sides of the Atlantic; it is also the codification of triumphal Calvinism in general. One must turn to the Westminster Confession not only to learn the original intention of the Reformed movement but also the form in which this movement as Calvinism has conquered the politically (if not the intellectually) dominant part of the Protestant world, and of the Christian world in general. In this sense, it belongs to those documents that must be regarded as essential for any relatively adequate knowledge of the Reformed confessions. No other Reformed confessional document was worked on as long and as carefully (three to four years, based on how one counts), with the possible exception of Bullinger's Second Helvetic Confession. Every phrase, every Bible citation, is introduced consciously and with deliberation. It is entirely justifiable for us to submit the final product to a thorough investigation. But this final product is a tragedy. It can only show us how Calvinism's triumph was its death. The consequences were never good ones when Christianity conquered the world. The actual significance of such a movement was that it was conquered by the world. Our discussion up to now has prepared us to see that this was the outcome at which Calvinism had to arrive. How it actually happened is *what* this document

June 22

of triumphant Calvinism ultimately documents. Only in *this* sense do I want to understand its position in relation to the five documents we discussed yesterday. |

The positioning of the *doctrine of predestination* at the *head* of the system has been firmly established.[363] In terms of its results, it is certainly correct to characterize this doctrine as the central Reformed doctrine.[364] But one should not forget in the process that it does not appear in Calvin until the third book in chapter 18,[365] where it functioned originally as only a means to greater precision and certainty. The one God is "infinite in being and perfection (reality and worth), a most pure spirit," "incomprehensible," "most free, most absolute,"[366] bringing about all things according to the decision of his immutable and righteous will to his own glory. His glory does not need any of the creatures made by him; rather, he manifests himself in them, by them, unto them, and upon them. He is the "alone fountain of all being"[367]; there is nothing accidental for him (nothing "contingent"[368]), and also nothing uncertain. Whatever obedience he might require of humans, angels, and all other creatures is his *right* to require. One must say that all of this is well formulated and awakens great expectations for what is to follow. The disappointment is quick to come, unfortunately. But let us listen to more: God is therefore not the source of evil, for he leaves to the creatures their creaturely will. The freedom or contingency of "second causes" ["causae secundae"][369] is not abrogated by his freedom but rather established by it. To the manifestation of his glory he has determined some people and angels for eternal life and others to eternal death, both in a definite number that can neither be increased nor diminished, in such a way that no cause or condition present in the creatures could determine them for the one or the other. This is not 'foreseeing' [praevisio] but 'predestination' [praedestinatio] in the strict sense.[370] Effective calling, justification, acceptance, and sanctification are thus only to be understood as the implications of election. Why this doctrine? The answer says expressly that the people who attend to the revelation and become obedient to it "*may, from the certainty of their effectual vocation, be assured of their eternal election*" (M 552,38 [–41]).[370a] It is for his own sake, then, that the religious person makes this highest statement about God; in order to escape the paradox of one's existence, the human transfers it into God. This intention of *reassurance*, which is profoundly pietistic and egotistic, is the worm in the timberwork, not the doctrine itself! The *human* created by God carries the divine law, the "light of nature" ["lumen naturae"] (chapter 1),[371] written in his heart, but "under a possibility of transgressing."[372] Obedience would mean salvation, fellowship with God, and dominion over all creatures. |

The general concept for the relationship between God and the world, which is thus superior to predestination, is *providence*. It requires that in the observation of all things one distinguish between the *"first causes"* [*"causae primae"*] and the contingent and natural *"second causes"* [*"causae secundae"*][373] that are not to be excluded but to which God for his part is not bound but is rather capable of acting in an extraordinary fashion 'above' [supra] or 'against' [contra] them. Divine providence extends over Adam's fall in sin just as it does over all the individual sins of humans and angels, not as mere "permission" ["permissio"] but as real "governing" ["gubernatio"] and "dispensation" ["dispensatio"],[374] except that the evil of such deeds does not derive from God but from the creature. In his hands, the same means can serve to strengthen the elect in faith and the rejected in their impenitence, and to that extent a distinction must be made between the general providence of God and that *special* providence which is directed toward the church. All of this would have been quite good and astute—Thomas Aquinas had already said it all[375]—if only they had not then proceeded to think of the God of revelation in analogy to the order of the world and nature as known to humanity, to derive the given from the nongiven in continuity. The concept 'cause' [causa] betrays this in spite of the distinction between 'first cause' [causa prima] and 'second cause' [causa secunda]. The God of revelation is the creator, the pure origin, not the 'first cause' [prima causa] of the world. In the Westminster Confession, the safeguards against this dangerous use of analogy are still present. But the moment could come in which this analogy would gain a terribly independent significance, and the skilled apologist could then dare to make God plausible to the erudite among religion's despisers by using the name 'Universal' [Universum].[376] The development anticipated here is closely related to the abuse of the doctrine of predestination for the purpose of gaining personal assurance of salvation. I spoke of this already when we were discussing Beza.[377] When the question of human *salvation* becomes the decisive perspective in Christianity, then it should be no surprise when also the question of human *truth* becomes decisive in an immodest and irrelevant way. |

Chapter 7 develops the *concept of covenant* after the pattern already known to us in the Irish Articles. So great is "the distance between God and the creature"[378] that even rational creatures could have nothing in common with the Creator without a special "condescension" ["condescentio"][379] of the Creator to them. The legal covenant made with Adam is invalid from the outset because of the fall into sin that preceded it(!). (One should note how here the attempt to develop a temporal history of salvation becomes entangled in difficulties at the first step. With the presupposition of the fall into sin, there is only *one* conceivable step forward, namely, the foundational one that abrogates the fall into sin. A developmental history *based* on the fall, regardless of how many steps it were thought to have, does *not* lead to this goal. If law and grace are separated temporally, which Calvin would not have allowed, then it is impossible to assert that the law in and of itself is a stage of *revelation*. (How should one conceive of a revelation that is ineffective from the outset, other than that it is *not* a revelation?) But grace itself, separated from the law and asserted as revelation, appears in a strange way to require more to make it effective. (*This* view of really effective revelation cannot succeed without the contribution of rational humanity!)[379a] This second, effective 'condescension' [condescentio] of God is then the "covenant of grace" ["foedus gratiae"].[380] The Westminster Confession remedies the problem by ascribing to this second covenant retroactive power. It was already present under the covenant of law in the promises, prophecies, sacrifices, examples, and so forth, that by the power of the Holy Spirit assured the elect about the coming Messiah and the forgiveness of sins. Thus, the unity of revelation, that unity that comprehends all time as well as the unity of law and grace, is saved for the moment. But what other outcome can there be than that this distinction of that special 'covenant of law' [foedus legis] should be represented as superfluous? What is spoken of as the progress of the new over against the old covenant, the new "ordinance" ["ratio"][381] in which the covenant is established in the New Testament—namely, preaching and the new sacraments that are praised as simpler and yet more efficacious, and the extension of revelation to all peoples—all that can really not suffice as the grounds for a fundamental distinction. The chapter closes then with the statement, "*There are not, therefore, two covenants of grace* differing in substance, but *one and the same under various dispensations.*"[382] They were at a crossroads. If they were serious about this "one and the same" ["unum idemque"], then the differentiation of a sequence of stages of divine instructions would have to be taken up and then dropped as an unnecessary terminological game. If they *fell* for the "*under various dispensations*" ["*non uno modo dispensatum*"], that is, if they took the historical appearance more seriously than that which was really appearing, then revelation would be dissolved into the history of religions, and that would entail the most serious practical consequences in the destruction of the unity of law and grace. In the Westminster Confession, the issue is walking on the razor's edge. The following generations opted for the unhappy second possibility. We are plagued by this up to today.

Chapter 9 develops the following view of *free will*. The human as he was created by God has a truly free will, that is, predisposed neither toward good nor evil. Through the fall of sin, he has lost the freedom toward the good to such an extent that he can neither convert himself nor prepare himself for grace. Through grace the human becomes capable again of desiring and doing "the spiritually good" ["spirituale bonum"].[383] But because of the remaining "corruption" ["corruptio"][384] of his nature, he cannot desire it perfectly but only in combination with evil. The human only attains to the perfect and unchangeable free willing of the good in the "state of glory" ["status gloriae"].[385] One should note here the intrusion of an historico-psychological way of looking at things. The situation is clear in Luther and Calvin: Either the human will is free or not free, and the unambiguous decision is that it is *not* free.[386] In Bullinger and Beza we encountered the thesis that the human receives free will again in rebirth.[387] But there is *no* further haggling over this point, regardless of the problem of real experience that emerges. In this affirmation, the basic issue is the wonder of God, and it is absolutely clear that this wonder can rightly persist in all its fullness even if all of experience should speak against it. It is, however, apparent that grace with its gift is drawn here into the territory of experience and psychologized. This grace then is capable of restoring to the human a certain kind of free will. But it is only an imperfect free will that must await the final entry into the "state of glory" [status gloriae]. There is a precise parallel in all of this to that first covenant of God with man in the revelation of the law, which doesn't help that much, unfortunately, because the misfortune that it has to overcome is too great. What kind of covenant is it that fails in this fashion? The covenant *of God*? What kind of grace is it that accomplishes so little? The grace *of God*? What might be the character of this 'state of glory' [status gloriae] that is drawn in at the end as deus ex machina, wherever it may come from? Is there not reason to suspect that the state of this promised freedom even at this third stage might be very relative? This is how it proceeds, how it *must* proceed when Christian doctrine is no longer quite certain of its subject, of the *divine* subject in Christianity, so that in spite of all monergistic assertions it must degenerate into the description of possible human relationships to this subject. I

And now, listen to the titles of chapters 10–20: "Of Effectual Calling," "Of Justification," "Of Adoption," "Of Sanctification," "Of Saving Faith," "Of Repentance unto Life," "Of Good Works," "Of the Perseverance of the Saints," "Of the Assurance of Grace and Salvation," "Of the Law of God," "Of Christian Liberty." What is all of this when we take it as a *whole*? It appears to be precisely what is called in dogmatics of that period and thereafter the "*order of salvation*" ("*ordo salutis*").[388] It describes the way of salvation, the process of appropriation and the effect of revelation as it takes place over time in the believing individual; it is thus a religious psychology arranged from the perspective of temporal-biographical sequence or phases of Christian experience. And what does it signify? Just as, in chapters 2–5, the intentionality of the Creator God has its analogy in the legal regularity of world and natural history, so apparently here the action of the Redeemer God has its analogy in the temporal sequence of religious processes, in the continuity of the reflexes of the revelation of grace in the soul of the human person. The objective content of the doctrines, which is not yet forgotten and cannot be repressed, makes it extremely difficult to work out an understandable exposition of the thinking all along the line. The description of the phases is for that reason still rather clumsy and unilluminating because the heyday of the exploration of spiritual and psychological experience had not yet emerged at that time. But even so, this scheme comes across as much more refined than the naive outline of the Heidelberg Catechism, "Misery–Redemption– Thanksgiving," or the description of the Christian struggle with temptation that Beza offered as the scheme of his soteriological doctrine! It is no longer merely the classical 'way of Luther' [Via Lutheri].[389] No longer is a single psychological moment identified and placed at the center, a procedure that certainly lends Beza's confession a certain edifying vitality and actuality, regardless of the reservations one might have about it. Instead, now, it appears that what happens when one becomes a Christian and persists as one shall be *demonstrated*. This may not be that successful in the details, but the meaning and intention of the whole thing is certainly clear. The earthly analogy of the divine action now begins to become important and interesting. The dark night of objectivism in which the Reformers, under the weight of the medieval tradition, had still remarkably enough remained, now begins to *fade*, and gradually, from very far away, the pleasant morning of that day dawns on which Schleiermacher, that self-styled "Moravian of a higher order,"[390] will discover, as the actual finisher of the work begun by Luther, that the essence of theology is the analysis of the pious self-consciousness.[391] This will be the day on which the Erlangen theologian Hofmann[392] will compose the statement that defines at least two centuries of theology: "I, the Christian, am the most appropriate content of my science as a theologian."[393] |

Let us then examine the details. The problem that preoccupied the Westminster theologians under the title, *"Of Effectual Calling"* [*"De vocatione efficaci"*][394] was again the relationship of grace that calls, whose sole power they wanted to assert, to the spontaneous experience of grace on the part of the person called, which they *also* wanted to assert, in total correspondence to the relationship between 'first cause' [causa prima] and 'second causes' [causae secundae] in the doctrine of God. Their solution was to assert both: Man is "altogether passive therein"[395] and yet moves toward grace "freely" ["liberrime"].[396] The resolution of the riddle comes at the point where this asserted passivity moves over into willingness, where man is quickened and renewed by the Holy Spirit. What is this asserted passivity, and what is the willingness that follows after it, and above all, what are the quickening and renewing that lead from the one to the other possibility if the riddle is so easily resolved, simply through this distribution into a temporal sequence? *Justification* is initially defined in a thoroughly forensic way as the forgiveness of sins, the 'accounting' [reputatio] and 'accepting' [acceptatio] of persons "as righteous" ["pro justis"],[397] the imputation not of their act of faith nor their new obedience but only of the merit of Christ for righteousness. The faith that lays hold of justification cannot remain empty and be a dead faith. This is the well-known correct transition to sanctification of which we shall speak later. What then is the meaning of the statement that the justification of the elect is decreed by God from eternity but that the elect *are not justified* until "in due time" ["tempore [. . .] opportuno"][398] the *'act'* [*actus*] of justification takes place through the Holy Spirit? Is justification a temporal 'act' [actus]? Is it consequent and credible when then the assurance is made that one cannot fall out of the status of justification once it is attained? Why not? That which begins in time stands under the compelling suspicion that it can also end in time! The Westminster Confession then inserts between justification and sanctification a special *"grace of adoption"* [*"gratia adoptionis"*],[399] and understands this to be reception into the number of the children of God, entry into this promised possession, access to the throne of God, the possibility of calling God "Abba, Father!" to participate in his mercy and providence, and so on—all things that, of course, the old Reformed confessions knew. Is it then a coincidence that they did not make an article of faith out of them, that is, out of the religious possessions as such, but rather that they moved from[400] the description of the divine gift, which contains everything, directly and immediately to the task assigned to man? From the old Reformed perspective in which to think of 'grace' [gratia] always meant to think of God, this was the only possible option. At the moment in which the person who has received grace begins to focus his interest on himself, this swift transition had to become problematic. In accordance with the sequence of human emotions, a reflective passage had to intervene now in which the grace of justification, rather than becoming immediately active as the grace of sanctification, had to be examined and enjoyed for a while as the "grace of adoption" ["gratia adoptionis"].[401] |

Sanctification follows then as a second step. It is affirmed with strong language as inseparable from effectual calling. It is defined as universal, comprehending the entire person, but in this life it is imperfect and leads only into the struggle between flesh and spirit. Yes, man's residual "corruption" ["corruptio"] can "for a time" ["aliquandiu"] prevail, but there remains a "regenerate part" ["pars regenita"][402] in man, thanks to the Spirit of Christ that continually provides help, and this part escapes victoriously so that growth in grace does not cease.[403] But is not sanctification here confused with holiness? It is clear that there is growth in 'holiness' [sanctitas], but is there in 'sanctification' [sanctificatio] through the Holy Spirit? What should we think of the statement that *"sanctification* is . . . *imperfect"* [*sanctificatio* [. . .] est *imperfecta"*],[404] and what are we to imagine the "regenerate part" ["pars regenita"] in man to be? Is regeneration a larger or smaller quantity?

June 26

And if we are to think about holiness, why is there no discussion here of repentance and obedience? Is this not a concealed naturalism when one speaks of "sanctification" (='holiness' [sanctitas]), of which there can be more or less, as something that happens to a person without setting that person back on his feet? In what follows, the attempt is made to work out this side of the matter in that the things that mainly happen to man ('vocation,' 'justification,' 'adoption,' 'sanctification' [vocatio, justificatio, adoptio, sanctificatio])[405] are followed by those things that are to be understood mainly as man's spontaneous action. First, there is *faith*. The terminology used, the *"grace* of faith" ["*gratia* fidei"],[406] is properly Reformed. Faith is the work of the Holy Spirit, accomplished (at least "ordinarily" ["plerumque"][407]) by the effect of Word and sacrament. But here we find again this quantitative perspective. Faith can be "different in degrees, weak or strong"[408] and still remain victorious, even growing in many into a "full assurance" ["plena [. . .] certitudo"].[409] This is quite right, seen psychologically! But is that the *"saving* faith" ["fides *salvifica*"][410] of which the title speaks? Is it not just as strong, regardless whether, psychologically, it is present as "full assurance" ["plena certitudo"] or only as large as a mustard seed? Can the *"grace* of faith" ["*gratia* fidei"] be larger or smaller? There follows then the extensive treatment of the doctrine of *"repentance unto life"* ["*resipiscentia ad vitam*"], the conversion to life, apparently as the supplement to the doctrine of sanctification. It too is defined as "grace" ["gratia"].[411] This is a good reminder of original Reformed intentions. But it does not become fruitful. For this 'grace of repentance' [gratia resipiscientiae] is then described as moralistically and methodologically as was the previous 'grace of santification' [gratia sanctificationis] naturalistically. To be sure, the sinner repents and converts, and it is certainly affirmed that without doing so he does not receive forgiveness. Both private and public confession is recommended. But it is not clear at all to what extent any of this is necessary. Apparently the only reasoning here is again that this side of things corresponds to experience. This means that the original unity in which the original Reformed dogma defined repentance and sanctification as human question and divine answer is no longer understood here. Thus, even though the dogma is formulated correctly and completely, and appears to have been enriched, it is actually in a process of hidden deterioration. |

Speaking of *good works* [chap. 16] the correct statement is made that they are good to the extent that they correspond to God's commandments. They serve to express the thankfulness of believers, to increase their assurance of salvation, to edify fellow humans, and to glorify God. There is no obligatory perfection, no merit for the attainment of the forgiveness of sins, not even through our best works. Even though our deed is mixed with our weakness, it is acceptable to God in Christ and worthy of reward. Thus far it is quite good, but it is then strange when the well-known doctrine that the Holy Spirit effects good works in the believers is supplemented with the statement that "besides the graces they have already received" there must be in addition "an actual influence of the same Holy Spirit,"[412] so that both good willing and doing might result. Then they should not wait for this special awakening by the Holy Spirit but should make the effort to awaken the grace that is already in them. Again, this is not a bad psychological description, but how does this description and its consequence (as it was in the Thorn Declaration[413]), this doctrine of an "infused grace" ["gratia infusa"], get into the Reformed confession? How strange as well is the precise description of the good works of those not yet regenerated! There can be those who formally conform to the commandments of God and are useful to themselves and others. But they do not serve to glorify God, and in spite of everything they are sinners, and they cannot be acceptable to God. Of course, if they did *not* do such works, they would sin *even more* gravely and they would offend God *even more* profoundly. Such casuistic hair-splitting must result from this increasing concentration of the focus upon the religious subject. |

The sections on the *perseverance of the saints* [perseverantia] and the *assurance of grace and salvation* show why the English were so interested in the doctrine of predestination that they placed a very pointed formulation of it at the head of their confession. These chapters 17–18 are truly a fortress of religious security based here on the consciousness of election, since neither the Catholic option of basing it on the church nor the Lutheran option of basing it on faith alone was possible. The "absolute decree" [decretum absolutum],[414] a concept with which the fathers at one time sought to secure the knowledge of *God's* freedom and majesty, has degenerated here into a proposition intended rather to provide the Presbyterian *Christian* an unshakeable freedom and majesty that enables him to navigate with the necessary insouciance through the vicissitudes of sinful earthly life. Those who have been accepted cannot fall finally and totally out of the "state of grace" ["status gratiae"][415] but will instead persevere until the end and attain to eternal life. The certainty and infallibility of this perseverance results from the "immutability" ["immutabilitas"][416] of the election decree, from the effectuality of Christ's intervention for them, from the Spirit and seed of God that remains in them, and from the total nature of the covenant of grace. Grave sins are possible, and they may result in God's wrath, the grieving of the Spirit, "to a certain point and a few degrees"[417] the loss of his graces and consolations, a wounded conscience, and temporal punishments. But (although there is also a hypocritical or imagined assurance) those who believe in the Lord Jesus, who love him truly and attempt to live before him with a pure conscience, can attain the certainty that they are in the state of grace. This certainty is not a mere presumption but an "infallible assurance of faith" ["infallibilis [. . .] fidei certitudo"],[418] based upon the truth of divine promises, upon the grace through which the promises receive "inward evidence" ["interna evidentia"],[419] and finally upon the testimony of the Holy Spirit. But each one should endeavor to "make sure" ["certam facere"][420](!) his calling and election through peace and joy in the Holy Spirit, through love and thankfulness toward God and through deeds of obedience. Even if this assurance can still be shaken, it cannot be taken away from the Christian nor be changed into despair. Here again, one can only say that this is all said well, astutely, and judiciously, and even affirm that it is all true. But how remarkably the believing confession of the great deeds of God has become here an almost technical instruction for the assurance that man will be saved! It is an assurance that apparently requires so much verbiage because something about it is not quite right. Within the Reformed context of thought, the inseparable unity of faith and obedience asserts itself even here, and it introduces a pervasive element of disquiet into the peace of this assurance, so that a "making sure" ["certam facere"] has to be added to the "infallible certitude" ["certitudo infallibilis"]. No 'making sure' [certam facere] can even approach the founding of 'certitude' [certitudo] in election, promise, the testimony of the Spirit, and so on. Here the fact that one is Reformed and not Lutheran or Catholic revenges itself, precisely where one would so much like to have what the others so splendidly have, each in his own way! It must be acknowledged that the English of the seventeenth century understood in a masterful and successful way how to struggle with this Reformed difficulty, and to a certain degree they came to terms with it.

It is characteristically Reformed that the 'order of salvation' [ordo salutis] of the Westminster Confession now reaches its climax and concludes in the chapters *on the law* and *on Christian liberty* [chap. 19–20] leading immediately to chapter 21, which addresses "*Religious Worship* and the *Sabbath-day*" ["De *cultu religioso* et de *Sabbato*"].[421] This is the classically Calvinist conceptual sequence: from faith to the law to the worship of God. But in classical Calvinism, everything is related to the knowing of God, to God's giving, commanding, leading, and ordaining, whereas here the theme is the human person in his receiving and having, accomplishing and presenting. In *this* context, as was already the case in the doctrine of 'repentance' [resipiscentia], it is unavoidable that the Reformed turn to ethics takes on a moralistic and legalistic appearance. God established the covenant of the law with Adam, in which he committed his law to him to be observed personally, totally, and carefully. After the fall, the law did not cease to be the perfect rule of righteousness. Because God is its originator, the Mosaic moral law obligates all people, including the nonjustified, to continuous obedience. Conversely, the justified also stand under the covenant of the law, even if not under the law itself. That means, the law is of "*great use*" ["*vehementer utilis*"][422](!) to them as revelation of the divine will, for the knowledge of sin and self, for their preservation in the fear of God that seeks his mercy, and finally for the sake of the promises of the law. There can be no conflict between the law and the gospel because the gospel causes them to do voluntarily what the law demands. This is all well and good, but neither Zwingli nor Calvin found it necessary to argue the believers' obedience of the law with the assertion that it was "of great use" ["vehementer utilis"] to them. Can it then be surprising that an obedience argued this way comes at least dangerously near to moralistic superficiality? In the chapter on Christian liberty, there is the fine statement, "God alone is lord of the conscience."[423] The meaning of Christian liberty is also well formulated in its statement, "[D]elivered out of the hands of our enemies, we might serve the Lord without fear in holiness and righteousness all the days of our life."[424] But what follows is an abrupt break in the content, in that Christian liberty may not be abused as a pretext for the overthrow of civil or, more importantly, of *ecclesiastical* ordinances or even to disseminate erroneous opinions. Constantly, both here and in what follows, the "light of nature" ["lumen naturae"][425] is appealed to as the first lawgiver, on whose authority rests ecclesiastical order, the service of worship, and the sanctification of the Sabbath. |

The Sabbath command in particular is traced back to the "law of nature" ["lex naturae"],[426] which calls for a certain time for the worship of God. Through God's "positive, moral, and perpetual commandment,"[427] the seventh day is set apart for that purpose, which is then transferred to Sunday, which is to be celebrated "to the end of the world, as the Christian Sabbath."[428] One should prepare for it inwardly and observe it with the greatest possible abstention from all activities, including amusing entertainment, focusing instead on the service of worship and works of mercy. We have here the famous, allegedly Calvinist[429] but in reality English Presbyterian, sanctification of the Sabbath in its authoritative expression.[430] It differs from Calvin's thought on this point not only positively through the weight it places upon the day and the seventh day (which Calvin expressly rejected),[431] and not only through the rigorism with which resting on Sunday is emphasized, but also negatively through the absence (1) of the reference to the eternal Sabbath of rest from our own works so that God might work in us, and (2) the social argument for Sunday rest in view of the working classes. |

The doctrine of *the church and the communion of saints* contained in chapters 25–26 strongly emphasizes the catholicity and universality of the visible church, with Christ's provision of its "ministry, oracles, and ordinances of God,"[432] the latter referring to the sacraments. Its visibility is here more and there less pronounced depending upon the greater or lesser purity with which in the particular churches the gospel is preached, the sacraments administered, and public worship celebrated. Church discipline *is lacking* here among the marks of the true church, although in chapter 30 it is foreseen and instituted. Instead, it is expressly stated that the purest church can become the synagogue of Satan, and to ensure that one knows what is meant, a special paragraph explains that the Roman pope is the antichrist, the man of sin and perdition according to 2 Thess. 2[:3–8].[433] In the doctrine of the communion of the saints, the aspect of the society is especially underlined and the church described as an association whose members are obligated to provide each other help in external matters.[433a] This fraternal fellowship, however, must extend itself to include all who call upon the name of Jesus, as far as God provides the "opportunity" ["opportunitas"] for it.[434] The conclusion discloses that this was not meant in an enthusiastic sense and that this Christian idealism has both feet on the ground in that it follows the Anglican Articles in rejecting the unsettling misunderstanding that through this ideal fellowship of Christians the private right to property and possessions might be abrogated or even infringed upon.[435]

Next to the *Westminster Confession*, it is worthwhile also to look briefly at the two Presbyterian *catechisms* in the same year, which are distinguished as the Larger and Shorter Westminster Catechisms.[436] They make even clearer the broad lines of the structure of the concept of Christianity with which we are dealing here. The first question asks in a thoroughly Calvinist way: What is the chief and highest end of man? And the answer is, at least, exactly one-half Calvinist: To glorify God and fully to enjoy him forever. But then [in the Larger Catechism] there follows in a very un-Calvinist way the foolish second question, "How doth it appear that there is a God?" The answer: The "light of nature" in man and the works of God reveal "plainly" ["luculenter"] that there is a God, but sufficiently and effectually for salvation this happens through his Word and his Spirit.[437] Then, after a few questions about the Scriptures, Question 5 asks what the Scriptures principally teach. The answer: What man is to *believe about God* and the *duties God* requires of man.[438] The two first Calvinist categories dominate this otherwise barren field completely. One should compare this with the truly catechical *questions* posed by Calvin, formulated conversationally with all kinds of variations but always aiming at a living knowledge. Here, in a monotonous and brusque way, the Westminster Catechism asks "What is? What should? What has God said, ordered, commanded?" The entire thing, including the first part, has truly become a book of laws with innumerable sections. The arrangement in detail, aside from this significant division into two parts, is almost that of the Confession. Here, as well, after a few questions about God and the Trinity, double predestination is placed at the head. By contrast, the doctrine of the church follows here immediately after Christology. In response to Question 62, the visible church is the "society" ["societas"][439] consisting of all those in all regions of the world and all ages who confess the true religion, including their children. It is remarkable that the invisible church is spoken of only *after* the visible and thus shifts into the background. Then follows the well-known sequence of the stages of experience, cresting in the doctrine of the assurance of salvation, except that faith stands after justification, which is appropriate. There is a further enrichment in the fact that all those elements that refer to the blessed enjoyment of God and his gifts are removed from the doctrine of "adoption" ["adoptio"][440] and made, under the title "communion in glory" ["communio gloriae"],[441] into the crown of the entire thing, placed above the assurance of salvation. What was moving and preoccupying the Westminster theologians is truly palpable here. Then, under the title "duties," follow the Decalogue, the sacraments, and the Lord's Prayer. It must certainly have made an impression upon the children when they learned in connection with the Sabbath command that, since all work and worldly pleasures were forbidden on Sunday, they would have to find their delight in spending all the time thus made free in public and household worship services![442]

Let us now attempt to summarize the findings of this section. We have been asking about the positive Reformed doctrine of Christianity, and what appears to be a very diverse series of answers has

June 28

paraded before us. It both appears to be and is a long way from the clear and sensible Zwingli to a Beza who is aroused in every fiber of his refined and cultivated soul, from the Bern Synod's undaunted trust in the regenerating power of the Spirit to the starchy Pharisaical confidence with which the pious Puritans of whom we just spoke assured themselves of their eternal salvation, their morality, and also of course their private property, from Bullinger's noble humanism to the Old Testament prophetic speech of John Knox—and how much separates all of them, and for the most part unfavorably, from their master in Geneva! It would not be helpful to try to arrange groups and types here. Confessions that are similar in one respect diverge from each other all the more in another respect. One could engage in eternal comparing and typing, but it would always be arbitrary and coincidental. Perhaps, however, if in spite of all these differences *one thing* is *the same* in all these documents, then one can pay attention to the movement in which the formulation of this one thing has taken place. There really can be no doubt that there is truly *one thing* that is the *same* in all these documents, something that forms them all as a unity over against the Augsburg Confession, that makes them into characteristically *Reformed* confessions. This one thing is, of course, the understanding of Christianity as the connection, grounded in God and effected in humans, of the invisible divine truth of life and the visible renewal of human life, of divine turning and human converting, of the knowledge of God and self, of New Testament and Old Testament revelation, of gift and task, of justification and rebirth, of covenant of grace and covenant of law, of faith and duty (Westminster Catechism), or however else it may be phrased. This *connection* is the positive Reformed doctrine of Christianity. |

Of course, it appears in other Christian confessions. But that is the point: It *appears* there, but here it is the theme. One cannot assert that of the *Roman Catholic* confession because the two-sidedness of the matter, the dialectic of the connection, is blurred by the dominant naturalistic view of infused grace, making sanctification into the outflow of justification and vice versa. It cannot be said of the *Lutheran* confession because there the first side of the matter, justifying faith, is abruptly shifted to the center, over against which the second side, the new obedience, appears to be peripheral if still indispensable. The Reformed confession is certainly not an attempt to mediate between the Roman and Lutheran confession. In a similarly abrupt way, grace is placed, in principle, over against nature and in the center. There is no cooperation here of God and man. The polemical approach against the old church's[443] mixing of Creator and creature is even more pointed, more severe here than in Lutheranism. Because the Reformed confession, when it speaks of grace, thinks fundamentally and essentially of what *God* does and sees faith fundamentally only from that side, as God's action upon man, it gains the necessary distance in order then to establish that faith is not God's *only* action upon man. This same God also makes man obedient for his service. To enrich the understanding even more, at least in Calvin's Catechism, this same God drives man to prayer and causes man to proclaim God's glory in the church through Word and sacrament. This is all the same God, and yet none of this (especially not the first and the second aspects: faith and obedience!) is to be confused or interchanged, for all of it is equally valid and equally important in its connectedness. Calvin dropped his concept of a fourfold relationship, which he was still considering in the 1545 Catechism, and it was never taken up by any successor. The question is worth discussing whether there might be here the most fruitful stimulus for a Reformed dogmatic or, better, for a comprehensive Reformed presentation of Christianity. In such a presentation, the fundamental 'To God alone be the glory!' [Deo soli gloria] and, against that, the wealth of human possibilities related to it, and the *many*-sidedness of the real dialectic of the relationship of God and the human might be more adequately treated than in the restriction to the two-sidedness at which the sixteenth and seventeenth centuries stopped. If we also stop at this connection then we can claim this as the Reformed view: The same God gives, the same God demands. The same God reveals himself in the gospel, the same in the law, in very different ways here and there, but the same, and in an inseparable connectedness he does *both*, not just the one. Therefore, in the center of Christianity [lie] *not* only justification, *not* only faith, but without mixture and yet undivided the doublet: faith *and* obedience. The Reformed Christian [is] a child of God *and* a servant of God, certain of his salvation *and* struggling in fear and trembling, his name written by God's finger in heaven *and* on earth. That is the common theme in the variety of Reformed confessions. |

If one then attends to the varying ways in which this one thing is understood, then we recognize, if not groups and types, still a certain movement, a movement that fluctuates upward and then downward. There is, first of all, an energetic grasping of the knowledge of Christ, which is expressed awkwardly and ambiguously. This is doubtless seen most powerfully and clearly, in spite of a certain narrowness of perspective, in *Zwingli's* depiction of the battle between spirit and flesh in the believer. Along the same line are the *Bern Synod's* doctrine of rebirth through the Spirit of Christ, the *First Helvetic Confession's* doctrine of believers' life fellowship with Christ, and the attempts offered by *L. Jud* and *Bullinger* from the most various of perspectives. The discourse addresses the restoration of the destroyed image of God in man, the covenant between God and man as strengthened in Christ, the law which becomes freedom in the believer, the 'law of nature' [lex naturae], conversion, and other themes. They all move in the same direction but without a systematic central concept. This emerges then in *Calvin,* where the line arrives at its vertex. Now the meaning of all these attempts becomes clear. To say it once more, it is not a question of mediating between Rome and Wittenberg. The contrast to Roman Christianity first gains here its truly principled, almost bitter sharpness. It is not a matter of a new monasticism or works righteousness. *But* it is certainly the attempt to take up, to understand, and to address properly the problem of the Middle Ages, which was also the problem for the enthusiasts and especially the Anabaptists, the problem of *life* in its inseparability from the problem of God. I emphasize that it is the *problem*, not the medieval and enthusiastic *resolution* of the problem. Luther rejected that in both directions. But the problem is taken *seriously*; it is *regarded* as a problem, a central and burning one, posed immediately in and with the problem of God, and to be thought through and worked on with the same seriousness and emphasis. This raises the danger that faith is no longer the one and the all but rather that with and in faith the steely seriousness of submission to God's will claims a place. It raises the danger that one can no longer linger on the sunny heights of the assurance of salvation, where the child of God, comforted by the gospel and certain of the love of his Father, is already saved. No, this already-being-saved is one possibility that Calvin both knows and proclaims, but it is only *one* and not *the* Christian possibility. The other, one other, is the labor and battle in view of God's commandments, which are not a provisional truth but rather in their way the *total* truth that lays a *total* claim upon man. In fact, faith is not the one and the all. *God* is the one and the all. Therefore, because God also commands, faith must be joined by something that is not faith: a disciplined pulling of oneself together, an intentional willing and working of man, a taking with full seriousness the human possibilities, not with a view to their purposes in and of themselves but with a view to the glory of God. In Calvin, I am saying, the entire attempt to understand Christianity arrives at clarity. |

This attempt experienced other strong and important expressions, but it was never expressed with such clarity again. The successors resemble their predecessors in that they place the basic thought under some specific perspective, under which it is then expressed by some of them very clearly *as well*, whereas for others, as we saw in detail, it becomes very *unclear*. In the *Heidelberg Catechism*, for instance, the connection between gift and task is worked out in an exemplary way, although the entire thing is placed under the non-Calvinist perspective of the question about sole comfort. One can perceive in the chaos of the *Erlauthal Confession* that the authors have understood very well the Calvinist approach that thinks all points from God, but their tumultuous untamed style never arrives at a serene and clear cognition and remains, in contrast to Calvin, a pile of great truths that are not able to create an *insight* into what is authentically true. In the *Scots Confession*, the "holy city" ["civitas sancta"], the Christianized Israel of faith with its struggle for God's glory, is, in a certain sense, perhaps the strongest expression of what the early Reformed intended. This is, of course, also one-sided, but Calvin's superiority lies in the fact that in his articulation of the unity of the Old and New Testament revelation there is no preference of the former, but rather truly a [unity of the two] is seen and incorporated in and with the first. In the documents of *Lasco* and the *Belgic Confession*, as we saw, the positive Reformed concern is expressed almost entirely in the strong emphasis upon church discipline, which is a reduction of the knowledge content that can only by appraised as an impoverishment. In spite of a variety of weak intentions, the *Irish Articles* express it with relative purity, as they make that life fellowship with Christ into the dominant perspective, as it was done in the beginning. In the *Hessian Catechism*, the parallelism of the 'knowledge of God and of ourselves' [Cognitio Dei et nostri] is at least asserted, even though it never manages to assert itself against the Lutheran dominance of its remaining contents. In *Beza*, the *Thorn Declaration*, and the *Westminster Confession*, its power is demonstrated at least negatively in the explosive effect it has upon the framework in which it is placed, that is, the very un-Calvinist doctrine of the assurance of salvation, which is either openly or secretly dominant, and the broadly drafted attempt to make Reformed theology into anthropology. Finally, in the *Anglican Articles* there is only the banal recognition that parallel to religion there must also be morality.

If we survey everything, then it is easy to ascertain that, as always in the history of the church, there is much less power and clarity than there is weakness and confusion. The process certainly does not proceed as a developmental progression from weakness to power but rather the opposite. It moves from unconscious and untamed power to maturity and exposition and then descends in a steep curve, although passing many a lovely place on the way. The Westminster Confession, which stands at the end, is doubtless and in spite of all criticism still in its own way a respectable document rich in insight. But one can no longer ignore what clearly now is beginning to unfold, and one senses that what will come later will be truly dreadful. The historical fate of the positive understanding of Christianity among the Reformed is virtually a classical illustration that answers the question about how it could happen that the faith of the fathers in the church of the Reformation could become so obsolete in such a relatively short time. One likes to blame the unbelief of the emerging modern world. That is quite right if one means with the term "world" mainly the church itself, not just the rationalist church of the eighteenth century but the church of the sixteenth century. One must clearly see that in the confessions the faith of the fathers already is fissured, its power is already broken, so that the bearers of the most famous names—I think for example of Beza— assisted in good faith and with the purest Christian attitudes to saw away at the branch on which they sitting and to bore holes in the ship in which they were traveling. Why was it possible in German-speaking Switzerland for the First and Second Helvetic Confessions to repress Zwingli's Instruction, which was theologically less refined but incomparably more dynamic? Did they not see that they were trading their firstborn rights for a mess of pottage [see Gen. 25:29–34]? Why did tiresome pedagogical quibbles about Calvin's Catechism of 1545 result in its finding so little resonance outside of Geneva? And why did the 1536 Catechism, which has so much to recommend it, find so little reception that it had to be rediscovered in its original form in the second half of the nineteenth century in the dust of a Paris library, in order then to be incorporated into the Corpus Reformatorum?[444] Why did the Hungarians, instead of thinking further along the lines of the good insights developed in their Erlauthal Confession, accept instead without any critique the confession of the famous Beza, a progress that, in terms of the content, was in fact a regress? Why could the successors of John Knox celebrate the Pyrrhic victory of Puritanism in the Westminster Confession so that they gave up their Scots Confession and exchanged the idea of the 'holy city' [civitas sancta] for the deficient idea of the 'order of salvation' [ordo salutis], the theology of the assurance of salvation? |

These forgotten and rejected documents are, coincidentally, those most worthy of attention and reading if one wants to learn about the original Reformed movement. The only other one about which this can *also* be said and which did receive better treatment is the Heidelberg Catechism. That happened not *because* of but *in spite of* the Calvinism of its authors and of its basic character, because its first question made it possible to interpret it non-Calvinistically *against* the sense of its authors and *against* its basic character, first in a Melanchthonian-Lutheran way, and then in a Pietistic-rationalistic way. The Heidelberg Catechism, as the Reformed churches soon were interpreting it,[445] could not remain the unshakable bulwark of Reformed faith that it certainly could and should have been if it were properly understood. If it were understood along the lines of the Christianity of the Westminster Confession, then the moment would *have* to come in which one said that *this* could be better expressed in the smooth language of modern piety rather than in the gruff words of the fathers, which like roots torn out of the nourishing earth can no longer nourish themselves. The question is heard, Why should there be a special Reformed theology and church? Can one not be a Lutheran just as well? It is a justifiable question when the Heidelberg Catechism is interpreted in *such* a way. It is not the dropping of the Heidelberg Catechism, as is now happening in Switzerland[446] in favor of modern catechisms and in Germany in favor of the Lutheran book,[447] that is so dreadful but rather what preceded that dropping and made it inevitable, that is, the hollowing out and emptying of the confession. That goes back to the sixteenth century, however. And the situation with the other confessions is similar. The dagger did in fact come from behind. When this is understood, one will no longer so easily utter cheap complaints and laments nor devote oneself anymore to some very deceptive hopes for a return of what once was. It would only be meaningful to read backward in Reformed theology (the situation is similar on the Lutheran side) if the capacity were there to read backward to Calvin. And if one really wanted to do *that*, then one would become aware that one is standing at the foot of a snow-capped mountain of awkwardness and difficulty. Whoever moves past the vulgar old and oldest Reformed movement and arrives at Calvin will become aware that there, as everywhere, where real sources flow into history, there is an enormous amount to learn. But there is nothing there to copy, to take over, to conserve. To be a Calvinist one must not *want* to be a Calvinist, but rather, one must *oneself* embark upon a way that will quickly appear to enthusiastic contemporaries to be inopportune, unpedagogical, and impractical, and with good reason. That is the most positive thing that can be said about the positive understanding of Christianity in the Reformed confessional documents.

3. THE CONTROVERSY WITH LUTHERANISM

We dealt first of all with a whole series of Reformed confessions that should only be understood as documents of the struggle against the old church. Then we dealt with the major thrust of those that were dedicated to the positive presentation of what was regarded as Christian, for the building up of the churches. Now we turn to a further series of documents in which polemics against the Evangelical sister church take all or most of the space. Even though the theme we now address appears to be unedifying, we dare not be put off by it if we want really to see and understand the early Reformed as they were. To say that the division of the Reformation churches and their mutual polemics are regrettable is true but superficial. What else is one to say other than this *was* the situation? Our regrets are too tardy and would have more than sentimental value only if, after inserting ourselves authentically and seriously into the situation then, we would know what the clever word might have been that would have resolved the disputes which were taking place at that time. We must merely ascertain that if one regards as well-grounded and meaningful the specifically Reformed style of attack and defense over against Rome and the specifically Reformed view of the positive essence of Christianity, then one must place as much advance trust in the men behind these thoughts that their stance on this new front, to which we are now coming, will be at least as well-grounded and meaningful, and not merely foolishness and quirkiness. It could well be the case that if one does not understand them here, then one does not understand them at all.

They too sensed this sentimental, and not only sentimental but very legitimate, regret that we feel today in regard to this conflict. In fact, the Reformed sensed it more strongly then did their opponents. Consider, in particular, how much Calvin struggled for peace with Wittenberg![1] But at one particular point they had to say, 'Not this!' [Quod non!], this far and no further, even if it meant the destruction of the unity of the Evangelical church. We must trust them and their opponents that this was a serious matter to them, that they were not fighting about irrelevancies but rather that they saw the entire truth, all of Christianity, at risk. If at a later period, the Union period at the beginning of the nineteenth century, one could announce with the stroke of a pen that, while these different doctrines might persist, they would no longer have divisive significance and should no longer be disputed,[2] then it sounds very nice but really proves nothing either in favor of the knowledge of those who could speak that way or against the knowledge of those who could not speak that way 250 years earlier. One should not hasten to discredit the actual importance of this old dispute. It might appear to be of little actual importance to us today because so many other points of Reformed knowledge are of so little importance to

June 29

us today. In spite of the almost universal storm of indignation on the part of modern Christendom,[3] the two churches and confessions do still continue to exist, even though the lines are clear here and more blurred there. Let us not ask why, nor how much the enduring power of that which already exists might play a role in this fact. It suffices that it is a fact. And here in Germany, at least, it is a fact that one must reckon with. It is not a matter of indifference for one who is more or less accidentally a Reformed theologian to have a clear sense of what it might mean that one is *this*, and thus coincidentally not a Lutheran.[4] The coincidental aspect of what one is could actually have a meaning, and if one understood it, then one would no longer be what one is coincidentally. And it is certainly a condition to be desired that one's identity is not a mere coincidence. And then if one, as a Lutheran or Reformed, finds it necessary to ponder who one is, then these old issues that were the stuff of the division back then—that is, for us *the* Reformed confessions devoted to the controversies with Lutheranism—cannot be a matter of indifference now. Whether they will provide us the desired insight is an entirely different question, about which we shall speak directly. But in any event, they must be of interest to us. |

The documents to be discussed here are the following: the *Zurich Confession of 1545*,[5] which was the response to the attacks directed by the older Luther himself with renewed intensity against Zwingli and the Zwinglians. The counterpart to that is Calvin's older *Confessio fidei de eucharistia* of 1537, from the period of the Wittenberg Concord Formula. Then there is the *Consensio mutua in re sacramentaria* of 1549, which was the documentation of the merger of the Genevan and Zurich Reformations against the German. The *Settlement of Sendomir* (in Poland) of 1570 is a further example of an attempt at rapprochement and union. There is then the entire series of German-Reformed documents: the *Nassau Confession* of 1578, the *Bremen Confession* of 1595, the *Baden-Durlach Confession* of 1599, the *Kassel Confession* of 1607, the *Bentheim Confession* of 1613, the *Confessio Sigismundi* of 1641, and the protocols of the *Leipzig Disputation* of 1631, all of them more or less parallel and contrast pieces to the Formula of Concord.

If one surveys these documents, approaching them on the basis of our findings up to now regarding the Reformed confessions, then the first impression must be one of great *displeasure*, displeasure that the early Lutherans and Reformed did not fight about the things about which[6] they *should* have fought, according to our expectations. I do not mean merely my expectations! Take any study of the world of early Reformed thought that you desire, *Max Goebel*[7] or *Schweizer*,[8] *Schneckenburger*[9] or, from more recent times, the works of *Troeltsch*![10] You will observe, when you deal with these researchers as they attentively and lovingly enter into this world, that they throw a bright light on the distinctive Reformed character over against the Lutheran. But they have no idea how to explain, based upon the distinctive character they have described—not *that* the great dispute was unavoidable, which they seem to grasp—but that *this* very dispute had to be conducted as it is documented by the confessions on both sides and by the entire history as well. What does the spirit of Calvinism—as it is portrayed by Max Weber[11] and Troeltsch in its sociological and cultural-historical significance, and whose difference over against the spirit of Lutheranism is understood only too well—have to do with the spirit in which Calvin wrote against Joachim Westphal[12] in Hamburg?[13] |

We have drawn more modest circles here, and while remaining within narrowly defined theological territory, we have unpacked as the distinctive polemical doctrine against Rome the concept of divine majesty, and as the distinctive positive view of Christianity the parallel relationship, described once more yesterday, between gospel and law, faith and obedience. At both points we have discovered something quite unusual precisely in contrast with Lutheranism, something very important and serious at both points, something that could and should be argued about. The first point would be the contrast between a theological (in the more narrow sense) and an anthropological perspective. The second would be the contrast between an overview that gives central significance in Christianity to the ethical problem, and an overview that is exclusively religious—whereby the ethical problem is *also* an issue for the latter but only *after the fact* and with greatly diminished power because of the specifically religious formulation of the question. Why did not the two churches battle *about this* if they had to fight about something? In their confessions, they did *not dispute at all* about the second point, which appears to us to be the more burning issue, the relationship between justification and sanctification. They battled *a little bit* about the first point, about the doctrine of predestination, but without that much energy and gravity. The Lutherans, coming from their original assumptions, could not contradict very sharply, and the German Reformed made it easy for them in this point with their great spirit of accommodation, without giving away anything essential. What we regard as the decisive issue, the contrast in the two concepts of God, never was raised in these discussions. Instead, there were pointed, bitter, and unresolved disputes, lasting long into the nineteenth century, about the *corporal presence of Christ in the Lord's Supper*, linked closely to the Christological question of the importance of the ascension and *Christ's sitting at the right hand of God*. One of the many things that amaze me in theology is that I find so little amazement about this fact in the well-known presentations of church and doctrinal history. Has it then been *explained*? I cannot recall having encountered a real explanation of this matter (what I would see as an explanation!). Or is it so *easily understandable* that there is nothing to explain and I am the only one to be amazed? Or is it obvious that one should forgo understanding and explanation of this matter in a more than externally pragmatic sense and be satisfied with the portrayal of the historical situation? Is not the separation of Lutherans and Reformed because of these two interrelated questions not one of the most consequence-laden events of recent intellectual history? How can one understand what subsequently developed if one does *not* fundamentally understand why this separation happened but rather acquiesces in the mere setting out of the facts, as though blind while seeing? |

To be sure, I cannot offer you much more than to point out this strange gap and to ask you, if you are capable of it, to be amazed with me, and then to offer, not a solution, but rather my provisional *attempt* at a solution, about whose questionable character I have no illusions. Before long we will have *Walther Köhler's*[14] great two-volume study of the Communion controversies of the Reformation, and we shall hope that it will not only provide new facts but also new insights. Our best approach will be to proceed here in a simple and analytical way, keeping it as brief as possible. Besides Communion and Christology, other themes are discussed in the documents mentioned. For example, in 1545, the Zurich theologians defended, against Luther, Zwingli's well-known teaching regarding the revelation that is also made known to illuminated pagans in Christ.[15] As already alluded to, they defended the authority of James's epistle, contesting claims that it is a strawy epistle,[16] and the Apocalypse, in whose spirit they should conduct themselves.[17] The German confessions conduct a delightful little battle against exorcism,[18] crossing oneself at baptisms,[19] the baptism of unborn infants,[20] the question of a host or bread at Communion,[21] whether one might receive the sacrament with one's hand,[22] candles and mass vestments,[23] doing away with the concept of the altar and the clergy's turning their back to the congregation at prayer,[24] "holding a cloth under the elements as done by some in the administration of the supper,"[25] and Communion for the sick (prohibited in Bremen, for example, as a "private act or concealed action"[26]). It is obvious that all of these things had some kind of relationship to the central question of the sacrament and to that extent were serious in nature (because of exorcism, which he did not want to give up, the pastor of Badeborn in Anhalt, *Johann Arndt*, subsequently the author of the famous book on true Christianity,[27] became a martyr of Lutheranism[28]). The tragic seriousness with which questions such as that of the form of Communion bread, whether round or square, could be taken was shown in 1817 in *Hanau* where this very question formed the high point of union negotiations, and its resolution the breakthrough to a happy merger. "In that moment," reports the official minutes of the meeting, "a holy enthusiasm coursed through the assembly. All hastened from their seats, thronged to embrace the Lutherans, and all embraced each other. Tears flowed from their eyes and in every breast there rose feelings of the unending beauty of Christian peace. It was a moment of the highest moral sunshine" (Heppe, Kirchengeschichte von Hessen II, 380). That was the situation when they reached agreement on this question. What might have been going on when the moral darkness was still so great that they thought they had to quarrel about it? The discussion of these things probably belongs more to the history of liturgics, and it could lead us far astray to shift the basic conflict into the light of *these* disputes. |

The question of the doctrine of predestination was, as we have already noted, a secondary battlefield in this case (we shall encounter it once more in this section at an important juncture), upon which nothing decisive took place. The two churches had not separated over this issue, nor over the Epistle of James, as remarkable as their varying positions on this biblical section were. The thesis of the salvation of noble pagans was and remained a specifically Zurich theological theme,[29] in spite of Bullinger, who advanced it somewhat hesitatingly once more in the Second Helvetic Confession.[30] It was otherwise sharply rejected by Calvin and the Calvinists.[31] We can limit ourselves to the investigation of the double question of Communion and Christology (both are never separated and always form one complex). *This issue* and only this was the theme of the controversy with Lutheranism. *Why so?* This is the "x" in the equation that we are seeking. I hope that you will not look upon it as an artificial anticipation of the answer when I tell you the direction in which I am *looking* in this difficult matter (there can be no talk about finding anything). |

Wherever *Christology* is the theme, then it appears to me, if I am right, that the real question is the *presupposition* of the matter as we ┌─────────┐ July 3 └─────────┘ discussed it in the previous section, that is, the presupposition of justification and sanctification, faith and obedience, prayer and human thankfulness. It is not the *first* presupposition, which is the reality of the living God, nor is it the *third* presupposition, which is the self-attestation of this God in the inward man. Rather, the *second* presupposition is an outward revelation of this God, a revelation that is in no sense immanent to man, not even in the sense of a transcendent a priori,[32] nor even in the sense of that self-attestation in the inward man, but in every sense transcendent. It is the presupposition of a finite, temporal, given revelation, which certainly cannot become revelation to man without the inward one but is truly not the same as that. Expressed in the language of ancient dogma, which is actually the language of the Bible, we are speaking here not of the *Father* nor of the *Spirit* but of the *Son*, who transfigures the Father before men [see John 17:4] and to whom the Father draws man through the Spirit [see John 6:44][33]—through the Spirit who is not only his but is also the Spirit of the selfsame Son [see Gal. 4:6]. To what extent does the Father speak to us *through the Son*? To what extent can we speak of a *revelation of God in the finite*, in the temporal, in the given? What do we mean when we confess this particular, earthly, bodily *Jesus of Nazareth*, as the Scriptures testify to him, as *God's Word to us*? To what extent do we know in him a *mediated*[33a] *presence of God*—one likes to say today, in "history?" But I would prefer to avoid this fatally ambiguous term, for what is at stake here is something greater, what the Bible calls *in the flesh* [John 1:14], in humanity, not to the extent that it is spirit (to which the term "history" alludes[34]), but rather to the extent that it is nature, creature, fallen creation. Christianity knows no other Spirit than the *Holy* Spirit, proceeding not only from the Father but also from the Son (filioque![35]), no unmediatedness of God than that which is also (not *only* but *also*) manifested in mediatedness, in time, in the flesh. Not in mediatedness in an absolute and general sense, for that would be naturalism and pantheism, nor in everything finite but only in *this* finite One, in Jesus Christ. Without the Father's movement to the Son through the Spirit there is no transfiguration of the Father through the Son before us. But the Father moves us to the *Son* through the Spirit and to nowhere else, and through the *Son* the Father transfigures himself before us and through no one else. Without the unmediated immanent presence of God there is no mediated transcendent presence, but where there is the former there must be the latter, and only in this presence of God *at all*: only as *finite*, temporal revelation taking place in the incarnation, which means the same as to say, only as *this very definite single* revelation, finally and exclusively bound to the name Jesus Christ. 'The Word has become flesh' [Verbum caro factum est] [John 1:14]. |

Between Lutherans and Reformed there was and is no separation about the *that* of this "Word become flesh" ["verbum caro factum est"], about the reality of the incarnation of God. But there was also no debate about the reality *of God the Father*, and yet the image one made of this Father God on both sides appears, as we saw in the first section,[36] not to be quite the same. Does not a good Lutheran who reads Calvin still react in a direct and naive way that the God proclaimed here is a terrible, almost sinister God in his distance and holiness?[37] That is an optical illusion. Calvin never meant it that way. But there is something to it, for the serene, steadfast, friendly nearness of God, which for the Lutheran is essential to *his* image of God,[38] is certainly interrupted here in a threatening way by the explanation that this near God is also, at any time, very far, that God's mercy is also his holiness, that the One who lives in darkness [see Exod. 20:21] is also the light of our life [see John 1:14; 8:12]. Let anyone accept this who can [Matt. 19:12]! It was just through this apparently mutual insistence upon Yes and No that Calvin testified to the real and living God. Reformed thought cannot evade posing a difficult riddle for Lutheran thinking and sensibility with this view of God. That was and is the situation with the first person of the Trinity. Unity in the "that," disunity in the "how"? The thrust of the dispute, if one can speak of one, was that the Reformed image of God reveals a movement comprising the greatest contrasts, of which today's Lutheranism no longer has any awareness. Luther himself certainly was aware of them. All of his earlier writings and many passages in his late works are the witness to this. The dispute did not break out. The argument about predestination[39] was only a weak indication that there was some sense at the time that they were not in complete agreement. Beyond that, early Lutheranism was itself, at least in part, still virile enough not to be offended by the severe seriousness of the Reformed concept of God. However, the question, the fissure, was there. |

There was also no real division with regard to the effective work of *God the Holy Spirit* in the believers. And yet—we are thinking here of our second section[40]—how very differently the two sides understood this work! We have seen, have we not, how the same testimony of the Holy Spirit liberates the Lutheran primarily from the 'horrible terrors of the conscience' [terrores conscientiae][41] and assures him of the forgiveness of sins, in order then *in addition* to call him to and guide him in good works of love. For the Reformed, this testimony does indeed mean the certainty of forgiveness, but not afterward so much as in and with that forgiveness (the word "love" occurs more seldom!) it casts the believer into the inner struggle with the flesh and the outer struggle to the glory of God. In this process, acting in accordance with God's commandments gains its distinctive significance, which the Lutherans easily caricature as a new monasticism and works righteousness, as moralistic Pharisaism, and as Baptist or even enlightened activism.[42] It is again an optical illusion! It could lead in that direction, just as its opposite could lead to quietism. Calvin was as little a Pharisee as was Luther a quietist.[43] But to be sure, 'some things stick' [aliquid haeret].[44] This unsettling placement of faith and obedience next to each other will always make it impossible for the Reformed to give the Lutheran the comforting answer to the question of the assurance of salvation that he is seeking. This is the situation, then, with regard to the third person of the Trinity. The dispute, if it had broken out, would have had to deal with the fact that the Reformed image of God the Spirit was so dynamic that it had to be frightening to the Lutheran. But this dispute did *not* erupt at that time. *Why* it did not happen is for me a question that I cannot really answer. In a very provisional sense, I can only explain it by saying that at that time this difference was felt to be very small and unimportant when contrasted with the contradiction we now must speak of, that is, the difference relating to *God the Son*, the second person of the Trinity. |

I repeat: Here, as well, there was fundamental agreement among everyone, including with the old church as they understood it then, about 'the Word became flesh' [verbum caro factum]. But they were *not* in agreement about the *interpretation* of this shared conviction. In saying that, I have said that they were not in agreement about the interpretation of the very center of Christianity. For the reality of the Father reveals itself, and the work of the Spirit is carried out, through the Son and out of the Son. The relationship to that which is not given comes about through that which *is given*, and the view into eternity comes *within time*. Christianity says, *this* given, *this* time, Jesus Christ. Is it not true that that century, more alert and more focused upon the essential than is our century, saw the difference at the point of its real origin and center, in the problem of mediated revelation, and thus had simply no time for the consequences that resulted? What can be the meaning of the 'Word becoming flesh' [caro verbum]? It is not meant in the sense of a general doctrine of identity, nor is it a straightforward equation between deity and humanity in general. Its meaning is that of Christian revelation: *this* flesh, the flesh *of Christ*, the eternal Father's Word to us. Was it so scholastic, so erroneous, so redundant, and so annoying to dispute about this?[45] Did not the disputants perceptively select that very issue that certainly is disputable, perhaps—do not be taken aback at this idea—even *had* to be disputed, if the problem was to be vitally grasped? *This* problem most emphatically does not bring peace upon earth but rather the sword [see Matt. 10:34]. Can there be any more urgent task for a theologian than *Christology*?[46] And once this task is recognized, can the disputation be avoided? Is it not the case that once intractable tasks have been posed, they must be disputed, even if they are incapable of solution? Does not the church need a theology that takes up this task, that engages this dispute? The age of the Reformation *was*, it appears, of this opinion. It might be worth considering whether the progress is all that great if we, as more peaceable contemporaries basking in the moral sunshine of our entire lack of real problems, are *no* longer of this opinion. Back then, this serious Christological question, the question about the "how?" of revelation within finitude, found its expression as the question of the meaning of the *Lord's Supper*.

[Review:][47] A glance at the content of those Reformed confessions dedicated to anti-Lutheran polemics must astonish us in two ways. First, we encounter the fact that the fathers were not arguing about the things that are important to us today as the differences between Lutheran and Reformed Christianity. These include primarily the concept of God, the different approaches to the problem of ethics that became clear to us in the last section, and in that context the different positions on the sociological questions that are chiefly articulated in the church constitutions. Whoever starts from these things that interest *us* might arrive at the most excellent and correctly seen conclusions about the contrast of the two evangelical confessions, but still nothing would be settled because the sixteenth and seventeenth centuries had no concept of this contrast that *we* have constructed, and certainly did not argue *about it*. There is a very serious question here whether we really understand the contrast, regardless of how correct our observations might be, if we put in that place where the contrast emerged, there at the site of the historical reality, a construction of our own making. Secondly, we encounter the fact that the fathers did in fact

| July 5 |

argue about certain things, primarily about the Lord's Supper and Christology. We stand before these debates as alienated and perplexed as probably Lasco, Beza, and Knox would be if they were to be confronted with
Troeltsch's and Weber's results and were to be told that *this* was how they
differed from Lutheranism. It appears that we and the fathers are talking
completely past each other. What appears to be remarkable to *us* left the
fathers cold, and, conversely, where the fathers seethed, we simply shake
our heads and offer our pragmatic, historical, and psychological explanations, which, as I must sharply emphasize, are *no* explanations at all. We
end up as the losers in this game. *Our* observations about the principal differences can, if they are correct, conceivably render useful *service* in *illuminating* and *understanding* the actual differences at that time. But if they do
not do that, if the actual difference back then remains *lying* there like an
untied knot in the center, than all of *our* observations, even the most correct
of them, are of *no* value. I see here a gap that ought not to be permitted in a
truly scientific, that is, truly knowledgeable study of the confessions, and I
am not prepared to be mollified easily and quickly about the presence of
this gap. More depends upon one at least *seeing* the problem here than may
be apparent at first glance. Please understand what I am now going to say
not as the solution but as the *attempt* at a solution, and not really even that,
but only the attempt at least *to come closer* to the *question* that did in fact
move the fathers into opposition to each other.

They fought about *Christology*, for the dispute about the *Lord's Supper*
was, as the texts unambiguously reveal, only the shadow side of the actual
dispute about their view of Christ. Clearly, Christ is one of the *presuppositions* of the things that we discussed in our section on the positive view of
Christianity, one of the presuppositions of justification and sanctification,
faith and obedience, prayer and thanksgiving. *One*, because these things
have several presuppositions. *One* of these presuppositions is, for example, the originalness, the initiating and finalizing reality of God, from
which all these relationships either derive or to which they all refer, or both
at the same time. Put in the language of Trinitarian dogma, God *the Father*.
Another *one* of these presuppositions is the fact that these relationships are
not suspended in midair, are not metaphysics and not mythology, but
rather this entire "from God" and "toward God" that is apparently to be
defined by them addresses the human, plays itself out in and on the
human, so that *I* am justified, sanctified, am a believer and am obedient,
whatever that might mean in detail. In the language of Trinitarian dogma,
God *the Holy Spirit*, dwelling in the heart of the believers. |

Let us first ask what the situation was with the early Lutherans and
Reformed in regard to these two presuppositions of Christianity. Were they
in agreement about the Father and about the Spirit? They certainly did *not
fight* about them. If we were to return to these presuppositions ourselves,

then we would certainly and most likely argue about them. We saw in our first section that the image of *God the Father* formed by each side was not in fact quite the same. A certain contrast tends to be sensed here today, in an immediate and naive way, especially by Lutherans, who have always been more sensitive to these differences as such. The God of the Reformed, Calvin's God, for example, frequently appears in a strange glow of distant and fearful holiness, of Scotist arbitrariness, of cruel philosophical negativity and abstraction. This is an optical illusion. Calvin never meant it in that way. But there is something to it. The serene, enduring, friendly nearness and gentleness of God, which are essential to the Lutheran for *his* image of God, are clearly and threateningly interrupted here by the declaration that precisely this near and gentle God is always also the distant and holy God, that God's grace is also his judgment, that the one who lives in darkness is also the light of our life [see 1 Kgs. 8:12; John 8:12]. Let those who are able to do so grasp [see Matt. 19:12] that Calvin thinks that he is testifying most clearly, most powerfully, most purely to the reality of God the Father by means of this *dynamic* image moving in the greatest contrasts. Reformed thought cannot avoid presenting to Lutheran thought and sensibility a difficult riddle here, if not an offense. But the dispute *about this* remained latent and did not find expression. The controversies about predestination were a weak suggestion that they did sense the contrast here. It was impossible for the Lutheran side fully to forget that if not Melanchthon then Luther himself had *also* stated what seemed to be offensive in Calvin. Luther also was building upon Occam and never denied that. One might have been alienated by the severe seriousness of the Reformed view of God because one did not return constantly to this side of the matter, to the 'hidden God' [Deus absconditus],[48] but rather, having once taken the step from Moses to Christ, one lingered now on the other, more friendly side, thinking and speaking on its terms.[49] Even so, at least in early Lutheranism, one was still sufficiently virile to acknowledge as justified the issue concealed in the dialectically dynamic Reformed faith in God the Father, so that they did not find themselves challenged to argue this. Still, they were not completely in agreement about the Father. |

What was then the case with the *second* presupposition mentioned, with *God the Holy Spirit*? Here we must remember the findings of our second section, where we saw how the image of the *work* of the Spirit in believers and in the church was not quite the same from one side to the other. The same testimony of the Spirit that above all leads the *Lutheran* out of the 'terrors of the conscience' [terrores conscientiae] and assures him of the forgiveness of sins, in order then, *also*, to call for and lead to good works, means for the *Reformed* the certainty of forgiveness as well, but precisely with and through this certainty it places him in the struggle with the flesh, which is at the same time the necessary battle for the glory of God. On the one side, faith alone dominates the field, and all human activity, for which the preferred term is *love*, derives solely from faith; on the other side, there stands next to faith in relative independence, although united with it in its divine origin, a resolute action according to God's commandments (the word "love" is noticeably less frequently used!). Is this the same Spirit? Yes and no. A suspicion hovers in the air that the Reformed Spirit wants to be a spirit of a new monasticism and works righteousness, of a moralistic Pharisaism, a Baptist or humanistic activism, while the Lutheran Spirit is a spirit of quietism and comfortableness. Optical illusions on both sides. Calvin was no Pharisee and Luther was no quietist. But 'some things stick' [aliquid haeret]. This parallel juxtaposition of faith and obedience on the Reformed side, corresponding to the juxtaposition of holiness and mercy in the concept of God, is in some way irritating. The Lutheran will not be able to find the calming answer to the question of the assurance of salvation. We saw how the later Reformed wrestled with this difficulty. Conversely, what the Lutheran has to say about law, new obedience, and good works has a certain sense of security, satisfaction, satiation, and a profound absence of the problematic, which is very difficult for Reformed ears to tolerate. That this is not merely a matter of irrelevant variations of mood and terminology but is rather a very serious difference is demonstrated by the contrasting structures of piety of the peoples shaped by Lutheranism over against those shaped by Calvinism.[50] But here as well, the dispute *never* broke out. Although mutual suspicions hovered in the air, *they* were never vented in the confessional documents of either side. The sources do tell us explicitly that they were not completely unified in the Spirit.[51] The more strongly we sense today that the conflict at that time was related to *these* two presuppositions, the *more* puzzling we must find it that for them these differences were quite unimportant next to *another* difference, which was in fact what ignited the dispute.

We have not yet named the *third* Christian presupposition, or rather, the second (because it stands between the other two in the middle). That it is even possible to speak of God and of our relationships with God appears to presuppose that the abyss between God and humanity has been fundamentally *bridged*; it presupposes the real *presence* of God the Father and God the Spirit in the *world*, in that which is finite, temporal, given. But that means, if it really were true, a finite, temporal given presence of God, a *contingent* presence of God—unique, concrete, limited like anything else in the world, but yet the presence *of God*. The idea of the *immanence* of God in the world and in humanity is not, in and of itself, the presence of God the Spirit. It could just as well be another expression for the world or humanity, a hypostasization of given reality. And the idea of the *transcendance* of God over against the world and humanity is certainly not, in and of itself, the presence of God the Father. It can just as well be another expression for that which is nonworld, nonhuman, the mere empty negation of given reality. That these ideas really refer to *God*, that is, that they are not merely ideas but the presence of the Father outside of us and the Spirit in us, needs to be *warranted*. But where else could that warrant come from, and who else could provide it, than God himself? And if it should be really given, then it must be given in such a way that the presence of the Spirit in us is unambiguously distinguished from the infinite positivity of given reality. It must be given in such a way that the presence of the Father outside of us is just as unambiguously distinguished from the similarly infinite negativity that is its unavoidable reverse side. If it is to be warranted that we are dealing here and there with the reality *of God*, then this reality clearly must itself be *finite, temporal, contingent, not* confusable with the infinity of the world nor with the infinite negation of the world but rather, over against both infinities as they mutually abrogate each other, conquering and reconciling in their midst that which is absolutely unique, unrepeatable, individual—*revelation*. That God has revealed himself, that is, that a certain particle of temporal and spatial reality is identical with God himself, that is the warrant that God is present in us and outside us, precisely at that point where we otherwise would only be able to think of the infinity of the world and its total questionableness. |

This is, however, the language of the doctrine of the Trinity: *the Son, Jesus Christ*, the Word that becomes flesh [see John 1:14]. He is the one with whom humanity has to do when humanity has to do with God, with God's *contingent revelation*. Here the decision is made about who and what the Father is, and who and what the Spirit is. The questions about the essence of the Father and of the Spirit[52] are secondary and derived questions. As questions of any substance, they can only be posed from this center, from the revelation of the Son, let alone be answered. Through the Son, the Father speaks with us, and the Holy Spirit lets itself be recognized as the Spirit of the Son. The question of God the Father and God the Spirit is decided at the question of the *incarnation*, at the question of what it means that Christ is true God and true man. To put it in the language of the *issue of the Lord's Supper* (for the issue of the Lord's Supper is only a translation or variation or illustration of the issue of the incarnation), it has to do with what it means to say, "this" ["hoc"], this thing here, this particle of nature, creature, fallen creation "is my body" ["est corpus meum"] [see Matt. 26:26 parallels]. This question—"What does that mean?"—was the point at which the Lutherans and Reformed divided in the sixteenth century. They agreed about the *that*. No one questioned the dogma of the Trinity in this dispute of the two parties. That the "Word became flesh" ["verbum caro factum"] was also beyond question. But they were not in agreement, decisively not in agreement, about the How. And to that extent, they were not in agreement in Christ, *precisely* not *in Christ*. It was the differing views of the Lord's Supper, and especially the way in which Christ is present in the elements, that first uncovered the fact that they understood revelation differently. They differed in their understanding of how God warrants his presence as Father and Spirit, outside and inside us, in Jesus Christ. The discussion of the Lord's Supper between Luther and Zwingli had already shifted over into a discussion about the relationship of the two natures in Christ.[53] The analogous theses on these two points with which they confronted each other formed now the mutual separation that was sensed to be and asserted itself as important and severe as long as there was any awareness of the central importance of the category of revelation. It was therefore not a matter of indifference whether one thought and spoke about it in this or that way. |

The Lutheran shibboleth in the Lord's Supper question was the thesis of the real presence of the body and blood of the ascended and omnipresent Lord in the visible Communion elements—underlined by the proposition about 'oral and unworthy partaking' [manducatio oralis et indignorum].[54] Both as a continuation and an implication of this for Christology, there was also the thesis of the ubiquity of his body and blood, always and everywhere possible according to the will of Christ.[55] The Reformed shibboleth in the Lord's Supper question was the interpretation of the Communion elements as symbols—underlined by the proposition that through the miracle of the Spirit (*only* through the miracle of the Spirit), the spiritual eating and drinking with the body and blood of the ascended Lord were happening, parallel to the bodily eating and drinking of bread and wine. This was connected with the Christological thesis of the humanity of Christ, which since Ascension Day and until the second coming is at the right hand of God, and thus is not omnipresent but rather at this particular place in heaven.[56] I cannot promise you that I will be successful in showing you that in the shibboleths of these controversial doctrines are reflected the differing views of revelation on both sides. We have moved almost an eternity away from the solid dogmatic thinking of our elders, so that we feel as though we were wearing suits of armor when we try to find our way back into their way of thinking. We do not know how to move around in this thinking, and we do not quite see the *meaning* of thoughts that were so very relevant then and clearly dealt with actual things. I would therefore only like to tell you the direction in which I am exploring and invite you to join me. The reason that the Reformation period was, in its way, a classical age in theology was not only that it pursued the question of the relationships between God and humanity with a seriousness and power that has not been attained since then. Not only that, it pressed on to the *presuppositions*, to the question of the *reality* in these relationships. Reformation theology's intent was certainly to be something completely other than merely phenomenological. The presupposition of each proposition was the strongest and most vital presence of God through which alone these propositions could be made true. For that reason, Luther moved the Lord's Supper to the center of interest (long before there was any dispute). But Calvin as well had always had a very definite and positive interest particularly in the Lord's Supper, while Zwingli had at the least a burning critical interest in the matter. |

What does the Lord's Supper mean for the thought shaped by the Middle Ages? Clearly, it is the proclamation, the objectification of the presence of God 'par excellence' [κατ' ἐξοχήν]. This positioned one—as an automatic outcome of the meaning of the Lord's Supper—directly before the special question of revelation: What does it mean that God, God himself in Christ, communicates himself (not in general, not everywhere, not in the entire world, and also not in our ideas, but rather) as that 'most concrete thing' [concretissimum], that he lets himself be known and enjoyed by us? This is the point from which it is then possible for us to speak about everything else that we are, have, and experience in relation to God. Everything that unfolds between the Word of God on the one hand and the faith and obedience of man on the other must be illumined and proven from this point. And here they made the tragic discovery that they were not in agreement. Whatever one might think about this emerging dispute, one cannot ignore the fact that with undoubted certainty this period uncovered the point at which the problem of all theology is located. It was a dispute that definitely had significance and high standards, so that even if there are many things about it that we cannot comprehend, we will have to acknowledge that it was dealing with essential issues. It was more essential than that which we find interesting in the differences among the fathers, and about which we would have fought if we had been there. This dispute was not ended by the triumph of truth, nor by the Christian peaceableness of later theologians, but rather by the fact that they were no longer moved by the essential that had moved the fathers, and most likely did not even understand it anymore. If one has no serious problems, then it is a cheap pleasure to be a theologian of peace. If the essentials were again to move us the way they did the fathers, then probably this dispute would resume at the same point. For the problems are still just as important and unresolved today as they were then.

The *Zurich Confession of 1545*[57] is the last confessional document of
July 6 | a pure, although cautious and moderate Zwinglianism. What the
early Lutherans found irritating and challenging in Reformed theology is expressed here bluntly, severely, thus clearly, beyond all misunderstanding, and inviting rebuttal. The Reformed themselves were irritated and challenged by the last polemical utterances of the late Luther.[58] The point of departure here, as it was in Zwingli, is the Chalcedonian doctrine of the natures: *Christ as true God and true man.* This is what I called yesterday the contingency of revelation; this definite particle of earthly reality, this

man Jesus, is indirectly identical with God. In this, Luther and the old church agreed. Where the difference begins to emerge is in the way that, here, the differentness of the natures in unity is much more strongly emphasized than their unification. It is not the 'union of persons' [unio personalis], not the indirect identity that interested the Zurich party, but rather that this identity is indirect. They strongly resist the idea that the properties of the one—meaning chiefly the properties of the divine nature—are transferred over to the other, to the human nature. They do not want to assert that there are two Christs,[59] but rather the one, only begotten Son. His work and our relationship to him are also conceived of as a unity. But every statement about him is intended to apply either to his deity or to his humanity. What they did not accept and instead contested was that there was some kind of third entity flowing out of the two. After making only these statements, we can already see that Reformed Christology relates to the Reformed concept of God and of the Spirit, in that here too that tension, that dialectical relationship of the two marginal possibilities, is characteristic. This is precisely what the Lutherans did not want, and so there was no agreement with them on this. Physically, according to his human nature, Christ left the world and sits at the right of the Father in heavenly being and will not be brought back into this earthly mortal being. To be sure, this is said of the body of Christ that was born of a virgin, crucified, died, and buried, that is, of Christ to the extent that he is God's contingent revelation. Transfigured but unchanged, not transformed into deity, not become Spirit but body and blood, put as clearly as possible: At one definite and defined place in heaven, this one departed from the world and is sitting at the right hand of God.[60] No one is contesting that in his deity he is omnipresent, but that is what he shares with God the Father and the Spirit; as contingent revelation, however, he is not omnipresent but concealed to us, except for the scriptural testimony to him. It cannot be denied that these are concepts with weighty implications. |

Let us first ascertain what this implies for the relationship of the believer to revelation in general. The characteristically Reformed holiday for Christ is Ascension Day; the characteristically Reformed expression for the relationship with Christ is Colossians 3:1: "Seek the things that are above"! This very clearly shapes our confession. It is not true that Reformed doctrine is spiritualistic.[61] That is, again, an optical illusion. Even Zwingli was not that. And our Zurich confession emphasizes strongly that the food and drink of souls unto eternal life is the true body and the proper blood of Christ given over to death for us.[62] To believe means nothing other than truly to eat the body of Christ and truly to drink his blood. The contingency of revelation, the fact that the Christian faith has to do with the 'most concrete' [concretissimum] Jesus Christ, years one to thirty, is emphasized more strongly here than by the Lutherans. If one wanted to denounce Lutherans as heretics, then one could accuse them of the gnostic vaporization of the historical Christ. "Be careful, Luther, Marcion is growing in your garden," Zwingli once cried out to his opponent.[63] In any event, one cannot insist more firmly on the real humanity of the Son of God than did the early Reformed. But now they emphasize just as firmly that this presence of the true body and blood of Christ is not fleshly but spiritual, not earthly but heavenly. Faith is a certain confidence of things that one does *not* see (Heb. 1:1)—this is another Reformed 'classical passage' [locus classicus].[64] "Lift up your hearts!" ["Sursum corda!"][65] and put your thoughts and faith in the one who died for us *once and for all* but who *now* sits at the right hand of God. To seek the body of Christ down here is to "cast down your hearts" ["Deorsum corda"]![66]

It was a *weakness* of Zwingli and his successors that they never got beyond a certain psychologism in the development of this thinking. It could really appear that the relationship of the believer to revelation was conditioned by, or even consisted of, a kind of bold uplift of the believing soul, higher and higher, until it finally finds and can enjoy the humanity of Christ enthroned in the distant heavens. This courageous 'Lift up your hearts!' [Sursum corda!] is, to be sure, a great and indispensable truth, but when it stands there alone as it does in our confession, then it is not difficult to confuse it with a certain optimistic religious enthusiasm whose incessant voice can often still be heard from the pulpits of German Switzerland.[67] The basic thought is quite clear, aside from better or poorer interpretation: spiritual eating, spiritual drinking, that is the faith, that is the Christian's relationship to contingent revelation.

This results then, consistently, in the *doctrine of the Lord's Supper*. The issue in the Supper is the eating and drinking of the true body and blood of Christ, but in a spiritual way, with a believing disposition(!) and thus, of course, only for believers. They direct their thoughts not to bread and wine, as though they were at home, but to that of which bread and wine *remind* them. Whoever comes with true faith to the Lord's Supper participates in the forgiveness of sins, in eternal life, in fellowship with Christ and all the saints. The unbeliever eats and drinks, because of his unbelief, judgment to himself [see 1 Cor. 11:29]. As believing is *eating*, eating is nothing other than *believing*.[68] It is not the hand or the mouth that take, receive, and enjoy the gift of God, but rather faith or the *believing soul* of man. *Faith* makes present the goods gained from Christ's body broken and blood shed. Faith nourishes the believers to eternal life. The faith of one's heart must indeed be brought to the Supper, and it is itself the meal that then takes place there, *even there*, we must add. The special dignity of the Lord's Supper is not that something special were given us there, but rather that it is instituted by Christ, certainly not in vain, for the exercising, planting, and strengthening of our faith. He institutes it as a visible, outward action, as a sign that is not itself the Lord but that *signifies* the Lord Jesus, true God and man, his body and blood, his martyrdom, cross, and death, and everything good that flows from it. The Lutheran doctrine of the real presence of the body and blood of Christ in the signs is expressly and finally rejected not only because it is useless but also because it torments the believers, embitters the Lord's Supper, and darkens and confuses the doctrine of justification through faith. "Beyond such simple, clear truth, what need is there of many splendid, high, and dark speeches and strange words?"[69] |

I need not say much about the weakness of this position. If the Lord's Supper signified for the Christian consciousness of that time the realization of the relationship of humans to revelation, then here, this realization has unambiguously changed into an "action,"[70] in which the "believing disposition"[71] plays a curiously important role. They did indeed also assert that "the Lord Christ, who is up in heaven, is not carried around down here in our hearts,"[72] by which they intended to say that the believing disposition and the faith that receives the body and blood of Christ were two different things. But the Zurich confessors are not able to clarify to what extent this protest is well-grounded. Aside from this ambiguity, the basic thought is clear. The realization of the relationship to contingent revelation takes place parallel to the external and visible action instituted by Christ, but not in such a way that this action is itself the realization. That is understandable enough. If the contingent revelation itself is at the right hand of God, concealed to the physical eye until the end of all things, and if the relationship to it is solely the very indirect and concealed relationship of faith with its 'Lift up your hearts!' [Sursum corda!], then faith *'in action'* [*in actu*] can never merge with the 'act' [actus] as such, but rather must stand *on its own*, again with reservations, again placed in hiddenness as a spiritual usage. The problem was that they opened themselves to the suspicion that they were replacing the outward 'act' [actus] of eating and drinking with the inward 'act' [actus] of the believing disposition. This suspicion, as relatively justified as it is both here and with regard to Zwinglianism in general, has nothing to do with the Reformed intention as such.

We turn now, for the sake of comparison, to a document of earliest Calvinism, to the *Confession of Faith concerning the Eucharist* [*Confessio Fidei de eucharistia*], 1537, composed by Calvin himself as an instrument of peace and union in a moment when both sides thought that they were coming close to agreement. It consists of only a few very succinct propositions and demonstrates at one stroke, so to speak, what was at stake (Calv. Op. IX 711–12).[73] The 'spiritual life' [vita spiritualis] that Christ grants us consists not only of *'vivification'* [*vivificatio*] by his *Spirit* but also of his making us participants in his life-giving *body through* the power of his Spirit. The word "Spirit" refers in this context apparently to the *divine* nature of Christ. Calvin intends to say that there is no *isolated* relationship to Christ, insofar as he is God. To be sure, there is *also* such a relationship, that is the 'vivifi-cation' [vivificatio] through the Spirit, that takes its form as the justification and sanctification of the human, in a word, in all of those *relationships* between man and God. But this relationship never stands alone. These rela-tionships are borne and realized through the power of the *presupposition*, the contingent revelation. The Spirit also creates our fellowship with the 'body of Christ' [caro Christi]; otherwise, it would not be the Spirit. Calvin con-tinues, when we are speaking of the fellowship of believers with Christ, then we mean that they have no less fellowship with his body and blood than with his Spirit and thus they possess the *whole* Christ. In order to attain to life in Christ, we "ought to be truly nourished"[74] through the body and blood of Christ. This is what Paul means (in Ephesians [5:30]) when he calls us flesh of his flesh and bone of his bone, a mystery that can never be ade-quately expressed in words. But (and now the Reformed "but" comes!), that does not alter the fact that our Lord, raised up to heaven, has concealed from us the spatial presence of his body ("has withdrawn the local presence of his body from us"[75]), which is completely unnecessary for that 'fellowship' [communio]. Contingent revelation is never and nowhere given to us; there is no human act, no seeing, touching, sensing, that would be directly identical with our relationship to that revelation. The 'body of Christ' [caro Christi], seen from the perspective of human, earthly, and temporal possi-bilities, is in heaven and remains there. *This* contingent entity does not become contingent next to other entities. And it doesn't need that, Calvin adds coolly. For, he continues, if we as we wander in our mortality ["pil-grims in mortality"[76]] are not in the same space with him ("are neither included nor contained in the same space with him"[77]), the power of his Spirit (i.e., of his divine nature!) is prevented by no obstacle truly to bring together and to unite what is separated by the obstacles of space (might one perhaps translate, through the differentness of the spaces, "things that are disjoined in local space"?[78]). Thus, we recognize that the *Spirit* of Christ is the executor of our fellowship with him (the "bond of our participation"[79]) in that it nourishes us with the substance of the body and blood of the Lord truly for immortality and vivifies us *in that* it makes us into participants in that substance. This fellowship of his body and blood Christ offers us under the symbols of bread and wine in his holy meal, to all who celebrate it 'rightly' [rite] according to his institution. |

That was the doctrine that Calvin, as long as he lived, taught with minor terminological variations, and from which not even the deeply desired agreement with Lutheranism could induce him to move. The identity of this doctrine with the Zurich doctrine just discussed cannot be denied. Up until a year ago, I thought that I could interpret this confession as a mediation between Luther and Zwingli.[80] But I can no longer do that. What Calvin offers is a clarification of the concern represented by Zwingli and his party, incomparably more profound and improved in every way, but not necessarily dependent upon it. It can certainly be argued that he was much more influenced by Luther than by Zwingli,[81] and the well-known disparaging remarks he made about Zwingli[82] do not surprise me at all. What he presented was the *Reformed* view with all its decisive hallmarks, brought here to classical expression. The Lutherans of the 1550s demonstrated correct instincts when they attacked him as strongly[83] as Luther had attacked Zwingli thirty years previously. What connects him with *Luther* and Zwingli is that antispiritualistic interest in the '*body* of Christ' [*caro* Christi], in the contingent revelation. No general religious truths about God outside of us and in us. No game with the infinities of immanence and transcendance. No work of the Spirit without the 'most concrete' [concretissimum], without the body and blood—of the Lord! Calvin also knows that our flesh and blood cannot inherit the kingdom of God [1 Cor. 15:50] but *this* flesh and blood nourish us to eternal life. It is, then, the *whole* Christ; a mere intellectual Christ, a Christ *idea*,[84] *is* not Christ. But then, and here the dissension begins, this flesh and blood are hidden from us. *Christ the Revealer* is in another space from ours, absolutely separated from the valley of mortality in which we are on pilgrimage.[85] We think involuntarily of the Calvinist God who lives in inaccessible light [1 Tim. 6:16], and of the Calvinist human, or rather, of the source of his faith and his obedience, of the place where his assurance of salvation rests, which is so absolutely far beyond him, so far as the place to which the clock's pendulum swings, and with which he can never swing. Clearly it is the same interest that is expressed in this Christology, but not just that; rather, we stand here at the very *source* of that doctrine of God and that doctrine of man. |

And now the *relationship of the human* to revelation. We note, within the same basic view, the decisive progress over against the Zurich Confession (from eight years later!). Just as decisively as there it states that we are *here* and the humanity of Christ is *there*, and therefore the Spirit and only the Spirit is the "bond of participation."[86] But there is no psychologism of any kind. The word "believing" that is used so frequently in the Zurich confession never occurs here. While it was asserted there that we cannot carry the humanity of Christ around in our hearts, this is made very certain here from the outset. It is foundational that there can be no talk of man's pathway to God but only of God's way to man. The *Lord* is the subject of the 'participation' [participatio] that takes place. Not our faith but the Spirit from above overcomes the differences of the spaces, making that which is far into something near, uniting us with the humanity of Christ, setting us in relation to the contingent revelation whose local presence we could under no circumstances ever assert. In his Institutes and other references to the Lord's Supper, Calvin spoke extensively of the "lift up your hearts" ["Sursum corda"] of faith; he made a broad place for it, especially where the discourse was edifying as, for example, in the liturgy for the Lord's Supper.[87] It was patently obvious that he could only conceive of the Spirit in correlation to faith. But when the context required that he formulate the foundational concisely, he could be content in beginning with the statement that the theme is "the communion which [believers] have with Christ,"[88] in order then to develop very precisely the thought that *in* this 'communion' [communio], an event is at stake whose subject is God and God *alone*. Next to this thought, the fact that the believers are the ones it concerns is only secondary and derived, and not, as it might appear in the Zurich Confession, of constitutive importance. *Christ* acts. He acts through faith *as well*; faith is subsumed under what Calvin calls "vivification" ["vivificatio"], to which then the new obedience belongs. But Calvin asks how this 'vivification' [vivificatio] *comes about*, and he sees and expresses much more clearly than did the Zurich confessors that the Communion of the flesh and blood of Christ is the *presupposition* of all 'vivification' [vivificatio]. Faith is not curiously suspended in the air for him as it was for them, where no one really knows *whence* it comes in order then to be strengthened, planted, and practiced. Calvin puts it unambiguously when he speaks of the *"vivifying* body" ["caro *vivifica"*]; the body of Christ vivifies, grounds faith, "in the power of the *Spirit* of Christ" [virtute *spiritus* Christi], but '*in the body*' [caro].[88a] Thus, man's relationship to contingent revelation is fully emphasized as the primary thing and does not appear merely as an appendix after the fact. To be sure, that "in the power of the *Spirit*" ("virtute *spiritus*") contains the Reformed reservation, that decisive "but," which connects Calvin with the Zurich confessors in spite of everything else, and sets him apart from the Lutherans. We are and remain the "pilgrims in mortality" ["perigrinantes in mortalitate"]; *we* remain those with empty hands. There is *no* equation of divine doing and human having, but rather God remains God. *His* is the Spirit that vivifies us through 'participation' [participatio] in the body and blood of his Son. |

And thus we come now to the assessment of the *special doctrine of the Lord's Supper* that, as with the Zurich confessors, appropriately follows from what has already been stated: bread and wine as '*symbols*' [symbola].[89] The word is unmistakably there, and it will remain. There is never anything other to say about bread and wine than that they are meaningful signs. Here too the gift of Christ is a parallel to what is taken by the hand and into the mouth; they do not merge, either by virtue of transubstantiation or consubstantiation. Thus, the particular dignity of the Lord's Supper is not based upon a reference to a special sacramental gift but rather to the fact that this supper is the supper of the *Lord, his* institution. Yet, here again, Calvin's special doctrine of the Lord's Supper has a different tone from that of Zurich. What is at stake here is the realization of the relationship to contingent revelation, and it works here believably. The statement that this is the supper *of the Lord* has a different sense from Zurich's because it is clear here that the *Lord* makes present body and blood and their consequences, not faith. Thus, Calvin can confidently say that it really is the 'substance' [substantia] of the body and blood of Christ that are present to us here; he later had a long and friendly debate with Zurich about this.[90] He could and had to say that the substance of the body and blood of Christ is *offered* to *all* who "rightly celebrate it according to his own proper institution."[91] He could not go further. He could not say that the body and blood of Christ are *received* by everyone, for reception depends upon the "power of the Spirit" ["virtus spiritus"], and that cannot be said of everyone who celebrates the Lord's Supper; it is in God's hands. But he could and had to go as far as he did. In contrast to Zwinglianism, the Lord's Supper is for Calvinism more important, more inalienable, more necessary to the extent that here the *primary* significance of contingent revelation is recognized more clearly. This has wide-ranging implications for the structure of the *congregation*. The Calvinist congregation is constituted as a Lord's Supper community. For that reason, the most visible expression of this basic conception was the call for *church discipline*, which was asserted relentlessly and tenaciously and finally successfully established.[92] This action, although it is never thought of as identical with the action of God, is shifted so totally into the *light* of God's action that the symbolic is no longer a matter of an *"only,"* but rather *as* symbolic it is enveloped and filled with ultimate seriousness.

The *'Mutual Consent in regard to the Sacraments'* (*Consensio mutua in re sacramentaria*) of 1549 (the Consensus Tigurinus)[93] displays more clearly and completely than either of the two last named documents how and what it was that Reformed theology and church *contended* for against Lutheranism. In the Zurich Confession of 1545, we got to know only the one Zurich faction of the Reformed movement, and Calvin's little 'Confession' (Confessio) of 1537 afforded us more an insight into the *positive* side of the line that divided the Reformed from Lutheranism than into its character as a *battle line*. In terms of the worth of its internal substance, I would rank the Confession of 1537 high above the much more famous and historically important Consensus of 1549. And if our purpose is *understanding*, which is what we primarily are after, then one will undoubtedly have to turn to the *former* statement. The relation between the two is somewhat like the one, described in our second section, between the Genevan Catechism, rarely used outside Geneva and half forgotten, and the generally well-known and well-recognized Heidelberg Catechism. The difference is that, in this instance, both documents, the esoteric one of 1537 and the more generally accessible one of 1549, were composed by Calvin himself. In order to learn what the real battlefront was, we shall have to turn to the latter. |

As the name implies, it is a compromise. For the sake of its particular purpose, however, this compromise is intended to sharpen the critical, polemical, negative side of the Calvinist position. What was at stake was the negotiation of an agreement between Zurich and Geneva. Calvin's doctrine of the Lord's Supper in its original and pure form had been largely misunderstood. What for Calvin had been simply the obvious and positive side of the matter was taken to be unclear, perhaps intentionally unclear, uniting formulas, and concealed concessions to Lutheranism. They thought that Calvin wanted to bind grace to the sacraments, to ascribe to the sacraments a special efficaciousness and thus restrict the efficaciousness that is God's alone. The negotiations about this took place between the fall of 1548 and the summer of 1549, especially between Bullinger and Calvin, in the form of written theses and antitheses accompanied by letters, conducted in a very loyal and mutually accountable fashion. They concluded with a complete agreement (Op. Calv. 7,693[–716]).[94] But as early as the spring of 1548, Bullinger, in one of these private letters, had openly consigned Calvin to the "Lutherans" ["Lutherani"] (713). When we look back at the process now, what the Zurich guardians of Zion imposed upon Calvin was a rather narrow-minded affair. It can only be understood historically when we recall the irritation of the Zurich party at Luther's latest attacks, and especially the ambiguous way that Bucer had played the role of mediator in the entire dispute.[95] They had the unpleasant feeling that in the earlier union negotiations they had lost face, then ultimately were brusquely rejected, so that now they wanted to ensure that there were clearly drawn fronts. It has always been a fatal mistake when such tactical considerations gain influence over the formulation of theological convictions, whether they result in more concessions or, as in this instance, in greater harshness. This is a way to serve partisan interests, but the issues of knowledge and of the kingdom of God will always come up short in such processes. |

Be that as it may, the intransigent attitude of the Zurich participants, who were determined totally to eradicate every trace of Lutheran leaven, put Calvin in a predicament. The last dispute with Luther had left an anti-Lutheran mood and movement in all of German-speaking Switzerland. In Bern, the remaining Lutheran sentiment among the clergy was totally expunged in 1546–1548,[96] and this same new system threatened to expand into Bernese Vaux and Neuchâtel, where Calvin's friends *Viret* and *Farel* were ministering.[97] If Calvin was regarded as a Lutheran in Zurich, these two were also threatened by the very close connection between Zurich and Bern, since any pretext was useful to the Bernese government to diminish the Calvinist influence in its western territories. In addition, Calvin's political involvement in the Huguenots' affairs led him to work toward an *alliance* between Bern, Zurich, and the French crown, so that it was impolitic to have the Bernese and Zurich theologians as opponents. Nevertheless,

Bullinger and his followers remained faithful in this matter to Zwingli's total rejection of all alliances with the French.[98] Finally, any hope of reaching an agreement with German Lutheranism had become so pointless by this time that Calvin, as the generous *politician of union* who he was, had now to attend to saving what could be saved. Since things could not be worked out with Wittenberg, he was eager at least to maintain or regain unity with Zurich. |

The conditions for doing so on his side were certainly there. As we saw last time,[99] he belonged to Zurich, in spite of the very important accents that we noted, and not to Wittenberg. The Zurich suspicions that crested in the accusation that, in Calvin's theology,[100] God's absolute efficaciousness could be threatened were a theological childishness beyond comparison. They had no sense for the dialectical refinement of his discussion of the presence of the body and blood of Christ through the power of the Holy Spirit. They only heard certain expressions that made them see red. Calvin was justified in his constant and reluctant inquiries into what they really thought he was all about and had they in fact read what he had written.[101] It was a rather weak excuse when Bullinger then soothingly responded that they were only trying to give him an opportunity to express himself so that they could hear his true opinion.[102] To give his doctrine the countenance that the Zurich faction liked, Calvin only had to leave out a few provocative expressions such as the explicit "body and blood of Christ" ["caro et sanguis Christi"] or even "substance" ["substantia"], which were not essential for his view. (A dialectical theology like Calvin's will never depend on such expressions in such a way that it could not replace them with others.) He clearly presented his own most authentic view in only one rather concealed place (Art. 23).[103] In order further to suit them, he needed only to emphasize more strongly the negations that were part and parcel of his position anyway. He did them the favor of providing the doctrinal countenance they wanted to see, and in so doing, he performed an important service for the Reformed movement without harming the truth. From the larger viewpoint of the theological enterprise, however, the process was not a pleasant one. |

Let us make the effort to rescue what can be rescued from the confession that came about in this way (M 159[–63]). Its final redaction was completed in July 1549,[104] and it consists of twenty-six articles, which are based upon the twenty articles of a confession that Calvin had submitted a few months previous to the Bernese Synod.[105] I shall make my analysis under three thematic perspectives: Christ the Revealer, the relationship of the human to him, and the special doctrine of the Lord's Supper. '*Christ in the flesh*' [*Christus in carne*] is our high priest and the atoning sacrifice made for us, our brother who lifts us out of Adam's misery to be children of God, the 'repairer' [reparator] who renews us through his Spirit so that God lives in us, the king who rules us with the scepter of his mouth. He is always to be understood as the one who *raises us up* to himself, to the true God, and to the Father, until God is all in all (Art. 4). With that, the specifically Reformed approach has been prepared: There is no concept of a local presence; "Christ regarded as man" is nowhere other than in heaven and thus neither visible nor tangible but is to be sought solely "with the mind and eye of faith."[106] To want to enclose him in the elements of this world is a "perverse and impious superstition" (Art. 21).[107] Calvin's further explanation is remarkable: He knows that "philosophically speaking" ["philosophice loquendo"] one cannot speak of a heavenly place as a place—"there is no place above the skies."[107a] What must be said is that the nature of Christ is as such *finite* ["finitum"],[108] like every human body, but it is as distant from us as is the heaven from the earth (Art. 25). |

Now we turn to the *relationship of the human person* to this contingent but also concealed divine revelation. Calvin proceeds here, again, from the decisive concept that Christ himself is the subject in this relationship. This effectively does away with the psychologism of the Zurich confessors. Christ unites us through faith with his spiritual body in that he justifies and sanctifies us (here the characteristic Calvinist doublet) through the power of the Spirit. But the only way in which this can happen is that he, as our head, shares his 'life' [vita] with us (Art. 3–4). Here is the same approach as in 1537: It is *Christ* who acts and brings about this fellowship, not human faith, as the Zurich approach could appear to imply. The fact that the Zurich group accepted this broad shift in emphasis reveals that they were open to discussion on this point and were at least not insistent on their psychologism. On the other hand, Calvin spares them from having to hear a discourse at this point about the body and blood of Christ, the "vivifying body" ["caro vivifica"], although given their presuppositions they would not have been able seriously to object to it. This results in a modest blurring of the positive fundamental thought here, and as that thought recedes, the defense against the idea of an other than spiritual fellowship with Christ is more strongly emphasized. |

It is from the perspective of this spiritual fellowship that the view of the *special doctrine of the Lord's Supper* then opens up. The Son of God, dwelling in us through his Spirit, makes all believers into partakers of all the blessings in him. The 'testifying' [testificatio] to this fellowship is preaching and sacrament (Art. 6). Article 7 defines the purpose of the sacraments. They are (following Zwingli's well-known definition)[109] the "marks and badges of Christian profession and fellowship or fraternity,"[110] an incitement to thanksgiving and the necessary practices of a new life. Their chief purpose is that God testifies to, represents, and seals his grace through them. They do not say anything different from what the word also says, but they place "living images" ["vivae imagines"] before our eyes, "bringing the object in a manner directly before them" in that they bring to our remembrance Christ's death and all its benefits.[111] Especially this article is indelibly marked with the character of compromise. When Calvin was doing his theology in his own way, he never placed human and divine 'testifying' [testificatio] next to each other in this way. By referring to the original draft, we can reconstruct that the passage about "the marks and badges" ["notae ac tesserae"]—a concept that Calvin otherwise regarded as very secondary[112] —was added in later.[113] In what follows in Articles 8 to 15 there is no trace of an attempt to develop these concepts systematically. Everything is built instead upon the idea of a divine testifying that takes place in the sacrament. This testifying is true, that is, what is depicted there for the senses actually *happens* in the Spirit. We grasp Christ as the source of all blessings, are reconciled with God, and are renewed to a holy life. The signs may therefore be distinguished from the truth that they signify, but they cannot be separated from it. Of course, water does not bring about baptism, nor do bread and wine bring about the Lord's Supper; rather, it is the promise that is connected with these signs. That is what one is to hold to. The signs alone would be empty masks. But even when one holds to them as promise, it must be emphasized that the sacraments effect nothing through their own power. God alone is the one who works through his power. He does not make use of the sacraments in such a way that he transfers some of his power to them, but rather he uses them to assist our capacity to comprehend so that he alone is and remains the one who acts and who is effective. Christ baptizes, Christ shares himself, and his Spirit is always and only the truly acting one, in a strict sense the only seal and pledge of the promise. "Not even the smallest portion of our salvation"[114] is transferred from the creator to the creature. (One should note here Calvin's effort to clarify what had been misunderstood. *None* of this was new thinking for him, but with this emphasis a polemical thrust was impressed upon his doctrine that the Zurich faction had found missing and that from now on would be inseparable from him.) |

Articles 16 to 20 define in greater detail *what* then is received in the sacraments. The main thing to say is that the divine effect only takes place in the elect; grace cannot be bound to the sacraments in such a way that whoever receives the signs receives eo ipso the matter. Christ alone is offered, and human disbelief does not overturn the truth of God. But it can happen that the capacity to lay hold of Christ is missing. Conversely, the truth of the sacraments persists for believers separate from the actual participation in them (this point was especially important to the Bernese Zwinglian Johannes Haller[115]). Faith must be present before one goes to the Lord's Table, and what one receives there is only a strengthening and an increase of faith. One should not think, then, that the effect of the sacraments occurs in some way simultaneously with one's receiving them. Baptism, for example, stands above the life of a person timelessly, valid both at the beginning and for one's entire life, and what it signifies may not actually occur until one is very old. (One reads all of this with the feeling that Calvin himself obviously had while writing it: These are obvious things, restrictions that result from his positive position, against which there can really be no objection. But, in that they were wrung out of him in an almost inquisitional way, they have a certain unpleasant breadth and worth, and do not add much of substance.) Articles 22–24 and 26 add in a similar sense still more details. Article 22: The words of the institution are to be explained, in line with the oldest and most approved writers of the church, as significative, "figurative" ["figurate"], as metonymy. Bread and wine "are" means, they "*signify*."[116] Without raising an eyebrow, Calvin agreed to the Zwinglian exegesis, and did so without any doubt because he regarded it as *correct*. In Article 23, on the eating of the body, we find the most genuine expression of Calvin's view, put here in its negative emphasis: The eating of his body and blood in faith through the power of his Spirit, as it is represented in the Lord's Table, is not a mingling or transfusing of his substance but a sharing of the life that derives from the sacrifice made by him once and for all. Article 24 rebuts with strong language the Catholic doctrine of transubstantiation and all other "gross figments and futile quibbles" that reduce the celestial glory of Christ or are incompatible with the truth of Christ's human nature. To ensure that one knows that the Lutheran doctrines of consubstantiation and ubiquity are meant, he says expressly that it is just as absurd to look for Christ 'under the bread' [sub pane] as it is to assume a transformation of the elements. According to Article 26, Christ cannot be adored in the sacrament. The sign is not the thing and "has not the thing either included in it or fixed to it."[116a] Thus, to worship the sign would always and inevitably be an act of idolatry.

| July 12 |

You were able to tell the day before yesterday that I do not place too high an estimate upon the substantive value of the Consensus Tigurinus, even though it is the most important document of the old Reformed theological front directed against Lutheranism and even though it is Calvin's own work. There is too much in it that was obvious to Calvin and that he only repeated to suit the Zurich group, while on the other hand much of that which is innovative in Calvinism is lacking here, so that it is not the work from which one should learn his doctrine of the Lord's Supper. For that, one must turn to the great seventeenth chapter in the fourth book of the Institutes, to the "Short Treatise on the Holy Supper of Our Lord Jesus Christ,"[117] to his exegesis of 1 Corinthians 11,[118] and also to the little "Confession of Faith concerning the Eucharist" of 1537,[119] whose few pages are more ingenious and substantive than the entire twenty-six articles of the Consensus of 1549. All the same, the Consensus does serve to demonstrate unambiguously that Calvin decisively aligned himself with the Reformed in the controversy with Lutheranism. He was also the one who had to bat-

tle through the strongest clash on this theme; I am referring to the controversy with J. *Westphal* of Hamburg,[120] which we will not be able to deal with
in the context of these lectures.

We turn now to the further stages of the controversy as it was documented in the Reformed confessions. It was characterized by the double
effort of the Reformed, on the one hand to do justice to Lutheran theology's
typical concern and interest in the reality of the presence of Christ, and on
the other hand to present positively its own view of the indirect form of
this real presence, or at least through cautious silence on certain points not
to deny it. To the extent that both endeavors were an expression of a striving for agreement and fellowship with the Lutherans, they failed to reach
their goal completely. The reason for this was not, as the history of the
church and doctrine has tended to assert since the eighteenth century, the
irreconcilable stubbornness of the Lutherans whose only response to
Reformed courting was a harsh "No!"; rather, it was based in the nature of
the thing itself.[121] Certainly both of these efforts, precisely in their connection to each other, were not *only* an expression of the striving for union,
which was an essential part of the Reformed movement from the beginning. There were, to be sure, special cases like the older Zurich contingent
who were an exception (and Bullinger never completely ceased to send out
feelers in this direction!).[122] These efforts were, however, also an expression
of the fact that Reformed theology, particularly in its position on contingent revelation, but from that central point throughout, was in principle a
dialectical theology. It incorporated into itself the Lutheran doctrine almost
to the very last word and could say Yes to it with a clear conscience. But
when the Lutherans wanted to hear this last word, say, a totally reassuring
answer to the question of the assurance of salvation, or an answer with no
qualifications to the question *what* the believer or unbeliever has between
his teeth when partaking of the Lord's Supper—bread or the body of
Christ—then the Reformed reserve asserted itself. Its intent was then to
point out that for the Reformed the matter, in which there was agreement,
also had a very different side that needed to be emphasized just as much.
This is what the Lutherans found to be so profoundly objectionable and
unacceptable in the Reformed. According to the Lutheran view, which
could not function without a certain dialectic as well, the *final* theological
statements must be undialectical and explicit. That was the demand that
the Reformed could not meet. The accusation of insincerity or unclarity
that was directed against them[123] was as groundless as that of a stubborn
preoccupation with consistency that the Reformed directed at the Lutherans. For the Reformed, the explicit and undialectical are fundamentally
only in *God himself*, while the Lutherans went further and asserted that they
could proclaim certain unambiguous *words* about God. Thus, as long as
they both still knew what they really wanted, both parties could with the

greatest seriousness talk past each other. The Reformed always had to introduce their necessary "But!" in response to the confident assertions of the Lutherans, and the latter always detected in this a sign of deficient logical consistency of faith, as long as the one side continued to engage the other and could do so with good conscience.

For the first document, I turn to the *Consensus of Sendomir* of 1570 (Augusti 254[–64]), negotiated by the Lutherans, Reformed, and Waldensians of *Poland* as an agreement on the Lord's Supper, the rare example of *union* really achieved in the sixteenth century in which the Augsburg Confession, the Second Helvetic Confession, and the Waldensian Confession were acknowledged to be of equal validity.[124] This miracle was only possible because the Lutherans involved were *Melanchthonians*, that is, those who, without sharing the consciously critical position of the Reformed, did not draw certain consequences and thus were able to enter into alliances or agreements with the Reformed here and elsewhere. This form of Lutheranism has, as is well-known, become historically insignificant since the Formula of Concord, and seen from the Reformed side as well it must be regarded as fortunate that such unions, based not on insight so much as on mutual weakness, did not emerge more frequently. We did not get a very positive impression of the Polish Reformed in our discussion of the Thorn Declaration, which was twenty-five years previous. |

A long quotation from a Saxon-Melanchthonian 'Confession on the Lord's Table' [Confessio de Coena Domini] of 1551 forms the bulk of this consensus, to which an introduction and an epilogue are appended.[125] The tenor of the document is accordingly that of an imprecise Lutheranism under whose capacious robes there was also room for a rather unsophisticated Reformed theology. At the decisive points it says that the signs in the sacrament are neither naked nor empty but offer and give (exhibere et praestare) to the believers in faith simultaneously (simul) in truth (reipsa) what they signify. (Virtually every word here is ambiguous and could be interpreted by both parties in their sense!) Further, a "substantial presence of Christ" ["substantialis praesentia Christi"] (but not of his body and blood!) is not only signified in the Lord's Supper but also truly presented, distributed, and offered to the partakers (but not eaten by them!) in that the symbols are added to the matter itself, which are themselves "by no means naked" ["minime nuda"].[126] (How one is to imagine this, symbols that are incorporated into the matter and yet are not *naked* symbols, is not explained!) In the citation from the 'Saxon Confession' [Confessio Saxonica] it is put somewhat more definitely, but then ultimately still indefinite in its dependence upon the well-known Communion article of the Augustana Variata: Christ is present in the Lord's Supper "truly and substantially" ["vere et substantialiter"], and his body and blood are truly offered ["vere exhiberi"] to the table guests.[127] Each one is left to make one's own sense of this wisdom! The Consensus of Sendomir does not merit serious theological attention not only because it is chiefly a copy of Melanchthon's work but also because it never addresses the Christological question, which is what lends both dignity and meaning to the disputes about the Lord's Supper. Let us then leave Poland and turn to the main section of our exploration here, which must be devoted to the *German* Reformed confessions, which in the nature of things bore the primary burden and passion of the controversy with Lutheranism.

We shall proceed chronologically and look first at the *Nassau Confession*, composed by the Synod of Dillenburg in 1578 (M 720[–39]).[128] Already in the second article we find a detailed exposition of the humanity of Christ. It *is* and *remains creature*, seen in and of itself, and is not equal with God either in its essence nor in its characteristics. The only thing to be said is that by virtue of certain prerogatives, this humanity is distinctive from all other creatures, including all angels and saints, chiefly through its inseparable union with the deity of the Son, through the work that he carries out in it, through its birth from the virgin, through its gifting with the fullness of the Holy Spirit, and finally through its transfiguration in resurrection and ascension. All of this must be *distinguished* from the eternal, infinite, essential characteristics of the divine nature. The exaltation of Christ, according to Article 3, relates to the entire person, God and human, and refers to his investiture as king, priest, and head of his church. His human nature continues to have its own definite share in this his continuing work. But the doctrine of the *ubiquity* of the body of Christ is a monstrous "literary invention" ("Gedicht," Art. 4),[129] unknown to the ancient, orthodox church, the Word of God, and the Augsburg Confession. Infinity, omnipotence, and omnipresence are characteristics of the deity that cannot be transferred to the humanity of Christ that is united with it. Article 5 addresses the *Lord's Supper*. In the Lord's Supper the issue is, in fact, fellowship with the body and blood of Christ, that is, with its substance and not only with its merit and power. What must be heard is "This is my body!" and not merely the commemorative signs of my body. The sign that the communicant receives is thus not *merely* sign and meaning, as it is explained here, but with it the true body of Christ is communicated *simultaneously* (this "*simul*" constantly appears in all these attempts to satisfy the Lutherans![130]). It is not as though the body of Christ were enclosed in the bread, for Christ does not dwell in bread but in the believing person, but rather that the sign of grace is God's ordained means, a pledge and testimony of the true fellowship of his body. Christ is voluntarily present in this his institution, where it is properly administered, and thus shares himself with everything that is proper to himself. |

The Nassau Confession also shows expressly and in many citations that it is *Melanchthonian*,[131] and of course its main authors were Crypto-Calvinists who had been banished from Saxony.[132] "*Crypto*-Calvinist" is the best definition of its contents. We find ourselves here visibly in that wing of the Reformed movement established by Bullinger and his followers. If sacramentalism was the red flag issue there, here it is bare symbolism. How might these two wings have moved apart from each other had Calvin not stood between them, who was not party to the horrors of either and, even more, was superior to and a match for the dangers of both! If the Zurich formulations sounded somewhat hollow because of their overzealousness, then these now under consideration did so as well because of the lack of clarity in their intention. The statement apparently intends to make clear why the fathers of Dillenburg did not want to follow the theology of the Book of Concord. But they do it, at least in the Communion article, almost exclusively in the form of a polemic against Zwingli, which could never have satisfied the Lutherans anyway. In so doing, their exposition of their own stance comes out rather blurred and confused. For example, one looks in vain in their Christology for a statement of the *concealed character* of the human nature of Christ, and the lack of one means that in their doctrine of the presence of Christ in the Lord's Supper it appears to be unnecessary to mention the power of the Spirit that overcomes that concealment, a point that is so important to Calvin. As a result, their assertion of this presence seems somewhat unbelievable, a situation that is not improved by their hide-and-seek game with the sign, which is not a naked sign because simultaneously something happens that is more than a sign. Aside from this reservation, it should be said that the two major points, the continuing *contingency* of the revelation of Christ (the creatureliness of the human nature of Christ in heaven as well) and the *parallelism* of sign and matter in the Lord's Supper, are clearly described in the Nassau Confession.

The 'Bremen Consensus' (*Consensus Bremensis*) of 1595 (M 739[–99]) stands in a close personal and thematic relation with the Dillenburg Confession. The same Saxon Crypto-Calvinist Pezel, who ministered in Nassau in the 1570s, took an influential position in Bremen in 1580. He had developed from Melanchthonianism to a more defined Calvinism.[133] Let us see to what extent that found expression in the Bremen Confession. One sentence from the introduction to the second part, dealing with the controversial doctrines, is important for my view of the entire dispute between the two churches. It says there that great divisions had been caused at the time "namely about the person of the Lord Christ *and what depends upon such articles*."[134] The examples that are then cited include the application of the benefits of Christ, divine providence, eternal predestination, the sins of the elect, and the ministry of Word and sacrament. The sentence shows not only that it was generally acknowledged by the theologians of that day that *Christology* was truly the divisive issue but also that it was occasionally recognized that this issue related to all the other controversies as the *superior* concern. Crypto-Calvinist Christology appears here to be enriched by the doctrine of the 'personal union' [unio personalis]. The unification of God and human in Christ is something other than that which generally maintains between Creator and creature. The Son of God takes on human nature so that it is now his own and inseparable from him and has no independent existence apart from his person. Just as we must protest against the Nestorian view of the unity of both natures, we must protest against the Eutychian mixing of both. The Lutheran ubiquitists are expressly accused, together with the Anabaptists and the Schwenkfelders (the Reformed can also do polemics if necessary!), of both the latter and the former heresy.[135] It is not by virtue of the human but of the *divine* nature that Christ is God, eternal, infinite, incomprehensible, and so on. The *human* nature, despite its exaltation, is neither deified nor does it participate in the divine being and divine qualities. With regard to his person, one must "know all things in two ways, omnia duplicia."[136] Having conceded that, the especially high, wonderful, and great glories of the human nature of Christ are certainly asserted over against all creatures. This then happens, following the order of the Nassau Confession, in the detailed development of the doctrine of the 'glory of the union, the offices, and the character' [gloria unionis, officii, habitualis] of Christ's humanity.[137] But, the conclusion emphasizes, there can be no talk of a mixing of the Creator with the creature. (Here again is one of those instances where the Reformed doctrine, having gone emphatically as far as conceivable in the direction of the Lutheran, turns aside at the last minute and refuses to speak the liberating word.) They concede the possibility of ascribing to the human Christ divine qualities, and to Christ the Son of God human qualities, when one either speaks of his person as an entirety or of his work, which is always the work of the entire person. In this dual concept there is also a Reformed doctrine of the 'communication of the properties' [communicatio idiomatum]. This is not so, however, in the third concept ('majestic type' = genus majestaticum), according to which human nature was said to have what only can be ascribed to the divine, primarily omnipotence, omnipresence, and infinity. "This new concept is the proper origin of all the senseless paradoxes which the ubiquitists amass without limits, to the great distress and confusion of the Church of God."[138] It results in the unending confusion of all the articles of our Christian faith, makes the true humanity of Christ into a phantom, destroys all comfort that we are to gain from it, puts the body of Christ on the cross and simultaneously invisibly in Rome and Jerusalem, inside and outside the maternal body of Mary, in every apple and pear, even in every beer and wine cask! "To this one might well ask, 'Which inferno is disgorging here?' "[139] This is honest religious indignation speaking here. But, of course, it deals just as unfairly with the intention of the Lutheran doctrine of ubiquity, even if individual Lutherans might really have always drawn the absurd consequences cited, as did conversely the Lutheran indignation at the "Calvinist certain somewhere" ("certum πoῦ Calvinisticum")[140] with the picture of the Reformed Christ absent and in heaven. Just as angrily, the Bremen party discusses the Concordistic-Lutheran view that the heaven into which Christ ascended was not a place distinguished from heaven or hell but rather only the heavenly kingdom and thus everywhere, so that Christ did not have to ascend the width of a shoe, nail, or hair in order to come to the Father.[141] "It is as if hell were in heaven, which no Christian can approve or allow, regardless of how one might patch it together or excuse it."[142] By contrast, the Bremen confessors want to understand resurrection and ascension as a literal "translation of locale" ["translatio localis"][143] from earth into the heights, through the visible heavens into the heavenly dwelling, so that the humanity of Christ afterward can never be with the apostle Peter in Rome, with Thomas in India, "simultaneously present in heaven, in hell, and on earth, in all creatures, wood, stone, cords, and beer kegs," but is rather "contented in heaven" ["contentum in coelo"].[144] |

I am telling you all of this not just for the sake of curiosity. Some of the meaning of the entire dispute becomes visible here. Why do the Reformed insist that the humanity of Christ after the end of his earthly life is transferred in its full and unlimited state into heaven? Why do they speak of his presence for us, of the aforementioned givenness of contingent revelation to us, only dialectically, in a twofold manner, "omnia duplicia"?[145] They fear, and not entirely without cause as the crass extremes of some Lutherans show, that, by accepting the direct givenness and presence of contingent revelation, ultimately that revelation will merge with contingent reality, so that the Creator might no longer be distinguished from the creature. They suspect in the speculative idealism of the Lutheran doctrine of the properties and of ubiquity with its daring anticipation of "God all in all" [1 Cor. 15:28], which goes back to Luther himself,[146] a speculative materialism that ultimately will speak of "nature or God."[147] By contrast, they want to remain critical idealists whose Christ becomes neither an omnipresent phantom nor All and Everything but who, "contented in heaven" ["contentus in coelo"],[148] is contingent *revelation* but not *contingency* as revelation. I repeat that this was a misreading of the intention of Lutheran doctrine, but that only addresses the polemical side of the matter. Depending on whether one shies more away from the extreme of Christ *absent* from the world or from Christ present as the *world*, and bearing in mind that there is no clear third option out there, one will have to decide today either for the Lutheran or for the Reformed view, conscious of the problems present in both. |

The effect of this Christology on the doctrine of *Word and sacrament*[149] is worked out in the Bremen Confession as follows. One must stick to a middle way leading between two errors. The one error is that of the Schwenkfelders and Enthusiasts with their harsh separation of the internal and the external, of the divine and creaturely

July 13

Word and worship of God, in which the latter becomes the mere practice, identification, and motto of the Christian. This implies also the boundary over against Zwingli or a Reformed approach like that of the East Friesian Confession of 1528.[150] The other error is that of the Lutherans espousing the concept of ubiquity, who move the Holy Spirit, the body and blood of Christ *into* the word of the preacher, and *into* the sacramental elements. With disapproval the saying of some is cited, "You must not say, mumble, mumble, but [say clearly] what the priest has in his hand!"[151] This saying is actually a quotation from Luther himself (from his "Warning to those in Frankfurt am Main that they should beware of Zwinglian doctrine," 1533, EA 26,299).[152] In reality, it has pleased God to *use* Word and sacrament for his service. Used properly, they *are* by God's institution *powerful signs* and seals of his *grace*, although they are earthly elements and foolish creatures. They can provide no service in and of themselves, but indeed they do so when God with the power of his Spirit inwardly preaches, baptizes, and feeds. |

Thus, in *baptism*[153] the distinction is made between the washing of the body with water and that of the soul with the blood and Spirit of Christ. But these *two kinds of washing* are not separated in the properly instituted usage of true baptism. There is no baptismal water that is enclosed in God's Word and thus sanctified (Luther[154]), nor transformed in its substance, which would have an effect corresponding to a natural power as is present "in precious stones, medicines or foods."[155] But this baptismal water is still a divine means through which in proper use our faith is assured of grace. Similarly one must distinguish in *the Lord's Supper between two kinds of food and eating*.[156] Our senses testify to the outward kind, and the promise of grace testifies to the inward. At the Lord's Supper, not just bread and wine but the truly crucified body and truly shed blood of our Lord Jesus Christ are presented and offered to us, together with all his gifts. This fellowship requires neither the assumption of a transformation nor of a hidden presence of the humanity of Christ in the elements as such, but solely *the* presence of Christ in his divine and human nature, which he himself promised as the means to their proper use. There is therefore also a double reception, a receiving of bread and wine with hand and mouth, and another receiving of the body and blood of Christ with faith. This faith is not directed toward a supernatural merging of body and bread, however, but is directed toward Christ's person and office. The merging of element and matter is not discounted but is understood as a *sacramental* union that has nothing to do with something physical or hyperphysical but stands and falls with the proper usage. It is exactly comparable to how Christology's statements about the divine-human person and its work do not mean the transfer of the properties of the one nature to the other. Just as the unity of deity and humanity in Christ is not the unity of an equation but rather is and remains a non-equation, so it is with the unity of matter and sign. At the same time, the Zwinglian view of the signs as *naked* signs and meanings is rejected, and following Calvin it is emphasized that this spiritual eating is more than faith in what Christ has done for us; it is, namely, the fellowship with his body and blood. Therefore, this is no mere celebration of remembrance or love, emphatically not a transformation, no bodily presence of Christ in the bread, no literal understanding of the words of the institution, no doubling of the body of Christ, no confusion of the 'thing signified' and the 'sign' [res significata, signum], no 'eating by the unworthy' [manducatio indignorum]. |

The advance represented by the Bremen Confession over the Dillenburg is unmistakable. It is not only an advance in the clarity and completeness of its statements but above all in its pure Reformed doctrine, if one takes Calvin as the norm. The explanations of Christology and the Lord's Supper draw the boundaries with clarity and evenhanded balance. What is said against ubiquity and consubstantiation is a good and, for that time, appropriate summary of the objections that the older Reformed generation had already raised. The strong emphasis upon the 'glory of the humanity of Christ' [gloria humanitatis Christi] and on the substantial presence of Christ makes visible the positive thinking that invests the polemical with enduring gravity. One might wish for a stronger accentuation of the contrast between the hiddenness of Christ in heaven and the miracle of the Spirit by which power he is present to us on earth. But it would have been truly astonishing if this second generation had dared to take up that bold concept of Calvin, which really first produces *full* clarity; after all, most of his own contemporaries had not understood it.

For the sake of comprehensiveness, I will mention the *Anhalt Articles* of 1597 (Ebrard, Salnars Harm. Conf. 75,189). Only two of these twenty-seven articles have dogmatic contents; all the rest deal with liturgical details (e.g., Art. 17: that the priest during worship should not turn his back to the people).[157] The two dogmatic articles (1 and 2) address Christology and the Lord's Supper and are exemplars of a clumsy polemic that justifiably evokes contradiction. The theologians who induced Prince Johann Georg[158] to adopt this confession could not have been very great heroes. Article 1 states, "*It is not possible that the body of Christ could be at the same time in heaven and on earth in the holy Communion, because it contradicts the property of a natural body.*"[159] The rejection of ubiquity is thus grounded on the argument that it is inconceivable. That was an egregious blunder. Reformed theology's interest in this rejection was based, on the one hand, on the maintenance of the true humanity of Christ, that is, on the *contingency* of revelation, and on the other hand on the maintenance of the contrast between Creator and creatures, that is, on revelation as *God's* revelation. Neither of these has anything to do with the *irrationality* of a natural and yet omnipresent body (which is what this "it is *not possible*" is directed at).

Lutheran theology's relationship to the prostitute reason[160] was fundamentally much too strained for such an argumentation to make any other impression than: There you have it, the Reformed are secret believers in reason, while we submit ourselves to the Word of God, with whom nothing is impossible. |

Article 2 states, "*One must* (in the Lord's Supper) *ascend in faith to heaven and there grasp the body of Christ.*"[161] This was surely a well-meant reiteration of Calvin's 'Lift up your hearts!' [Sursum corda!][162] but put so nakedly and bluntly it could only evoke the Lutherans' scornful response about the Calvinistic "captured in heaven" ["raptus in coelum"].[163] It portrays this faith that climbs so boldly up to heaven and "grasps" the body of Christ— as though that were possible—as a kind of overenthusiastic idealism. It ascribes to the human a capacity and will to arise to God. Against all of this, the doctrine of justification would have to make serious objections, if this 'Lift up your hearts!' [Sursum corda!] were not preceded primarily and foundationally by the work of the *Spirit* from *above*, as worked out in Calvinist doctrine. The poorly conceived way in which the 'Lift up your hearts!' [Sursum corda!] stands alone in the Anhalt Articles shows the fatal consequences of the way that German Reformed theology neglected that primary element of Calvinist theology, as we have already observed. Based upon the concept of intrinsic faith, the grasping of the body of Christ could, in fact, only be made understandable as an enthusiastic human act, reaching out beyond one's boundaries. The German Crypto- and More-than-Crypto-Calvinists probably never really sensed how close they stood in this point to the Zurich faction, for whom they otherwise had very little sympathy.

We move now from Anhalt farther south, to the confession of Margrave Ernst Friedrich von Baden-Durlach of 1599 (the "*Staffort Book*," M 799 [–816]). This Margrave Ernst Friedrich did in fact write his own confession, comprising 555 quarto pages(!), and had it printed for the edification of his subjects at his own press set up in the castle of Staffort. From all that we know, he must have been an interesting personality, the further study of whom would be worthwhile. His father, Karl II the Pious, had introduced Lutheranism, and his guardian, Duke Friedrich of Württemberg, had signed the Formula of Concord in his name, and with him all the clergy of the land. But when the young Ernst Friedrich reached his majority and assumed rule, he began to study Calvin, became persuaded of the correctness of this doctrine, and decided to make his territory Reformed. This confession emerged as sovereign decree directed to the pastors and schoolteachers. His subjects proved to be very resistant to the imposition of this new instruction. The city of Pforzheim, in particular, openly refused to obey, so that Ernst Friedrich was constrained to carry on the battle against the ubiquity doctrine not with pen and ink but with spear and musket. The consequence of this military crusade was that he suffered a fatal stroke, which for his opponents was undoubtedly the theme of the most edifying observations, and his successor hastened to restore Lutheranism to its old rights.[164] Judging by the confession, the Margrave must have been not only a man of outstanding theological erudition but also truly a fine and independent thinker. It definitely belongs among the most remarkable examples of Reformed confession; by virtue of the quick-witted common sense with which it argues, the lack of theological hemming and hawing, and a notable openness to the issues, it definitely overshadows many of the other documents written by schooled theologians. |

Its Christology[165] also proceeds from the *"personal union"* [*"unio personalis"*] of the God-Man. The deity of Christ is strongly underlined: He is "truly God Jehova" ["*verus Deus Jehova*"],[166] whose being is intrinsically his and who gives and preserves the being of all creatures. As such, he became man and is now an indivisible person, God according to his deity, man according to his humanity. What may then be said about Christ as God and as man, based upon the 'fellowship of properties' [communicatio idiomatum], is related *to this one person* and not to the two natures as such. A 'real communication in the *natures*' [communicatio realis in *naturis*] (Lutheran) *would have to be reciprocal*, that is, the human nature would have to communicate its properties no less to the divine than conversely. But then, 'there would be something accidental in God' [Deum cadere accidens],[167] and he would be burdened with coincidence, finitude, and contingency, which is not acceptable, as was already known to the Gentiles based on the light of nature. Furthermore, it is important to consider that the *redemption of humanity* was the work of Christ "in accordance with the *natural*" ["secundum respectum *naturalem*"], that is, through the man Christ, who was "*local, tangible, limited*" ["*localis, palpabilis, circumscriptus*"], and not through a *non*spatial, *non*comprehensible, and *un*limited person, "in accordance with the *supernatural*" ["secundum respectum *super*naturalem"].[168] Otherwise he would not have suffered for our sins and we would not be healed by his wounds. The question must then be asked, *With which humanity* did the deity unite itself for the 'personal union' [unio personalis]? Was it with the knowable defined one or with the unknowable, undefined, omnipresent one? If it was with the latter, as the Lutherans asserted, then apparently the first one is set aside, or should the deity have united itself simultaneously with both finite *and* infinite humanity? If one does not want to accept that proposition, then it is apparent that God did not become truly human at all. The Lutherans ask if then the divine nature did not necessarily have to make the human partake in its omnipotence and its other divine properties? To be sure, the Margrave responds, but not through the pouring out of one nature into the other (here as well, not physical-hyperphysical), but solely in the 'personal or hypostatic union' [unio personalis sive hypostatica]. Therefore, "the *whole* and not the half Christ is truly and in fact omnipotent, omnipresent, and God."[169] This is, however, only as *the one whole Christ*, not his humanity *in and of itself*. Here as well, the high gifts that are proper to the humanity of Christ in and of itself are mentioned (what in the Bremen Confession is defined as the 'glory of the union' [gloria unionis])[170]; *but* these gifts, it says, are themselves created and not infinite. So (in agreement with the Bremen doctrine of the 'glory of the offices' [gloria officii][171]) the work of Christ is the work of the *whole* person. According to his deity and his humanity, Christ is the mediator, the redeemer, the savior, the intercessor; according to both natures he is worshiped and prayed to, and *yet* in this work both natures carry out the *different thing* that is *proper* to each, the human in its humanity, finitude, and creatureliness, even though a special human. |

The conclusion and climax of the entire treatise is formed by a series of thoughts about the concept of the *"vivifying body of Christ"* [*"caro Christi viv-ifica"*],[172] which we have already encountered in Calvin.[173] To what extent is the body of Christ life-giving? Certainly not by virtue of a power infused into and dwelling in him. According to John 6:51, the bread that Christ gives his own is the flesh that he *will give*, namely, that he will *give in death* for the life of the world. Christ *dies* in the flesh, and *thus* his flesh becomes 'vivifying' [vivifica], but not through any 'strengths' and 'qualities' [vires, qualitates] inherent in it. This was a thought that Zwingli constantly insisted upon,[174] and it can safely be assumed that the Margrave was actually following a Zwinglian tradition here that can probably be traced back to the contacts maintained between Zurich and the house of Baden-Durlach during the second half of the 1520s.[175] This concept is then expanded by a second one: Only through its *unification with the deity* did the body of Christ gain for us eternal life. Solely as 'finite' [finita] it could not have born the "infinite burden" ["onus infinitum"] of the divine wrath.[176] Furthermore, we know that *in the Old Testament, God* always had his believers among the beloved patriarchs, prophets, kings, and all of Israel, who were saved no less than we are in the New Testament. If this is true, then it is in the same way, that is, they too have eaten the 'vivifying body of Christ' [caro vivifica Christi]. If it is clear that in the case of the Old Testament believers this cannot be related to qualities inherent in the body but only to the power of his death, then that is also valid for us. Therefore, we also are not saved "by reason of the inherent virtue of the body" ["ratione virtutis carni inhaerentis"].[177] Further, how could the *flesh of Christ have been killed* if it were indwelt with an "infinite and divine power" ["vis infinita et divina"]? It *was* killed, however, therefore. . . . Further, how can an "extinct power of life"[178] *'vivify'* ("vis vita extincta", *vivificare*)? The life power of Christ *was* extinguished when he was killed and buried. Therefore, that is not what 'vivifies' [vivificat]. Finally, we are made alive by the action of the one who also made the dead humanity of Christ alive in the resurrection. This making alive was the power of the deity. Therefore, we are made alive through the power of the deity of Christ. |

July 17

Let us now turn our attention to the *doctrine of the Lord's Supper*[179] that follows immediately after the Christology. The Margrave boldly combines Augustine and Melanchthon's Apology to oppose the stance of the Concordists. His definition of *sacrament* is *"a ceremony or outward sign or a work through which God gives that which the divine promise offers, which is connected to that same ceremony."*[180] What is received, eaten and drunk in the Lord's Supper is not just the visible signs of bread and wine, but when properly done it is the body of Christ offered for us on the cross. There is therefore a double eating, outwardly and inwardly. Whoever believes the promise truly receives what it affirms. For, as the Margrave says with Chrysostom, "It is the power of faith that it can view what is distant from this place."[181] He energetically contends that the controversial sixth chapter of John applies to the Lord's Supper. If one is to be saved and live eternally, then one must eat Christ's body and drink his blood with true *faith*. This consequence of John 6 must under all circumstances be true of the Lord's Supper. "Since the unbelievers and the godless do not have such faith, for that reason this cannot be a sacrament for them,"[182] but rather they receive only outward, visible signs. If they could really eat the body of Christ and really drink his blood, then they would participate in the promise of grace. Their end in the damnation of hell and the slough of fire and brimstone reveals that this was not so of them. Thus, the 'eating by the unworthy' [manducatio indignorum] is *dropped*, that point of Lutheran doctrine[183] that appears to have caused the Margrave the most difficulty.

Clearly there are all kinds of objections to raise to this sovereign's baroque theology. The Margrave learned from the theologians much too well the secret of syllogistic argument, and he wields it at points with an almost virtuosic self-confidence that does not fit the seriousness of the subject. One can also say that the way in which he combines Zwinglian, Calvinist, and Melanchthonian themes with each other betrays the hand of the theological dilettante. The appeal to the light of nature, which had already prevented the Gentiles from reducing God to the finite, was of course not a good thing. His Christology succeeds more than his somewhat fragmentary doctrine of the Lord's Supper. But such reservations are overruled by the generally refreshing impression one gains of this man and his confession. He grasped in a relatively independent way the necessity of the Reformed reservation over against Lutheran Christology and Communion theology, and he was able to give it relatively independent expression. In particular, his doctrine of the 'body of Christ' [caro Christi] that is not 'vivifying' [vivifica] through its own power but through that of the deity, together with the references to the death of Christ and to the Old Testament believers, shows that he had grasped the crucial point.

The confession of the *Kassel General Synod of 1607* (M 817[–21]) leads us again into the territory of *Hessian* Reformation history, which is dark in more than one regard. Here too a ruler, namely, *Landgrave Moritz* the Learned, played an important role. (It is a peculiarity of the German Reformed movement of this period that there was an entire series of rulers in various provinces who were interested not only in politics but very genuinely in theology: Friedrich III of the Palatinate, Ernst Friedrich of Baden-Durlach, Moritz of Hesse, Johann Sigismund of Brandenburg, and Johann the Elder of Nassau-Dillenburg.) Landgrave Moritz was a well-educated and well-traveled man who carried on a lively correspondence with Beza and other prominent Reformed personalities outside his province, especially in France. For him, the Reformed movement was a matter of personal conviction—which even *Vilmar*, who was very adverse to him, had to admit—after his father, Landgrave Wilhelm, had gradually moved over to the Reformed side.[184] Unfortunately, Moritz did not get as intensively involved as had the house of Baden-Durlach; for political reasons he had to be less open and radical than the latter. In our discussion of the Hessian Catechism, which was promulgated at the same time, we saw the effort made in Hesse "to be Zwinglian and to appear to be Lutheran," as Vilmar once scornfully put it.[185] The older Hessian theology appears in this confession as well in a rather puzzling light. |

One is somewhat put off upon perceiving that the turn to the Reformed movement in Hesse found its expression in the implementation of the following three or four "points of improvement"[186]: (1) the prohibition of dangerous and unedifying disputations and arguments about the person of Christ, (2) the total wording of the Ten Commandments including the separate counting of the second, (2a) removal of all pictures and images still present, and (3) breaking of the bread at the Lord's Supper.[187] Which pious Lutheran could be offended by such harmless improvements? But point 1 really means the rejection of the doctrine of ubiquity. Point 2, and point 2a based on it, was the fundamental proclamation of the pure spirituality of Christian worship. And point 3 underlined the demonstrative character of the celebration of the Lord's Supper as an act of commemoration in which the *bread* is broken, which obviously could not happen were the body of Christ itself present. The Synod of 1607 was convened to implement the program more concealed than expressed in these points, although undoubtedly intended. Its result was our confession, which treats in five articles the Decalogue, images, Christology, predestination, and the Lord's Supper, with special emphasis upon the scriptural principle throughout. This is chiefly where the personal theology of the Landgrave is expressed. Accordingly, the Christological article[188] finds it only necessary (1) to assert that the Holy Scriptures never speak of the humanity of Christ as being everywhere at the same time and then suddenly present, (2) to make the confessors' intention known that it is their desire to speak of the great mystery of the person of Christ with Scripture and to remain silent with Scripture, and (3) apparently to contrast statements such as "I am with you always" and "Where two or three are gathered together . . . " with statements such as "I am leaving the world! I am no longer of this world! I go to prepare a place for you!" |

The Communion article[189] emphasizes very strongly the use of real bread as the only scripturally valid method (the host usually found among Lutherans was often understood as a concealed removal of true bread with which the doctrine of the real presence was supposed to be enhanced for the senses!) For, "we should receive the blessed bread with our physical mouth, chew it with our teeth, taste it with our tongues, and leave it in our stomachs, for that is what it properly means to eat with one's mouth."[190] Their thinking was that it should be unambiguously clear that, as far as the senses are concerned, it is a matter of bread and nothing but bread. (We might note in passing that in the first years following these points of improvement, they used for Communion in Hesse a bread that was difficult to break, to eat, and to digest, so-called "iron cake."[191] Thus, the Reformed also made use of the same means of which they accused their opponents, which was to strengthen their doctrine through a tangible demonstration not only 'for the eyes' [ad oculus] but also 'for the teeth and the stomach' [ad dentes et stomachum]!) It follows then that because this bread not only is called but is a sacrament of the body of Christ and is in this usage not "a bad and common bread," "this eating is called and is not a common, but a sacramental eating."[192] Since then the Lord demands and desires faith that we are not only eating bread with our physical mouth but his body given for us with the mouth of a believing heart, we believe that we "are partaking *next* to and *with* the physical eating of the *sacrament* of the body of Christ (=of the bread!) simultaneously the true body [and blood] of Jesus Christ, not only in our imaginations or our mere thoughts, but in truth. . . . For that reason the Lord Jesus [Christ] truly feeds us with his holy flesh, not absent but present to us in his holy Supper."[193] This twofold eating is in accordance with Scripture, but a third thing is not, the 'eating by the unworthy' [manducatio indignorum], according to which blasphemers, magicians, and other unbelievers eat the body of Christ with their mouths in a mysterious way, but without any usefulness or benefit. This doctrine should be left alone. "But we do not wish to fight with or condemn any church that might teach or hold to it."[194] |

We shall not want to reckon this Kassel Confession among the great achievements of Reformed confessional formulation. If the Anhalt Articles were a deterring example of an awkward, unavoidably misunderstandable reduction of Reformed thought, then the Hessian Articles are an equally fatal counterexample of a badly overcautious silencing if not dissimulation of the essential points of Reformed doctrine. Neither could make much of an impression on the Lutherans. Like any proper confession, the Reformed confession cannot be surreptitiously smuggled in via some points of improvement in the hope that people will unwittingly get used to them and wake up one day as good Reformed Christians. This was the apparent intention, however. Perhaps Vilmarianism[195] was the late but just punishment of heaven for this misguided tactic. I would like to point out a few more details to substantiate my general rejection of this document. It is not acceptable to use the Reformed principle of Scripture in the particular manner in which it is done here in the Christology. Instead of formulating their own views grounded on Scripture, they simply quote a few Bible passages as a way to dismiss the view of their opponents by saying that it is a "discourse unknown" to Scripture.[196] This is especially unallowable when they portray the opposing view as an absolute ubiquity in its crudest and most extreme form. The opponents could easily respond that this had never been Lutheran doctrine, and the *real* Lutheran doctrine of ubiquity (which expresses not the absolute presence of the body of Christ in the world but rather its presence there where the doctrine wants it) could easily be advanced in the shadow of such an exaggeration. The sharp lines of the Reformed view were not made understandable through such Bible quotations. It would be impossible for students and pastors to *derive* from this confession what should guide them as Reformed, so that both the polemical and the positive purpose of this article would not have been met. If we remember how much hard effort was made by the authors of the Dillenburg, the Bremen, and the Baden-Durlach documents to sound a clear trumpet tone precisely in their Christology, the comparison to the Hessian is a very negative one, especially when we also consider the worldly difficulties that threatened their dogmatics. |

In the article on the Lord's Supper, the emphatic discussion about the true bread and the sacred ceremony of bread-breaking leaves at first an unpleasant, divisive impression. *Either* something very unimportant is ceremoniously expressed here, so that many Lutherans, who either noticed nothing or did not care to notice, agreed to the formulation with the obvious and allowable reservation that they would interpret it how *they* wanted to. *Or* something very harmful is advanced here under an apparently harmless appearance, which is what led many others to refuse to agree to it.[197] When one has finally distilled the meaning of the decisive statements out of their long and complicated construction, then it is clearly and correctly Reformed: real presence of Christ but double eating, parallelism of spiritual and physical eatings. But how concealed this meaning is under the strong words that appear to point in a very different direction! How could anyone who really wanted to learn something be instructed by this? And how justifiably enraged an upstanding Lutheran would have to become here! The paragraph about the 'eating by the unworthy' [manducatio indignorum] is certainly unambiguous enough, but then what is to be made of the little concluding sentence that they neither want to fight with nor condemn anyone on this matter? As though the writers of the confession had not known that

for them and their opponents *everything* depends on a Yes or No to this doctrine, so that it was highly inappropriate to lay out the contradiction here
only then to cover it up immediately with the blanket of a tolerant friendli-
ness toward all. This mild dismissal was of no service to the Lutherans and
was even less helpful to clarity in their own ranks. A dogmatics that does
not dare to state that an opposing doctrine is positively and clearly wrong
is simply *not* a dogmatics.

The short *Bentheim Confession* of 1613 is also a curious piece in the archives
(M 833–34). It contains in its twelve articles—which according to Müller are
still the obligatory confession in the Bentheim territories[198]—if I read them
properly, not a single proposition that a Lutheran could not also sign, even if
he might find some things missing. Article 3 repeats in three lines the Chalcedonian Christology without uttering a single treacherous word about the
unity and distinctiveness of the two natures. Articles 5–7 develop the doctrine
of the threefold office of Christ, perhaps in Article 7 with a mild implication
that Christ shares his grace "through the Spirit in the Word and Sacraments"
["Spiritu Verbo et Sacramentis"][199] with true believers and penitents. Article
8 contains the favored Calvinist statement about the justification and redemption of the Old Testament believers through faith in Christ.[200] But this is also
what Melanchthon taught.[201] Articles 10–11 speak of election but cautiously
only of election to salvation, adding superfluously that it is God's will to save
all believers and penitents, which obviously is not contestable but really has
nothing to do with the problem of predestination. It is finally Article 12 that
strikes a Reformed note: In the means of salvation, the beginning, middle, and
end are entirely ascribed to God, not, however, to the powers and works of
humans and their merits, neither wholly nor partially, as though the pious
and the believers could work with God to accomplish their salvation. But
which Lutheran would not *also* have said this, if it were rightly understood?
There is no article about the Lord's Supper at all!! When one observes such
things, then one must say that the evil Lutherans cannot be blamed if
Reformed consciousness has gradually grown weak in many places in Germany.[202] (If it is still relatively strong in Bentheim, then that cannot be traced
back to the fathers but to the relatively recent influence of Kohlbrügge.[203]) It
may well be that at the Reformed universities the truth was articulated more
clearly than in the two confessions we have just discussed. But if Reformed
theology was abandoned by the confessing Reformed *church* in this way, then
it is no wonder that the former with its schools became redundant over
time.[204] We can only note the Bentheim Confession as a third fatal example:
To say nothing at all is *also* not good Reformed theology!

Historically, the most important of the German Reformed defen-

| July 19 |

sive confessions is undoubtedly the so-called '*Confession of Sigismund*' (*Confessio Sigimundi*) or '*Of the Mark*' (*Marchica*) of Elector
Johann Sigismund of Brandenburg, 1614 (M 835[–43]).[205] His conversion

from the Lutheran to the Reformed church aroused the greatest attention and controversy of the various similar processes (Baden, Hesse), and it had the broadest consequences. At one time, Johann Sigismund had been required to make a vow to his grandfather, Elector *Johann Georg*, a zealous friend of Lutheranism, that he would remain true to the Formula of Concord. But a change began to develop under his father, *Joachim Friedrich*. It was the time in which Brandenburg began to pursue the independent political line that found its classic exponents later in the Great Elector and in Frederick the Great. Our confession is related very closely to this process that was of such decisive importance not only for German but for world history. For it led to a political linkage between Brandenburg and the Reformed Palatinate and the Reformed Netherlands in opposition to Lutheran Electoral Saxony, which was faithful to the emperor. Thus, Reformed church and theology entered into the perspective of the house of Hohenzollern. Johann Sigismund studied in Heidelberg, worked there on the critical response of the Zurich theologian Rudolf Hospinian to the Formula of Concord, the famous "Concordia discors,"[206] and was won over to Calvinism finally by his cousin, Landgrave Moritz of Hesse. One must assume in this instance as well that the political considerations attending this step were strongly accompanied by sincere personal conviction and that this is what primarily motivated him. The nobility of Brandenburg resisted mightily, also not for purely religious reasons but rather in continuation of Brandenburg's traditional tension between the crown and the estates. When reminded of the vow he had once taken to remain a Lutheran, and of various proofs of his having confirmed that promise, Johann Sigismund replied, "No declarations are valid in the affairs of God."[207] He also wrote to them that he had earlier believed everything that was said to him from the pulpit. "But when we then examined these documents and compared them to the divine Scriptures, our eyes were opened, praise God, so that we now knew how to distinguish the truth from the untruth."[208] The strong opposition led him, however, not to insist that his country follow his personal step, although, as he wrote, he would be entitled to "the introduction of religion as the highest royal right, freely and without limitation."[209] "We shall, however, leave you to your conscience without restriction and confusion and will, conversely, not permit you as my subjects to impose upon my conscience."[210] This became the occasion when, voluntarily and involuntarily, the old legal principle "whoever the ruler his religion" ["cujus regio ejus religio"][211] was violated for the first time, resulting in a parity arrangement for the Lutheran and Reformed church in the same state. This meant that the Lutheran pastors' custom of reviling their opponents from the pulpit was now legally forbidden,[212] which prohibition resulted later in the Lutheran martyrdom of Paul Gerhardt,[213] and similarly of Johann Arndt as a result of the repression of exorcism in Anhalt.[214] To justify his personal step, the Elector promulgated our confession, "so that it may be made known in all Christendom that his Electoral Grace opens up the gates of his realm to the King of glory" (M 836,6). A certain Superintendent Füssel seems to have been decisively engaged in the composition of it.[215] In the course of the seventeenth century, it joined the Thorn Declaration and the Records of the Leipzig Conversation as the criterion for the confessional stance of the Reformed Church of Brandenburg. |

The *Christology*[216] begins with the concept of *personal union*. It is the presupposition upon which everything that can be said about *God* and about a true *human* can be said about Christ, for example, that he is with us and will remain to the end of the world in accordance with his infinite nature, his divine majesty, and his powerful support, but not according to the nature by which he ascended into heaven and from whence he shall return. For *this* nature could not be everywhere without destroying its properties, even in their highest glory. In general, *"abstract locutions"* [*"locutiones abstractivae"*][217] (statements about the *one* nature of Christ per se!) should be avoided, since they necessarily bring about a false extension, comparison, and finally eradication of one or the other nature or natural characteristic. And this "was taught neither by the orthodox fathers nor by Luther."[218] |

The *doctrine of the Lord's Supper*[219] proceeds in a parallel fashion from the idea of *sacramental union*, the connection (parallelism) of the eating and drinking of bread and wine with the *mouth*, and of body and blood of Christ with *faith* in this divine action, which *as such* is the basis for the sacrament, instituted by God. Thus, bread and wine *are "sacramentally"* the body and blood of Christ, namely, as signs, but not as bare and empty signs but rather instituted as a "memorial of trust, of thanks, and of love."[220] But since *faith* is the mouth that receives the body and blood of the Lord, the sacrament cannot benefit the impenitent, for which a diplomatically well-chosen sermon of the younger Luther is quoted. It is the same one that Zwingli often cited against Luther, where he said, "Just as the sacrament is a proper food, whoever does not receive it with one's heart through faith is not helped by it, for it does not make someone into a believer but rather requires that he already be pious and a believer."[221] Great emphasis here is also made upon the fact that at the Lord's Supper one should use simple *house bread* and not unleavened bread or oblates, so that it is clear that just as bread strengthens and maintains the human body, so the body of Christ is really a heavenly food that nourishes, feeds, and maintains. Just as important is the *breaking of the bread* as a constantly true picture of the first Lord's Supper: This is my body which is *broken* for you. For this, Luther is also cited[222] here somewhat less happily, for it really can*not* be shown that Luther had ever taken a positive interest in this custom, even if he occasionally mentioned it. |

Aside from dealing with Christ and the Lord's Supper, the confession also addresses Baptism[223] and predestination,[224] the latter with a certain eclecticism. God's eternal gracious election is affirmed for the believers, expressly in the strict sense of pre*determination*, not simply pre*knowledge*. On the other hand, the 'absolute decree' [decretum absolutum] with regard to the godless is rejected; God had seen these from eternity and even prepared the eternal fire of hell for them, but the cause of their sin and destruction rests in themselves and in Satan. "Here his Electoral Grace rejects each and every opinion and saying, in part blasphemous and in part dangerous, to the effect that man must with his reason climb up to heaven and examine in some special register or in God's secret chancery or council room who is foreseen for eternal life and who not, since God has sealed the book of life so that no creature can look into it."[225] I cite this passage because it, and the entire section on predestination, is characteristic of the way in which generally one grappled with this problem in Germany. One emphasized firmly and in very Calvinist tones predestination to salvation, avoided predestination to damnation, without giving clear information about the rationale for doing so, and then appealed to the mystery of God that we cannot explain. I scarcely need to say that Calvin himself never thought that one could climb up to heaven with one's reason and there ascertain with the book of life who were elect and who not.[226] But that such a book of life *exists*, even if we cannot look into it, is something he certainly did assert,[227] and the German Reformed did not contest it, except that, as we said, they had no burning interest in this question over against Lutheranism and were thus always prepared to be broadly accommodating in this matter.[228] |

Generally, with regard to the central questions of Christ and the Lord's Supper, the Confession of Sigismund, if not especially profound, belongs among the clearly Reformed confessions of Germany. The conclusion of the document is a justification of the Lutheran-Reformed parity introduced in Brandenburg.[229] The Elector was certain that his confession conformed to the Word of God and wished nothing more than that his faithful subjects might be blessed and illumined by the light of infallible truth. Yet faith was not every man's affair but a work and gift of God, and it was not allowed to anyone to rule over the conscience (the attitude of the nobility did contribute something to this insight!). Thus, the course and progress of the truth should be commended to God alone. The Elector would hope, desire, and command that those subjects who do not understand the disputed matters of religion, "should renounce blaspheming, reviling, defaming the 'orthodox and reformed' [orthodoxos et reformatos] whom one loudly calls Calvinist out of pure envy, . . . they should be patient with the weak where they believe that they are strong . . . and what they have not themselves read nor adequately understood up to now, they should not call heresy and condemn."[230] |

We conclude our third section appropriately with the records of the *Leipzig Conversations of 1631* (Augusti 386[–410]). It was at the time of a high point of the Thirty Years' War, after Gustav Adolf entered the battle, when a convention of all the evangelical imperial estates took place in Leipzig to discuss the political situation. This opportunity was used by the Reformed court preachers of Elector Georg Wilhelm of Brandenburg, *Johann Berg*, and of the aforementioned Landgrave Wilhelm of Hesse, *Theophilus Neuberger*, and with them the Marburg professor *Johann Crocius*, to extend a feeler to the theologians of Electoral Saxony, among whom at the time the senior court preacher D. Mathias Hoë von Hoënegg was the leader.[231] People called him the "high priest" or also the "oracle of the Holy Spirit" ["oraculum spiritus sancti"].[232] Among the many things to be said about him, some of them not all that positive, I will mention only that he was a great polemicist before the Lord and had proven in print that the Calvinists "at ninety-nine points are in agreement with the Arians and the Turks."[233] They certainly had come to the right place when they turned to this remarkable character. Hermelink was of the opinion that what then happened was the greatest comedy of his life, and we can add that, in 1636, when the conversation came to an amicable conclusion, he did in fact remark with a sigh, "This is now the fourth year that I have not published a polemical writing against the Calvinists."[234] Representing the Lutherans were also the two Leipzig professors, *Polykarp Leyser*[235] and *Heinrich Höpffner*. |

They began with a very ceremonial preliminary negotiation. The Reformed pointed out the rejoicing of the papists at the divisions in the evangelical camp, and raised the desire of their princes to end or at least to soften the confessional disputes. Would it please the Lutherans to discuss with them without prejudice and harmlessly as "a pure and honest private action"[236] how far one might come toward and achieve such a good intention. They were "of a mind to do and accomplish everything [that could be done] to build up and facilitate this intended work, without prejudice to the conscience."[237] The Lutherans responded that it was also no secret to them how fatal the growing dispute was, and that they wished "that God might give and grant wholesome ways and means for agreement," and they were "more than willing" to do their part, while reserving their concern for matters of divine truth. This was indeed "a work of high importance" that did not only concern them and that they could not engage on their own, but only in consultation with their Electoral Prince and his privy counselors, "because the matter impinges upon the 'public state' [statum publicum]."[238] The Reformed then responded that they were not seeking anything dangerous or harmful, but that they expected that, once a good beginning were made, other theologians in Germany would join them, and they hoped that his Electoral Highness in Saxony would "not be in opposition to this work."[239] That was indeed not the case, and even His

Majesty's Lord Privy Counselors were agreeable in that it was to be certainly nothing more than a private and harmless conference with the intent to consider whether and to what extent one would be in agreement with the Augsburg Confession and whether and how one might move closer to one another. |

So, with three persons representing each side, they convened for their first real meeting on March 3 in the residence of the Saxon senior court preacher in the name of the Most Holy Trinity. The negotiation began with the Reformed declaring their willingness to confess the Augustana Invariata, and if required to sign it! But—note the Reformed reservation—they did not want to cast aside the edition of 1540 and 1541, which means that they maintained the right to interpret the Invariata in terms of the Variata.[240] They then left these dangerous initial questions and decided to talk through the paragraphs of the Augsburg Confession, one after another. They were in agreement in the first article, dealing with *God*. All the same, the Reformed, in view of the anti-Trinitarian proximity to the left wing with which one liked to confuse them,[241] delivered a declaration of their Trinitarian orthodoxy and of their faith that God was 'simply' [simpliciter] omnipotent, that nothing was impossible for him except what according to his Word was contrary to his nature and his will.[242] In the second article, addressing *original sin*, they determined that original sin was real sin in all people from birth on, even in the children of believers. Zwingli's special teaching on this point[243] was expressly dropped by the Reformed. |

Then they moved on to the third article, dealing with *Christ*, where understandably they remained one and one-half days.[244] The Reformed initially declared their completely Chalcedonian Orthodoxy and that they took everything literally which was in the article and expressed the wish that one should be satisfied with this summary confession. (One will have to intervene that this was not a good wish! All of the German Reformed confessions, with the exception of the Bentheim Articles, show conclusively that the Reformed knew that they stood here in a decisive and serious contradiction to Lutheranism. How was it possible now, in the very moment where they had their opponents at sword's point, that they should *not talk about it*? What else did they have to discuss? one might ask. What would be the point of an agreement if they did not want to reach on agreement *on this point*, about which they notoriously had been *arguing*?) It was not a laudable achievement of the participating Reformed that they had to hear their opponents tell them that they were dealing with high and major points about which they were *not* in agreement, and thus they were literally forced to take a position. Since the days of Bucer,[245] it has been a major weakness that the Reformed have often proceeded more irenically than substantively, and have left the impression that Luther could not have been all that wrong when he often accused them that they apparently wished that the beer were back in the keg.[246] The discussion of Christology was then carried out in such a way that they first agreed on twelve paragraphs that they could affirm in common, after which the Lutheran and Reformed contingency each presented a separate statement. We now are so well acquainted with the material that it is neither all that difficult nor uninteresting to attempt to think through these three presentations today.

Lutheran and Reformed   First of all, then, *what they have in common*.[247] The personal union of the Son of God with a perfect human nature consisting of body and soul was not only 'verbally' [verbaliter] but with true conviction

L.   affirmed by both sides. No separation of the two natures ever took place from conception onward, not even in death: the Son of God is never with-

R.   out his flesh. The natures, or their properties, are just as little to be inter-mingled with each other, even though they are united. The divine nature is not the human nature, and vice versa; both natures *and* their properties

L.   remain what they are in eternity. One can and should say, for example, that the Son of God, the Lord of glory, the prince of life, the eternally praise-worthy God suffered *according to his flesh*, that is, that he took upon himself the suffering of the flesh so that the blood shed for us is not mere human

R.   blood but the blood of the Son of God. But one should not say that the deity

R.   itself suffered. The *whole* Christ, without division of the natures, is all-knowing, all-powerful, present everywhere, without these properties per-taining to the human nature *as such*, but rather in such a way that they are ascribed to the whole *person* for the sake of the personal union of deity and

*L.   humanity. *This whole Christ is to be worshiped, rules, **descended into

**R.   hell, ascended spatially and visibly into heaven as a particular place insti-

*L.   tuted by God and located in the heights, *without being restricted to it. The right hand of God is not a created place, and Christ's sitting there is not a physical or spatial sitting, but rather the right hand of God is God's majesty, power, and omnipotence, and Christ's sitting there is his ruling and gov-erning according to both natures. According to both natures he also carried out the work of mediation and redemption, his human nature never excluded, so that the flesh of Christ is truly 'vivifying flesh' [caro vivifica].

Secondly, the *separate Lutheran statement*.[248] Christ is also, accord-

| July 20 | ing to his human nature, truly omniscient, omnipotent, and omnipresent, but in such a way that these properties are conceived

L.   of not as natural ones but rather as properties of the *person* communicated through the personal union and exaltation. To utter divine predicates of Christ is only meaningful in relation to this *human* nature, so the Luther-ans argue that "the highest is not exalted but the flesh is exalted to the high-est,"[249] not outside the person but *in* the person. |

R.   Thirdly, the *separate Reformed statement*.[250] It is conceded that from eter-nity Christ is already all that these predicates say about him, according to his deity. They do *not* say *anything new* about his deity as such. Nor do they about his humanity *as such*! The exaltation of the whole Christ to the right hand of God means, in relation to his humanity, its *transfiguration*, its elevation above all other creatures, while in relation to deity it means its complete transfiguration and revelation *before us humans*. The omnipresence of the whole Christ as mediator and head of his church does not mean that Christ according to his humanity, the *human* nature of Christ, his body according to its *substance*, is present with all creatures, either in the state of humiliation or of exaltation, either because of the personal union or because of his sitting and ruling at the right hand of God. The omniscience and omnipotence given to the human nature is *not the same* as that of the divine nature. The Reformed stated at the time that they would most prefer to remain with the formulations that are expressly used in the Bible, in the most ancient general conciliar decisions, and in the Augsburg Confession. |

Was this really a joint agreement or not? One can say both that they agreed about what they did not agree on, *and* they did not agree about what they did agree on. The point in which they did agree was the *'personal union'* [*unio personalis*], the reality of God's becoming human, Jesus the Christ, the contingent revelation, the 'vivifying flesh' [caro vivifica]. What then did they really agree on? On the fact that they were not in agreement about this one definite point that they were considering together. They were not talking past each other. They did in fact mean the same thing. But they meant it in different ways. The *Lutherans* admit that the issue at stake is the human person who is *God*, that is, the contingent *revelation*, the '*vivifying* flesh' [caro *vivifica*]. But then they push further: It is about the *man* Jesus Christ who is God, the *contingent* revelation of God, the 'vivifying *flesh*' [*caro* vivifica]. What especially interests them in the 'personal union' [unio personalis] of the God-man is that in him God is *revealed, present, given*; therefore, they press precisely the *divine* predicates of the *human* nature, the identity of the baby in the manger with the one who sat in the Father's bosom, that is, the immediate *nearness* of the distant God given in Christ. The *Reformed*, on the other hand, admit that the issue at stake is the *human* Christ who is God, the *contingent* revelation, the 'vivifying *flesh*' [*caro* vivifica]. But they are then seized by the disquiet that goes in precisely the reverse direction for the Lutherans; their concern is about the human who is *God*, the *contingent* revelation, the '*vivifying* flesh' [caro *vivifica*]. What interests them about the 'personal union' [unio personalis] of the God-man is that *God* is revealed, present, and given here (more than his being *revealed*, his being *present*, his being *given*!), and so they resist ascribing divine predicates as such to the human nature, and they are especially focused on the identity of the man Jesus with the *resurrected, exalted* Christ, that is, on the distance of the God who is immediately near in Christ. |

So they were in agreement and disagreement on precisely the same point, simply because this one point, Jesus-Christ, contingent-revelation, 'vivifying-flesh' [caro-vivifica], is *one* point, the 'personal union' [unio personalis], which was acknowledged by both sides. But in thinking it through, in attempting to *talk* about it, this point necessarily had to separate into *two* points. If one began at one of the two, then one would necessarily arrive at the Lutheran view, and if one began at the other of the two, then one would necessarily arrive at the Reformed view. One might say that the partners approached each other, each beginning from one's own point of view, met each other for just a moment at the middle, and then arrived at the place from which the other had started. They were both saying the same thing as long as it signified simply the one point Jesus Christ, following the line of the Chalcedonian formula. But this one point was for both sides of such burning importance that they could not avoid interpreting it, conceptualizing it, speaking clearly about it. And then they were no longer saying the same thing, or rather, in that they were saying the same thing, something emerged on both sides that was offensive for the other. On the *Lutheran side,* it was an *undialectical step forward,* the uninhibited definition of the human nature of Christ with the predicates of deity, a total unifying of revelation with the contingent in which it reveals itself. On the *Reformed* side, it was a *dialectical step back,* the Reformed reservation, the 'Calvinist extra' [extra Calvinisticum],[251] according to which the humanity does not participate in the predicates of deity in the full sense. Thus, a certain reserve is secured for the Godhead as *God*head, a concealment in revelation, one might say. |

One should not too quickly concur with the one side or the other. One is dealing here indeed with very difficult problems, which, in part, we must learn to *see* again. It is even less acceptable to move quickly to the middle with the thesis that both sides were right. Three hundred years ago they would have been delighted to take up that middle position, when it was not uninvolved spectators like us but the contenders themselves who wanted to do so. Neither of the parties had any awareness that they were occupying an extreme position; both thought that they were entirely in the center. The concessions that they made to each other almost rendered the differences unrecognizable. This we see when we study the statements about which they reached agreement in Leipzig. They demonstrate *how* close to each other they were, how much both were actually saying one thing. And yet the division precisely in this one thing was unavoidable. It is almost a reflection of the great subject *itself* that we have before us when we look at the dialectic of this dispute as it presents itself at this its highest point! Whoever could say here, not as a theory but as a realized cognition, that both were right would have to be greater than Luther and Calvin, both of whom were not in such a happy place. For us the situation is likely to be, based on instinct or insight or habit, that we tend to assign *more* validity to the one *or* the other side and thus feel ourselves, for better or for worse, to be Lutherans or Reformed. It is not necessary today to add the express admonition that one should avoid being either a bigoted Lutheran or Reformed. The contrary danger is much greater, which is that one simply no longer sees the problems of the fathers and no longer understands their actual relevance. The result is that one thinks that the confessional contradiction has been overcome even though one would have absolutely no way of answering the question *to what extent* it were really overcome and what is then the resolution of the question of contingent revelation, which is what divided the confessions back then. |

The Prussian Union theology did not, in any event, provide that resolution. The only way to a legitimate union would be the continuation of the Leipzig conversation in *our* language, presupposing everything that has happened in the meantime: the emergence of a pure historical consciousness, of a critical philosophy, and not least the new discovery of the eschatological character of Christianity. What a focusing and deepening of the old question would result from these three changes in the situation! It should be said, however, that it would have to be the continuation of the *conversation* and not of the *dispute*, but a continuation of the conversation conducted with the full seriousness and emphasis of the dispute. The conversation back then revealed that it was not possible for either side to claim triumphantly to have been right. Thus, it was a good thing that they went their separate ways not in anger but with polite bows and appeals to the God of truth and of peace. The fact that they *went their separate ways*, that in the midst of the Thirty Years' War they dared to be so impractical, so little opportunistic that they did *not* embrace each other but rather determined that they both agreed and disagreed about the 'union of the natures in Christ' [unio naturarum in Christo], is a serious admonition for something which modern Protestantism has broadly forgotten, for an unconditional theological objectivity. It is not necessary that we again deride each other as Arians and Turks,[252] but it is necessary that a serious grappling for the truth should begin on both sides, that truth which stands, mysteriously unifying and separating, between the two great types of Protestant Christianity. I need not say how much from both directions, from both Luther and Calvin, would have to be thought through anew, given the presuppositions of modernity, and how very different the *historical* picture of the conflict would be now if the question of the sixteenth and seventeenth centuries should be revived for us today. As far as the future of intellectual history is concerned, one can posit neither wishes nor prophecies, and I would like to ask you not to understand my remarks as such. But one may and one can say when looking back at the past that here a beginning is waiting for a continuation, that something has been postponed here which cannot be, for that reason, set aside.

Now I have anticipated what I really wanted to say as a conclusion of this entire section, because it lent itself best to the discussion of the third article. I still must report to you about the process of the remainder of the conversation. Article 4 (on justification)[253] produced a little hesitation, although not at that point where we would probably hesitate but rather with the clause, "that Christ suffered for us." The Lutherans asked, in view of the doctrine of predestination whether Christ had died for all people? The Reformed said yes. Was God's will that all people should be saved through faith not just an ostensible will (again, this was focused on pre-destination)? The Reformed said no. No one is excluded who does not exclude himself through his unbelief. Articles 5, 6, 7, and 8 went by without problems. Consider what that means! We are dealing here with the articles on the office of preaching, the new obedience, and the church. If the usual views of the historical relationship were correct, according to which either the differing view of the relation between religion and ethics or of the sociological structure constituted a division between the parties,[254] then the Reformed would certainly have had much to object to! They would have had to speak out about the entirely lacking principle of Scripture; they would have objected to the fifth article's approach to the preaching office, with its hierarchical approach so strange for Reformed sensibilities; based on the Reformed view of sanctification, they would have had to remark about the inadequacies of Article 6 where, with all the emphasis upon faith and the forgiveness of sins, there is virtually no mention of the new obedience; they would have insisted that the two 'marks of the church' [notae ecclesiae] in the seventh article be expanded to include the third, church discipline; and they would never have let Article 8 pass muster where the purity of the church is exclusively defined in terms of ecclesial office. There is nothing of that. They "accepted the Electoral Saxon document completely, without any changes, as that which was taught at all times in their churches."[255] It can be shown black on white that this was *not* the case in the German Reformed churches. Why then were there no objections? Why were there also none from the Lutheran side, when they were otherwise visibly eager to pounce on any divisive matter that the Reformed might have wanted to discard under the table? Reformed dis-simulation cannot be ruled out. But one must apparently assume that the period in question saw no problems or at least nothing fundamentally divi-sive, where we might see enormous divisive mountains with our specta-cles, and that they saw *the* problem at a point where our history is silent, partially out of pity and partially out of a lack of understanding. At Arti-cle 9, on baptism[256]—they were getting closer to the burning bush—the Reformed appeared to have made an independent move. They emphasize the necessity of baptism for the sake of its divine institution and promise, and also that the *power* of baptism is not 'by the doing of the act' [ex opere operato] nor by external sprinkling but again due to divine institution and promise. One might be puzzled that the Lutherans found nothing to say in response. |

All of March 7 was devoted to Article 10, on the *Lord's Supper*.[257] The negotiations began with the Reformed accepting the article in the version of the Invariata,[258] "word for word,"[259] which created no problem if they were dealing with the shorter Latin text. They then expressly rejected the doctrine of the transformation of the elements (no one mentioned the Lutheran awkwardness that this doctrine is expressly stated in the corresponding article of the Apology[260]), the doctrine of concomitance, of the sacramental presence of Christ in the elements 'beyond their usage' [extra usum], all spatial and physical presence of the body of Christ, and all adoration of the bread. They then confessed positively the presence not only of the elements, not only of naked signs, not only of the power and effect of Christ, but of the true and essential body and blood itself, which (and here they made a decisive error) "is truly and presently offered, distributed, and consumed *by means of* the blessed bread and wine,"[261] by virtue of the 'sacramental union' [unio sacramentalis] (the parallelism) that consists not only of meaning nor of sealing but takes place in the passing out of the earthly elements. The Lutherans found nothing to object to in this. They also reached agreement on these propositions: The spiritual eating comprehends not only the power and the effect but also the being and substance of the body and blood of Christ, and it, the eating and drinking *of faith*, is indispensable. Simultaneously with this spiritual eating, the external also happens. The Reformed soundly reject the idea that the organ of such eating was the mouth and that both the worthy and the unworthy experience it. But they concede that the true body of Christ is received by means of(!) the bread, but "not with the mouth rather solely through faith"[262] (here their willingness to be accommodating again takes its toll)! The *Lutherans* then develop their idea in this fashion: *By means of* the elements, the body and blood of Christ are eaten, and drunk *orally* (they are logical!). But in this eating, the mode of the actual consumption must be differentiated: While the mouth eats the elements, it also eats the body and blood of Christ by virtue of the blessing of the elements, in a heavenly and supernatural way known only to God, and thus without any physical and natural swallowing, chewing, or consuming. This was the artful tactic with which later Lutherans sought to avoid the real chewing and swallowing of the body of Christ, as Luther himself had occasionally taught,[263] and still maintain the oral eating of the body of Christ. It was at the fine line between the spiritual eating of body and blood by means of bread and wine that was the Reformed concession, and the nonphysical 'oral eating' [manducatio oralis] known only to God with which the Lutherans countered, that they separated with an express reference to Marburg in 1529.[264] It would have been easy for a generation with less character to have said, "We mean the same thing, so let us be brothers!" But no, the fathers admitted openly to each other that although they were very near to each other, they did not mean the same thing, and they risked putting the truth *over* peace. I

In Article 11, dealing with repentance, the Reformed gave the desired notice that they could acknowledge the Lutheran rite of confession as a free and good ceremony.[265] They were in complete agreement on Articles 12–28, again an impossibility if the old Protestants had been thinking the way they would have had to, based on our assumptions. In relation to Article 19, the Reformed declared that God was not the origin of sin and that they rejected Calvin's double decree.[266] This led to a sequel related to the question of predestination that was not foreseen in the Augsburg Confession.[267] The Reformed responded to this in the rather inadequate way we have already encountered in the Confession of Sigismund.[268] They said that they emphasized election to salvation strongly and exclusively; they ascribed the guilt of the damned to them themselves; they related the question of election not to the secret decree of God but rather to his revealed Word and the fruit of faith; they rejected the foolish consequences of a concept of election understood in such a way. These were all things that Calvin had said, and said better,[269] and that should not have permitted the German Reformed to be spared serious thought about divine judgment as the *ultimate* truth. The counter declaration of the Lutherans[270] on this theme differs only in that they changed predestination to damnation expressly into a mere fore*knowledge* of the unbelief of those affected, just as predestination to salvation is a 'predestination based on the foreseeing of faith' [praedestinatio ex praevisa fide].[271] The Reformed could not then accede to this more deficient although more logical doctrine of the Formula of Concord. But the whole thing was more like an epilogue, and *this* difference would not have separated the parties. The divisive issues remained Christology and the Lord's Supper. They took their leave accompanied by solemn reservations and protests regarding the consequences of the process but still in a friendly and loyal way, promising to practice Christian love, "in all faithfulness and without jeopardy."[272] A similar conversation had taken place in Berlin around 1670, also without results.[273] It was not the triumph of truth but of indifference, which then in the eighteenth and nineteenth centuries produced the peace so much desired.[274]

4. THE BATTLE AGAINST MODERN CHRISTIANITY

July 24

The Reformation was neither the last phase of medieval Christianity, as Troeltsch saw it,[1] nor the first phase of modern Christianity, as popular modern theology sees it.[2] Regardless of the traces of the medieval and the modern that cling to it, the Reformation stands over against both, at least in its core and its original intention, as something new and alien, a third entity.[3] The young Luther does not fit neatly with either Dante or Goethe, Saint Thomas or Schleiermacher. He stands on his own, and in contrast to him the enormous contrasts between the medieval and modern approaches merge in a remarkable way into *one* front. Was he battling against the Middle Ages or modernity in his struggle with Erasmus? Should one not set aside this either/or and respond that, in Erasmus, both in their characteristic unity were positioned over against him? In his battle with the enthusiasts of his day, whom some justifiably see as the predecessors of modern Christianity,[4] he used with instinctive certainty the same arguments that he used against the old church. Looking at both fronts he saw faith in reason, monkery and works holiness, endangerment of the certainty of faith, and autonomous rebellion against the eternal truth and order of God. For him the papists were clandestine enthusiasts, as were the enthusiasts hidden papists. Like a bolt of lightning, his original intuition strikes between the ages as something that neither the old nor the new man, neither the captive nor the liberated spirits grasp: the sinful person made just before God through grace in faith. Neither the earlier typical medieval nor the later typical modern had counted on the immediate actuality of God's relationship with humanity, although there are certainly lines leading both backward and forward from this knowledge. Both sides begin with the human person, with nature, with reason in its best sense and build further on this safe and broad foundation, with the help of revelation. Christianity appears as a great pedagogy, a pathway along which the human partly walks, is partly led, and is partly carried along by supernatural power. It is indeed the highest and greatest thing in the world, but in the *world* it has other things next to it. It is and wants to be a historical force, even if it also characterizes itself as the salvation-historical force. The human person is first of all a human person and *then* a Christian, and always still a *human person* next to his Christianity, even if in a definite relationship to it. And as a human person he is obviously the measure of his Christianity as he is the measure of all things.[5] All medieval and modern supranaturalism should not deceive us as to the fundamental character of this common fact. If one wants to see how easily and brilliantly medieval Christianity could be modern, without sacrificing anything essential to it, one should study the basic principles of the Jesuits, which differ from the similar instructions of the Freemasons or today's anthroposophists only in that the Jesuits are much more clever and profound in their relation to the common goal of perfecting the human with God's help, or however the alleged supernatural factor might be called. If you want to get to know a typically medieval and at the same time modern, typically un-Reformation and *anti*-Reformation teaching from *our* day, in a somewhat different mixture than that of Erasmus, then read Friedrich Wilhelm Foerster.[6] |

The Reformation in its original intention begins with revelation, with the Word, and with faith. It is thoroughly unpedagogical. It does not begin with human interests, among which emerges finally, ultimately, and as the highest point, the interest in God; rather, it begins with God's interest in the human person. It does not show the way that the human should seek and follow, but rather, the way that God has already found to him. It is impractical: It demands of humans either too much or too little, depending on one's view. In terms of its intention, it is very difficult if not impossible for it to integrate itself into what humans otherwise want. With its conception of life it stands there like an erratic block between the splendor of the medieval and the no less splendid modern consciousness. It proclaims that the human is *not* the measure of all things, least of all Christianity, and positions him before the reality *of God*. The Reformation is only truly itself in this battle position. One must, in fact, say that it lived from that conflict. |

When the Helmstedt theologian Calixt began to speak about the reconciliation of the Christian churches,[7] when the last persecution of the Huguenots was over,[8] when again there was an up-to-date Protestant Christianity that fit the changed modern situation, God was certainly not dead. There must be such peaceful passages in history where the permanent crisis in the relationship between God and humanity is only latently present and at work, known only to the "quiet in the land"[9]—but by then the Reformation was over. That there could be a Christianity that had made its peace with the modern conception of humanity, that itself had become modern, is as impossible from the standpoint of the living, unfolding Reformation as that Calvin would have put his name to Trent.[10] Seen from the perspective of the Reformation, the emergence of modern Christianity was *possible* only as the enemy that had to be opposed and battled against. We may have our reasons to want to be modern Christians *in spite of all that*, but we must be clear about the fact that, seen from the Reformation's view, we are positioning ourselves precisely against Luther with *Karlstadt*, and against Calvin with a *Socinus*, a *Blandrata*, a *Castellio*, a *Bolsec*, a *Servetus*,[11] or against the fathers of Dort with the *Remonstrants*. In the portrayals of this last Pyrrhic victory of Reformation Christianity over the enemy from the left, we sense even in a man like *Seeberg* the unmistakable sympathy of the modern man for those figures who are closer to us both intellectually and personally, people like Coornhert, Wtenbogaert, Arminius, Hugo Grotius, and Episcopius.[12] These truly noble and highly respectable men would have graced appropriately any modern Protestant (even positivist!) pulpit or professorial chair! Who would be so presumptuous today as to expel such spirits with the peremptory "You are dismissed! Go! Go! ("Dimittimini, ite, ite!") with which Bogerman[13] at the memorable 57th meeting of the synod ejected Episcopius and his fifteen comrades from the assembly—where they had only appeared as the defendants—and thus out of the church.[14] But we must then admit that the fathers of Dort were doubtless *right* when they described the doctrine of these men as thoroughly Semi-Pelagian, and thus as a revival of Catholic Christianity. But who then are *we*, and where do *we* stand in relation to the Reformation if we should find these men to be most sympathetic to our position now? If Troeltsch had expanded his well-known thesis[15] that these figures and the related anti-Reformation circles of the sixteenth and seventeenth centuries were the actual predecessors and ancestors of our Christianity, with a further thesis to the effect that with them we must make our commitment to Semi-Pelagianism and thus to solidarity with the anti-Reformational Middle Ages, then his theology would have truly been a word of redemption. The request, "Tell me thy company,"[16] would need once to be put very bluntly to modern Protestantism in order to get it *either* to return to the Catholic Church, to which only because of a small misunderstanding it does not belong today, *or* to consider how it might again be or could become Reformation Christianity. I need scarcely to say that this does not imply the reintroduction of the Canons of Dort.

By the very nature of things, the battle against *this* enemy, modern Christianity, fell primarily, or better, *entirely* to the lot of early *Reformed* Protestantism. Zwingli and Calvin were undoubtedly modern men, both of them students of Erasmus.[17] The new world of the Renaissance was a serious matter for them, which it never was for Luther, just as conversely for them the Middle Ages were already over. All of Reformed Christianity is to be understood as the attempt to understand the human person, who through the Reformation was again placed before the immediate reality of God, as *human*, in the *world*, in *history*, but not at peace with so much as at *war* with the world, and yet in *relationship* to it. In a way very different from Lutheranism, it is looking at *modern* man, at the *modern* world, although certainly in its very primitive beginnings. It stands in the midst of the turmoil that had descended upon old Europe. Virtually everywhere, the early Reformed were already in some way outwardly liberated from the old unity and tradition, as citizens of dynamic city-states, as defiant or persecuted political minorities, as members of the newly developing trade and merchant states. Everywhere they interacted with the great emancipation from the structures of authoritarian subordination, as medieval culture was now viewed, and in contrast with which the Renaissance person set out confidently to build a totally new world. The Reformed movement is at many points very similar to such emancipative and progressive movements. It will not have been a coincidence that Reformed Christianity could only put down deep roots where the Middle Ages were definitely over, politically, economically, and culturally. In the German language area, this was in Switzerland, along the Rhine River, generally in the west, but not in the north and the east. Its biblicism is reminiscent of humanism, its dialectic is reminiscent of philosophy, its emphasis upon an independent ethic is reminiscent of the moralism of secular contemporaries. I say, "is reminiscent," but no more than that. What we see is that they took the neighbor on their borders seriously since they had to live and talk with him. But they did it by *guarding* their borders. They would not let him in; they were totally different from him and wanted to be so precisely because they knew him so well. When it came to differentiating themselves from the Christianity of the day, be it humanist, moralist, open to revelation, secretly rejecting revelation, or evading it, Calvin and his successors and students did not draw the line any less sharply than did the Lutherans. One must in fact say that they drew the line more sharply, in a more detailed way, and with greater anxiety. They knew better whom they were dealing with precisely because they had so much in common with their opponents, personally, politically, and culturally. |

The dispute that they conducted in the name of all of Protestantism focused more and more upon one point, the concept of God. At Dort the hotly debated issue was once again predestination. It was the doctrine that we defined in our first section as the doctrine of the anti-Roman battle. I see evidence in this for the correctness of the view that medieval and modern Christianity belong together, at least in terms of the self-awareness of the early Protestants. The same decisive concept of the majesty of God that had once been hurled at the old opponent now had to be defended against the new one. The arena in which the battle surfaced was *Holland*, which at that time was *the* modern state in Europe. It had just emerged from the wars for liberty against Habsburg Spain, was thoroughly republican and also capitalist, as far as these terms may be used for that period, and it was on the verge of becoming a sea and trade power of the first rank. (Hermelink points out that the entire dispute that climaxed at Dort took place in the midst of the formation of the East and West Indian Companies, commercial endeavors that must have had a fantastic impact on the consciousness of that time.)[18] Add to that the self-confident, stolid, and yet flexible, practical, and goal-driven types of people whom we know from Rembrandt's paintings. Now I have already said that this Holland was a very remarkable center in terms of the religious and doctrinal history in those centuries.[19] All the possible mystical, Baptist, and spiritualist threads converge here, most of them with roots going back to the pre-Reformation period. Here is where Erasmus had his home. This is where Zwingli's doctrine of the Lord's Supper got its thorn, the "signifies" ("significat").[20] This is where the so-called Calvinist Libertines emerged and spread.[21] The radical East Friesians on the left wing of the Reformed movement took their inspiration here.[22] How much more could be mentioned here! |

Shaped by persecution, Calvinism had initially established itself around the middle of the sixteenth century. No sooner had things become outwardly peaceful again than a strong resistance to it emerged from this side, for the first time along a broad front. It was not borne so much by unstable refugees like Bolsec and Servetus as by peaceful, honorable, and thoughtful men. But it was nonetheless a decisive resistance, the first perceptible wave of the emerging modern world that would find it impossible to make peace with Reformation Christianity. Let me briefly describe some of the people who were part of this process. There was, around 1560, *Jacob Acontius*,[23] who renounced all confessional statements in favor of the Bible alone because of the moral purposefulness of all its Christian doctrines. Every person, but especially lazy pastors, is inwardly a papist. Synodal majorities lead as a rule to the victory of Satan. In the question of the Lord's Supper, both the Reformed *and* the Lutherans are right. But there should be no one-sidedness, no impetuousness, no domination by the theologians! Beyond the present struggles lie the ideas of tolerance and hope for the ecclesial unity of the various parties. Then there is the statesman *Dieryck Coornhert* (1522–1590),[24] who was also the representative of a superior piety and tolerance. The most important thing is the practical Christianity of daily life. God and free human will must work together. Just as human sin is real, restoration through the "true medicine man" ("Medezijnmeester")[25] Christ must also be real and not just imputed, for such would be a delusionary righteousness. But in point of fact, Christ makes people morally healthy, and precisely that is justification. A God who destines a portion of humanity for condemnation is unacceptable, comparable to a medical doctor who first poisons the well and then, when everyone is sick, demonstrates his art by healing some. No, in contrast with irrational creatures, the human person is subject to no absolute necessity. But then, in his emphasis on sanctification and moral perfection, Coornhert appears to be in full agreement again with Reformed church doctrine. There is *Jacob Arminius* (1560–1609),[26] a student of Beza. When he was commissioned by his provincial synod to rebut two Delft theologians who were attacking absolute predestination, the encounter left him confused about the matter as well. As a professor in Leiden he got involved in serious struggles with his colleague Franz Gomarus,[27] who was the most important and most consistent of the Calvinists. His motto was "paradise is a good conscience,"[28] and his doctrine stated that the work of rebirth took place in a gradual development guided by God. Predestination was a prescience of God over believing persons as they persisted in their faith. We hear well-known sounds from the court preacher *Johann Wtenbogaert* (1557–1644).[29] Whatever we do, no dogmatizing! Rather, edify! No binding of the spirits through confession and catechism! Following the death of Arminius, he was the actual leader of the party. We could mention, in addition, *Kaspar Koolhaes* (1536–1615),[30] who called all who believed in Christ brothers but did not want to sign the Belgic Confession; *Konrad Vorstius* (d. 1622),[31] who succeeded Arminius in his office and was suspect because of his connections to the Socinians; *Simon Episkopius* (d. 1643),[32] the speaker of this movement at the Synod of Dort and professor in Leiden; and last but not least *Hugo Grotius*,[33] who became very famous as a teacher of international law, an exegete, apologist, and mediator in controversies. On Janury 14, 1610, all the adherents of this intellectual current joined together in what is called the *Remonstrance*,[34] a declaration against the official church that rejected the Belgic Confession and the Heidelberg Catechism as unconditional norms of faith, ascribed to secular authority the right to mediate church disputes, and finally proposed five articles on grace that were to become the object of the emerging battle.

The *Synod of Dort* took place from November 13, 1618, to May 9, 1619, thus lasting half a year. One hundred fifty-four sessions are enumerated in the records. There were about eighty Dutch participants and twenty-seven representatives of other Reformed churches invited as advisors. Of the Dutch, I mention the well-known theologians *Gomarus* and *Voetius,* and of the foreigners *Cruciger* from Hesse, *Alting* and *Scultetus* from the Palatinate, *Breitinger* from Zurich, *Rütimeyer* from Bern, and *Diodati* from Geneva.[35] The moderator was Johannes *Bogerman.* The leader of the Remonstrants, who were present from the twenty-second to the fifty-seventh sessions as the accused, was Simon *Episkopius.* Louis XIII had prohibited the French Reformed to attend.[36] Brandenburg chose not to participate out of consideration for its Lutheran majority.[37] It was a church assembly of a universality and solemnity that Protestantism has not experienced either before or since. It would be better not to look upon modern festivities such as the Genevan Calvin Jubilee of 1909[38] as a parallel. The actual occasion for the convening of this assembly was the question of whether the theology of the Dutch opposition party, documented in the Remonstrance, should be tolerated in the Reformed church or not. The Remonstrants contested the synod's competence to answer this question, but the synod ignored this objection and answered the question with a No expressed in five chapters addressing predestination, redemption, the fall, conversion, and the endurance of the saints, together with the removal of the Remonstrants from all churchly offices, enacted in the 137th session. In addition to these decisions, they (1) declared that the Heidelberg Catechism should be the official book of instruction for all Reformed churches, (2) authorized a new Dutch translation of the Bible, and (3) made it obligatory for all preachers to subscribe to the official doctrine of the church. Following the general meeting, the Dutch National Synod also was convened, but it never reached agreement regarding a church constitution and book of order binding for all the provinces. |

We turn now to the five doctrinal chapters that are divided into ninety-three canons.[39] They are the classical document of what the Reformed church at that time wanted to be and not to be over against modern Christianity. It was without doubt the *monument of the victory,* at that time, of early Reformed Protestantism, but since this was a Pyrrhic victory and did not last, it was just as doubtlessly the *mausoleum* of the early Reformed movement. For my explanation, I shall draw, in addition to the Canons of the Synod, on the *Articles* of the Remonstrants of 1610,[40] the *Theses* used by the Remon-

July 6

strants to explain their position to the synod,[41] and also the *"Rejection of Errors"* (*"Rejectiones errorum"*),[42] which are appended to every chapter of the synodal confession. These latter serve as an illustration of what they wanted to confront and reject *beyond* what was formulated in the Remonstrants' theses.

1. *Predestination.* (a) The *position of the Remonstrants.*[43] The divine decree made before creation states that in, because of, and through Christ all those will be saved who believe in him and persist in their faith, whereas unbelievers, those who are alien to Christ, remain in their sin and under wrath. *Before* the decision that God makes about every person comes the ascertainment of one's obedience or disobedience. Independent of this divine decision, the human is thus fallen and grace is offered to him. It is not because of a *necessity* in God but because of one's *faith* or *no faith* that some are saved and others damned. Faith in the one instance and no faith in the other are not merely divine *means.* Rather, whoever believes is then elected also by God, and whoever does not believe is rejected. It is to be assumed that the children of believers who die before they can use their own reason will be saved. |

We confront this congenial doctrine immediately with (b) the *errors* (*Errores*),[44] both articulated and assumed, that the synod identified in this thinking. Election, they claim, is *not* the same thing as God's will to save believers. It does not have multiple meanings, so that it emerges provisionally in the offer of grace, only to be bound to the faith of the person as final election. It is also not to be reinterpreted as though God should have chosen, among the various human possibilities, precisely the act of faith as the work well pleasing to himself. It does not depend upon the proper usage of the "light of nature" ("lumen naturae")[45] in an honest and humble obedience of faith. Faith, obedience, holiness, piety, endurance are not its conditions and causes. It is therefore not changeable, so that the elect could again be lost. And the *assurance* of election also does not depend upon changeable and contingent conditions. One should *not* deny that God has decided, according to his just will, to *leave* certain people in the condemnation that lies upon the generation of Adam. And one should *not* say that it was the special dignity and competence of a people that would have led God to share the gospel with them before others. |

Finally, (c) the *positive teaching* of the synod.[46] The human race is lost in and with the sin of Adam. God would be doing injustice to no one were he to damn everyone. It is God's *love* that he sent his son into the world so that those who believe in him should not perish [see John 3:16]. The cause of unbelief is in the *human* and only in him. Faith, however, is *God's* gift. According to his eternal decision, he carries out among all people, who are equally lost, a separation, in which he softens the hearts of some and leaves the others in their hardheartedness. That is election: God's eternal intention, formed according to the "sovereign good pleasure" ["liberrimum beneplacitum"][47] of his will, out of pure grace, to set apart, to call, to make into believers, to justify, to sanctify and ultimately to glorify a "certain number" ["certa multitudo"][48] of particular people, who are not better and more worthy than the others, to be saved in Christ. For what purpose? To demonstrate his mercy! That is not based upon God's foreseeing the faith of believers but rather that mercy itself is the source of all good. No 'qualitas' [quality] or 'disposition' [dispositio] of a person decides his election but rather the 'good pleasure' [beneplacitum] of God to draw this and that person to himself. Nothing can be altered or changed in this election. The elect cannot be lost, just as the number of the elect cannot be diminished. Both are true as certainly as God himself is unchangeable. Faith in Christ, childlike fear of God, remorse at one's sin, hunger and thirst for righteousness, joy in the Spirit are all the fruit of election by which the elect are known. This knowledge and this certainty lead the children of God only deeper into humiliation before God, to worship the endlessness of his mercy, into purification and the love of the One who first loved them. It is impossible to deduce fleshly security from it: Whoever does not walk along the ways of the elect is and remains thus under judgment. This doctrine is to be preached in the church as revealed, with restraint and with "reverence and piety" ["religiose et sancte"][49] in its place and at its time, but to the glory of God and for the lively comfort of his people.

On the other side are the *non*elect, those *passed over* by the divine election, whom God according to his free, just, and unchangeable good pleasure, which is beyond all reproach, *leaves* in the general state of human misery, does not give saving faith or the grace of conversion, and thus damns and eternally punishes for the 'declaration' [declaratio] of his justice. This is the "decree of reprobation" ["decretum reprobationis"] by which God is by no means made the "author of sin" ["autor peccati"][50] but rather reveals himself as the righteous judge and avenger. No person who does not yet have an assured faith should therefore look upon himself as rejected, but should make use of the means that God has given us for our strengthening and in the meantime hope and wait for the power that brings him perfect grace. God will not extinguish the dimly burning wick [see Isa. 42:3]. This doctrine should rightly be a terror to those who forget God or are sold out to the world. Believing parents should not doubt the election of children who die young, not because they were holy by nature but because they are comprehended with their parents in the covenant of grace. Whoever murmurs ["obmurmurare"][51]) against the grace of election or the rigorousness of rejection should be answered with Romans 9:20, "Who are you, O man, who answers back to God?" [NASB] and with Romans 11:33, "Oh, the depth of the riches both of the wisdom and knowledge of God! How unsearchable are His judgments and unfathomable His ways!"

I need not say much by way of explanation of the differences on this point. There are two different worlds that collide with each other here—the thoroughly biblical-ecclesial language of the Remonstrants will not have deceived you about this—on the one hand, the human person is the measure of all things, and on the other, God is. On the one hand, faith as a human act is in the center, and on the other, the divine 'good pleasure' [beneplacitum] out of which come faith and all other good things. On the one hand, a humanly righteous and rational relationship with God, and on the other, God to whom alone all righteousness and reason are ascribed. On the one hand, the human standing in a mild equality with God; on the other, God's mercy as the only thing with which the human stands or falls. Whether one calls what emerges here medieval Semi-Pelagianism or a modern Christianity of feeling and reason, it ends up as the same thing, and it stands in decisive contrast with the Reformation itself. There is no way to deny that what is expressed in the Canons of Dort is the authentic concern of the Reformation. Their case against the Remonstrants is entirely justified and consistent from the perspective of Luther and Calvin. The consequences from the opposed doctrine drawn in the 'rejection of errors' [Rejectio errorum] are also correct. Dort's own doctrine is, as a whole, nothing other than the comprehensive, level-headed, judicious, thorough expression of what had to be said about the majesty of God, if one were not willing to haggle. With this dogma the Reformed church had raised the banner against the old church some eight or nine decades earlier. With the same dogma it was now setting out the boundaries over against the emerging new church. It is difficult to see what right one might have to call oneself Reformed today if one is not able to engage in the essentials of this thinking with affirmation. |

There are a few details to which we must yet attend. One can see how incorrect it is to speak of the Reformed doctrine of God as speculative.[52] What interests the Dortians is obviously not the Occamist or apparently Occamist arbitrariness of God[53] but his mercy, which must be *entirely* free in order to be mercy, so that the human rests *entirely* in God's hand. Further, election and rejection are not related to each other in these canons in an equilibrium as similar acts of God. Rather, God's *action* is election; God's *non*action is merely *to leave* the rejected in the condition that is by rights that of all people—that is rejection. That does not deprive the idea of the double decree of its necessary incisiveness, but it does take away the rational coldness, that philosophical clarity which makes this idea so objectionable in many other formulations. The rejected are simply the "nonelect" ["nonelecti"], "those who are passed by" ["praeteriti"].[54] The idea that "God is the author of sin" ["deus autor peccati"] can in this way be successfully rebutted.[55] Unbelief bears the guilt. The relationship with God remains a living one. It does not become mechanical. |

At one point, to be sure, I cannot agree with the fathers of Dort. It is not an unimportant point. They share with their opponents an interest in the psychological state of the individual, that is, in the question of whether this or that person might be elect. In our discussion of the Westminster Confession[56] in particular, we saw how this interest became dominant in the second and third generation of Reformed theology. There is no doubting that they respond with the *Reformation* answer to this question. But in my view, the actual interest in this *question* was the first crack in the wall of the church itself. They were thinking anthropologically rather than theologically when they made the 'absolute decree' [decretum absolutum], which is a profound statement about God, into a doctrine not just about humanity but about this or that person—even if they did so with logical consistency. The doctrine of a 'limited number' [numerus clausus] of the elect is, in particular, not good doctrine; it ties God down to particular people when the meaning of the entire doctrine is precisely the freedom of God. This is not the place for me to develop my own thinking about this matter (Romans).[57] I was pleased to see, however, that my particular approach on this point is not among the nine rejected 'errors' [Errores] on predestination, so that it has nothing in common with the theology of the Remonstrants, as I trust you will accept in good faith! But I would like to add that the Canons of Dort are much superior to the Westminster Confession. Especially the dangerous doctrine of the assurance of election is presented here in a balanced way and does not emerge as the central point and crown of the entire thing, as is the case in the intolerable approach of the English.

2. *The death of Christ and reconciliation.* (a) *Remonstrants.*[58] Christ died for humanity in general and for each individual, earning reconciliation and the forgiveness of sin for all, but only the believers participate in it. They appeal to John 3:16 with its "whoever *believes* in Him" and 1 John 2:2 [NASB], "He Himself is the propitiation for our sins; and not for ours only, but also for those of the whole *world*." For them, the decree of God's grace merges with the redemptive work of Christ. They want nothing of a 'hidden God' [Deus absconditus] through whose decree the extent of the effectiveness of this work of redemption should have been determined. No, in him the Father established the covenant of grace for all humanity while preserving his own righteousness and truth. There should not be any limitation of the grace of God, but there should be something else. Its taking effect is conditioned by faith. There is no forgiveness on the basis of this covenant until humans "actually and truly believe in Christ."[59] If there were rejected ones for whom Christ had not died, how could one blame them for their unbelief? For their faith, according to the Remonstrants, could only consist in their believing that Christ had *not* died for them. |

(b) *'Rejection'* (*rejectio*).[60] Reconciliation is not a general but rather a special and individual truth. The two claims of Jesus cannot be separated: "I give my life for the sheep!" [John 10:15], "and I know them" [John 10:27]. Christ and his own belong together from the outset. There is no abstract historical redemption to which the redeemed would then have to come, but they are already comprehended in the redemption. Reconciliation is not the creation of a possibility for God to move toward humanity so that it would then depend upon the 'freedom of the will' [liberum arbitrium] of each individual whether or not one made use of this possibility, leaving the question open whether perhaps all or no one is really reconciled. Reconciliation also does not mean that now the obedience of the law is replaced by the obedience of faith. No, we are made just through grace. A justification through faith as a human act that is pleasing to God is a "new and strange kind of justification" ["nova et peregrina iustificatio"], introduced by the "impious Socinius" ["impius Socinus"]![61] Moreover, reconciliation is not to be understood as though original sin were no longer in effect or no longer damnable. No, both are maintained next to each other: acceptance into the "grace of the covenant" ["foedus gratiae"] *and* "guilt of that sin" ["reatus peccati"].[62] It is also impermissible to say that *from God's side* the goods gained through Christ's death have been given to all people, but that *from humanity's side* there is a difference in the acceptance of these goods. |

(c) The *positive doctrine* of the synod in relation to all of this is as follows.[63] Thinking in a strictly Anselmian[64] way, God is merciful and just. The sin committed against his majesty requires eternal punishment. We cannot accomplish the satisfaction. Therefore, God gives us his son. His death is the sole and perfect satisfaction because he is God and man (Heidelberg Confession, second section!).[65] The promise that all who believe in him will not perish [see John 3:16] goes out to all peoples and persons with the command to repent and to believe. Unbelief is not a burden for Christ but for the human who does not believe. But faith comes only from God's grace, which he owes no one. It is a fruit of the reconciliation accomplished on the cross. Election, reconciliation, and faith form a closed circle. As only those who are already reconciled can believe, only those who are elect are reconciled. The efficacy of the death of Christ benefits only them, in point of fact. They form the church, which, founded by his blood, is his bride, loves him, and praises him, in eternity.

The only thing that one can say about this chapter is that it is the implementation of the Lutheran concept, "the two, faith and God, have inevitable connection,"[66] from a Calvinist perspective. Faith may not claim any independent significance. It is clear that here modern anthropocentric fideism is meant, just as then among the 'errors' [Errores] the Socinian doctrine is in fact mentioned. With so much emphasis upon the act of faith itself, the death of Christ as the basis of reconciliation might well become entirely unnecessary. Here again you should note how the relationship of reconciliation to the individual (Kierkegaard[67]), which is certainly an excellent thing in and of itself, threatens to become somehow problematic and sectarian when these individuals begin to present themselves as known not only to God but to other persons and above all to themselves, a step that is not hard to take. In effect, they set themselves apart from the 'corrupt mass' [massa perditionis][68] as a visible group of the elect and reconciled. What follows—I am not saying that this was intended by the Canons of Dort but that this step is not hard to take—is the intolerable picture of God's grace and glory in the restrictive enclave of a free church fellowship or a chapel community,[69] a development that we know only too well in modern Pietism. Thus, I could also sign the second chapter of Dort with the reservation that no consequences may be drawn from it for *this or that particular person*, that it really, and especially in the structuring of churchly practice, is left to the Lord, who knows his own [see 2 Tim. 2:19].

3 and 4. Fall and Conversion. (a) *Remonstrants.*[70] They also empha-

July 27 size here that the human does not have faith by virtue of his "free will" ["liberum arbitrium"][71] but that one must be reborn and renewed by God in order to believe. Grace is the beginning, the middle, the end of all good, as "prevenient, motivating, accompanying, and cooperating grace,"[72] but not, and this is the essential thing, as "irresistible grace" ["gratia irresistibilis"].[73] At this point, the Remonstrants moved toward Calvinism as far as they could. One must look very carefully at some of their statements in order not to take them as Calvinist. We shall see when we look at the 'rejection' [Rejectio] that the other side was not deceived and that they formulated the difference as it was in fact really there. They say that the human does not have faith "in and of itself"[74] but must be renewed by God in order to comprehend, to desire, and to carry out that which is healing and right. But they do not make the positive(!) point that faith is a gift of God. Grace is the beginning, the middle, and the end, and all good is to be ascribed to it, in the reborn person as well! But the following sentences betray that they do not understand the term 'grace' [gratia] as something that is outside of and confronts the human in a primal and creative way but rather as a principle that accompanies and cooperates with him, along the lines of Goethe's "love from on high *is also his!*"[75] Not all zeal and striving outside of faith is empty and worthless or even dangerous or harmful, but rather hearing the Word of God, mourning one's sin, seeking the "healing grace" ["gratia salutaris"] is "most useful" ["utilissimum"] and "completely necessary" ["maxime necessarium"][76] for the attaining of faith. |

It initially sounds very Calvinist when the freedom of the will to do good is energetically denied. But one must see what the Remonstrants are really saying: [There is also no][76a] freedom of the will to do wrong, which means that they understand the will as a neutral thing, a natural drive, which is as such determined and not free. This has nothing to with the Reformation's 'servile will' [servum arbitrium], the enslavement of the will to the wrong. But it certainly is compatible with a partial freedom that can be posited *after all*, assuming the participatory love from above. Such grace is therefore not irresistible. It certainly gives to the human supernatural powers; it leads him "actually to believe" ["actu credere"].[77] But the human can also reject it, can not believe, and thus can perish through one's own guilt. On the other hand, this grace is available to every person to the extent that one needs it for one's salvation, even for the person who does not make use of it "in the act itself" ["actu ipso"].[78] According to the amount of grace given, the human could do a great deal more good and avoid a great deal more bad than is in fact the case. The 'calling' [vocatio] that is extended to all people is really seriously meant for all, and there is no one to whom it is externally extended with the secret will to prevent him from being converted; there is no "secret will of God" ["arcana voluntas Dei"], no "holy charade" ["sancta simulatio"] on God's side, no "two-faced person in God" ["duplex persona in Deo"].[79] In other words, the relationship to God is completely unambiguous and transparent: God offers himself, and now it is the human's turn, and only his, to offer himself. God does not will evil—here the Remonstrants had an easy game to play. From God's perspective, one cannot assert that "it is impossible not to sin with respect to the divine decree."[80] God does not will that someone should blaspheme him. If it were God's authentic and concealed will that someone should sin, then this person would incur guilt if he were to fulfill God's commandments and thus rebel against God's authentic and concealed will. (We see here that the Remonstrants also knew how to draw dreadful consequences from their opponents' statements, but these were consequences that no intelligent predestinarian would ever have drawn; instead, these ideas have persisted in the thinking of those who, since the days of Paul [see Rom. 6:1], have steadfastly sought to ignore the real meaning of the dogma.)

(b) The *'rejection'* [*Rejectio*].[81] It dwells primarily on *original sin*. One should not deny that it is, in and of itself, reason enough for the condemnation of the entire human race. The *human will* is not to be imagined as having no qualities so that at the fall no essential damage was really done to it. No, *before* the fall, in the human created in the image of God, the will had the whole range of the divine gifts of the Spirit, and now it is fundamentally destroyed, that is, it has lost these divine gifts; neither before nor afterward is it a neutral entity. The unregenerate person is really *dead in sin* and is not capable of hungering and thirsting after righteousness, not capable of bringing to God the sacrifice of a contrite and humbled spirit. It is not true that there is a "*common grace*" ["*gratia communis*"], a "light of nature" ["lumen naturae"] that fallen man could use in order to attain "gradually" ["gradatim"] to the gospel and salvation.[82] And it is *not* true—both experience and Scripture testify to the contrary—that God thus levels the path leading all people to revelation, to faith, and to repentance "sufficiently and effectively" ["sufficienter et efficaciter"].[83] There is no staircase from reason to revelation. The biblical argument for this, rather remarkably, is Acts 16:6–7, where Paul and his companions were prevented by the Holy Spirit from proclaiming the Word of God in Asia. And after they came to Mysia they tried to go to Bithynia, but the Spirit would not let them. *Faith* is not a human act but rather a divine gift in the sense of a "quality imparted by God" ["qualitas infusa a Deo"].[84] *Grace* is not merely a "gentle persuasion" ["lenis suasio"][85] of the person through which God might bring human nature into appropriate agreement with his own will using moral reasoning. Nor is it an action by which God renounces his omnipotence and leaves it to human capacity whether one will experience one's rebirth or not. There is no sense here in which grace and free will somehow compete in conversion, that God's grace might be waiting upon man's will. (One sees in this third and fourth chapter especially clearly how the synod's rejection apparently and consciously *caricatures* the Remonstrants' position, projects its cautious Semi-Pelagianism on the wall as massive Pelagianism—that is, without the "Semi"—to make known that *this is how* they are being understood. Since no names are mentioned, it is perhaps a somewhat drastic but not forbidden procedure to say in a sharply contoured way what they did *not* want to say.)

The positive teaching of the synod[86] is especially detailed in this double chapter. *The first human*, who was created in God's image, is described by saying, "the whole Man was holy" ["totus sanctus"],[87] knowing spiritual things, with a just heart and will and pure in all his affects. "By the instigation of the Devil" ["Diaboli instinctu"][88] and misusing his free will, he *falls away from God* and deprives himself of all those properties. Now his knowledge is characterized by "blindness of mind, horrible darkness, vanity, perverseness of judgment," his will is "wicked, rebellious, obdurate," and his affects are "impure."[89] And so now are all his children, for "a corrupt stock produced a corrupt offspring,"[90] not because one imitated the other as Pelagius thought but rather "by propagation"[91] his corruption was reproduced through God's just judgment. So all people are conceived in sin, born as children of wrath, are incapable of goodness, inclined to evil, dead in sins, and lacking grace are unable even to *desire* to lose their corrupt nature. What has remained are *"the glimmerings of natural light"*[92] to distinguish between that which is respectable and reprehensible, and to practice outward virtue. But man is not even capable of the proper use of "things natural and civil,"[93] let alone the saving knowledge of God. There is only enough to make man inexcusable before God. Even the sense of the "light of nature" ["lumen naturae"] repeated in the *Mosaic Decalogue* only uncovers the dimensions of sin and offers no means of healing. |

What the 'light of nature' [lumen naturae] and the law cannot do, God now does in the power of his Spirit *through the Word*, which he gives to a few in the Old Testament and to many in the New Testament, without regard for their worthiness but according to his free pleasure. Why this person then and not that one? One should not ask curiously about this but rather worship the righteousness of his judgment. The call that God issues is meant seriously; here the synod is in agreement with the Remonstrants. If it is *not heard*, then the guilt is not with Christ and his gospel, nor with God and his calling, but in the person called, as foreseen in the parable of the diverse soils [Mark 4:3–20, parallels in other gospels]. It is, indeed, to be attributed to God when his call is *heard* to his eternal election, to the "efficacy" ["efficacia"][94] of his call, to the gift of faith and repentance that *he* gives. The implementation of that which God's pleasure has decided for the persons of his election now consists indeed of a *new birth*, above all of the pouring out of a new "quality" ["qualitas"][95] into their will, of its transformation into a good tree that can produce the fruits of good works. It is a "supernatural work, most powerful, and at the same time most delightful, astonishing, mysterious, and ineffable,"[96] no smaller or less than the creation or the resurrection of the dead. Whoever experiences it is "certainly, infallibly, effectually"[97] reborn and now does, in fact, believe. His will "in consequence of [God's] influence becomes itself active,"[98] that is, by the power of grace it is true that he himself believes. How this actually happens will never be completely comprehensible for the believer in this life. Now, however, the object of faith *and* faith itself, "the *will* to believe and the act of believing," come from God.[99] And God owes this grace to no one; rather, whoever receives it owes eternal thanks to God and will be very careful not to boast before others as though he had elected himself. But just as the human as a sinner is human, he is and remains human in grace, that is, not a stump or a block. God does not coerce or force him but rather "spiritually quickens, heals, corrects, . . . bends"[100] him, so that where there was formerly rebellion and resistance, now obedience prevails. That God does all this alone does not exclude but rather includes his doing this through the means he has instituted—Word, sacrament, discipline—for, according to his pleasure, he wills to take *this* path.

5. *The perseverance of the saints* [perseverantia sanctorum]. (a) The *Remonstrants* teach[101] that through the gift of grace believers receive a powerful help in the battle against Satan, sin, and the world. Christ stretches out his hand to them, supports and sustains them. Is there not then the possibility that they might fall again? In 1610, the Remonstrants were really raising only this question.[102] In the theses for the synod, they speak more emphatically. After God has given humans all the necessary help 'to persevere' [perseverare], they now say that it does not depend upon him whether or not they really do. Even true believers can lose their faith, and it happens not that seldom. Believers can also be lost in eternity, although of course previous to that they can again be received back in grace. It is dangerous for piety and good morals to teach that believers could only sin in weakness, could not fall out of grace, that election could not be reversed by anything, that all the sins of the elect are already forgiven, and so forth. All of this would open the window to a fleshly security. One can only be certain of one's faith and one's good conscience at the present time. One might be concerned about the future through watching and praying, but one cannot really tell, in this

"school of Christian soldiers" ["schola militiae christianae"][103] in which we are located, where one might gain a sense of certainty for the future, nor can one know what such a certainty might be needed for. |

(b) *The rejection* [*Rejectio*][104] of the synod follows directly upon the Remonstrant theses here, in contrast to the previous chapter. They reject the idea that perseverance is to be accomplished by us with our "free will" ["libera voluntate"].[105] They reject the idea that God only helps us and then leaves it up to us to help ourselves. True believers cannot "finally and completely" ["totaliter et finaliter"][106] fall away and be lost; they cannot sin against the Holy Spirit. One should not say that one needs a 'special revelation' [specialis revelatio] in order to be certain of one's future perseverance—with that the synod shoots over the heads of the Remonstrants to hit Roman Catholic doctrine.[107] It is not true that the doctrine of 'certitude' [certitudo] is a sleeping potion for the flesh. A temporary and frail faith is *not* "justifying and saving faith."[108] There is no repetition of rebirth, and Christ did not say in vain, "I have prayed for you, [Peter,] that your own faith may not fail" [Luke 22:32]. |

And now (c) *the positive doctrine* of the synod.[109] It begins cleverly with the statement that it is true that the elect live in the flesh, in the body of sin, although free from the slavery of sin. Even the holiest do not lack the sins of weakness and thus have reason to be humbled, to take refuge in the cross, and to mortify the flesh. In their own power they are not able to persevere in grace. They need to watch and to pray, for God does not prevent their falling into temptation. They insult God, they are guilty of death, they grieve the Holy Spirit, they break the practice of faith, they severely wound their consciences, they lose at times the "sense of God's favor" ["sensus gratiae"].[110] But God, who is rich in mercy, does not take his Holy Spirit away from his own. The immortal seed out of which they were reborn remains in them, and through his Word and his Spirit, God leads again to repentance. Thus, not because of their merit but through God's mercy, they are able never to fall completely out of faith and grace, and when they fall, they are capable of not remaining in that fallenness. "With respect to *themselves*" they might well be lost, "but with respect to *God*"[111] this cannot happen. It is only as members of the church that they can be *certain* of this, not through a special revelation but simply through faith in the promise. It is not necessary that they always have a *feeling* of this "certainty" ["certitudo"],[112] let alone of fleshly security. On the contrary, this certitude leads to careful attention to the ways of the Lord and to zealous use of the means of help that are made available to them. The chapter and the entire confession concludes with these words:

> The carnal mind is unable to comprehend this doctrine of the perseverance of the saints, and the certainty thereof, which God hath most abundantly revealed in his word, for the glory of his name and the consolation of pious souls, and which he impresses upon the hearts of the faithful. Satan abhors it; the world ridicules it; the ignorant and hypocrites abuse,

and heretics oppose it. But the spouse of Christ hath always most tenderly loved and constantly defended it, as an inestimable treasure; and God, against whom neither counsel nor strength can prevail, will dispose her to continue this conduct to the end. Now to the one God, Father, Son, and Holy Spirit, be honor and glory forever. Amen.[113]

Very seldom has a churchly assembly of such diverse constituencies been able to express its common convictions in such a thoroughly united, cohesive, and outwardly comprehensive form as did the fathers of Dort. It must be remembered that they were certainly not of one heart and one soul. There was a majority and a minority, a right and a left wing, with the Dutchmen Gomarus and Maccovius on one side, and on the other the English and the Hessians in particular.[114] The former would have preferred a more severe formulation of the idea of predestination, the so-called supralapsarianism by which the divine decree applied to humanity before the fall, that is, to those free protoplasts who enjoyed all the divine gifts. The latter, especially the Germans, sought to have this more severe doctrine repudiated. The synod acquiesced to neither tendency wholly, and generally taught in an infralapsarian way but also did not completely exclude supralapsarianism. One has to approve of this decision. Given the way that Dort understood predestination, namely, with the consistent emphasis on the *predestined character* of particular individuals, the doctrine of Gomarus and Maccovius would have meant the proclamation of a religious determinism that was otherwise avoided as best one could. There was good reason for their inability completely to reject supralapsarianism: To focus on the concept of God, on the one who predestines rather than upon those who are predestined, results unavoidably in the emphasis upon the unconditional elective freedom of God over against the first human as well, that is, the created person as such.[115] |

One critical remark must be made with reference to chapters 3–5. We must acknowledge that the doctrine of the assurance of salvation or election, especially in chapter 5, is presented with every possible safeguard against misunderstandings. The Dortians certainly recognized the dangers and ambiguities of this doctrine and reacted to them with strong assertions that it is *not* meant in this or that way. For my sense of things, however, there remains an element of dissatisfaction, which is of course closely related to the formulation of the doctrine of predestination itself. Between chapters 3–4 on the one hand and 5 on the other, there is an obvious contradiction. The irresistibility of grace, the reality of a "divinely infused quality" ["qualitas infusa divina"],[116] which is proper to the will of the converted, is emphasized in such a way on the one hand that it is then somewhat confusing, as right as it may be, to hear that those who are holiest can "with respect to themselves" ["quoad ipsos"][117] fall into the gravest sins but are ultimately protected from falling completely out of *grace*. If they wanted to say this in chapter 5—and they certainly were right in wanting to do so—then it would have been preferable if they had omitted from chapters 3–4 the ideas of "infused qualities" ["qualitates infusae"][118] and the "habits" of believers[119] imparted by God, which are confusingly reminiscent of Roman Catholic concepts. In their place they should have spoken of the forgiveness of sins and of the justification of believers founded *upon it*, not upon a real sharing of new life. The new life, the newly born person cannot be anything other than *faith*, as chapter 5 then clearly shows. That there is so little said about faith and the forgiveness of sins in Dort, and in contrast so much about what the elect and believers allegedly *are* and *have* on the basis of their election, is for me the most problematic point of this otherwise very beautiful confession. Because of their interest in the concrete situation of the pious individual, they came too close to their opponents and then had to save themselves through a somewhat unfortunate withdrawal from the dead-end into which they had maneuvered themselves; they could not do so without leaving the impression that they had initially tried more than they could really accomplish. A little forensic salt rather than the somewhat oily 'infused justice' [iustitia infusa] *earlier on* would have made the entire argument of chapters 3–5 more credible. They would then, of course, have had to make much clearer in chapters 1–2 that, in contrast with the Remonstrants, they were interested in theology and not in anthropology. The inexorably expanding deterioration of Reformation knowledge that later beset the Reformed church as well as the Lutheran church did not come at them from outside; the worm was in the woodwork of the church itself. Thus, it is not without melancholy that we read of the joyful ringing of the bells from all the church towers that greeted the conclusion of the confession at the time.[120] The bells of death were already ringing with them. It is part of the tragedy of all historical things that there can apparently be no pure decisions within time that do not carry within themselves the seeds of their future corruption.

We have arrived at the end of our course. In actuality, it really should begin at this point, as the coherent investigation of the various doctrinal points throughout *all* the confessions with which we have become acquainted in various groupings and under very particular perspectives. This opens up for you a rich field for private study now or later, and I hope that it has become clear to you how worthwhile it is to research the thinking of the Reformed fathers. Although they were not exempted from the 'confusion of humans' [confusio hominum],[121] which itself forces us to believe in the 'providence of God' [providentia Dei] in order not to lose courage, they lived in a world of rich and profound insights and learnings. It is a very different question as to how things now stand with us, the Reformed and also the non-Reformed children. If we look at our theology, then what we see first of all is a pile of ruins. Perhaps the best thing that can be done at this moment is to work on a historical orientation for what a real theology *would* look like. Beyond that, it is possible earnestly to *stand quietly* before the eternal questions and answers which once required of our fathers that they confess. We can do that, even if we are not able to utter their confessions with our lips. I am persuaded that we *must* do that even if we have only somewhat and only historically understood them. When that is done, more seriously perhaps by a *young* generation that knows better what real questions and answers are than do many older folks, then we need *not* be ultimately fearful about the future of theology and the church, in spite of all serious concerns about their present internal confusion.

NOTES

PREFACE

1. In the Barth Archives, Basel.

2. H. Vorländer, *Aufbruch und Krise: Ein Beitrag zur Geschichte der deutschen Reformierten vor dem Kirchenkampf*, Beiträge zur Geschichte und Lehre der reformierten Kirche 37 (Neukirchen, 1974), 12–29.

3. See Vorländer, *Aufbruch und Krise*, 29ff.

4. K. Barth, *Das Bekenntnis der Reformation und unser Bekennen*, ThExh 29 (Munich, 1935), 20.

5. K. Barth, *Das Bekenntnis der Reformation*, 24.

6. Bw.Th. I, 412.

7. K. Barth, *Gespräche 1964–1968*, Gesamtausgabe, section 4, ed. E. Busch, (Zurich, 1997), 151.

8. Scholl, H., ed., *Die Theologie Calvins*, Gesamtausgabe, section 2 (Zurich, 1993) [cited as Th.C.], ET: *Theology of Calvin*.

9. Bw.Th. II, 162.

10. Ibid., 179.

11. *Anfänge der dialektischen Theologie*, vol. 1, ed. J. Moltmann, Theologische Bücherei, 17/I (Munich, 1962), 143; ET: *The Beginnings of Dialectic Theology, Part I*, ed. James M. Robinson, trans. Keith R. Crim (Richmond: John Knox, 1968), 121.

12. In the foreword to the 3d edition of the *Epistle to the Romans*, cited in *Anfänge der dialektischen Theologie*, 148, ET: *Beginnings of Dialectic Theology*, 448.

13. V.u.kl.A. 1922–1925, 604–43; ET: "The Desirability and Possibility of a Universal Reformed Creed" (1925), in Karl Barth, *Theology and Church*, trans. Louise P. Smith (London: SCM Press, 1962), 112–35.

14. KD I/2, esp. 693–740, ET: CD I/2, 620–60.

15. J. F. G. Goeters, *Reformierter Lehrstuhl und Studienhaus in Göttingen*, in *Die evangelisch-reformierte Kirche in Nordwestdeutschland: Beiträge zu ihrer Geschichte und Gegenwart*, ed. E. Lomberg, G. Nordholt, A. Rauhaus (Weener, 1982), 274.

16. V.u.kl.A. 1922–1925, 202–47.

17. Ibid., 203.

18. H. Vorländer, *Aufbruch und Krise*, 9.

19. E. Wolf, "Bekennende Kirche," in RGG, 3d ed., 1:985.

20. In this volume as well we have added paragraph indentations to Barth's manuscript, which has very few, for the sake of reading ease. At times this has been done where he made a dash to indicate the transition from one section to the next; otherwise we have based the indentation on the paragraph contents. In the latter

case, the insertion of an indentation is indicated by a vertical line at the end of the paragraph (|). Where he has carried out some orthographical modernization of the texts he cites, we have incorporated his changes here without reference; as a rule they differ only minimally from the original text. Latin citations or texts in his manuscript have no quotation marks, but we have added them here wherever they are actual quotations. Square brackets inside quotations enclose emendations of the editors. They indicate that Barth left something out of a quoted text without noting it. Ellipses without parentheses indicate an omission that Barth himself made and noted.

21. In citations made by Barth from the relatively accessible edition of E. F. K. Müller (=BSRK), this edition provides only the exact location of the quotation. Where Barth paraphrased or translated texts from older editions of Reformed confessions that are difficult to find today, such as Augusti and Ebrard, we have printed the original passages in the notes where it appeared to be useful.

1. THE SIGNIFICANCE OF THE
CONFESSION IN THE REFORMED CHURCH

1. Formula of Concord, BSLK 735–1100, ET: K/W 481–660.

2. Augsburg Confession, BSLK 31–137, ET: K/W 27–105. Following Barth's practice, in this ET the term "Augustana" will be used interchangeably for "Augsburg Confession."

3. The numbers inserted in the text here and hereafter are Barth's references to his sources in SBLK. The corresponding locations in BSLK are 3,24–33, ET: K/W 5[2]; 5,21–24, and 745,2–5, ET: K/W 6–7[7]; 768,31–33, K/W 486–87[4]; 835,12–18, K/W 527[5].

4. =BSLK 833–34., ET: K/W 526–27[1–2].

5. Enders, vol. 8, 53–54 (=WA.B 5,442, 12–18 [Nr. 1626]), ET: LW 49:354. Italicization is Barth's.

6. =WA.TR 2, 45, ET: *Table Talk*, trans. Wm. Hazlitt (Philadelphia: Lutheran Board of Publication, 1873), 283[DXXIV].

7. =BSLK 3, 31–34. Barth's translation from the Latin differs from the German text [we have rendered Barth's German version—Trans.]: " . . . publice ad omnes homines Christianam doctrinam profitentes adeoque in totum terrarum orbem sparsa ubique percrebuit et in ore et sermone omnium esse coepit," ET: K/W 5[2]: " . . . was set forth for all estates of the Empire and was disseminated and has resounded publicly throughout all Christendom in the whole wide world."

8. =BSLK 831, 10–14. Barth's translation from the Latin again differs from the received German text. "Neque in animo habemus hoc scripto aut quocunque alio a commemorata iam confessione vel transversum, ut aiunt, unguem discedere, vel aliam aut novam confessionem condere," ET: K/W 525[5]: "We do not intend to deviate in the least from the Confession either in this document or in any other, nor do we intend to submit any other, new confession."

9. =BSLK 833,24–28, ET: K/W 526[2].

10. See BSLK 835,6–44, ET: K/W 527–28[5–6].

11. See BSLK 835,46–836,17, ET: K/W 582[7].

12. See BSLK 836,18–35, ET: K/W 528[8].

13. See BSLK 838,18–839,7, ET: K/W 529[11–13].

14. The page numbers given by Barth are a summary reference for the citations in n. 10–12.

15. =BSLK 835,18, ET: K/W 527[5].

16. See BSLK 835,22–27, ET: K/W 527[5].

17. M. Luther, *Von Conciliis und Kirchen* (=WA 50,551,29), ET: LW 41:58. The following citations up to note 22 are taken from this Luther document. The page numbers entered by Barth refer to the appropriate places in EA.

18. =WA 50,551,25–33, ET: LW 41:58; WA 50,562,36–563,1: ET: LW 41:72.

19. =WA 50,563,1, ET: LW 41:192. Barth's italicization.

20. =WA 50,616,28, ET: LW 41:134.

21. =WA 50,623,10–11, ET: LW 41:141–42.

22. =WA 50,616–17, ET: LW 41:134.

23. BSLK 3,45–4,2, ET: K/W 5[3]. Barth's italicization.

24. BSLK 835,10–11: "e verbo Domini [. . .] desumpta," ET: K/W 527[5].

25. WA 50,551,29, ET: LW 41:58.

26. BSLK 835,20–21, ET: K/W 527[5].

27. See BLSK 830,3–4, ET: K/W 524[1]. Barth's italicization [however, neither the Latin nor the German text contains the literal phrase "at the time of" that Barth emphasized—Trans.].

28. =BSLK 769,30, ET: K/W 487[8]. [The ET speaks of "symbols" and "writings," and thus the plural form "witnesses" is used. Barth's insertion of the Latin phrase reveals that neither the German text nor the ET refers to the "doctoribus," "the teachers who lived at that time."—Trans.]

29. =BSLK 838,10–17. Barth's translation from the Latin text [which we have literally rendered—Trans.] differs from that in the official German translation of the Latin: " . . . ut unanimi consensu approbatam certamque formam doctrinae habeamus, quam Evangelicae Ecclesiae nostrae simul omnes agnoscant et amplectantur, secundum quam, cum e verbo Dei sit desumpta, omnia alia scripta iudicare et accomodare oportet, quatenus probanda sint et recipienda"; ET: K/W 529[10]: " . . . unanimously and commonly held, reliable form for teaching to which all our churches commonly pledge themselves. The extent to which all other writings are to be approved and accepted shall be judged and evaluated on the basis of and according to this form, for it is taken from God's Word."

30. =BSLK 840,15–21, ET: K/W 530[16]. [The last phrase paraphrased by Barth reads in the ET "regarding what our churches unanimously hold fast and have decided concerning these controverted articles."—Trans.]

31. Seeberg 536: "It is constantly emphasized that both the symbols and the books collected in the Book of Concord are only authoritative because they are taken from the Word of God and can be validated from it ([SBLK] 569,5, ET: KW 527[5]; 590,6.8.9, ET: K/W 544–45[6][8][9]). They are only *witnesses of the truth* [*testes veritatis*], but the Scripture is the foundation ([SBLK] 571,13, ET: K/W 529[13]). Thus, they do not possess judicial authority, but rather the significance of the confessions lies in the fact that they demonstrate how the doctrine of Scripture has been understood in the various periods of time and for what reasons the doctrines contradicting it have been repudiated ([SBLK] 518,8, ET: K/W 486[2]).

32. =BSLK 834,18–19, ET: K/W 527[3].

33. =BSLK 767,14–19, ET: K/W 486[1]. [Barth inserts in the German text the

phrase from the Latin original 'nullam omnino aliam' ('in no wise any other than') before the reference to the Scriptures, to emphasize their sole authority; the ET renders this "alone."—Trans.]

34. BSLK 769,23–24., ET: K/W 487[7].

35. =BSLK 767,14–17, ET: K/W 486[1]; 769,19–27, ET: K/W 487[7]; see 834,16–22, ET: K/W 527[3].

36. =BSLK 769,19, ET: K/W 487[7] [the ET omits "luculentum" = "brilliant"—Trans.].

37. =BSLK 838,29–839.7, ET: K/W 529[11–13].

38. BSLK 838,45–839,7, ET: K/W 529[13].

39. Pencil notation on the margin of the manuscript: "518,8 [=BSLK 769,32, ET: K/W 487 (88)] duntaxat allein." The sentence to which the notation refers is as follows (BSLK 769,28–40): "Cetera autem symbola et alia scripta, quorum paulo ante mentionem fecimus, non obtinent auctoritatem iudicis; haec enim dignitas solis sacris litteris debetur: sed duntaxat pro religione nostra testimonium dicunt eamque explicant ac ostendunt, quomodo singulis temporibus sacrae litterae in articulis controversis in ecclesia Dei a doctoribus, qui tum vixerunt, intellectae et explicatae fuerint, et quibus rationibus dogmata cum sacra scriptura pugnantia reiecta et condemnata sint," ET: K/W 487[8]: "The other symbols, however, and other writings listed above are not judges, as is Holy Scripture, but they are only witnesses and explanations of the faith, which show how Holy Scripture has at various times been understood and interpreted in the church of God by those who lived at the time in regard to articles of faith under dispute and how teachings contrary to the Scripture were rejected and condemned."

40. =BSLK 832,37–38: "*verbo Dei et Augustanae Confessioni* orthodoxae," ET: K/W 526[10]. Barth's italicization. [Both the German and English translations in the Book of Concord render "orthodoxae" as "Christian."—Trans.]

41. =BSLK 1093,4–7: " . . . cum prophetica et apostolica doctrina atque cum pia nostra Augustana confessione in Verbo *Dei* probe fundata . . . " ET: K/W 657[8]: ". . . to the writings of the holy prophets and apostles and to our Christian Augsburg Confession, which is completed based on *God's* word."

42. =BSLK 835,10–11: "quia e verbo Domini est desumpta," ET: K/W 527[5]; 838,15, ET: 529[10]. [The Book of Concord translates "desumpta" with "taken from" and "drawn from."—Trans.]

43. =BSLK 830,47–49, ET: K/W 524–25[4].

44. See on this BSLK 831,3–11, ET: K/W 525[5].

45. See above, p. 2; see also the preface to the Formula of Concord, BSLK 739–66, ET: K/W 5–17, esp. 760,37–761,24, ET: K/W 15[23].

46. According to BSLK XL, there were 8,182 signatures. See also P. Tschackert, *Die Entstehung der lutherischen und der reformierten Kirchenlehre samt ihren innerprotestantischen Gegensätzen* (Göttingen, 1910), 569.

47. Leonhard Hutter (1563–1616), Lutheran theologian from Nellingen near Ulm, served from 1596 on as theology professor in Wittenberg. '*Malleus calvinistarum*' ('The Hammer of Calvinists') is not the title of a document by Hutter but rather the pseudonym given to him as the author of several polemical writings directed against Reformed doctrine. See Krüger/Hermelink, 258.

48. Barth translates the text from a quotation in K. Hase, *Hutterus Redivivus oder Dogmatik der evangelisch-lutherischen Kirche: ein dogmatisches Repertorium für Studierende*, 10th ed. (Leipzig: Breitkopf & Haertel, 1862), 125 n. 3: "Auctorem Libri Conc[ordiae] primarium constituimus non hominem aliquem, s[eu] theologum,

s[eu] politicum: sed ipsum Deum Sp[iritum] S[anctum], fontem et largitorem omnis boni, usque adeo, ut divinitus inspiratum ipsum appellare minime dubitemus, eo tamen servato discrimine, quod Sc[ripturam] S[acram] et L[ibros] S[ymbolicos] s[eu] ecclesiasticos intercedit."

49. *Ibid*: "nimirum, sensu latiori L[ibri] S[ymbolici] ab auctoribus nonnullis vocantur θεόπνευστοι (a) *ratione objecti*, quoniam continent et exponunt verbum Dei Prophetis et App. [Apostolis] olim immediate inspiratum, et quidquid ex verbo Dei per manifestam consequentiam elicitur; (b) *ratione mediatae illuminationis*, neque enim dubitamus, quin Deus speciali concursu influxerit in mentes fidelium doctorum qui Symb[olum] conscripserunt, mentes eorum illustravit, et voluntates ipsorum flexerit, ut verissima saluberrimaque dogmata mente conceperint et calamo expresserint," ET: "Without doubt, in a broader sense the Symbolic Books are described by many as inspired in relation to their authorship (a) *for the obvious reason* that they contain and expound the Word of God of the prophets and apostles that was at one time directly inspired, together with everything which is elicited from the Word of God as obvious consequence; (b) *for the reason of mediate illumination*, for we do not doubt that God through a special working has influenced the minds of the pious doctors who wrote the Symbols, has illuminated their minds and guided their wills so that the truest and most salubrious dogmas were conceived in their minds and written down with the pen."

50. =BSLK 834,16–25, ET: K/W 527[3].

51. BSLK 834, 6–7: " . . . pro symbolis et communibus confessionibus semper habita sunt . . . " ET: K/W 526[2]: " . . . [that have been regarded] as creeds or confessions . . . at all times."

52. BSLK 834–35, ET: K/W 527.

53. BSLK 769,31–32, ET: K/W 487[8]: "witnesses . . . of the faith," see BSLK 838,45–839,1, ET: K/W 529[13], "testimonies of the truth."

54. A. Knapp, *Evangelischer Liederschatz für Kirche, Schule und Haus: eine Sammlung geistlicher Lieder aus allen christlichen Jahrhunderten*, 2d ed. (Stuttgart/Tübingen, 1850), 450–51. (nr. 995), verses 3 and 5. The lyricist was Christoph Carl Julius Asschenfeldt (1792–1856), whose last office was provost of Flensburg and superintendent for the German-speaking part of the duchy of Schleswig. The German lyric is as follows (Barth's italicization):

"*Reine* Kirche, unsre Kirche! / Mahlschatz ist das Wort aus Gott,—/ Ist ihr Schwert und ihre Krone / Wider aller Feinde Rott'. / Ihre Kammern sind gefüllet, / Reich an Licht und Trost und Kraft, / an Gerechtigkeit und Frieden / Und an tiefer Wissenschaft.

"*Sichre Kirche*, unsre Kirche! / Mauer um sie, Heil und Wehr / Augsburgs siegendes Bekenntnis, / Wie ein Bollwerk um sie her! / Auf dem heil'gen Bibelgrunde / Steht die feste Gottesstadt; / Drei Jahrhunderte bezeugen's, / Daß sie Gott zum Schirmer hat!"

55. BSRK 79–94, ET: Hinke 2:33–61.

56. BSRK XXIV–XXV. [There is, unfortunately, no English translation of the useful historical introduction to the Reformed Confessions provided by Müller in the BSRK.—Trans.]

57. The four upper German cities of Strassburg, Konstanz, Lindau, and Mem-

mingen, which were not willing to accept the Augsburg Confession because of the view of the Lord's Supper represented by its Article X, entered into the Augsburg religious negotiations with the *Confessio Tetrapolitana* composed by M. Bucer and W. Capito (BSRK 55–78, ET: Cochrane 51–88. It was intended to be a middle position between the Lutheran and Zwinglian stances.

58. See Tschackert, *Entstehung der lutherischen und der reformierten Kirchenlehre*, 254–55.

59. EA 62,82 = WA.TR 3,128,8–10, ET: LW 54:186–87.

60. *Waldenser-Bekenntnis* (1655), BSRK 500–505, citation is at 504,11: "selon la declaration qu'en a donné l'auteur," ET: Schaff 757–70; the phrase quoted is on 768.

61. *Confessio Augustana Variata (1540)*, in R. Stupperich, ed., *Melanchthons Werke in Auswahl*, vol. 6 (Gütersloh: Bertelsmann, 1955), 12–79. See on this W. Maurer, *Confessio Augustana Variata*, in ARG, Year 53 (1962), 97–151. The plan for renewed religious conversations in the year 1540 at which the Augsburg Confession was to serve as the basis of discussion led Melanchthon to produce a substantially revised version, known as the Augsburg Confession Variata (CA Variata). In it, he distanced himself from the blunt concept of the real presence in the eucharistic question. There are various versions of the "Variata" in existence.

62. *Consensus Sendomiriensis* of 1570, Augusti 254–64; see there, 254; Niemeyer 553–61; see 553–54. In this consensus, the Polish branch of the Moravian Brethren (Unitas Fratrum) joined together with the Lutherans of Great Poland as well the Reformed of Little Poland.

63. *Declaratio Thorunsiensis*, Augusti 411–42, see there 413; Niemeyer 669–89; see there 670. It formulates the Reformed position at the Religious Consultation at Thorn (1645) after a common Protestant front had not come together since the Lutherans insisted on holding to the CA Invariata.

64. Salnar, *Harmonia Confessionum Fidei Orthodoxarum et Reformatarum Ecclesiarum [. . .] Quae omnia, Ecclesiarum Gallicarum, et Belgicarum nomine, subiiciuntur libero et prudenti reliquarum omniun, iudicio* (Geneva, 1581), ET: Salnar/Hall. See BSRK XIII.

65. K. Laurentius, *Corpus et Syntagma Confessionum Fidei, quae in diversis Regnis et Nationibus, Ecclesiarum nomine fuerunt authentice editae* (Aureliae Allobrogum, 1612). See BSRK XIV.

66. See BSRK XIII, 28 and BSRK XIV,18.

67. J. Calvin, letter to M. Schalling, April 8, 1557 (Nr. 2607), CR 44 (=CO 16), 430: "Nec vero Augustanam confessionem repudio, cui pridem volens ac libens subscripsi, sicuti eam autor ipse interpretatus est," ET: "I also do not reject the Augsburg Confession, which I long ago happily and willingly signed, as it is expounded by its author" (see Rudolf Schwarz, ed. , *Johannes Calvins Lebenswerk in seinen Briefen* [Neukirchen, 1962], 3:885).

68. J. Calvin, *Defensio sanae et orthodoxae doctrinae de sacramentis eorumque natura, vi, fine, usu, et fructu* (1555), OS II, 271: "Et ne privata singulorum scripta evolvere et excutere necesse sit, in Consensu nostro reperient lectores quidquid continet edita Ratisbonae confessio, quam Augustanam vocant: modo ne crucis metu ad captandam papistarum gratiam flectatur. Verba sunt: in sacra Coena cum pane et vino vere dari Christi corpus et sanguinem," ET: "Exposition of the Heads of Agreement," "Mutual Consent of the Churches of Zurich and Geneva as to the Sacraments" [Consensus Tigurinus], *Tracts and Treatises II*, 225: "And to make it unnecessary to turn up and examine the private writings of each, readers will find in our Agreement every-

thing contained in the Confession published at Ratisbon, and called the Confession of Augsburg, provided only that it be not interpreted as having been composed under fear of torture, to gain favour with the Papists. The words are—'In the holy Supper, the body and blood of Christ are truly given with the bread and the wine.'"

69. Barth thus revised the view he had expressed a year earlier, that Calvin had signed the Invariata. See Th.C. 538–39, and note 19 there on this problem; ET: *Theology of Calvin* 398; in regard to this problem see note 18.

69a. *Letters of John Calvin*, ed. Jules Bonnet, trans. M. R. Gilchrist (New York: Lenox Hill, reprint, 1972), 4:223.

70. =WA.B 5,319,7–8; letter to Elector Johann of May 15, 1530 (Nr. 1568), ET: LW 49:298.

71. *Nassauisches Bekenntnis [Nassau Confession]*, BSRK 720–39.

72. 1599, excerpted in BSRK 799–816.

73. BSRK 739–99.

74. See BSRK 740,27–36.

75. BSRK 740,39–41.

76. Cited in H. Heppe, *Kirchengeschichte beider Hessen* (Marburg, 1876), 1:376 (in the continuation of note 2 from 375); the German there says "gewahrten" instead of "bewährten" ["perceived" instead of "proven"; the years 1540 and 1542 are meant—Trans.].

77. *Confessio Sigismundi*, BSRK 835–43.

78. See BSRK 740,38–39.

79. See BSRK 836,28–29.

80. BSRK 836,32–34; the year 1530 is meant—Trans.

81. See Ebrard 12–13 ET: Salnar/Hall xxxviii–xxxix.

82. BSLK 64,1–8, ET: K/W 44[1–2].

83. See above, nn. 62 and 63.

84. Pencil notation on the manuscript margin: "Took place however at Leipzig in 1631 (Aug. 389)." Barth is referring here to the Leipzig Colloquium, March 3–23, 1631. Augusti 389–90: " . . . since in the beginning the Electoral-Brandenburg and Royal Hessian [i.e. the Reformed] theologians voluntarily declared that with mouth and heart they subscribed to the Confession submitted at the Diet in the year 1530 on June 25 to Emperor Charles V of worshipful memory, by the evanglical Electors and Estates at Augsburg, and that when and where desired they were willing to sign it without reservations, that they would not be opposed to give witness to their consensus by signing that example of it found in the *Chur-Sächsischen Augapfel*. And they were all the more desirous of doing so not only because they had registered their submission to the Augsburg Confession in their place but also in that their most gracious lords in Electoral Brandenburg and in the Principality of Hesse had always publicly confessed and promoted it in their churches and schools." See lecture 3.3, pp. 197–206.

85. With the signing of the Peace of Westphalia on October 24, 1648, the Augsburg Religious Peace of 1555 was expressly extended to the Reformed, who now were counted among the "adherents of the Augsburg Confession" ("confessioni Augustanae addicti"). See Loofs 929.

86. This citation cannot be referenced; perhaps it has to do with a characteristic turn of speech of one of Barth's Göttingen colleagues, to which he alludes ironically here.

87. In his letter to Duke Albrecht of Prussia of May 6, 1548 (WA.B 8,215,32ff.), Luther

mentions, for example, with the inclusion of a few upper German cities, all of those "Swiss" who promote a eucharistic doctrine that differs from his. Perhaps Barth is also thinking of the fact that some at the time sought, without foundation, to explain the term "Huguenot" as related to "Eidgenosse" [The Swiss term for a member of the confederation]. See on this the article on "Hugenotten" in RGG, 1st ed., 3:166, ET: S/H 5:393. See also W. Hadorn's article, "Reformierte Kirche" in RGG, 1st ed., 4:2110: "Reformed here means first of all 'Zwinglian' and 'Swiss' and later 'Calvinist.'"

88. BSRK 1–7, ET: Cochrane 36–44.

89. OS I, 162–223, ET: Inst. II,xix,2:1449–84, entitled "The Five Other Ceremonies, Falsely Termed Sacraments . . . " [Although the ET is based on the version of 1559, the editor notes, "The text of the present chapter has only a few sentences not in that of 1536" (1448 n. 1)—Trans.]

90. See Th.C. 258–60, ET: *Theology of Calvin* 192–93. [The key sentence should read in the ET: "1. The direct impression that one has is that a man is speaking here who is *completely finished* with Catholicism" (Barth's italics)—Trans.]

91. Manuscript: "1540," Barth dates the Regensburg Religious Consultation, from whose files this quotation comes, erroneously one year earlier.

92. CR 33(=CO 5), 654. The original is in French, which Barth has translated.

93. J. Calvin, *De fugiendis impiorum sacris* (1537), OS I, 325: "Et quid inde lucri vel tibi, vel aliis redeat, si atheon te esse suspicentur, quem nulla tangi religione existement? Verum, ut illam suspicionis causam ne ultro dataque opera praebeas consulo, ita si forte fortuna illuc incideris, satius multo fuerit, quidvis de te suspicentur, quam idololatram conspiciant," ET: "The Unlawful Rights of the Ungodly, and the Purity of the Christian Religion," *Tracts and Treatises III,* 407: "For what gain can accrue to yourself or others from being suspected to be an atheist, utterly devoid of all religious feeling? But, while I advise you not voluntarily, or of set purpose, to give ground for such suspicion, still, if by circumstances you are accidentally brought into a dubious position, any suspicion is better far than to let them see you acting the idolater!"

94. Ibid., 303: "quam ut a radice evellantur universa, et una [. . .] litura corrigantur, quae ex eius disciplina prodierunt," ET: *Tracts and Treatises III,* 378.

95. This sentence is entered in pencil on the margin of the manuscript, BSRK 428, 5–8.

96. See F. W. Kampschulte, *Johann Calvin: Seine Kirche und sein Staat in Genf*, vol. 1 (Leipzig, 1869), 328–35; further, Th.C. 532–44, ET: *Theology of Calvin* 393–402.

97. On Zwingli's plans, esp. in 1529–1530, directed against the Habsburgs, who were papal loyalists, and his intention to form a "Protestant" axis with Landgrave Philipp of Hesse; see G. W. Locher, *Die Zwinglische Reformation im Rahmen der europäischen Kirchengeschichte* (Göttingen and Zurich, 1979), 514–21.

98. See V.u.kl.A. 1922–1925, 622–23 nn. 70 and 71; cited is a lecture given by Barth to the Annual Meeting of the Reformed Federation of Germany, held at Duisburg-Meiderich, June 3, 1925, in which he obviously used material from this book.

99. See Th.C. 533, ET: *Theology of Calvin* 394–95.

100. See J.-B. Bossuet, *Histoire des variations des églises protestantes: Défense de cette histoire; Advertissemens aus protestans, et instructions pastorales sur les promesses de J. C. à son Eglise,* 5 vols. (Paris, 1770), esp. vol. 2, 361ff, 429ff, ET: *The History of the Variations of the Protestant Churches,* 2d ed. (Dublin: Richard Coyne, 1836), 2:189–90, 235–37. Barth knew of Bossuet's judgment through Augusti 599 (epilogue).

101. See O. Spengler, *Der Untergang des Abendlandes: Umrisse einer Morphologie der Weltgeschichte*, vol. 1: *Gestalt und Wirklichkeit* (Vienna and Leipzig, 1918), and vol.

2, *Welthistorische Perspektiven* (Munich, 1922), ET: Oswald Spengler, *The Decline of the West*, trans. and ed. Charles Francis Atkinson (London: George Allen & Unwin, 1932), vol. 1, *Form and Actuality*, and vol. 2, *Perspectives of World History*.

102. Pencil notation on the margin of the manuscript: "See Pestalozzi, Bullinger 186, 188." C. Pestalozzi, *Heinrich Bullinger: Leben und ausgewählte Schriften*, Leben und ausgewählte Schriften der Väter und Begründer der reformirten Kirche, Part 5 (Elberfeld, 1858). Regarding the formulation of the Basel Confession of 1536 by Bullinger, Myconius, and Grynäus, 186: "These articles have been composed by us, servants of the Word, not in *the* opinion that we wanted to impose them upon or prescribe them for all churches, or that we should catch someone in words and force him to speak in a special way which would be pointless and incomprehensible for the churches. Rather, we have wanted to express, confess, and explain mutually our faith and understanding of the true Christian religion." Quotation of a letter from Bullinger to Bucer, February 1536 (p. 188): "One cannot describe how the confession has been received here with profound expressions of blessing and thanksgiving to God, not only because of the unity which has been achieved for us and the fellowship with you, but also because you have made known to us the happy prospect that *Luther*, Melanchthon, Osiander and the other pious and brave defenders of the Gospel *will require nothing further from us*. What happiness for me if I should experience the day on which you presented me certain testimonies of that! . . . Turn off the scorners in Wittenberg. Things are going there much too crudely."

103. This sentence was entered later in pencil; BSRK 229,11–12: "Nulle église ne doit prétendre aucune domination ou seigneurie sur l'autre," ET: Schaff 377.

104. The new foundation of the chair for Reformed theology in Göttingen would not have been possible without the financial help of American Presbyterians. See E. Busch, *Karl Barths Lebenslauf: Nach seinen Briefen und autobiographischen Texten*, 4th ed. (Munich, 1986), 135; ET: Eberhard Busch, *Karl Barth: His Life from Letters and Autobiographical Texts* (Philadelphia: Fortress Press, 1976), 123; Goeters, *Reformierter Lehrstuhl und Studienhaus* (see above, n. 15), 271.

105. =BSLK 833, 9–17, ET: K/W 526[1]. Barth was translating from the Latin version. [We have inserted the Latin phrases in the ET that he inserted in his German translation.—Trans.]

106. Barth's manuscript has the German verb "werden," which the German editor has corrected to the singular "wird."

107. M. Luther, letter to Michael Stifel of December 31, 1525 (Nr. 957), = WA.B 3,653, 6–9, ET: LW 49:141.

108. M. Luther, *Antwortschreiben an die Christen zu Reutlingen* (1526), = WA 19,122, 12–14: "Denn wyr wissen, das der heylige geyst, eyn got der eynickeit ist, vnd eynerley synn, grund vnd lere gibt."

109. See Augusti 580 (epilogue).

110. See BSRK XXIII, 16–22.

111. See Kampschulte, *Johann Calvin* (see above, n. 96), 1:307.

112. Geneva Catechism of 1442/45, BSRK 117–53, ET: *Tracts and Treatises II*, 33–94.

113. On the biography of Knox; see section 3.2, p. 278, n. 333.

114. On the biography of Lasco; see section 3.2, p. 268–9, n. 167.

115. On the biography of Olevianus; see section 3.2, p. 269, n. 179.

116. BSRK 724,31; 726,34.

117. BSRK 775,43.

118. BSRK 803,31; 812,26.

119. BSRK 836,42; 837,45; 838,13.31.

120. BSRK 550,20–22, ET: Schaff 757–70, esp. 768; see also Isa. 44:24–45:8.

121. H. Bullinger (1504–1575) was the successor to Zwingli. The Second Helvetic Confession (BSRK 170–221, ET: Cochrane 220–301), which he wrote in 1562 and published in 1566, resulted in his linking the Reformed churches of most of Switzerland together with a strong common bond.

122. Quoted in BSRK XXXI,40–41: "passim per omnes ecclesias Germaniae, Galliae, Angliae, et ceterorum regnorum regionumque."

123. In the preface to *Catechismus seu christianae religionis institutio ecclesiae Genevensis* (1538), OS I, 431: "Quod si imperatori Christo nostra obsequia approbare cupimus, piam inter nos conspirationem ineamus necesse est, ac mutuam pacem foveamus, quam suis non commendat modo, sed etiam inspirat." ET: "But if we desire to prove our obedience to Christ our Leader, we must enter into a godly compact among ourselves and foster mutual peace, which he not only commends to his own, but also inspires in them," the ET by Ford Lewis Battles of this catechism is found in I. John Hesselink, *Calvin's First Catechism: A Commentary* (Louisville, Ky.: Westminster John Knox Press, 1997), 1–38, citation on 5.

124. BSRK 862, 20–23: "Salva unitas corporis mystici et Spiritus . . . , et in eadem tuenda sancta conspiratio et contesseratio . . . ," ET: "The unity of the mystical body and the Spirit is entire . . . and in it the holy compact and contesseration is preserved." [The ET of the Helvetic Consensus Formula of 1675 is in Leith 308–23, but this citation is in the preface to the Consensus, which is not included in this edition.—Trans.]

125. See BSRK XXXI,49–XXXII,1.

126. See Ebrard, 1–2.; Salnar/Hall xxix–xxvi.: mutual acknowledgment of the Gallican and Belgic Confessions.

127. Regarding the obtaining of external expertise in the case of Hieronymus Bolsec (d. 1584), who was arrested for his disputation of Calvin's doctrine of predestination, as well as for the case of Michael Servetus (d. 1553), who was tried because of his disputation of the doctrine of the Trinity, see E. Stähelin, *Johannes Calvin: Leben und ausgewählte Schriften,* Leben und ausgewählte Schriften der Väter und Begründer der reformirten Kirche, Part 4, (Elberfeld, 1863), 1:413, 449–52.

128. E. Troeltsch, *Protestantisches Christentum und Kirche in der Neuzeit,* in P. Hinneberg, ed., *Die Kultur der Gegenwart,* Part 1, Sect. 4, 1st half (Berlin/Leipzig, 1906), 351.

129. BSRK 843–61, ET: Bray 457–78, also an abridged version in Schaff 581–97.

130. See E. F. K. Müller, *Symbolik: Vergleichende Darstellung der christlichen Hauptkirchen nach ihren Grundzügen und ihren wesentlichen Lebensäußerungen,* (Erlangen/Leipzig, 1896), 420.

131. See above, n. 64; ET: Salnar/Hall.

132. See above, n. 65.

133. *Confessio Saxonica* 1551; see BSRK XIII,28, XIV,18.

134. *Confessio Wirtembergensis* 1552; see BSRK XII,28, XIV,18.

135. In Ebrard's revision these two confessions were not included; see Ebrard V [but they are in Salnar/Hall—Trans.].

136. See BSRK XIII,18–22. Further, Ebrard III–V, ET: Salnar/Hall xvi–xvii; J. Wirsching, "Bekenntnisschriften," in TRE 5:501, 45–51.

137. BSRK 741, 8–12.

138. See BSRK XIII, 24–25, ET: Salnar/Hall; the history of English translations is briefly reviewed in Hall's preface, Salnar/Hall, ix–xii; see xvii–xviii.

139. See Wirsching, "Bekenntnisschriften," 5:501,55.

140. See list of abbreviations under Augusti.

141. See Augusti 650–51.

142. See list of abbreviations under Niemeyer.

143. P. Schaff, *Bibliotheca Symbolica Ecclesiae Universalis: The Creeds of Christendom, with a History and Critical Notes*, 3 vols. (New York: Harper & Row, 1877; reprint, Grand Rapids: Baker Book House, 1966).

144. See list of abbreviations under BSLK.

145. See list of abbreviations under SBLK.

146. See BSRK V.

147. See list of abbreviations under Augusti.

148. See Augusti 584–85.

148a. BSRK 199,40: "Fides catholica non est nobis tradita humanis legibus, sed scriptura divina, cuius compendium est symbolum apostolicum," ET: Schaff 277; BOC 5.141.

149. J. Calvin, *Pro G. Farello et collegis eius adversus Petri Caroli calumnias—Defensio Nicolai Gallasii* (1545), CR 35 (=CO 7), 312: "conceptae intus fidei testificatio." The following quotations are from this document. Both the translation and emphases are Barth's. [See J. Calvin, "Gegen die Verleumdungen des P. Caroli (1545)," in *Reformatorische Anfänge, 1533–1541*, ed. E. Busch et al., vol. 1, Calvin Studienausgabe 1/1 (Neukirchen, 1994), 225–61, our citation is on 233].

149a. Calvin, *Pro G. Farello*, 312: "*ipsissima scripturae veritas*, exquisitis ac solennibus verbis religiose composita."

150. Letter of the Genevan pastors to the Bernese, February 1537 (Nr. 49), CR 38/II (=CO 10/II), 83–84; no ET, but see R. Schwarz, ed., *Johannes Calvins Lebenswerk in Briefen* (Neukirchen, 1961), 1:53–55. Letter from Calvin to a Bernese pastor, February 1537 (Nr. 50), CR 38/II (=CO 10/II), 86.

151. OS I, 71–75, noted in the manuscript erroneously as [CO] 1,79–82, ET: *Institutes (1536)*, 45–48[7–9]. For the correction; see Th.C. 423–24, ET: *Theology of Calvin* 312.

152. The Lausanne pastor P. Caroli accused Calvin and Farel of the denial of the Trinity. See Th.C. 420–71, ET: *Theology of Calvin* 309–45.

153. =CR 38,II, 103: letter from Myconius to Bullinger, May 20, 1537 (Nr. 60).

154. On the controversy between Calvin and the anti-Trinitarian M. Servetus and on his position in the legal process resulting in Servetus's execution in Geneva on October 27, 1533, see Calvin's *Defensio orthodoxae fidei de sacra trinitate* (1554), CR 36 (=CO 8), 458–644. See Servetus's letters to Calvin as well as the Genevan court proceedings in CR 36 (=CO 8), 645–720 and 721–872. [Although no ET; see on the trial of Servetus and his correspondence to Calvin and the court, R. Willis, *Servetus and Calvin: A Study of an Important Epoch in the Early History of the Reformation* (London: Henry S. King, 1877), 314–488.—Trans.]

155. BSLK 50,3–18, ET: K/W 36–37[1–4].

156. BSLK 414,25–26, ET: K/W 400[4].

157. BSLK 768,8–21; 834,26–39, ET: K/W 486[3]; 527[4].

158. BSRK 164,3–8.

159. BSRK 723; 740,14–18.

160. BSRK 740,37–39.

161. BSRK 836,27–31.

162. BSRK 222,41–44: "Et suyvant cela nous avouons les trois symboles, ascavoir des Apostres, de Nice et d'Athanase, pource qu'ilz sont conformes à la Parole de Dieu," ET: Schaff 362[V].

163. BSRK 527,8–11, ET: Schaff 528[7].

163a. BSRK 56,10–12, ET: Cochrane 56[II, lines 1–9].

164. BSRK 79,37–39, ET: Hinke 236.

165. BSRK 236,21–22, ET: Schaff 393.

166. BSRK 186,3–9, ET: Schaff 854, also Cochrane 247.

167. BSRK 935,20–22.

168. BSRK 458,1–4.

169. BSRK 508,11–14, ET: Schaff 492.

170. BSRK 804,45–46.

171. Barth probably means here the Bern Synod of 1542 (BSRK 31–55), not the Bern Theses of 1528 (BSRK 30–31, ET: Cochrane 45–50).

172. BSRK 249–63, ET: Cochrane 166–84.

173. Instruction et Confession de foy (1537), OS I, 396: "Et il ne peult pas guaires challoir par quel autheur ou autheurs ait este compose ce sommaire de la foy, lequel ne contient du tout vien [rien?—Trans.] de doctrine humaine . . . ," ET: *Instruction in Faith* 46: "It can hardly matter which author or authors have composed this summary of faith. It contains no human doctrine."

174. Genevan Catechism (1542), BSRK 118,9–12, ET: *Tracts and Treatises II*, 39.

175. BSRK 327 7–11: "Tridentinum anno 1547 et 1546 celebratum de Iustificatione, de fide, operibus [. . .]," "Item multa alia concilia et decreta veritate scripturae approbata."

176. BSRK 172,17–18, ET: Schaff 834; see also BOC 5.011.

177. BSRK 258,22–40, ET: Cochrane 178.

178. BSRK 430,34–36; 430,41–431,3.

179. BSRK 513,12–20, ET: Schaff 500[XXI].

180. BSRK 536,10–16, ET: Schaff 539–40[76].

181. BSRK 609,17–24: "Quae quidem decreta et decisiones [scil. Synodorum et Conciliorum], modo verbo Dei consenserint, cum reverentia sunt ac summissione excipienda; Non quidem solum quod verbo Dei sint consentanea, verum etiam gratia potestatis ea constituentis, ut quae sit ordinatio Dei ad id in verbo suo designata," ET: Schaff 609[3,XXXI): "Which decrees and determinations (e.g, of synods and councils [German editors' emendation]), if consonant to the Word of God, are to be received with reverence and submission; not only for their agreement with the Word, but also for the power whereby they are made, as being an ordinance of God appointed thereunto in his Word."

182. BSRK 513,15–16, ET: Schaff 500–501[XXI].

183. "Testimony of inwardly conceived faith" ["Conceptae intus fidei testifactio"]; see above, n. 149.

184. See BSRK 186,12, ET: Cochrane 247, line 25.

185. See above, n. 19, ET: LW 41:72: " . . . the holy church of God in former times . . . "

186. See, e.g, BSLK 742,17–18, ET: K/W 5[4]; 834,42–835,2, ET: K/W 527[5]; 983,5–7, ET: K/W 598[34]; 984,36–37, ET: K/W 600[41].

187. BSRK 869,40, ET: Leith 308–23.

188. BSRK 870,12.

189. E.g, the *Constitution of the Free Church of Vaux* (1847), BSRK 903,34, *Declaration of the French General Synod* (1872), BSRK 910,24.

190. See above, n. 149.

191. F. Brunn, *Gottes Wort und Luthers Lehr*, 2d ed. (Zwickau, 1892), 1, calls it "a long-known saying."

192. =BSLK 832,37–38, ET: K/W 526[10]; 1093,6–7, ET: K/W 657[8].
193. BSRK 1–6, ET: Cochrane 36–44.
194. BSRK XVII,26–27.
195. 1523, BSRK 7–29, ET: Pipkin 49–75.
196. BSRK 110, ET: Cochrane 120–26.
197. BSRK 111–16: "*Confession de la Foi* la quelle tous bourgeois et habitans de Genève et subjects du pays doibvent jurer de garder et tenir," ET: Cochrane 120–26.
198. OS I, 426–32, ET: I. John Hesselink, *Calvin's First Catechism: A Commentary*, trans. of catechism by Ford Lewis Battles (Louisville, Ky.: Westminster John Knox Press, 1997), 1–7.
199. See Th.C. 386–98, 400–406, ET: *Theology of Calvin* 284–93, 295–99.
200. See OS I, 429: "Aequum esse, ut in actione tam sancta [sic] populo suo praeirent [namely, the Council members], cui se omnis virtutis exemplar esse oportere noverat," ET: Hesselink, *Calvin's First Catechism*, 4: "It is proper that the magistrates should in such a holy action precede their people [namely, the Council Members, (emendation by German editors)], for whom they knew they ought to be the pattern of all virtue."
201. See Th.C. 391, 403–5, ET: *Theology of Calvin* 288–89, 297–98. [The Bernese Oberland is the relatively small mountainous area in south central Switzerland between the Aare and Rhone rivers.—Trans.]
202. OS I, 432: "Indignissimum est enim, ut in quibus libertatem Dominus reliquit, quo maior esset aedificandi facultas, servilem praeterita aedificatione conformitatem quaeramus. Atqui ubi ad summum illud tribunal ventum fuerit, ubi reddenda erit olim functionis nostrae ratio, minima erit de caeremoniis quaestio: neque omnino haec in rebus externis conformitas . . . ad calculum vocabitur . . . ," ET: Hesselink, *Calvin's First Catechism*, 6: "For it is most unworthy of us to seek a servile conformity, having passed over edification, in those whom the Lord leaves freedom in order that there might be a greater readiness to be edified. And yet when that last judgment-seat will have been reached, where once for all an account of our performance will have to be made, it will not at all be a question of ceremonies nor conformity in external matters, but the lawful use of freedom will be strictly reckoned."
203. OS I, 432, ET: Hesselink, *Calvin's First Catechism*, 6.
204. BSRK 930–35, esp. the title: 930,4–7: "Summa unde bekenninghe Christliker leer der predicanten In Oostfrieslandt, warinne men sien mach wo si nicht noch Gades wort noch Sacramenten verachten, als hem valschelyck opghelecht werdt," ET: "Summary of the Confession of Christian doctrine of the preachers in East Friesia, in which they explain that they do not despise either God's Word or Sacraments of which they have been falsely accused."
205. George Aportanus (d. 1530), of Zwolle, earlier a member of the Brethren of the Common Life, from 1518 on teacher and then Reformed preacher in Emden. See BSRK XXII,7–9.
206. Zwingli took from a letter of the Dutchman C. H. Hoen (Honius) in 1523 the tropic exegesis of "est" (="significat") in the words of the institution of the Lord's Supper. See CR 91 (=Z 4), 512–19. See Gottfried W. Locher, *Zwingli's Thought: New Perspectives, Studies in the History of Christian Thought*, ed. Heiko Obermann (Leiden: E. J. Brill, 1981), 221.
207. *The Canon of Dort of 1619*, BSRK 843–62, ET: Bray 455–78. The public reading, following a prayer, took place on May 6, 1619, in a worship service in the Great Church, to which the populace came in great numbers. See BSRK LXIV,33–35. The ringing of the bells at the proclamation of the canons cannot be documented in any of the literature used by Barth.

208. See K. Barth, *Wunschbarkeit und Möglichkeit eines allgemeinen reformierten Glaubensbekenntnisses* (1925), in V.u.kl.A. 1922–1925, 604–43, esp. 616, ET: "The Desirability and Possibility of a Universal Reformed Creed" (1925), in K. Barth, *Theology and Church*, trans. Louis P. Smith (London: SCM Press, 1962), 112–35, esp. 116.

209. See above, n. 149.

210. *Platform der Savoy-Declaration*, BSRK 656,7; ET: *The Savoy Declaration*, Schaff 728[XXVI].

211. See BSRK XXIV,31–33; XXXVII,9–12; XXXIX,40–43.

212. See Ebrard 7–10.

213. See above, n. 59.

214. BSLK 833,2–3, ET: K/W 526. [The Latin title of this section is "De Compendiaria Doctrinae Forma, Fundamento, Norma atque Regula," which is rendered in the ET, "Concerning the Binding Summary, Basis, Rule, and Guiding Principle"; "form" is not literally translated but Barth's point is made by the ET "binding summary."—Trans.]

215. Letter to Gregor Casel of November 5, 1525 (Nr. 942) (=WA.B 3,604,35–36: "Spiritus enim non sic trepidat aut disputat," ET: *Luther's Correspondence and Other Contemporary Letters*, trans. and ed. Preserved Smith and Charles M. Jacobs (Philadelphia: Lutheran Publication Society, 1918), 2:347.

216. BSRK 2,16–18, ET: Cochrane 36[lines 5–7]; Barth's italics.

217. Zwingli, *Eine kurze christliche Einleitung*, S 1,543 (=CR 89 [Z 2], 629), ET: Pipkin 49. Barth's italics.

218. *Der Berner Synodus von 1532. Das wichtigste Denkmal der Reformation in Bern, eine Anweisung zur rechten Führung des evangelischen Predigtamtes* (Basel, 1870), 177. (=G. W. Locher, ed., *Der Berner Synodus von 1532: Edition und Abhandlungen zum Jubiläumsjahr 1582* [Neukirchen-Vluyn: Neukirchener Verlag, 1984], 1:26–27); Barth's italics. In BSRK 31–55, the articles of the Bern Synod are printed without the introduction from which Barth took this quotation.

219. BSRK 100,14–20, ET: Cochrane 89–96.

220. The preface is not included in the version of the Second Helvetic Confession (1562) printed in BSRK 170–221, ET: Cochrane 224–301 [which also fails to include the preface—Trans.]. Barth used the translation found in F. A. Beck, *Die Symbolischen Bücher der evangelisch-reformierten Kirche: zum ersten Male aus dem Lateinischen vollständig übersetzt und mit historischen Einleitungen und Anmerkungen begleitet*, 2d ed. (Neustadt a.d. Orla, 1845), 1:65–69; see esp. 68–69: "Above all we testify publicly that we are always ready to discuss in greater detail everything and anything that we have included here with whomever wishes to do so, and to anyone who better instructs us from the Word of God we shall submit not without thanks and be obedient in the Lord, to whom be praise and honor."

221. Pencil notation on the margin of the manuscript: "also Postfatio Zürcher Consensus 1544 Op. Calv. [CO] 7 [=CR 35,] LI: "If anyone should present something better, then we promise that we shall be willing to be corrected and to receive that which is better, so that everyone may readily know that we desire nothing other than that all disagreements should be resolved positively and that the one truth of God should be heard by everyone."

222. As cited in n. 220, vol. 2 of Beck, ET: Cochrane 165; see also Schaff 439.

222a. "Classis" is a frequently used Reformed term for a regional church governing body.

223. J. V. Bredt, *Neues evangelisches Kirchenrecht für Preußen*, vol. 2: *Die Rechtslage nach 1918* (Berlin, 1922), 742.

224. G. Finsler, *Kirchliche Statistik der reformierten Schweiz* (Zurich, 1854), 41–42, as well as 584 (under "Nachträge und Berichtigungen"); Barth's italics.

225. See Finsler, *Kirchliche Statistik*, 41.

226. BSRK 169,44–45: "Homines enim nos esse probe reminiscimur, et ob id facile posse labi errare, nescire et decipi," ET: "For we humans must modestly remind ourselves that we are truly human, and thus easily fall into error, know nothing, and deceive ourselves."

227. BSRK 169,36.

228. BSRK 869,38–39: " . . . dubium vel novum aliquod dogma fidei in Ecclesiis nostris hactenus inauditum," ET: Leith, 322: ". . . some doubtful or new dogma of faith hitherto unheard of in our churches."

229. See BSRK LXV, 26–29.

230. See BSRK XXXIV,45–XXXV,6; in 1619 the confession was officially recognized by the Synod of Dort.

231. See BSRK XLVI,40–XLVII,46.

232. *The Points of Difference of the Congregationalists, 1603*, BSRK 541,34–38, where the point is made over against all ecclesial tradition, " . . . that all Churches and people (without exception) are bound in Religion only to receave and submit unto that constitution, Ministerie, Worship, and order, which Christ as Lord and King hath appainted unto his Church: and not to any other divised by Man whatsoever."

233. Usually this catechism is dated in the year 1537 (see OS I, 378–79; BSKO 1). According to E. F. K. Müller (BSRK XXVII, 31–43), this catechism (OS 1,378–417, ET: John Calvin, *Instruction in Faith 1537*), together with an excerpt from it, the "Confession of Faith" (Confession de la Foy), was already approved by the Geneva Council on November 10, 1536, but it was not publicized until the spring of 1537. Barth dates the text in a similar fashion (Th.C. 366–67, ET: *Theology of Calvin* 271–72), and so in this lecture he consistently connects it to the year 1536.

234. Since Calvin found the first catechism to be inadequate, he replaced it in 1541–1542 with a new one, again written in French (CR 34 (=CO 6) 1–146; BSKO 3–41). This appeared in 1545 in altered form in Latin (OS II, 59–157; BSRK 117–53, ET: *Tracts and Treatises II*, 33–94.

235. On the various editions, see OS III, VI–XLVIII.

236. SBLK LXIX in the edition of 1860.

237. CR 34 (=CO 6), 250. Translated by Barth from Latin: "Quorsum enim viveremus, si nihil aetas, nihil usus, nihil assidua exercitatio, nihil lectio, nihil meditatio conferret? Quorsum autem proficeremus, nisi ut fructus inde aliquis ad alios quoque perveniret? Imo si nescit Pighius, hoc illi testatum esse velim: nos huc dies noctesque incumbere, ut quae fideliter a nobis tradita sunt, in modum etiam, quem putamus optimum fore, foremus," ET: John Calvin, *The Bondage and Liberation of the Will*, ed. A. N. S. Lane, trans. G. I. Davies (Grand Rapids: Baker Books, 1996), 29.

238. *Inst.* IV,xiii,13,2:1177. The last two sentences have been added to the manuscript in pencil. The italics in the Calvin citation are Barth's.

239. See above, n. 54.

240. Abraham Kuyper (1837–1920), Reformed theologian, defended the authority of the unabbreviated Reformed confession against liberalism, modernism, and mediatory theology, and thus brought about the formation of the "Gereformeerde Kerken in Nederland," which split away from the "Hervormde Kerk."

240a. The Lutheran and Reformed churches in the Prussian territories were compelled by the king to form regional "United Churches" in the early nineteenth century.—Trans.

241. See Bw.Th. II, 150: Zwingli should "be set in a direct line with . . . Schleiermacher," his talk of the "numen" [numinous] was "simply *one* gigantic attempt, carried through with astonishing vitality, to avoid the 'offense' and to wring the neck of the paradox of revelation" (Barth on February 28, 1923). ET: *Revolutionary Theology in the Making: Barth-Thurneysen Correspondence*, trans. James D. Smart (Richmond: John Knox Press, 1964), 137.

242. Alexander Schweizer (1808–1888) and Alois Emanuel Biedermann (1819–1885), professors of dogmatics in Zurich, both belonging to the liberal direction. See K. Barth, *Die protestantische Theologie im 19. Jahrhundert: ihre Geschichte und Vorgeschichte* (Zollikon and Zurich, 1947, 6th ed. 1994) 516–23, ET: *Protestant Theology in the 19th Century: Its Background and History* (Valley Forge, Pa: Judson Press, 1973), 569–76 [dealing only with Schweizer].

243. Richard Adalbert Lipsius (1830–1892), professor of systematic theology in Leipzig, Vienna, Kiel, and Jena; Otto Pfleiderer (1839–1908), professor of systematic theology in Berlin. Barth had grappled with both of them in his essay *Der Glaube an den persönlichen Gott* (1913) in *Vorträge und kleinere Arbeiten 1909–1914*, complete ed., section 3, ed. H.-A. Drews and H. Stoevesandt (Zurich, 1993), 494–554.

244. Frédéric Godet (1812–1900), professor of New Testament in Neuchâtel, first on the state faculty, from 1873 on the faculty of the free church; Adolf Schlatter (1852–1938) became professor of New Testament in Tübingen in 1898.

245. Max Goebel (1811–1857), author of the *Geschichte des christlichen Lebens in der rheinisch-westphälischen evangelischen Kirche*, 3 vols. (Coblenz, 1849–1860); Heinrich Heppe (1820–1879) was professor of church history in Marburg and author *inter alia* of *Geschichte des deutschen Protestantismus in den Jahren 1555–1581*, 4 vols. (Marburg 1851–1859); *Geschichte des Pietismus und der Mystik der reformirten Kirche, namentlich der Niederlande* (Leiden, 1879). [The only work in English by Heppe is his *Reformed Dogmatics: Set Out and Illustrated from the Sources*, rev. and ed. Ernst Bizer, trans. G. T. Thompson (Grand Rapids: Baker Book House, 1978); Karl Barth wrote the foreword to the German edition which appeared in 1935.— Trans.]

246. Johann Heinrich August Ebrard (1818–1888), professor of dogmatics in Zurich and Erlangen, critic of theological liberalism; Hermann Friedrich Kohlbrügge (1803–1875), pastor of the "Dutch-Reformed" congregation in Elberfeld who after changing from the Lutheran to the Reformed church proceeded emphatically to make Luther's doctrine of justification the center of his preaching and theology. See K. Barth, *Die protestantische Theologie im 19. Jahrhundert*, 579–87, ET: *Protestant Theology in the 19th Century*, 634–42.

247. August Friedrich Christian Vilmar (1800–1869), theology professor in Marburg, "passionate protagonist for a specifically Hessian Lutheranism" (Barth, *Protestantische Theologie im 19. Jahrhundert*, 570–78, quote on 571, ET: *Protestant Theology in the 19th Century*, 625–33, quote on 626).

248. Virgil, *Aeneis* I, 118: "Apparent rari nantes in gurgite vasto . . . ," ET: Virgil, *Aeneid I–VI*, Loeb Classical Library 63, trans. H. R. Fairclough (Cambridge, Mass.: Harvard University Press, 1916), 248–49.

249. Claus Harms (1778–1855), pastor in Kiel; Johann Gottfried Scheibel (1783–1843), Lutheran leader of the opposition to the Union in Breslau, Dresden, and Nuremberg; Friedrich Julius Stahl (1802–1861), pastor and consistory member in Berlin, publisher of the Kreuzzeitung [Cross Newspaper]; Wilhelm Löhe (1808–1872), pastor in Neuendettelsau; Andreas Gottlob Rudelbach (1792–1862), pastor and theology professor in Copenhagen; Adolf von Harless (1806–1879), theology professor in Erlangen and

Leipzig, president of the Consistory in Munich; Gottfried Thomasius (1802–1875), theology professor in Erlangen; Heinrich Schmid (1811–1886), theology professor in Erlangen; Carl Friedrich Zezschwitz (1825–1886), theology professor in Leipzig and Erlangen; Johann Christian von Hofmann (1810–1877), theology professor in Erlangen; Hans Larsen Martensen (1808–1884), theology professor and bishop in Copenhagen; Karl Friedrich August Kahnis (1814–1880), theology professor in Breslau and Leipzig; Christoph Ernst Luthardt (1823–1902), theology professor in Breslau and Leipzig; Friedrich Adolph Philippi (1809–1882), theology professor in Dorpat and Rostock; Franz Hermann Reinhold von Frank (1827–1894), theology professor in Erlangen; Albrecht Benjamin Ritschl (1822–1889), theology professor in Bonn and Göttingen.

250. A. von Harnack, *Zur gegenwärtigen Lage des Protestantismus* (1896), in his *Reden und Aufsätze* (Giessen, 1904), 2:139: "In this regard he [Ritschl] is for the time being the last Lutheran church father; what is distinctive about him was the way that he strengthened and related to each other the two elements of Protestantism, the doctrinaire, and the individualistic religious."

251. Under the influence of W. James (1842–1910), among others, and of the psychology of religion he developed, a "realistic liberalism" was formed at the time (D. C. McIntosh, H. N. Wieman), which sought to comprehend religion empirically in human experience (J. E. Smith) or in the evolutionary history of love (C. S. Peirce). Barth might have learned about this through the work of his fellow student K. Bornhausen, *Religion in Amerika: Beiträge zu ihrem Verständnis* (Giessen, 1914), 14–15 and perhaps through the book written by his vicariate supervisor A. Keller, *Dynamis: Formen und Kräfte des amerikanischen Protestantismus* (Tübingen, 1922), see 12–14.

252. Finsler, *Kirchliche Statistik* (see n. 224), 45; Barth's italics.

253. Finsler, *Kirchliche Statistik*, 199; Barth's italics.

254. As a consequence of the Basel War, which produced many victims and ended in 1833 with the division of the canton into the city of Basel and the region of Basel (Basel-Stadt and Baselland), the separate Reformed church of Baselland was formed. The regulations cited above were written in this way because the pastorates in Baselland were occupied by former citizens of the city of Basel.

255. The words "the spiritual life of so-called Christian society at the time" are entered in pencil on the margin of the manuscript.

256. See n. 149.

257. See the preface by J. T. Müller, SBLK V.

258. Barth is undoubtedly thinking of the "Free Churches," mentioned in BSRK LXIX–LXXI and passim, which emerged in the second half of the nineteenth century in protest against the dilution or surrender of the church's confession by theological liberalism. The term "free church" in this context can be used for the English and American church situation in only a very restricted sense.

259. According to BSRK LXIX, lines 32–33, the confession, which is an appendix to the "Constitution of the Evangelical Free Church of Geneva," dates from 1848. [This is also the date given by Schaff 781ff, who, like Müller in BSRK omits the preface from which Barth takes and translates this citation.—Trans.]

260. Finsler, *Kirchliche Statistik*, 568; the German term in Finsler is "übereinstimmend" ("in agreement with each other"), while Barth uses "einmütig" ("unanimously") ["Unanimously" renders both German terms correctly.—Trans.].

261. BSRK 871–927; the Confession of the Calvinist Methodists (1823) [871–99 (in English)]; the Declaration of the Congregational Union of England and Wales (1833) [899–903; see also Schaff 730–34]; the Constitution of the Free Church of the Vaux

(1847) [903–5]; the Confession of the Free Evangelical Church of Geneva (1848) [905–7], ET: Schaff 781–86; the Confession of the Free Evangelical Church of France (1849) [907–8]; the Confession of the Free Italian Church (1870) [909–10, ET: Schaff 786–88]; the French General Synod (1872) [910]; the Free Church of Neuchâtel (1874) [911]; the Cumberland Presbyterian Church (1883) [912–27 (in English)].

262. "Mômmiers" = those who practice mummery, that is, hypocrites. This was a derisive nickname for the adherents of the revival movement in French Switzerland. Barth is referring here to the confession of the Evangelical Free Church of Geneva of 1848 (BSRK 905–7, ET: Schaff 781–86). This church emerged on the one hand from the Eglise du Témoignage (Church of Witness), which was forced out of the Genevan state church in 1829 and was formed under the influence of Pastor H. A. C. Malan, and on the other hand from the Genevan Evangelical Society, which was founded under the influence of Pastor L. Gaussen to focus on the religious life. See on this W. Hadorn, *Kirchengeschichte der reformierten Schweiz* (Zurich, 1907), 266–68. According to W. Oechsli, *Geschichte der Schweiz im Neunzehnten Jahrhundert* (Leipzig, 1913), 2:524, the journal *Feuille d'Avis de Genève* first used the term on October 7, 1817, in reference to Malan and his followers.

263. F. Meyer, article on "Schweiz" (Switzerland) in RE, 3d ed., 18:57 [lines 16–21]: "In no Swiss regional church is its doctrine bound anymore to an official confession of faith but rests instead upon the general acknowledgment of evangelical truth. . . . Catechisms from the Reformation period are just as seldom in general or obligatory use." On the "removal" of the confessions at the end of the eighteenth and beginning of the nineteenth centuries in the various Swiss cantons, see W. Hildebrandt and R. Zimmerman, trans. and eds, *Das zweite Helvetische Bekenntnis: Confessio Helvetica Posterior* (Zurich: Kirchenrat des Cantons Zurich, 1966), 156–61.

264. Since all the Reformed cantonal churches in Switzerland had set confessional commitments aside, this can only refer to the fundamental principles or foundations of the cantonal church orders. Barth had been working since the summer of 1920 on the revision of the church order of the Reformed church of the Canton Aargau, and argued for including a biblical citation at the beginning of the introduction as a "gentle illumination" but not "as a confession," see Bw.Th. I, 412.

265. See n. 218.

266. The beginning of a Pentecost hymn ascribed to Hrabanus Maurus (ca. 776–856).

266a. "Verpflichtung," the theme of this section, implies an act of obligation that is binding, often with judicial implications. We have translated it "commitment." —Trans.

267. This sentence is entered in pencil on the margin of the manuscript; BSRK 475,38–40: "Haec est vera illa et Apostolica authoritas . . . , quae non super locum et personas, sed super puram doctrinam e libris sacris derivatam, extruitur."

268. BSRK 475,45–46: "Quae vera authoritas ubicunque dari et demonstrari non potest, frustra ibi personalis illi praetenditur et defenditur . . . ."

269. The principle that "religion is a private affair" was officially articulated in the Gotha Program of the German Social Democratic Party in May 1875.

270. See Troeltsch, *Protestantisches Christentum*, (see lecture 1, n. 128). As a summary, he comments on the "new concept of the church" of modernity that "the church is becoming a religious fellowship."

271. See n. 149.

272. Ibid.

273. According to Hadorn, *Kirchengeschichte der reformierten Schweiz*, 247–58, this

was the "basic principle" of the Reformed church in the "period of the Helvetic Confederation" (since 1798).

274. C. Stuckert, *Kirchenkunde der reformierten Schweiz*, Studien zur praktischen Theologie 4, Booklet 2: "Kirchenkunde des evangelischen Auslandes I" (Giessen, 1910), 64. According to R. Stähelin, this usage continued until 1826; see the article on "Basel, Konfession von" (Confession of Basel) in RE, 3d ed., 2:426 [line 57].

275. Manuscript says "of," changed by German editor to "in."

276. BSRK IL,43–48; see also the title of the 'Confession of the Frankfurt Foreigners Congregation' (*Bekenntnis der Frankfurter Fremdengemeinde*) of 1554 (BSRK 657,4–7): "Professio Fidei Catholica, quam publice approbare, ac subscriptione confirmare oportet priusquam aut Ecclesiae accenseantur, aut sacramenta ulla in parte communicent in Ecclesia Peregrinorum Francofordiae," ET: "Confession of the catholic faith which should be publicly acknowledged and confirmed by signature, either before they join the church or participate in any sacraments in the Frankfurt Foreigner Church."

277. BSRK XXXVI,29–31: Since King James VI was suspected of Roman tendencies, he was required to make an oath to the Covenant.

278. BSRK 265,8–9: "We protest and promeis solemnetlie with our heartes, under the same aith, hand-wreit, and paines . . . " (. . . sancte, ex animo, eodem adacti sacramento, eademque poena proposita, policemur, et consignatis chirographis promittimus) (Schaff 485).

279. *Der Berner Synodus von 1532* (see n. 218), 17 (in the edition by G. W. Locher [n. 218], 1:26–27).

280. See H. R. Lavater, "*Der Synodus in der Berner Kirche bis zum Anfang des 18. Jahrhunderts*," in G. W. Locher, ed., *Der Berner Synodus von 1532*, vol. 2, *Studien und Abhandlungen* (Neukirchen-Vluyn: Neukirchener Verlag, 1988), 304–19 (see n. 218).

281. BSRK 170,4–10.

282. BSRK LI,21.29–32.

283. Augusti 266: "IV. Nullus Superattendens, aut Senior, quemquam ad ministerium et munus pastorale mittere, aut patronus quisquam, sive coetus noster, pro ministerio recipere audeat, nisi eum, qui sit rite ordinatus, et certum habeat testimonium consensuique subscribat, et secundum eum sese gerat.—V. Quilibet Superattendens sive etiam Senior districtus, habeat librum consensus ad id paratum, in quo et ipse nomen suum propria manu adscribat, et omnes ministros ad Inspectionem suam pertinentes, subscriptos habeat. Quod quidem illico post hanc Synodum facere debent et imposterum semper in missione ministrorum idem observabunt." ET: "No Superintendent or Senior should be so audacious as to send someone into pastoral ministry and office, nor any patron accept someone in ministry without our assembly, if such a one is not ordained according to the rite, and does not have a certain credential and has not signed the Consensus, and does not conduct himself in accordance with it. V. Every Superintendent or Distict Senior is to provide a book in which he has written the names with his own hand and which all the ministers and inspectors of his district have signed. They should certainly do this after this Synod and observe this practice hereafter in the sending of ministers."

284. See n. 123.

285. See Th.C. 565 (index; see under "Abendmahlsgemeinde"), ET: See *Theology of Calvin* 412, (index, see under "Eucharistic Community").

286. See on the Zurich Disputation (1523) and the Bern Disputation (1528), O. Farner, *Huldrych Zwingli* (Zurich, 1954), 3:347–58, as well as (Zurich, 1960),

4:267–88. On the Bern Synod (1532), see H. R. Lavater, *"Die 'Verbesserung der Reformation' zu Bern,"* in Locher, ed., *Der Berner Synodus,* 2:35–117.

287. See BSRK XXX,46–XXXI,1; LI,45–LII,21.

288. Barth's italics.

289. Friedrich von Schiller, *Wilhelm Tell,* V.388, ET: *William Tell,* trans. W. F. Mainland (Chicago: University of Chicago Press, 1972), act I, scene 3, line 388, 21.

290. The reference is to the mandate of the Zurich Council of May 8, 1528, which is printed in E. Egli, *Actensammlung zur Geschichte der Zürcher Reformation in den Jahren 1519–1533* (Zurich, 1879), (Nr. 1383), 597. See n. 224.

291. See, e.g, the complicated struggles in relation to efforts to set aside the Heidelberg Catchism in the Canton Aargau, in R. Probst, *Der aargauische Protestantismus in der Restaurationszeit: Beiträge zum Verhältnis Staat-Kirche* (Zurich, 1968), 110–13.

292. BSRK 899,13–900,3, ET: Schaff 730.

293. BSRK 910,1–7, ET: Schaff 788 [Schaff renders the Italian rather freely as "testimony of a Christianity purely evangelical" and describes the church as "The Free Christian Church in Italy," while Müller's title is the "Chiesa Evangelica Italiana."—Trans.].

294. BSRK 903,32–35: "elle se rattache . . . aux églises evangéliques qui au 16ème siècle ont exprimé leur foi avec un accord si admirable dans leurs livres symboliques, et, en particulier, dans la Confessions de foi helvétique."

295. BSRK 907,30–33; 908,1–4.

296. BSRK 910, 21–25.

297. See Stuckert, *Kirchenkunde der Reformierten Schweiz* (see n. 274), 67–68.

298. This vow was taken on November 4, 1908, before the governmental executive who was responsible for the affairs of the established church in the city of Bern.

299. T. Hugues, *Die Conföderation der reformirten Kirchen in Niedersachsen* (Celle, 1873), 101. Parentheses are Barth's.

300. BSRK 870, 10–14. Parentheses and brackets are Barth's.

301. On the Heidelberg Catechism, see M. Lauterburg, "Katechismus, Heidelberger," in RE, 3d ed., 10:171,37–39; on the Second Helvetic Confession, see E. Böhl, *Confessio helvetica posterior* (Vienna, 1986), XV–XVI; on the Westminster Confession, see B. B. Warfield, "Westminster Synode," in RE, 3d ed., 21:183[20–26].

302. See n. 149.

303. This is an allusion to J. W. von Goethe, *Faust* I,V,682–83 (Nacht), ET: von Goethe, J. W., *Faust I and II,* ed. and trans. Stuart Atkins (Boston: Suhrkamp/Insel, 1984), 213: "If you would own the things your forebears left you, you first must earn and merit their possession."

2. THE PRINCIPLE OF SCRIPTURE AND ITS GROUNDS

1. Friedrich von Schiller, "Das Lied von der Glocke," V,414–17, ET: "Song of the Bell," in Friedrich Schiller, *An Anthology for Our Time,* ed. Frederick Ungar, trans. H. W. Longfellow (New York: Frederick Ungar, 1959), 248.

2. This is a saying derived from Heraclitus, passed on in this form in Simplicius, *Commentarius in Aristotelis Physicorum libros IV posteriores,* ed. H. Diels (Berlin, 1875), 1313.

3. See lecture 1, p. 17; 237, n. 149.

4. A. Ritschl, *Über die beiden Principien des Protestantismus* (1876), in *Gesammelte Aufsätze*, vol. 1, (Freiburg i.B./Leipzig, 1893), 234–47; see also Chr. Dogm. 553, n. 6.

5. Pencil notation on the manuscript margin: "Different from Art 5 of the Augustana!" The formulation there is as follows (BSLK 58:2–7, ET: K/W 40[V., German text], 41[V., Latin text): "To obtain such faith God instituted the office of preaching, giving the Gospel and the sacraments. Through these, as through means, he gives the Holy Spirit, who produces faith, where and when he wills, in those who hear the Gospel" [ET of German text]. "So that we may obtain this faith, the ministry of teaching the gospel and administering the sacraments was instituted. For through the Word and the sacraments as through instruments the Holy Spirit is given, who effects faith where and when it pleases God in those who hear the gospel, that is to say, in those who hear that God, not on account of our own merits but on account of Christ, justifies those who believe that they are received into grace on account of Christ. Galatians 3[:14b]: 'so that we might receive the promise of the Spirit through faith'" [ET of Latin text].

6. As in the introduction to the Epitome of the Formula of Concord, BSLK 768,29–30, ET: K/W 487[4].

7. Pencil notation on the manuscript margin: "For the catholic church is the witness of the heavenly doctrine" ["Ecclesia catholica tantum es testis doctrinae coelestis (*Erlauth*. M [=BSRK] 353,2)"].

7a. The German words for "witness as person" (Zeuge), "witness as content" (Zeugnis), and "to witness" (bezeugen) have the same root syllable (as do their corresponding terms in New Testament Greek), which Barth uses effectively for emphasis.

8. See lecture 1, p. 29.

9. This formula was coined, with reference to the doctrine of justification, by V. E. Löscher; see W. Köhler, *Dogmengeschichte* (Zurich, 1951), 2:329.

10. See A. Hausrath, *David Friedrich Strauß und die Theologie seiner Zeit*, Part 1 (Heidelberg, 1876), 329–423.

11. The text here is dealing with the ordination and, in Graubunden, the synodal oaths; see the texts in Stuckert, *Kirchenkunde der reformierten Schweiz* (see lecture 1, n. 274), 68.

12. The allusion is to Friedrich Schleiermacher, *Über die Religion: Reden an die Gebildeten unter ihren Verächtern* (Berlin, 1799; new ed. by R. Otto [Göttingen, 1967], 6th ed., 52, ET: *On Religion: Addresses to Its Cultured Critics*, trans. John Oman (Louisville, Ky.: John Knox Press, 1994), 40: "Offer with me reverently a tribute to the manes of the holy, rejected Spinoza!"

13. This sentence is entered on the manuscript margin in pencil. [The German edition does not give the reference, which is BSRK 902,8, ET: Schaff 733, under "Principles . . . "—Trans.]

14. BSRK 1,14–2,2, ET: Cochrane 33. Barth's italics.

15. BSRK 6,30–34, ET: Cochrane 44; Barth's italics.

16. At line 19: " . . . then of both the New and the Old Testaments . . . "; Barth's italics.

17. See H. Bullinger, *Reformationsgeschichte*, ed. J. J. Hottingen and H. H. Vögeli (Frauenfeld, 1838; reprint, Zurich, 1984), 1:432; W. Hadorn, *Kirchengeschichte der reformierten Schweiz* (Zurich, 1907), 77.

18. DS 1501: "traditiones, continua successione in ecclesia catholica conservatas," ET: Denzinger 244.

18a. BSRK 29,29–30, ET: Pipkin 74–75.

19. Barth provides a thorough review of the pre-Reformation period in Th.C. 86–92, ET: *Theology of Calvin* 64–68.

20. Pencil notation on the margin of the manuscript: "An intermediate stage recognizable in the Conf. of the *Bohemian Brethren* with their 'Catechism,' which first appeared in the version of 1609 as an 'Excerpt from the Document' (Aug. 277, M 455,8) and in the *Waldensian Conf.* of 1655, Art. 33 (M 504,3 [ET: Schaff 768[XXXIII]])." Augusti published the Bohemian Confession (Confessio Bohemica) of 1535 on 275–326, with its Article 2 entitled "De Catechismo" on 277–79. The article begins, "Hinc *Catechismum* docent, hoc est, catholicam et orthodoxam patrum doctrinam: quae *Decalogus* est mandatorum Dei, et *fides Apostolica*, in duodecim articulos digesta, et tradita in *Symbolo* per *Nicenam Synodum*, atque adeo alias confirmata et exposita. Denique *Precatio dominica*. Haec autem omnium sanctissima, bonam beneplacentemque Dei voluntatem esse, constanter affirmant," ET: "They teach this *Catechism*, that is, the catholic and orthodox doctrine of the fathers: which is the *Decalogue* of God's commandments, and the *Apostolic faith*, sub-divided into twelve articles, and passed in the *symbol* of the *Nicene Synod*, and confirmed and expounded in others as well. In addition, the *Lord's Prayer*. They confirm that all this is in agreement with the entire, most holy, good, and beneficent will of God." By contrast, the beginning of the Confession of the Bohemian Brethren of 1609, in Article 2 ("De catechesi"), contains the wording to which Barth refers: "*Catechesis quid, et quae ejus partes? Catechesin deinde Ministri Ecclesiarum nostrarum docent, illam nimirum Christianam, simplicem, antiquuam, Ecclesiae Catholicae perpetuam doctrinam, summatim ex verbo Dei collectam. Quam iure optimo, nucleum, et clavem sacrae Scripturae ipsi appelare solent*," ET: "*What is the Catechism, and what are its parts?* In this catechism the ministers of our churches learn the simple, ancient Christian doctrine, which has been perpetuated in the Catholic Church, and which is drawn together from the Word of God. They customarily call this teaching, in accordance with the highest command, the core and key of the Holy Scripture."

21. On Zwingli; see Locher, *Die Zwinglische Reformation* (see lecture 1, n. 97), 68–72. In the case of Calvin, it is more a matter of a general humanist orientation (see Th.C. 181, 187, 259, 263, 309, 537, ET: *Theology of Calvin* 137, 142, 192–93, 195–96, 228, 397). In this he was influenced more by Lefèvre d'Etaples than by Erasmus (see Th.C. 178–79, and passim, ET: *Theology of Calvin* 135–36, and passim).

22. On this "older view" of the Reformed shift, which is controversial today; see U. Gäbler, *Huldrych Zwingli: Eine Einführung in sein Leben und sein Werk* (Munich, 1983), 46–47, ET: Ulrich Gäbler, *Huldrych Zwingli: His Life and Work*, trans. R. C. L. Gritsch (Philadelphia: Fortress Press, 1986), 45–49[3].

23. See Th.C. 188–89, 320, ET: *Theology of Calvin* 142–44, 235–36.

24. See Th.C. 90, 105, 110, ET: *Theology of Calvin* 67, 78, 82.

25. See CR 59 (=CO 31), 21: "Ac primo quidem, quum superstitionibus papatus magis pertinaciter addictus essem, quam ut facile esset e tam profundo luto me extrahi, amimum meum, qui pro aetate nimis obduruerat, subita conversione ad docilitatem subegit," ET: J. Calvin, *Commentary on the Book of Psalms*, trans. J. Anderson (Grand Rapids: Wm. B. Eerdmans, 1949), 1:xl: "And first, since I was too obstinately devoted to the superstitions of Popery to be easily extricated from so profound an abyss of mire, God by a sudden conversion subdued and brought my mind to a teachable frame (which was more hardened in such matters than might have been expected from one at my early period of life)."

26. See Th.C. 179–85, ET: *Theology of Calvin* 136–40.

27. See O. Farner, *Huldrych Zwingli*, vol. 3, *Seine Verkündigung und ihre ersten Früchte 1520–1525* (Zurich, 1954), 29–45.

28. See Th.C. 349, ET: *Theology of Calvin* 258.

29. On Haller; see below, p. 258, n. 36.

30. Guillaume Farel (1489–1565), reformer of western Switzerland, in Geneva from 1532, later in Neuchâtel; Antoine Froment (1508–1581), in Geneva from 1532 as teacher, preacher, later as notary; Pierre Viret (1511–1571), Farel's coworker from 1539 on, primary influence in Lausanne. On the influence of Farel and Froment in Geneva before Calvin's arrival, see E. Stähelin, *Johannes Calvin: Leben und ausgewählte Schriften*, Leben und ausgewählte Schriften der Väter und Begründer der reformierten Kirche, Part 4, Section 1 (Elberfeld, 1863), 115–20.

31. Minutes of the Geneva Council from May and June 1536, CR 49 (=CO 21), 201, 203; see Th.C. 347, 409, 483, ET: *Theology of Calvin* 257, 301–2, 355.

32. See W. Shakespeare, *Hamlet*, act 1, scene 5, in W. Shakespeare, *Complete Plays and Poems*, ed. W. A. Neilson and C. J. Hill (Cambridge: Houghton Mifflin, 1942), 1056, line 76.

32a. BSRK 30,9–11, ET: Leith 129.

33. BSRK 55,26–30, ET: Cochrane 56; Barth's italics. [The italicized words are stronger in German: "to take refuge," "to flee."—Trans.]

33a. BSRK 145,33–35: " . . . est enim spiritualis doctrina, quaedam veluti ianua, qua ingredimur in coeleste eius regnum," ET: *Tracts and Treatises II*, 82.

33b. BSRK 170,35–36, ET: Cochrane 224.

34. " . . . la seule règle de bien croire et de bien vivre . . . " ET: "the sole rule of right believing and right living."

35. See, e.g, the *Confession of the Calvinist Methodists* of 1823, BSRK 872,19; the *Confession of the Cumberland Presbyterian Church* of 1883, BSRK 912,8, ET: *Encyclopedia of American Religions: Religious Creeds*, 1st ed. (Detroit: Gale Research Co., 1988), 231; the *Confession of the American Congregationalists of 1883*, BSRK 928,30–32, also in Schaff, 914[V] [These citations in BSRK are all in English.—Trans.].

36. " . . . la reigle de nostre foy et religion," ET: Cochrane 120: "the rule of faith and religion."

37. E.g, BSRK 222,26–27 [Gallican Confession, 1559]: ". . . reigle trescertaine de nostre foy . . . ," ET: Schaff 261[IV]: "the sure rule of our faith"; BSRK 526,14 [Irish Articles]: "rule of faith," also in Schaff 526[1]; BSRK 222,34 [Gallican Confession, 1559]: " . . . reigle de toute vérité . . . ," ET: Schaff 362[V]: "rule of all truth"; BSRK 500,3[incorrect, should be 35—Trans.] [Waldensian Confession]: " . . . Saint Ecriture . . . c'est-à-dire pour regle de notre Foy . . . ," ET: Schaff 758[III]: "Holy Scripture . . . that is to say, for the constant rule of our faith"; BSRK 612,35–36 [Westminster Larger Catechism, 1647]: " . . . Scripturae sacrae . . . sunt verbum Dei, unica illa fidei ac obedientiae regula . . . ," ET: BOC 7.113, 195: "The Holy Scriptures of the Old and New Testaments are the Word of God, the only rule of faith and obedience"; BSRK 872,114–19 [Confession of the Calvinist Methodists, 1823]: "All the Scriptures . . . are the only infallible rule of faith and obedience."

38. E.g., BSRK 817,10; 836,24: 'Guideline' [Richtschnur]; BSRK 657,26; 817,11: 'foundation' or 'basis' [fundamentum]; BSRK 739,28: Ground.

39. BSRK 146,15 [Genevan Catechism of 1545]: 'method' [ratio], ET: *Tracts and Treatises II*, 83; BSRK 904,1 [Constitution of the Free Church of the Vaux, 1847]; BSRK 910,26 [Declaration of the French General Synod of 1872]: 'authority' [autorité];

BSRK 928,31 [Confession of the American Congregationalists, 1884]: 'standard,' also in Schaff 914[V]; BSRK 454,30 [Bohemian Confession, 1609]: 'norm' [norma].

40. BSLK 834,16–22, ET: K/W 527[3]: "First, we confess our adherence to the prophetic and apostolic writings of the Old and New Testaments, as to the pure, clear fountain of Israel, which alone is the one true guiding principle according to which all teachers and teaching are to be judged and evaluated."

41. =BSLK 767,15, ET: K/W 486[1].

42. BSLK 833,1–3: "De compendiaria doctrinae forma, fundamento, norma atque regula," ET: K/W 526: "Concerning the Binding Summary, Basis, Rule, and Guiding Principle"; BSLK 834,17–19: " . . . scripta Veteris et Novi Testamenti ut limpidissimos purissimosque Israelis fontes recipimus . . . ," ET: K/W 527–28[3]: " . . . writings of the Old and New Testaments as to the pure, clear fountain of Israel"; BSLK 838,45–839,2: "ut enim verbum Dei tanquam immotam veritatem pro fundamento ponimus . . . ," ET: K/W 529[13], " . . . we base our teaching on God's Word as the eternal truth."

43. In the places cited the term "rule" ["regula"] is expressly reserved for the Scriptures (see also BSLK 837,12–13, ET: K/W 528–29[9]), but the confession is bound to the Scripture in such a way that one can say of it that it is a "single, universally accepted, certain, and common form of doctrine, 'to which all our Evangelical Churches subscribe and from which, and according to which, because it is drawn from the Word of God, all other writings are to be approved and accepted, judged and regulated' " ["secundum quam, cum e verbo Dei sit desumpta, omnio alia scripta iudicare et accommodare oportet, quatenus probanda sint et recipienda"] (BSLK 838,12–17, ET: K/W 529[10]).

44. See Th.C. 205–6, 369, ET: *Theology of Calvin* 155, 273.

45. See above, n. 18.

46. Inst. I,xiii,1:120–59.

47. See A. Schweizer, *Die Glaubenslehre der evangelisch-reformirten Kirche dargestellt und aus den Quellen belegt* (Zurich, 1844), 1:155–56, 1:241–42.

48. See Inst. I,ii,1,1:30–41.

49. At that same place (40) it states that God is not to be recognized as Father and Giver of salvation "until Christ the Mediator comes forward to reconcile him to us" ["donec ad eum nobis pacificandum medius occurrat Christus"]. In Inst. I,vi,1,1:70, the point is made more precisely that even the knowing of God the Creator comes "from the word" ["ex verbo"].

50. See Th.C. 214–30, ET: *Theology of Calvin* 162–72.

50a. CO, XXII, (–CR vol. 50) 35[–36], ET: *Instruction in Faith* 23, in which the next cited phrases appear—Trans.

50b. " . . . et renverse entièrement toute la sapience celeste laquelle autrement [clairment] y reluist," ET: *Instruction in Faith* 24.

50c. BSRK 221,38–39: "secondement et clairment par sa parole," ET: Schaff 360[II].

50d. BSRK 233,18: "longe manifestius et plenus," ET: Schaff 384[II].

51. BSRK 500,26.31–34: "Nous Croyons . . . II. Que ce Dieu s'est, manifesté aux hommes par ses oeuvres, tant de la Creation, que de la Providence, et par sa Parole, revelée au commencement par Oracles en diverses sortes, puis redigée par écrit és Livres qu'on appelle l'Escriture Sainte," ET: Schaff 758[II]: "We believe, . . . that this God has manifested himself to men by his works of Creation and Providence, as also by his Word revealed unto us, first by oracles in divers manners, and afterwards by those written books which are called the Holy Scripture."

52. The passage on the Erlauthal Confession is written on the manuscript margin in pencil. BSRK 267,14–17: "Cognitio Dei fit ex creaturis communiter, sed haec cognitio non salvat. Specialiter et interne ex verbo patefacto, ex sacramentis in Filio Christo per Spiritus S[ancti] operationem, et revelationem in salutem per fidem cognoscitur."

53. BSRK 542,14–543,5; see also BOC 6.001.

54. BSRK 612,31–33 [Westminster Larger Catechism]: "Ipsissimum in homine naturae lumen, operaque Dei esse Deum luculenter manifestant; solum autem ipsius verbum Spiritusque eum hominibus revelant sufficienter ac efficaciter ad salutem," ET: BOC 7.112: "The very light of nature in man, and the works of God, declare plainly that there is a God; but his Word and Spirit only do sufficiently and effectually reveal him unto men for their salvation."

55. BSRK 943,30–34; see also "Brief Statement of the Reformed Faith," 1902, Art. II (Revision of the Westminster Confession), in Schaff 922.

56. BSRK 928,21–26 [Confession of the American Congregationalists, 1883]; see also Schaff 914[IV].

57. Barth's italics.

57a. "Gschrift" is German Swiss dialect for "Schrift" = "Scriptures," literally "that which is written."—Trans.

58. According to Zwingli (CR 88 [=Z 1], 498,2–6) *three* Bibles (Latin, Greek, Hebrew) were on the table at the first Zurich Disputation of January 29, 1523. See on this Locher, *Die Zwinglische Reformation* (see lecture 1, n. 97), 111: "The issue here was not an academic disputation but rather a civil legal process." Its purpose was to overcome the uncertainty of public proclamation resulting from the legal protest directed against Zwingli's preaching. It was notable that, on the one hand, Scriptures rather than the 'body of law' [Corpus Iuris] and, on the other hand, the council rather than the bishop were the decision makers. "In a formal and legal sense the council, functioning as referee, established the common foundation valid for itself and for both parties. Theologically, the decision was already made by virtue of the 'principle of Scripture,' for from the evangelical perspective the dispute was actually about the question of God's Word or human tradition. Legally, the council proceeded along the lines of the late medieval 'reforming law' [ius reformandi] of the magistrate."

59. BSRK 155,10–19.

60. BSRK 222,5–24, ET: Schaff 360–61[III].

61. BSRK 233,31–234,13, ET: Schaff 385–86[IV].

62. BSRK 501,2–12, ET: Schaff 759[III].

63. BSRK 526,28–29, ET: Schaff 526[2].

64. BSRK 507,9–30, ET: Schaff 490–91[VI].

65. BSRK 543,15–544,6; see also Schaff 601–2[II], and BOC 6.002.

66. *Confession of the Calvinist Methodists*, 1823, BSRK 872,1–14; *Confession of the Cumberland Presbyterian Church*, 1883, BSRK 912,9–32, ET: *Encyclopedia of American Religions: Religious Creeds* (Detroit: Gale Research Co., 1988), 231.

67. BSRK 171,42–45, ET: Schaff 238[9]; see also Leith, 134.

68. BSRK 234,24–34, ET: Schaff 234[VI].

69. BSRK 544,11–18; see also Schaff 602[III], and BOC 6.003.

70. BSRK 507,19–27; see also Schaff 491[VI].

71. Augusti 414.

72. *Vorrede auf die Episteln S. Jakobi und Judä* (1522/1546), WA.DB 7,384–87, ET: "Preface to the Epistles of St. James and St. Jude," LW 35:395–99; *Vorrede auf die*

Offenbarung S. Johannis (1522), WA.DB 7,404, ET: "Preface to the Revelation of St. John," LW 35:398–99.

73. Barth's italics.

73a. BSRK 2,28–30, ET: Cochrane 36[V].

73b. BSRK 30,12–15, ET: Cochrane 49[II].

74. BSRK 111,14–18, ET: Cochrane 120[1]. In the manuscript there is a passage here struck out by Barth: "It was an aberration when the *Tetrapolitana* of 1530 limited this exclusive stance to those human stipulations and orders which are expressly *condemned* by Scripture, and then continued, 'For such as agree with the Scripture, and were instituted for good morals and profit of men, even though not expressed in Scripture in words, nevertheless, since they flow from the command of love, which orders all things most becomingly, are justly regarded *divine* rather than human' (M 69,4[–14] [BSRK 69,4–14, ET: Cochrane 71–72]). Such timidity on this point was however an exception among the Reformed."

75. Latin in BSRK, Barth's translation into German.

76. See above, p. 18–19; see also Schaff 362.

76a. Schaff 388.

76b. See Schaff 362.

77. Augusti 415: "Multo minus spiritum privatum ipsorum fidelium scripturae judicem aut fidei regulam esse statuimus . . . ," ET: "We stipulate that in relation to the much less significant private spirit of those believers, the Scripture is the judge and faith is the rule."

78. Augusti 414: "Nullum hodie verbum Dei exstat, aut certo ostendi potest, de dogmatibus fidei, aut praeceptis vitae ad salutem necesariis, quod non sit scriptum, aut in scriptures fundatum, sed *sola traditione* non scripta ecclesiae commissum," ET: "There is today no Word of God, nor can one be shown with certainty, about the dogmas of faith, or a doctrine of life which is necessary for salvation, that was not written or founded in Scripture, but rather was passed on solely through *tradition* as an *unwritten* secret of the church."

79. BSRK 93,15–17: "Sacris enim literis et ecclesiae secundum ipsas ex spiritu iudicanti, nostra submittere, nobis non minus iucundum et gratum est, quam aequum et iustum," ET: Hinke 2:58 (Account of the Faith, 1530): "For it is no less agreeable and delightful than fair and just for us to submit our judgment to the Holy Scripture, and the church, deciding in harmony with these by virtue of the Spirit."

80. BSRK 23,11–13, ET: Pipkin 67. Barth's italics.

81. BSRK 54, 10–33; Barth's italics.

82. Locher, ed. *Der Berner Synodus von 1532* (see pp. 24; 240, n. 218), 1:146–47.

83. Ibid, 1:147–48.

84. BSRK 526,28–33, also in Schaff 527[4].

85. BSRK 454,37–39.

86. BSRK 409,46–50; 410,31–36.

87. Augusti 414.

88. BSRK 546,17–30, also in Schaff 604–5, and BOC 6.008.

88a. BSRK 24,41–45, ET: Pipkin 69.

88b. BSRK 174,26–42, ET: BOC 5.020–5.022.

88c. BSRK 710,22–27, ET: BOC 4.098.

88d. BSRK 636,7–12, ET: BOC 7.267 (Q. 157), 222.

89. "Les extremes se touchent" is the title of chapter 348 in L. S. Mercier, *Tableau de Paris*, vol. 4 (Amsterdam, 1782).

89a. BSRK 91,1–2: "Credo prophetiae sive praedicationis munus *sacrocsanctum* esse, ut quod *ante omne officium* sit summe necessariam," ET: Hinke 2:56: "I believe that the work of prophesying or preaching is *most sacred*, so that it is a work most necessary, *above all others*."

90. BSLK 61, ET: K/W 42[German text], 43[Latin text].

91. Pencil notation on the margin of the manuscript: "See here *Scot. Art.* XVII, Scripture principle as the foundation of the doctrine of the visible church, subordination of the two other 'notes' [notae]: sacrament and discipline (M 256,45–46[–257,26]), ET: BOC 3.18.

91a. BOC 5.220.

92. BSRK 171,10: "Praedicatio verbi [Dei] est verbum Dei," ET: BOC 5.004.

92a. BOC 5.004, translates the Latin "annunciatur" with "preaching."—Trans.

92b. BSRK 171,10–18: "verum tamen et bonum manet nihilominus verbum Dei," ET: BOC 5.004.

92c. BSRK 146,5–26, ET: *Tracts and Treatises III*, 83.

93. See above, pp. 51–2, n. 81—Pencil notation on the manuscript margin: "In England through an official Postille (39 Articles, Art. 34, M 518,9[–19]), ET: Schaff 509–11 [in the current English editions, this is Article XXXV, "Of the homilies" —Trans.].

94. Pencil notation on the manuscript margin: "*Erlauth.* (M 345,42[–346,4])": "Scripta Prophetarum et Apostolorum, vel Evangelistarum non carptim ac concisim proponimus, ac mutilata documenta ex eis non sumimus, nec more papistico ut farta concidimus, aut mutilamus, discerpimus, traditionibus immescendo. Ut sic testimonia mutilata excisa a toto corpore non intelligantur, et in alienum sensum detorqueantur, ut multae rixae et logomachiae oriri solent ex textu non intellecto et concepto, aut detruncato." ET: "We assert that the Scriptures of the prophets and apostles, as well as of the Evangelists, are not to be torn and cut, and we do not use mutilated portions from them, and we do not divide them up in the fashion of papists as fillers, nor do we mutilate or tear them apart by connecting them to traditions. In this way the mutilated testimonies, wrenched out of the entire body, are not understood and are distorted into an alien meaning, so that often much disputation and argument arises from the text, which is not understood and comprehended, but destroyed."

95. Ebrard 29: "One should no longer preach a Gospel and an Epistle, but instead another text from the Bible, for this is a papist innovation."

96. See pp. 41–2 above.

97. BSRK 101,16–18, ET: First Helvetic Confession (1536), Cochrane 100[2]; Schaff 211–12[II] has the Latin and German versions—Trans.

98. BSRK 172,8–10, ET: BOC 5.010.

99. BSRK 257,39–258,7, ET: Schaff 463–64; see also BOC 3.18.

100. BSRK 546,34–42, ET: Schaff 605; see also BOC 6.010.

101. *First Helvetic Confession*, BSRK 101,16–18, ET: Cochrane 100[2]; *Second Helvetic Confession*, BSRK 172,12–13, ET: Schaff 833; see also BOC 5.010ff.

102. BSRK 258,5–7: "nos enim nullam interpretationem recipere aut admittere audemus, quae pugnet aut cum aliquo ex praecipuis fidei nostrae capitibus, aut cum perspicua scriptura, aut cum charitatis regula," ET: Schaff 464, BOC 3.18: "We dare not receive or admit any interpretation which is contrary to any principal point of our faith, or to any other plain text of Scripture, or to the rule of love."

103. E.g., *Westminster Confession*, BSRK 546,4–16, Schaff 604–5 (I.VIII); see also BOC 6.008; *Second Helvetic Confession*, BSRK 172,10, ET: Schaff 833(II); see also BOC 5.010.

104. See above, p. 29, n. 253.

105. BSRK 900,10, ET: Schaff 731[I].

106. Pencil notation on manuscript margin: "See Rob. Bach, Ref.K.Zeitg., 1922, Nr. 39–41": R. Bach, *Unsere Bibelnot und Calvin's Schlüssel zur Schrift: das innere Geisteszeugnis*, in Reformierte Kirchenzeitung, Year 72 (1922), 225–27, 229–32, 233–37.

107. Augusti 94: "Scriptura canonica, verbum Dei Spiritu S[ancto] tradita et per prophetas apostolosque mundo proposita, omnium perfectissima et antiquissima Philosphia, pietatem omnem, omnem vitae rationem, sola perfecte continet," Latin and German versions in Schaff 211, ET: Cochrane 100[1]: "The holy, divine, Biblical Scripture, which is the Word of God inspired by the holy Spirit and delivered to the world by the prophets and apostles, is the most ancient, most perfect and loftiest teaching and alone deals with everything that serves the true knowledge, love, and honor of God, as well as true piety and the making of a godly, honest, and blessed life." [Cochrane's ET is based on the German text, which is longer than the Latin cited by the German editors.—Trans.]

108. BSRK 154,44–48: "The holy Biblical Scripture . . . is the very oldest, most perfect, and highest teaching."

109. On the concept of "original history" that Barth took over from Fr. Overbeck; see Chr. Dogm, 309–21, esp. 309, n. 1 and 2.

109a. BSRK 188,29–31: "Deus enim ab aeterno praedestinavit," ET: Schaff 858; see also BOC 5.092.

110. BSRK 527,1–2, 5–7; see also Schaff 527[5].

111. BSRK 506,32–34; see also Schaff 489.

112. BSRK 545,11–33; 545,37–546,2; see also Schaff 603–4, and BOC 6.006–6.007.

113. BSRK 836,25.

114. BSRK 257,43–258,5; see also Schaff 463–64, and BOC 3.18.

115. BSRK 409,26–28.

116. Augusti 413–14.

117. BSRK 872,14–19.

118. BSRK 902,8–18; see also Schaff 731.

119. BSRK 919,1–5, ET: *Encyclopedia of American Religions: Religious Creeds*, 1st ed. (Detroit: Gale Research Co., 1988), 231.

119a. Schaff 545, and BOC 6.006.

119b. Schaff 506.

119c. Schaff 545, and BOC 6.007.

119d. BSRK 81,47: "Nihil hominem certum de gratia Dei facere potest quam Deus ipse," ET: Hinke 2:39.

120. BSRK 222,33–34: " . . . duquel elle seule prend son autorité et non des hommes," ET: Schaff 362.

120a. BSRK 170,28–29: "autoritatem sufficientem ex semetipsis non ex hominibus habere," ET: Schaff 831, and BOC 5.001.

120b. BSRK 234,20: "comprobationem [. . .] in se ipsis habent," ET: Schaff 387.

120c. BSRK 544,20–27: "Autoritas scripturae sacrae . . . pendet . . . a solo ejus autore Deo, qui est ipsa veritas: eoque est a nobis recipienda, quoniam est verbum Dei," ET: Schaff 602, and BOC 6.004.

121. Pencil notation on manuscript margin: "*Leo Jud* 1541: This is placed by the Holy Spirit in the hearts of those who wrote it and have left it for their posterity (Lang 91)."

122. Pencil notation on manuscript margin: "*Leo Jud*: Who explains the Scripture? The Holy Spirit, for it opens the spirit and the understanding (Lang 91)."

123. *Geneva Catechism*, BSRK 145,39: "certa veritas e coelo profecta," ET: *Tracts and Treatises II*, 82.

123a. BSRK 234,21–22: ET: Schaff 387(V).

123b. BSRK 501,13–17, ET: Schaff 759–60(IV).

123c. BSRK 544,30–545,8, ET: Schaff 602 (V), also BOC 6.005.

123d. BSRK 612,2–8, ET: BOC 7.114.

124. See Th.C. 222–23, ET: *Theology of Calvin* 167–68.

125. What follows is based on Inst. I,vii,1,1:74–75.

125a. Inst. I,vii,1,1:74: "E coelo fluxisse, acsi vivae ipsae Dei voces illic exaudirentur."

126. What follows is based on Inst. I,vii,2,1:76. Based on the comparison made there, Calvin arrives at this observation: "Indeed, Scripture exhibits fully as clear evidence of its own truth as white and black things do of their color, or sweet and bitter things do of their taste" ["Non enim obscuriorem veritatis suae sensum ultro Scriptura prae se fert, quam coloris sui res albae ac nigrae: saporis, suaves et amarae"].

127. What follows is based on Inst. I,vii,4,1:78: "Summa scripturae probatio passim a Dei loquentis persona sumitur."

127a. Inst. I,vii,4,1:78: "sed sacrum Dei nomen proferunt."

127b. BSRK 170,29–30: "Deus loquutus est . . . et adhuc loquitur," ET: BOC 5.001.

127c. Schaff 385[II].

127d. BSRK 546,4–14: "Instrumentum Vetus Hebraea lingua," "Novum Graeca," "A Deo inspirato," ET: Schaff 604[VIII], also BOC 6.008.

127e. BSRK 862,33–863,17, ET: Leith 309–11[I–III].

128. BSRK LXV,6–7. Louis Capelle II (1585–1658), scion of a Huguenot family of scholars and Hebrew scholar at the academy of Saumur, blazed new trails in the historical-critical study of the Old Testament text with his publications: *Arcanum punctationis revelatum sive de punctorum vocalium et accentuum apud Hebraeos vera et germana antiquitate* (Lyon, 1624); *Critica sacra sive de variis, quae in Sacris V.T. libris occurunt, lectionibus libri sex; in quibus ex variarum lectionum observatione quamplurima s. scripturae loca explicantur, illustrantur, atque adeo emendantur non pauca . . .* (Paris, 1650).

129. See Augusti 596–97; Beck, *Die Symbolischen Bücher* (see lecture 1, n. 220), 2:324–25; Seeberg 707–8; F. Trechsel, "Helvetische Konsensformel," in RE, 3d ed., 7:647, lines 28–35, on resistance to it as early as the seventeenth century; see also 7:651,59–654,16.

130. See BSRK LXV,14–16.

131. See Barth's letter of May 18, 1923, Bw.Th.II, 162, ET: in *Revolutionary Theology in the Making*, 141: In the second section of this lecture, "I have managed to extract an edifying and gratifying side even from the notorious Helvetian consensus formula of 1675 with its prohibition of textual criticism and its literal inspiration that extended to the very vowel points in Hebrew."

132. Inst. I,vii,4,1:78–80.

133. Inst. I,viii,1:81–92.

134. Inst. I,viii,1,1:81 [Barth paraphrases this Latin phrase from the title of the section: "Probationes, quatenus fert humana ratio, satis firmas suppetere ad stabiliendam scripturae fidem," ET: "So far as human reason goes, sufficiently firm proofs are at hand to establish the credibility of Scripture."—Trans.]

134a. Inst. I,vii,4,1:79: "*Idem ergo spiritus qui per os prophetarum loquutus est, in corda nostra penetret necesse est, ut persuadeat fideliter protulisse quod divinitus erat mandatum.*"

135. Inst. I,vii,5,1:80.

136. Inst. I,vii,5,1:80.

136a. BSRK 222,26–29: " . . . intérieure persuasion du St. Esprit, qui nous les fait discerner d'avec les autres livres ecclésiastiques," Schaff 361.

137. Inst. I,vii,5,1:81: "Si hunc intelligentiae thesaurum filiis suis reconditum esse Deus voluit, nihil mirum vel absurdum si in hominum vulgo cernitur tanta inscitia et stupiditas. . . . Quoties ergo nos conturbat credentium paucitas, ex opposito veniat in mentem, non alios comprehendere mysteria nisi quibus datum est," ET: "If God has willed this treasure of understanding to be hidden from his children, it is no wonder or absurdity that the multitude of men are so ignorant and stupid! . . . whenever, then, the fewness of believers disturbs us, let the converse come to mind that only those to whom it is given can comprehend the mysteries of God."

138. See Inst. III,xxi,7,2:930–32; III,xxiii,4,2:951–52.

138a. Schaff 317–18, 324–25, and BOC 4.031, 4.054.

139. G. E. Lessing, *Über den Beweis des Geistes und der Kraft*, Lessings Werke, Part 23, Theologische Schriften 6,1, ed. J. Petersen and W. von Olshausen (reprint, Berlin and elsewhere, 1925), (Hildesheim/New York, 1970), 47, 49; ET: G. E. Lessing, "On the Proof of the Spirit and of Power," in *Lessing's Theological Writings*, trans. H. Chadwick (Stanford: Stanford University Press, 1957), 55: "That, then, is the ugly, broad ditch which I cannot get across."

140. See Unterricht II, 267, n. 65; V.u.kl.A. 1922–1925, 518, n. 58.

141. See Chr. Dogma, 181, n. 41.

142. Inst. I,vii,1,1:74: " . . . ac si vivae voces Dei illic exaudirentur."

3. REFORMED DOCTRINE AS A WHOLE

1. See on this Th.C. 66–92, ET: *Theology of Calvin* 50–68.

2. See above, pp. 8–10.

3. See on this also Barth's lecture, "Reformierte Lehre, ihr Wesen und ihre Aufgabe," 1923, in V.u.kl.A, 1922–1925, 202–47, esp. 212–13.

4. See Seeberg 633–38.

5. BSRK 947 [this is the index, listing a typology of doctrines—Trans.].

6. Barth inadvertently used the number 3 twice and thus came up with a list of six rather than seven types.

1. The Debate with the Old Church

7. Barth uses the term "old church" as the designation for the RomanCatholic Church.

8. BSRK 1–6 (Zwingli's Theses), ET: Cochrane 33–44; 30–31 (Bernese theses), ET: Cochrane 45–40; 930–35 (East Friesian preachers); 55–78 (Tetrapolitan), ET: Cochrane 51–88; 95–100 (Basel), ET: Cochrane 89–96; 110 (Lausanne), ET: Cochrane 112–16; 111–16 (Geneva), ET: Cochrane 117–26.

9. BSRK XXII,3–4

10. See BSRK XXI–XXII, where further bibliography for Georg Aportanus, Johann Rhode, and Heinrich Rese is given.

11. See Locher, *Die Zwinglische Reformation* (see p. 234, n. 97), 292–93 and 633, as well as above, pp. 22f.

12. See BSRK 3,13–16; 6,1–9; 6,10–16, ET: Cochrane 38[XVII], 42–43 ["Concerning Purgatory"], 43 ["Concerning the Priesthood and Its Consecration"].

13. BSLK 66,1–8, ET: K/W 44 (German text) and 45 (Latin text); 97,34–98,16, ET: K/W 72 (German text) and 73 (Latin text).

14. BSLK 53–54, 56, ET: K/W 36–39, 38–41.

15. =BSLK 415,21–416,4, ET: K/W 301[5]. Barth uses here and hereafter the letter "M" as an abbreviation for SBLK.

16. See Luther's testimony in the preface to volume 1 of the Opera Latina of the Wittenberg Edition (1545), WA 54,186,3–13, ET: from Luther's "Autobiographical Fragment, March, 1545," in *Martin Luther*, ed. E. G. Rupp and B. Drewery (New York: St. Martin's Press, 1970), 6.

17. See M. Luther, *Von der heiligen Taufe Predigten* (1534), WA 37,661,20–27; see also WA 36,284,31–33, ET: *Sermons of Martin Luther*, ed. J. L. Lenker (Grand Rapids: Baker Book House, 1988), 4:79[27]: "For we are now within a sphere and on ground, where there is no question as to what I shall do or leave undone, I already know well enough, that I have not done, nor do I do, what the law requires; but here is the question, how may I acquire a gracious God and the forgiveness of sins?" WA 52,236,18–22.

18. BSLK 172,49–51: "Adversarii nusquam possunt dicere, quomodo detur spiritus sanctus," ET: K/W 131[63].

19. BSLK 172,46–47: "Haec consolatio est nova et spiritualis vita" [the original begins "Nam illa consolatio . . . "], ET: K/W 130[62].

20. The reference is again to BSRK 57,1–2, ET: Cochrane 57–58[III].

21. BSLK 56,3–4: " . . . hanc *fidem* imputat Deus pro iustitia coram ipso," ET: K/W 40 [German text], 41 [Latin text]; Barth's italics.

22. BSRK 57,45–46, ET: Cochrane 58[III]; Barth's italics.

23. See lecture 2. Barth later revises the view presented here on the place of the scriptural principle in Lutheran dogmatics. See KD I/2, 508, ET: CD I/2, 460: In this emphasized formulation of the Scripture principle the issue is not, therefore, "something which is specifically Reformed; this becomes clear later, when insistence on the Scripture principle came to be more generally adopted." A comparison of the older dogmatic works of Orthodoxy reveals that "the Lutherans put the Scripture principle at the very peak of their theological system even more ardently and obviously than did the Reformed."

24. BSRK 2,13–3,12, ET: Cochrane 36–37.

25. BSRK 2,42, ET: Cochrane 37[10].

26. BSRK 2,36, ET: Cochrane 37[8].

27. BSRK 79,1–94,41, ET: Hinke 33–61.

27a. BSRK 81,5–8, Hinke 36.

27b. BSRK 81,9–82,2, Hinke 38–39.

28. BSRK 81,10: "quod Deus meus est," ET: Hinke 38.

29. BSRK 81,11: "ab ullius creaturae occasione," ET: Hinke 38.

30. BSRK 82,3–19, ET: Hinke 39–40 ["Thirdly . . . "].

31. BSRK 82,6–7: "nihil enim aeque firmum ac *Deus* est," ET: Hinke 39; Barth's italics.

32. Zwingli, S, IV, 42–78; CR 93/V (=Z 6/V), 1–163, ET: Hinke 235–93; the document was not published until 1536.

33. See, e.g., the *Scottish Confession* of 1560, Article I, "Of God," BSRK 249,33, ET: Schaff 439–40; in their content similar, the *Gallican Confession* of 1559, BSRK 221,31, ET: Schaff 359–60; the *Belgic Confession* of 1561, BSRK 233,6, ET: Schaff 383–84.

34. Zwingli, S, IV, 45; Zwingli, Z, 6/V, 55, ET: Hinke 238.

34a. Hinke 238.

35. Zwingli, S, IV, 46–47; Zwingli, Z, 6/V, 61; ET: Hinke 241; in the German edition, Barth translated the Zwingli citation.

35a. CR 93/V 116–18, ET Hinke 263–64.

36. Berchtold Haller (1492–1536), from 1513 in Bern and from 1521 on in contact with Zwingli, became the Reformer of Bern. Franz Kolb (1465–1535) was banished from Bern in 1522 because of the Reformation zeal of his preaching; in 1527 he was called back to serve next to Haller. In the invitation to the Bern Disputation of January 6–26, 1528, both are mentioned as defenders of the Ten Theses (or "Conclusions") (BSRK 30,3–8, ET: Cochrane 45–50 [Schaff 208–10, in German and Latin]). The theses, drawn up by both (BSRK XIX,32), were "strongly influenced" by the 18 Theses of Johannes Comander, composed for the Disputation at Ilanz on January 7, 1526, and they, for their part, "depend upon the Zurich theses of 1523" (BSRK XXX,32–36). This is esp. true of the first Bern thesis, cited in the text, which reads as follows in the Ilanz formulation: "The church of Christ is born of the Word of God, and it is bound to abide in the same, and not to listen to the voice of any stranger" ("Ecclesia Christi genita ex verbo Dei, et in eodem debet manere, nec audire volem cujusquam alieni") (P. D. R. de Porta, *Historia reformationis ecclesiarum raeticarum*, Tom. I, Chur 1771, 102).

37. BSRK 30,9–11, ET: Cochrane 49[I].

38. BSRK 30,15–18, ET: Cochrane 49[III].

39. BSRK 930,4–7. For the title of the confession, see p. 239, n. 204.

40. BSRK 930–35.

41. BSRK 932,26–27: "om te betugen ende te verdeengen de vrijheit ende purheit des geloffs in Christo."

42. BSRK 934,18–25: "wat god nied selve is ende doet." Barth's citation refers to the entire confession.

43. Only the concluding "summary" ("summa") (BSRK 934,18–25) was for a while "read . . . every Sunday" in some East Friesian congregations (BSRK XXII,48–50).

44. BSRK 934,31–39.

45. Andreas Bodenstein von Karlstadt (ca. 1480–1541), initially an ally and then a foe of Luther, published in 1524 a series of mystical tracts. On May 15, 1529(?) Luther wrote to J. Jonas (WA.B 5,69,13, ET: *Luther's Correspondence and Other Contemporary Letters*, trans. and ed. Preserved Smith and Charles M. Jacobs (Philadelphia: Lutheran Publication Society, 1918), 2:482–83), "Carlstadt has for some time been settled in Frisia. He is joyful and triumphant" ["Carlstadius in Frisia laetus et triumphans . . . consedit"].

46. The Basel Confession of 1534, BSRK 95,1–100,26, ET: Cochrane 91–96, and BSRK XXV–XXVI [see Cochrane 89–90 for a brief historical introduction].

47. Oswald Myconius (1488–1522), the successor to Oecolampadius in Basel.

48. BSRK 110,1–35, ET: Cochrane 115–16 [Barth refers to this document in terms of the event for which it was written, "The Lausanne Religious Discussion," in English the usual term used is "The Lausanne Articles."—Trans.].

49. See Th.C. 352–55, ET: *Theology of Calvin* 261–64.

50. BSRK 110,7: "entnervt die vis Christi," ET: Cochrane 115[I].

51. BSRK 110,16, ET: Cochrane 115[IV]; Barth's italics.

52. This remark refers certainly to the Bernese state church system, which was defined by a decidedly patriarchalist view of governance ("the gracious lords"). Characteristic of this system was the claim formulated in the drama written by N. Manuel, a work that was significant for the beginnings of the Bernese Reformation.

Against the background of harsh criticism of the papacy, it is expected of "the authorities" that "they lead the sheep rightly / knowing that they are thy servant," for "Lord, thou alone art the door / through which we shall go into heaven" (F. Vetter, ed., *Niklaus Manuels Spiel evangelischer Freiheit; Die Totenfresser; Vom Papst und seiner Priesterschaft* [1523], [Leipzig, 1923], 88). It should be added that the Bernese regime, understanding itself in this way, later caused Calvin "more bitterness, irritation, inner and outer distress" than "all the other experiences of his life," Stähelin, *Johannes Calvin* (see lecture 1, n. 127), 2:98–112, 125–47; the quotation is on 98.

52a. BSRK 111–16, ET: Cochrane 120–23.

53. BSRK 111,14–18: " . . . sans y mêler aucune chose qui ait été controuvée du sens des homes [. . .], sans y ajouter ne diminuer," ET: Cochrane 120.

54. BSRK 111,26, ET: Cochrane 120.

55. For more on this confession; see Th.C. 386–98, ET: *Theology of Calvin* 283–93.

56. BSRK p. 113,13–14: "nous sommes tousjours povres et misérables pécheurs devant la fade de Dieu," ET: Cochrane 122[IX].

57. See the first thesis in Luther's 95 Theses on Indulgences, WA 1,233, ET: LW 31:83–85.

58. BSRK 113,21: "Tout nostre bien en la grâce de Dieu," ET: Cochrane 122.

59. BSRK 113,34, ET: Cochrane 123.

60. BSRK 113,40: "Invocation de Dieu seul et intercession de Christ," ET: Cochrane 123.

61. BSRK 500,22–505,8, ET: Schaff 757–70.

62. BSRK 504,28–29, ET: Schaff 769.

63. The title of this list is "Addition to this Confession" ("Additions à la sus-dite Confession"), BSRK 504,26, ET: Schaff 769–70. "Syllabus errorum," the announcement published by Pope Pius IX in the encyclical "Quanta Cura" on December 8, 1864, on errors related to the secularization of the Christian world: "Syllabus complectens praecipuos nostrae aetatis errores qui notantur in Allocutionibus consistorialibus, in Encyclicis aliisque apostolicis Litteris sanctissimi Domini Nostri Pii papae IX" (DS 2901–80); ET: Denzinger 435–42[1701–80]: "Syllabus or Collection comprising the particular errors of our age, which are noted in consistorial allocutions, in Encylical and other Apostolic letters of His Holiness, our Lord Pope Pius IX."

64. See BSRK 585,5–8, ET: Schaff 770, last par.

65. BSRK 504,44, ET: Schaff 770[10].

66. Barth mistakenly quotes the following sentence as "13."

67. Barth speaks mistakenly of "thirteen" statements.

68. See, e.g., Seeberg 633–34 n. 4.

69. A basic theological formula in Karl Barth's early theology; see Römerbrief 1, pp. 47, 79, 97, and passim; Römerbrief 2, pp. xiii, 56, 326, 328, and passim (in 1923 ed., xiv, 54, 324, 326, and passim), ET: Romans 11, 83, 346.

70. Barth is presupposing here and summarizing, with a certain accentuation, what he had already presented in detail in Th.C., ET: *Theology of Calvin* 13–49.

71. Gottschalk the Saxon (Gottschalk of Orbais, 806/8–866/70) was condemned for his doctrine of the free, double predestination of God, at the Synod of Mainz in 848 and of Quierzy in 849; he was then emprisoned by Hincmar in Hautvilliers.

72. See on this Th.C. 66–92, ET: *Theology of Calvin* 50–68.

73. Ca. 1290–1349.

74. Died in 1358. See Loofs 616.

75. Died in 1349. See Tschackert *Die Entstehung der lutherischen und reformierten*

Kirchenlehre (see p. 230, n. 46), 36, and Loofs 612; see also Th.C. 72–73, ET: *Theology of Calvin* 54–55.

76. Heinrich von Seuse (Suso, ca. 1295–1366): "Got ist als ein cirkellicher Ring, dess Ringes Mittelpunkt allenthalb ist und sin Umswank niene," cited in K. R. Hagenbach, *Lehrbuch der Dogmengeschichte*, 6th ed., ed. K. Benrath (Leipzig, 1886), 333, ET: K. R. Hagenbach, *Hagenbach's History of Christian Doctrines*, Clark's Foreign Theological Library, new series, 3 (Edinburgh: T.& T. Clark, 1880) 2:188: "God is a circular ring, the center of which is everywhere, and the circumference nowhere."

77. BSLK 560,2–3, ET: K/W 386[3].

78. BSLK 560,13–15, ET: K/W 386[2], Barth's italics.

79. See above, pp. 62–64; [see also Inst. I,vii,4,1:78–81—Trans.].

2. The Positive Doctrine of Christianity

1. The Reformed confessions mentioned in the next lines will be among those discussed in the course of lecture 3.2, and their sources will be noted as they appear.

2. See the new preface to Luther's Larger Catechism, BSLK 545,1–555,30, ET: K/W 379–83.

3. See Th.C. 210, ET: *Theology of Calvin* 158.

4. J. Calvin, *Sermons sur l'epitre aux Galates* (32d sermon), CR 78 (=CO 50), 683–84, ET: *Sermons on Galatians by John Calvin*, trans. Arthur Golding (1574) (Audubon: Old Paths Publications, 1995), 684–85. In the lecture, he quoted the French as follows: "Or nous nous prosternerons devant la (saint) majesté de notre bon Dieu, en cognoissance de nos fautes, le priant que de plus en plus il nous les fasse sentire; et que nous en soyons tellement touchés que ce (nous) soit pour nous [. . .] cherchions en nostre Seigneur Jesus Christ tout ce que nous voyons nous defailler: et qu'il y ait une telle humilité qu'estans du *tout* abatus, et ayant anéanti *toute* fausse présomtion de laquelle nous pourrions être trompé, nous ne tendions à autre fin, sinon d'être receus par la *pure* miséricorde de notre Dieu, pour parvenir à l'héritage eternel. Et que nous tâchions de cheminer tellement sous ses commandements que cependant il lui plaise de nous supporter selon notre fragilité, jusqu'à ce qu'il nous en ait du tout dépouillé. Ansi nous dirons tous, Dieu tout puissant, père céleste . . . " Barth's insertions are marked with <>; the italics are his.

5. See J. Calvin, *Le catéchisme de l'Eglise de Genève*, CR 34 (=CO 6), 1; the ET of the Latin version of this confession is in *Tracts and Treatises II*, 33–94; see esp. 37 [the French version appeared in 1541, and the Latin version in 1545—Trans.].

6. See p. 236, n. 127.

7. See pp. 208–224.

8. The term is explicitly alluded to at a few places in the Heidelberg Catechism (Questions 20, 52, 54, BSRK 687,20–24, 696,14 and 33–34, ET: Schaff 313 (Q. 20), 324 (Q. 52), 324–25 (Q. 54), but not fully discussed. See Seeberg 652, and Tschackert, *Die Entstehung der lutherischen und der reformierten Kirchenlehre* (see lecture 1, n. 46), 418.

9. BSRK 224,32–45, ET: Schaff 366–67[XII].

10. See n. 8 above and Barth's discussion in KD II/2, 89, ET: CD II/2, 82–83.

10a. In the Müller edition of the Reformed confessions used by Barth, the paragraph divisions and titles in Zwingli's *Instruction* differ from the order provided by Pipkin; Pipkin divides the first section into "Mandate," "A Short Christian Instruction," "Sin," and "Law," all of which is under "Sin" in Barth's version. Thereafter the divisions agree.—Trans.

11. P. Melanchthon, *Loci communes rerum theologicarum seu Hypotyposes theologicae*

(1521), CR 21,81–227, addresses in his most important sections the following themes in this order: "Of Man and of Free Will," "Of Sin," "Of the Law," "Of the Gospel," "Of Grace," "Of Justification and Faith," "Of the Distinctions between the Old and New Testaments," "Of the Abrogation of the Law," "Of Signs"; ET: *The Loci Communes of Philip Melanchthon*, trans. Charles L. Hill (Boston: Meador Publishing Co, 1944), 63–267.

12. BSRK 7,29–30, ET: Pipkin 50; Barth's italics.

13. BSRK 10,23, ET: Pipkin 53.

14. BSRK 11,7: "alldieweil wir Adams Balg tragen," ET: Pipkin 53.

15. BSRK 16,16, ET: Pipkin 58; Barth's italics.

16. BSRK 16,16–17, ET: Pipkin 59.

17. BSRK 16,39–40, ET: Pipkin 60; Barth's italics.

18. BSRK 18,9–10, ET: Pipkin 61.

19. BSRK 18,14–23,29, ET: Pipkin: 62–67.

20. BSRK 20,20–27, ET: Pipkin 64.

21. BSRK 23,20, ET: Pipkin 67.

22. BSRK 23,25–26, ET: Pipkin 67.

23. K. Holl, *Die Rechtfertigungslehre im Licht der Geschichte des Protestantismus*, Sammlung gemeinverständlicher Vorträge und Schriften 45; (Tübingen, 1906, 2d ed., 1922), 3–27, esp. 13; K. Holl, "Die Rechtfertigungslehre in Luthers Vorlesung über den Römerbrief mit besonderer Rücksicht auf die Frage der Heilsgewißheit," in K. Holl, *Gesammelte Aufsätze zur Kirchengeschichte, I, Luther* (Tübingen, 1921; 2d and 3d eds, 1923), 111–54. See Karl Barth, *Ethik II* (1928/1929), ed. D. Braun, Gesamtausgabe, section 2 (Zurich, 1978), 33–40, ET: *Ethics*, ed. Dietrich Braun, trans. G. W. Bromiley (New York: Seabury Press, 1981), 275–78.

24. BSLK 53–54,56,60,75–81, ET: K/W (German and Latin texts), 36–41[II–IV], 40–41[VI], 52–57[XX].

25. Interpretations of the Augsburg Confession are found in several German confessions, such as in the *Nassau Confession (Dillenburg Synod)*, BSRK 723,31–43; 727,32–728,28; *The Staffort Book*, BSRK 810,11–16; 813,16–28; the *Confession of the Cassel General Synod*, BSRK 821,34–37; the *Confessio Sigismundi*, BSRK 836,31–34.

26. BSRK 31–55.

27. Wolfgang Capito (1478–1541), reformer of Strassburg next to and with M. Bucer. For his important role in the formulation of the Bern Synod; see BSRK XX,37–48; further, see E. Saxer, "Capito und der Berner Synodus," in G. Locher, ed., *Der Berner Synodus von 1532: Edition and Abhandlungen zum Jubiläumsjahr 1982* (Neukirchen-Vluyn, 1988), 2:150–66.

28. See A. Lang *Puritanismus und Pietismus: Studien zu ihrer Entwicklung von M. Butzer bis zum Methodismus*, Beiträge zur Geschichte und Lehre der Reformierten Kirche, vol. 6 (Neukirchen, 1941), 13–14.

29. Nikolaus Ludwig Count von Zinzendorf (1700–1760), founder of the Moravian Brethren community at Herrnhut.

30. *Büdingische Sammlung Einiger In die Kirchen-Historie Einschlagender Sonderlich neuerer Schriften* (Büdingen, 1742), 1:705–70; reprint: N. L. von Zinzendorf, *Ergänzungsbände zu den Hauptschriften*, vol. 7, in E. Beyreuther and G. Meyer, eds, *Büdingische Sammlung* (Hildesheim, 1965), 1:705–70.

31. N. L. von Zinzendorf, *Materialien und Dokumente*, ed. E. Beyreuther et al., series 4, vol. 3: *Herrnhuter Gesangbuch* (Hildesheim and New York, 1981), hymn 2056, 1930–1941. The hymn is also printed in Locher, ed., *Der Berner Synodus non 1532* (see above, n. 27), 343–53.

32. Copies of the title page are found in the various editions of the "Berner Synodus" since 1532 in the edition named in n. 27, *Der Berner Synodus*, 1:383–91.

33. See BSRK 36,43–44; see Locher, ed., *Der Berner Synodus von 1532*, 48.

34. BSRK 37,26–27; see Locher, ed., *Der Berner Synodus von 1532*, 51.

35. BSRK 41,1–2; see Locher, ed., *Der Berner Synodus von 1532*, 64.

36. BSRK 41,16; see Locher, ed., *Der Berner Synodus von 1532*, 64.

37. See A. Lang *Der Evangelienkommentar Martin Butzers und die Grundzüge seiner Theologie* (Leipzig, 1900), 120–32.

38. See E. Hirsch, *Die Theologie des Andreas Osiander und ihre geschichtlichen Voraussetzungen* (Göttingen, 1919), 61,210–11

39. BSRK 101–9, ET: Cochrane 100–111.

40. Kaspar Megander (1495–1545), a close friend of Zwingli, was, beginning in 1528, a professor of theology and preacher in Bern, from which he returned to Zurich at the end of 1536 because of the occasional tendencies toward Lutheranism in Bern.

41. Simon Grynäus (1493–1541) was a friend of Melanchthon and Bucer, a Greek scholar, and called to Basel in 1529 by Oecolampadius.

42. BSRK XXVI,11–39.

43. E. F. K. Müller, "Helvetische Confessionen," in RE, 3d ed., 7:641,23–45; ET: S/H 5:216–17. For detailed information about the negotiations at that time between Luther and the Swiss regarding a "Wittenberg Concord" dealing with the Lord's Supper (1536), and about Bucer's mediating role in the process, as well as about the importance in this context of the First Helvetic Confession and the Smalcaldic Articles written by Luther in 1537; see E. Bizer, *Studien zur Geschichte des Abendmahlstreits im 16. Jahrhundert* (Gütersloh, 1940; 3d ed., Darmstadt, 1972), Beiträge zur Förderung Christlicher Theologie 2/46, 11–233.

44. "Preserved" (BSRK 104,6, ET: Cochrane 104[12]) in the sense of "being taken under one's care, being well provided for."

45. ET: Cochrane 103[11]; Barth's italics.

46. See BSRK 104,22, ET: Cochrane 105[13].

47. The discussions of the confession in the Augustinian monastery, on which site the Museum of Natural History stands today, took place from January 30 to February 4, 1536 (BSRK XXVI,16–17, 29–30). On Calvin's stay in Basel at the same time, only a few hundred meters from that meeting site, see Th.C. 208–9, ET: *Theology of Calvin* 157–58.

48. "Der kürtzer Catechismus," in A. Lang, *Der Heidelberger Katechismus und vier verwandte Katechismen (Leo Juds und Microns kleine Katechismen sowie die zwei Vorarbeiten Ursins)*, Quellenschriften zur Geschichte des Protestantismus, part 3 (Leipzig, 1907), 54–116. Leo Jud (1482–1542), one of the closest colleagues of Zwingli and Bullinger, preacher at the St. Peter's Church in Zurich, often active as a translator, particularly of Hebrew, played a significant role in the formulation of the First Helvetic Confession.

49. See with regard to this entire survey Questions 1–16 in Lang, *Der Heidelberger Catechismus*, 55–59.

50. Lang, *Der Heidelberger Catechismus*, 59.

51. In German, the term "Prest" is used—Zwingli's term for sin ("Sünde")—to be understood not as "infirmity" or "weakness" but as "incurable breach"; see Locher, *Die Zwinglische Reformation* (see p. 234, n. 97), 215–17.

52. BSRK 170–221, ET: Schaff 831–909.

53. BSRK 171,39–42 (doctrine of scripture), ET: Schaff 833; 172,14–23 (church tradition and councils), ET: Schaff 833–34; 173,40–174,3 (Trinity), ET: Schaff 836; 174,41–44 (images and idols), ET: Schaff 837; 181,14–19 (free will), ET: Schaff 847; 183,46–50 (Christology), ET: Schaff 851, and so on. See also BSRK XXXII,13–15, and C. Pestalozzi, *Heinrich Bullinger: Leben und ausgewählte Schriften nach handschriftlichen und gleichzeitigen Quellen* (Elberfeld, 1858), 420–22.

54. On the concept of covenant in Bullinger, see G. Schrenk, *Gottesreich und Bund im älteren Protestantismus vornehmlich bei Johannes Coccejus: Zugleich ein Beitrag zur Geschichte des Pietismus und der heilsgeschichtlichen Theologie* (Gütersloh, 1923), 40–44.

55. See Pestalozzi, *Heinrich Bullinger*, (see lecture 1, n. 102), 420.

56. BSRK 179,23–181,19, ET: Schaff 844–47[IX].

57. See BSRK 180,29, ET: Schaff 846.

58. BSRK 180,37–38: "Aguntur [...] a Deo, ut agant ipsi, quod agunt," ET: Schaff 846.

59. BSRK 186–87, ET: Schaff 854–56[XII].

60. BSRK 187,6, ET: Schaff 856.

61. See BSRK 186,17–18: "lex naturae digito Dei in corda hominum inscripta," ET: Schaff 856[XIII].

62. BSRK 187–88, ET: Schaff 856–62.

63. BSRK 188–91, ET: Schaff 858–62[XIV].

64. BSRK 190,32: "in studio *vitae novae*," ET: Schaff 861; Barth's italics.

65. BSRK 189,6: "poenitentia est *vera* ad Deum conversio," ET: Schaff 859; Barth's italics. [Barth's Latin is a paraphrase of the longer sentence in the confession: "And surely this is true repentance—namely, an unfeigned turning unto God and to all goodness."—Trans.]

66. BSRK 191–92, ET: Schaff 862–64[XV].

67. BSRK 192,6–20: "Iustificatio per solam fidem," ET: Schaff 863[XV]; BSRK 191,37–43: "Iustificamus propter Christum," ET: Schaff 863[II]; see also BOC 79[XV, 5.107]; [Schaff's edition omits the paragraph titles like this one, which Barth is citing, and which are included in later editions of this confession.—Trans.]. Note that "justification according to Christ" is treated before "justified by faith alone."

68. BSRK 192,21–23: " ... ubi pro credere ponit manducare, et pro manducare credere. Nam sicut manducando cibum recipimus, ita credendo participamus Christo," ET: Schaff 863–64: " ... where he puts eating for believing, and believing for eating. For as by eating we receive meat, so by believing we are made partakers of Christ."

69. BSRK 192,36–37, ET: Schaff 864.

70. BSRK 193–95, ET: Schaff 864–68[XVI].

71. BSRK 195–99, ET: Schaff 868–75[XVII].

72. BSRK 196,30, ET: Schaff 870; Barth rendered this Latin phrase in German.

73. See H. Zwingli's statement, "Qui verum dicit, ex Deo loquitur," in Zwingli, *Sermonis de providentia Dei anamnema* (1530), Zwingli, S IV,05 (=Z 6/III [=CR 93/III] 110,13–14), ET: Hinke 154: " ... [H]e who speaks the truth, speaks from God." Building on this, he propounded the proposition of the "salvation of noble pagans" ("Seligkeit edler Heiden"), Zwingli, *Christianae fidei a Huldrico Zwinglio preaedicatae brevis et clare expositio* (1531), Zwingli, S IV,65 (=Z 6/V [=CR 93/V] 132,3–4), ET: Hinke 272, in "A Short and Clear Exposition of the Christian Faith." See p. 285, n. 15.

74. BSRK 198,42, ET: Schaff 873.

75. See on this Th.C. 365–86, ET: *Theology of Calvin* 271–84.

76. Pencil notation on the manuscript margin (referring to the word in the manuscript "together" underlined in pencil): "*not* good so."

77. Pencil notation on the manuscript margin: "(Sig.: A36, B45)." This means that in the following section, Barth assigned the code A to the Catechism of 1536 [1537] and the code B to that of 1545. See n. 78.

78. The First Genevan Catechism (on its dating; see p. 241, n. 33) has the title *Instruction et confession de foy don't on use en leglise de Geneve*, CR 50(=CO 22), 33–74 (=A); =OS I, 378–417, ET: *Instruction in Faith*. The (second) Genevan Catechism, *Catechismus ecclesiae Genevensis, hoc est, formula erudiendi pueros in doctrina Christi*, appeared in 1545 in Latin, CR 34 (=CO 6), 1–160, OS II, 59–157 (=BSRK 117–53; =B), ET: Geneva Catechism (1545), in *Tracts and Treatises II*, 33–94. Occasionally Barth refers to the French version of the Second Catechism of 1541–1542, CR 34 (=CO 6), 1–160 (=BSKO 3–41). The Gallican Confession (1559) carries the title, *La confession de foy des Eglises du Royaume de France*, CR 37 (=CO 9), 731–52 (=BSRK 221–32), ET: Schaff 356–82 (in French and English, also titled "The French Confession of Faith").

79. See H. Walther, *Lateinische Sprichwörter und Sentenzen des Mittelalters in alphabetischer Anordnung* (Göttingen, 1963), 1:679, nr. 5556.

80. OS I, 378, ET: *Instruction in Faith* 17.

81. ET: Geneva Catechism (1545), *Tracts and Treatises II*, 37; Barth's italics.

81a. The wordplay Barth that uses here cannot be captured in English: "Gabe" means "gift," and "Aufgabe" means "task," that is, that which has been given to someone to do; logically, therefore, the gift comes before and constitutes the task.—Trans.

82. See Horace, Epistolae I, 18,84: "Tua res agitur, paries cum proximus ardet," ET: *Works of Horace*, trans. C. Smart (London: Bell & Daldy, 1864), 269: "For it is your own concern when the adjoining wall is on fire."

82a. The German word "Erkenntnis" describes a form of knowledge that is dynamic, involving and transforming the knower. It is more than mere "cognition" and includes nuances of "recognition" and "acknowledgment." For our purposes, we will often translate "Erkenntnis" with "knowing," although it does not adequately render the sense of the original; see John T. McNeill's discussion of the title of the First Book of Calvin's Institutes (I,i,1,1:135: "The Knowledge of God the Creator"), where in footnote 1 he suggests "existential apprehension" as the best translation for the Latin "cognitio," which is "Erkenntnis" in German.—Trans.

83. OS I, 378: "que nous *cognoissions* la *majesté* de notre Créateur," ET: *Instruction in Faith* 21; Barth's italics.

84. " . . . finis praecipuus vitae humanae . . . ut *deum*, a quo conditi sunt homines, *ipsi* noverint," ET: Geneva Catechism (1545), *Tracts and Treatises II*, 37; Barth's italics [the *ipsi* that Barth stresses is not rendered in the ET; we have added it in brackets—Trans.].

85. OS I,378, ET: *Instruction in Faith* 21.

86. The German manuscript says, "seeks apparently through this unheard of thing through us . . . " and was changed by the German editor.

87. BSRK 117,10–11: "ideo creavit, . . . quo glorificetur in nobis," ET: Geneva Catechism (1545), *Tracts and Treatises II*, 37, lines 4–5.

88. BSRK 117,11–12: "vitam nostram . . . in eius gloriam referri," ET: *Tracts and Treatises II*, 37, lines 5–7.

88a. ET: Schaff 359–60[I].

89. See BSRK 117,21: " ... *vera et recta cognitio* Dei," ET: Geneva Catechism (1545), *Tracts and Treatises II*, 38, line 7; Barth's italics.

90. See BSRK 117,23: "rite Dei honorandi ratio," ET: Genevan Catechism (1545), *Tracts and Treatises II*, 38, line 9.

91. BSRK 117,24–28, ET: *Tracts and Treatises II*, 38, lines 10–15.

92. See the structure of the catechism: I. On Faith (BSRK 117,6, ET: *Tracts and Treatises II*, 37); II. On Law (BSRK 129,7, ET: *Tracts and Treatises II*, 56); III. On Prayer (BSRK 137,43, ET: *Tracts and Treatises II*, 70); IV. On the Sacraments (BSRK 145,6, ET: *Tracts and Treatises II*, 81, 83).

93. BSRK 117,24–28: " ... in eo sita sit [...], studeamus [...], invocemus [...], agnoscamus ... " ET: *Tracts and Treatises II*, 38, lines 10–15.

94. In the German manuscript, "itself out," deleted by the German editor.

95. See, on this, Th. C, 94–122, esp. 110–11, ET: *Theology of Calvin* 70–90, esp. 82.

96. See Augsburg Confession, chap. 20, BSLK 78,9, ET: K/W 55[17].

97. Institutio christianae religionis (1536), OS I,37: "Summa fere sacrae doctrinae duabus his partibus constat: Cognitione Dei ac nostri," ET: *Institutes of the Christian Religion (1536)*, trans. Ford Lewis Battles (Grand Rapids: Wm. B. Eerdmans, 1986), 15.

98. H. Bauke, *Die Probleme der Theologie Calvins* (Leipzig, 1922), 97.

99. See Loofs 881: "Calvin never concealed the fact that he valued Luther more highly than Zwingli. To a much greater degree than Zwingli ever was, he was a 'Lutheran.'" Loofs appeals for this to CR 39 (=CO 11), 24.438 (letter of February 26, 1540 to Farel, and September 11, 1542, to Viret); see R. Schwarz, ed., *Johannes Calvins Lebenswerk in seinen Briefen*, 2d ed. (Neukirchen, 1961), 140–41, 229–30.

100. Only in the first version of 1536: Of the law, of faith, of prayer, of the sacraments ... (=OS I, 20).

101. OS I, 390: "Le seigneur donc après nous avoir par la loi admonesté de notre imbécillité et impurité il nous console par la *confiance* de sa vertu et miséricorde," ET: *Instruction in Faith* 34; Barth's italics.

102. OS I, 390: " ... ainsi nous *l'embrassons* par foi et le recognoissons comme *à nous* donné, ET: *Instruction in Faith* 35; Barth's translation and italics.

103. BSRK 117,40, ET: *Tracts and Treatises II*, 2:38; Barth's italics.

104. CR 34 (=CO 6), 11, ET: *Tracts and Treatises II*, 2:38; Barth's italics.

105. See BSRK 226,24: "*approprier* les promesses de vie qui nous sont données *à notre usage*," ET: Schaff 371. The original French text is cited in the German footnote: " ... d'autant que les promesses de vie qui qui nous sont donnees en luy sont appropriees à notre usage ... " showing that Barth's quotation rearranges this text. However, his version is virtually identical with the English rendering of the French in Schaff.—Trans.

106. See, e.g., M. Luther, Hauspostille (1544), WA 52,516: "Where there is the promise, and we accept it with all our hearts, there is right and vital faith." "Learn here what faith is, namely, nothing other than that we accept what the word promises as certain and true, that it will never be absent whether or not we see it or feel it" (517). "There you see what faith really is, if you want to define and portray it rightly, for it is nothing other than to hold as true what Christ promises you" (520).

107. BSLK 53,1; 54,1; 56,1; 60,1; 75,12, ET: K/W 36(37), 38(39), 40(41), 52–57.

108. OS I, 392: "Car ainsy la diffinition de la foy doibt estre prinse de la substance de la promesse, laquelle foy tellement sappuye sur ce fondement que iceluy oste incontinant elle ruineroit ou plus tost se sesvanoiroit. Pourtant quand le Seigneur par la promesse evangelique nous presente sa misericorde, si certainement et sans

nulle hesitation nous nous confions en luy qui faict la promesse, nous sommes dictz apprehender sa parolle par foy," ET: *Instruction in Faith* 38: "For thus the definition of faith must be taken from the substance of the promise. Faith rests so much on this foundation that, if the latter be taken away, faith would collapse at once, or, rather, vanish away. Hence, when the Lord presents to us his mercy through the promise of the gospel, if we certainly and without hesitation trust him who made the promise, we are said to apprehend his word through faith."

109. OS I, 392: "une clarté du St. Esperit," ET: *Instruction in Faith* 39.

110. OS I, 390, ET: *Instruction in Faith* 38–39.

111. SBLK 46,29 (=BSLK 80,18): "per fidem accipitur spiritus sanctus," ET: K/W 57[29].

112. OS I, 393: "perpetual *objet* de la foi," ET: *Instruction in Faith* 40; Barth's italics.

113. OS I, 393: " . . . non pas que nous recevions dedans nous quelque iustice, mais parsque la iustice de Christ nous est attribuée," ET: *Instruction in Faith* 40.

113a. "Ne Christum a se ipso distrahamus!" ET: Genevan Catechism (1545), *Tracts and Treatises II*, 55.

114. OS I,394: "La penitence es *tou jours* conjointe avec la foi de Christ," ET: Genevan Catechism (1545), *Tracts and Treatises II*, 56.

114a. BSRK 128,14–15: "Tota evangelii doctrina duobus his membris continetur: fide et poenitentia," ET: Genevan Catechism (1545), *Tracts and Treatises II*, 56.

114b. BSRK 125,16–20, ET: *Tracts and Treatises II*, 50.

115. Pencil notation on manuscript margin: "Parallel to the same thought in the doctrine of *'perseverance' (persévérance)* in Gall. Art. 21 [BSRK 226,30–38, ET: Schaff 151], Cat. 1536 Art.? 1545 Art. ?" The question marks behind the latter two texts probably mean that Barth was not sure whether the comments on "perseverance" in this text were really a "parallel to the same thought." The Catechism of 1536 speaks in the context of *prayer*, "Of perseverance and prayer" ("De la perseverance en orayson") (OS I,410–11, ET: *Instruction in Faith* 64); the Catechism of 1545 touches upon the theme in the context of the petition, "Lead us not into temptation" (BSRK 144,41–45, ET: Cochrane 81).

116. BSRK 129,1–2: " . . . veram hanc legitimam esse regulam colendi Dei, ut eius voluntati obsequamur," ET: Genevan Catechism (1545), *Tracts and Treatises II*, 56.

117. "Que cest que Esperance." OS I, 403, ET: *Instruction in Faith* (1537), 42. Barth cites from this section in what follows.

118. BSRK 227,3–5: "La foi non seulement ne refroidit l'affection de bien et sainctement vivre: mais l'engendre et l'excite en nous, produisant *necessairement* les bonnes oeuvres," ET: Cochrane 152; Barth's italics.

119. See, e.g., WA 40/I,45,11, ET: LW 26:7; 44,486,25, ET: LW 7:251; 54,185,19, ET: *Martin Luther*, ed. E. R. Ruppert and B. Drewery (New York: St. Martin's Press, 1970), 6.

120. See Th.C. 219–20, ET: *Theology of Calvin* 164–65.

121. OS I, 383: " . . . prescrit . . . qui es le service de sa majesté, lequel lui est agréable," ET: *Instruction in Faith* 24–25.

122. BSRK 227,16, ET: Schaff 372–73[XXIII].

122a. BSRK 136,49–50, ET: *Tracts and Treatises II*, 68.

123. OS I, 394, ET: *Instruction in Faith* 42.

124. See BSRK 137,21, ET: *Tracts and Treatises II*, 69.

125. See BSRK 137,28, ET: *Tracts and Treatises II*, 69.

126. See, e.g., Seeberg 564–66 and 637–38, and Tschackert, *Die Entstehung der lutherischen und reformierten Kirchenlehre* (see p. 230, n. 46), 425.

127. See, e.g., WA 40/I,45,11; 112,2; 291,3; 297,3–4, ET: LW 26:7,52,172,177; 'righteousness of the law,' 22:7.

128. See Seeberg 937.

129. See also Th.C. 407, ET: *Theology of Calvin* 300.

130. OS I, 385–86, ET: *Instruction in Faith* 27–29; BSRK 132,1–133,26, ET: *Tracts and Treatises II*, 61–63.

131. Inst. II,viii,28,1:394.

132. BSRK 132,9–18, ET: *Tracts and Treatises II*, 61.

133. BSRK 133,8, ET: *Tracts and Treatises II*, 62.

134. OS I, 386, ET: *Instruction in Faith* 29.

135. OS I, 386, ET: *Instruction in Faith* 29.

136. OS I, 385: " . . . repos spirituel par lequel les fidèles doyvent cesser de leurs propres oeuvres afin de laisser oeuvrer le Seigneur en eux–mêmes," ET: *Instruction in Faith* 28.

137. The excursus printed here in small type is enclosed with brackets in the manuscript.

138. See BSRK 137,44–139,30, ET: *Tracts and Treatises II*, 70–72.

139. BSRK 117,7, ET: *Tracts and Treatises II*, 37.

140. BSRK 138,40, ET: *Tracts and Treatises II*, 71.

141. See BSRK 139,12, ET: *Tracts and Treatises II*, 72.

142. OS I, 410–11, ET: *Instruction in Faith* 64–65.

142a. OS I, 411: "Il nous sera seul assez pour toutes choses, d'autant qu'en soi il contient tous biens, lesquels au temps advenir il nous revelera pleinement," ET: *Instruction in Faith* 65.

143. BSRK 145–53, ET: *Tracts and Treatises II*, 81–94; OS I, 411–13, *Instruction in Faith* 65–69.

144. The reference is to the first part of the Geneva Catechism (1545), "Of Faith" ("De fide").

145. BSRK 125,23–24, ET: *Tracts and Treatises II*, 50.

145a. BSRK 126,24[–27], *Tracts and Treatises II*, 52.

146. BSRK 125,26–27: "corpus ac societas fidelium, quos Deus ad vitam aeternam praedestinavit," ET: *Tracts and Treatises II*, 50.

147. See BSRK 125,39, ET: *Tracts and Treatises II*, 51. [Barth uses the infinitive form of the inflected verbs in the citation; the ET translates 'reformat' with 'forms.'—Trans.]

148. OS I, 401, ET: *Instruction in Faith* 52–53.

149. The reference is to the fourth section of the Genevan Catechism (1545), "Of the Sacraments," ET: 81–94, where Part 4 is translated in two sections, "Of the Word of God," and "Of the Sacraments."

150. The reference is to the relevant articles of the confession, BSRK 227,36–229,37, ET: Schaff 374–78[XXV–XXXIII].

151. See OS I, 86: The one, believed church is the "whole number of the elect" ["universus electorum numerus"], ET: *Institutes* (1536), 58; OS I, 87: "people of God's elect" ["populus electorum"], ET: *Institutes* (1536), 59. The literal source for Barth's citation is BSRK 256,9: "company of the chosen" ["coetus . . . electorum"] in the Scots Confession (1560), Schaff 458[XVI].

152. BSRK 227,39, ET: Schaff 374[XXV].

153. BSRK 229,3–4, ET: Schaff 376[XXIX].

154. See *Les Ordonnances Ecclesiastiques de l'Eglise de Geneve* (1561), OS II, 325–89, here 328.

155. BSRK 229,34–35: " . . . pour nourir concorde, et tenir chacun depuis le premier jusqu'au dernier en obéisance," ET: Schaff 378[XXXIII].

156. See Cyprian, Ep. 73,21 (CSEL 3/II, 795): "Salus extra ecclesiam non est," ET: Cyprian, "On the Unity of the Church," 6, in *Fathers of the Third Century, Ante-Nicene Christian Library* [American], ed. Alexander Roberts and James Donaldson (Grand Rapids: Wm. B. Eerdmans, 1989–1990), 5:432.

157. BSRK 228,2–3: " . . . mais pource qu'il lui plaît nous entretenir sous telle charge et bride," ET: Schaff 374[XXV], where the French varies as follows: "mais parce qu'il lui plâit nous entretenir sous telle bride."

158. BSRK 228,11: " . . . encore que le Magistrats et leurs édits y soient contraires . . . ," ET: Schaff 374–75[XXVI].

159. BSLK 61, ET: K/W 42[VII, ET of German] and 43[VII, ET of Latin].

160. BSRK 228,18–21: " . . . s'accordent à suivre celle Parole et la pure religion que en dépénd et qui profitent en icelle (die sie bekennen) tout le temps de leur vie, croissans et se confermans en la crainte de Dieu selon qu'ils ont besoin de s'avancer et marcher tousjours plus outre," the phrase in parentheses ("that which they confess") was inserted in German ("die sie bekennen") by Barth into the French citation, ET: Schaff 375[XXVII].

161. BSRK 228,31, ET: Schaff 376[XXVIII], who translates vérité as "word."

162. See BSRK 228,36: " . . . petite trace de l'Eglise en la papauté . . . ," ET: Schaff 376[XXVIII].

163. Seeberg 628–32; for a very abbreviated and ultimately unsatisfying version of this material; see Seeberg/Hay 414–17.

164. See, e.g., BSRK 230,4, ET: Schaff 379[XXXIV]; OS I, 390, 394, ET: *Instruction in Faith*, 36[10]; 42[16].

165. BSRK 117,7,11–12, ET: *Tracts and Treatises II*, 37.

166. See Seeberg 626: "Precisely the early and middle form of Lutheran doctrine is what influenced Calvin both directly and indirectly. He then reproduced it in a way which is more faithful to the origin in Luther than are Melanchthon's Loci." See also Loofs 880–81.

167. John Laski or à Lasco (1499–1560) was a Polish aristocrat who, after his studies in Bologna and Basel (with Erasmus) converted to the Reformation in Louvain; from 1543 to 1550 he was superintendent of the East Friesian Church in Emden, and from 1550 to 1554 of the four refugee congregations in London. The reason they emerged was the persecution in their home countries of Dutch and Walloon Protestants who found asylum in England under Edward VI. In 1550, Marten Micron (1523–1559) became the pastor of the Dutch refugee congregation after he was driven out of Belgium and arrived in London via Strassburg and Basel. After the appearance in 1546 of a catechism written primarily by Lasco, Micron wrote a catechism for his congregation in 1552, which led to a new version in 1559. When Mary Tudor came to the throne in 1553, the Protestants were again persecuted in England, and the refugee congregations fled to the Continent. Micronius went to Norden, while Lasco with his congregation made an adventuresome escape in 1554 and came to Emden, where he wrote a new catechism for the East Friesian Church. Others who fled from London found refuge in Frankfurt. The confession of faith for-

mulated by the refugee congregation here in 1554 had to be signed by every person desiring to become a member. In 1555, Lasco became the pastor of this congregation before he returned to Poland in 1556. See BSRK IL–L, and Lang XXXIX–LII.

167a. BSRK 660,4–5: "hominem [. . .] creavit, ut ab ipso unice coleretur et glorificaretur."

168. The outermost brackets were placed by Barth.

169. See BSRK 664,13.

170. BSRK 664,8.

171. BSRK 675,19.

172. See BSRK 663,26–27

173. BSRK 666,30–667,4.

174. BSRK 657,23–26.

175. See P. Bartels, *Johannes a Lasco, Leben und ausgewählte Schriften,* Leben und ausgewählte Schriften der Väter und Begründer der reformirten Kirche 9 (supplement), (Elberfeld, 1861), 27–29, 32–34.

176. BSRK 663,3–24.

177. BSRK 657,24–25.

178. BSRK 682–719, ET: Schaff 307–55; BOC 4.001–4.129. [Citations from the Heidelberg Catechism will be given both in Schaff and in the *Book of Confessions* (BOC), since the latter contains the wording of the modern translation now in use in most Reformed denominations in North America.—Trans.]

179. Friedrich III of the Palatinate (1515–1576), Electoral Prince in Heidelberg from 1559 on, who converted first from the Roman church to the Lutheran confession, and then favored the Reformed direction. Zacharias Ursinus (1534–1583), student of Melanchthon in Wittenberg; after itinerant study in Basel, Geneva, and Zurich, he was a teacher in Breslau, and from 1561 professor of theology in Heidelberg. Caspar Olevianus (1536–1587) studied law in France and then theology in Geneva and Zurich; beginning in 1561–1562 he was professor of dogmatics and from 1562 pastor and church counselor [administrator] in Heidelberg.

180. BSRK 682,20, ET: Schaff 307, BOC 4.001.

181. See H. Heppe, *Geschichte des deutschen Protestantismus in den Jahren 1555–1581,* 1:444: "Melanchthon's system was the guiding thought of the plan of the [Heidelberg] Catechism. Christian doctrine was communicated there in a thoroughly soteriological way in the three chapters on man's misery, redemption, and thankfulness. With regard to the Lord's Supper, no other doctrine was propounded than Melanchthon's." Barth presumably knew Heppe's thesis through Lang's introduction (Lang CI–CII).

182. The following examples: BSRK 699,25–700,13, ET: Schaff 328–29 (Q. 65–67), BOC 4.065–4.067; 694,33–695,15, ET: Schaff 322 (Q. 47–48), BOC 4.4047–4.4048; 706,9–21, ET: 337–38 (Q. 85), BOC 4.085.

183. See above, p. 84. See P. Althaus, *Die Prinzipien der deutschen reformierten Dogmatik im Zeitalter der aristotelischen Scholastik* (Leipzig, 1914), 63, n. 1: "This thesis is confirmed through the perception that in the soteriological orientation of the Cat.Pal. . . . German-Lutheran influences are present. Gooszen [*De Heidelbergsche Catechismus. Textus receptus met toelichtende teksten* (Leiden, 1890)] is in this context right when he differentiates an anthropological-soteriological direction in Reformed Protestantism from actual Calvinism: The point of departure and the outline of the catechism are not Calvinistic. . . . Regarding the basic outline of the Catechism, Reu [Quellen zur] Geschichte des kirchlichen Unterrichts in der evangelischen Kirche

Deutschlands I, [Gütersloh] 1904, 201ff., presented proof of genuinely Lutheran origins, so that the judgment of Calovius (Syst. II12: quae distributio paulo convenientior videtur magisque nostrae accedit, ET: 'the outline appears a little more in agreement with and comes closer to our own') is brilliantly confirmed. . . . For the point of departure as well German-Lutheran and certainly Melanchthonian influences are probable. One may say that the soteriological form of the analytical procedure is in its approach defined by non-Calvinist, perhaps Melanchthonian impressions. However one might judge this, the form is more congenial to Lutheranism than to Calvinism, whose tendency it does not quite express."

184. BSRK 682,28–683,2, ET: Schaff 308 (Q. 1), BOC 4.001; Barth's italics.

185. BSRK 117,7, ET: *Tracts and Treatises II*, 37.

186. Questions 23–58, BSRK 688,10–698,8, ET: Schaff 314–26, BOC 4.025–4.058.

187. BSRK 715,14–23, ET: Schaff 349 (Q. 155), BOC 4.115; Barth's italics.

188. BSRK 683,17, ET: Schaff 308, BOC 4.002/4.003.

189. BSRK 683,22–33, ET: Schaff 308 (Q. 4), BOC 4.004.

190. BSRK 683,34–684,4, ET: 309 (Q. 5), BOC 4.005.

191. BSRK 706,23, ET: Schaff 338, BOC 4.085/4.086.

192. BSRK 707,32–34, ET: Schaff 339–40 (Q. 91), BOC 4.091; Barth's italics.

193. BSRK 685,22, ET: Schaff 311, BOC 4.011/4.012.

194. BSRK 690,30, ET: Schaff 317 (Q. 31), BOC 4.031; Barth's italics.

195. BSRK 691,13–17, ET: Schaff 318 (Q. 32), BOC 4.032; Barth's italics.

196. BSRK 693,28–694,2, ET: Schaff 321 (Q. 43), BOC 4.043; Barth's italics.

197. BSRK 694,13.17–18, ET: Schaff 321 (Q. 45), BOC 4.045.

198. BSRK 695,24–27, ET: Schaff 323 (Q. 49), BOC 4.049; Barth's italics.

199. BSRK 697,8–9, ET: Schaff 325 (Q. 55), BOC 4.055; Barth's italics.

200. BSRK 700,32–701,2, Schaff 332–33 (Q. 70), BOC 4.070; Barth's italics.

201. BSRK 702,35–703,2, Schaff 332–33 (Q. 76), BOC 4.076; Barth's italics.

202. BSRK 705,10–11, Schaff 336 (Q. 81), BOC 4.081.

203. *Der kürtzer Katechismus*, in Lang 79: "God requires good works of us, and has prepared and called us to walk in them, that is our service, and as such a thanksgiving that we give to God, for we creatures have always been obliged to serve our Creator."

204. *Emden Catechism*, in BSRK 675,37–39: "And also that they admonish us again on our duty towards God and our neighbor, and are moved to thankfulness, love, faithfulness, and obedience for his sake." See also M. Micron, *De kleyne Catechismus*, in Lang 141: "Firstly, that we should always be thankful to God for his great benefits."

205. BSRK 699,17.19–21, ET: Schaff 328 (Q. 64), BOC 4.064; Barth's italics.

206. BSRK 706,29–32, ET: Schaff 338 (Q. 86), BOC 4.086.

207. For a discussion of the resistance and difficulties under which the General Synod of 1607, urged on by the Calvinist-leaning Landgrave Moritz of Hesse-Kassel, adopted a new confession (BSRK 817–21) and a "revision of the Small Lutheran Catechism," which is the Hessian catechism under discussion, see BSRK LV,31–LVI,17. The version of the catechism in BSRK (see LVI,17–21) is not the original but the version of 1736 and 1897, which was possibly revised.

208. Barth is alluding here to a statement of Luther that he wrote in his appeal to the pope after the hearing before Cajetan in October 1518: "to the pope who is not well informed . . . for the better information of the pope" ("a . . . Papa non bene informato . . . ad Papam . . . melius informandum"), WA 2,32,31–38.

209. BSRK 823,6–7; Barth's italics.

210. See H. Heppe, *Kirchengeschichte beider Hessen*, (see p. 233, n. 76), 12–21.

211. BSRK 822,22–26; Barth's italics.

212. See above, n. 97.

213. BSLK 507,34–510,24, ET: K/W 351–54 (1–22); the explanatory sentence referred to is "We are to fear, love, and trust God above all things."—Trans.

214. BSRK 825,27–30; Barth's italics.

215. The German manuscript has "lernen" (to learn) rather than "lehren" (to teach); text changed by the German editors.

216. Questions 10–12, BSRK 827,11–23.

217. See E. R. Grebe, *Geschichte der hessischen Renitenz* (Cassel, 1905), 40–44.

218. During Philipp II's bloody suppression of Protestantism in the French and German Netherlands ("Belgium"), this confession was written by Guy de Brés (Bray) (1522–1567, who died a martyr's death), and directed to the sovereign as an apology for the persecuted faith. In 1568, the confession "won over . . . the Protestantism of the Netherlands for its basic Calvinist stance" (BSRK XXXIV, 34–36) and edged out in the process the "Netherlands Confession" formulated in 1566.

219. BSRK 240,42–241,12, ET: Schaff 407–8[XXII]. [Note that Schaff's version is based on the revisions at the National Synod at Dordrecht in 1618–1619.—Trans.].

220. BSRK 227,8: "par la conduite de St. Esprit," ET: Schaff 372[XXII] [Both Schaff and BSRK have "his Spirit" ("son Esprit") rather than "Holy Spirit" ("St. Esprit"). —Trans.]

221. BSRK 227,1: "grâce de vivre sainctement et en la crainte de Dieu," ET: Schaff 382[XXII].

222. BSRK 936,39–48.

223. Belgic, Art. XXVII–XXXII, BSRK 243,29–245,33, ET: Schaff 416–24; Netherlands Confession of 1566, Art. 7, BSRK 936,49–937,8 and Art. 17, BSRK 939,25–34.

224. BSRK 265–376. The confession, which was an apologetic statement directed against the bishop of Erlau (in Hungarian, Eger) A. Verantz, was written by the preachers P. Melius and Gr. Szegedy in Debrecen and appeared with two different titles, one of which is reproduced in n. 229 below; see BSRK XXXVII,2–25.

225. BSRK XXXVII.

226. BSRK 288–94; 303–10.

227. BSRK 342–44.

228. On Luther, see J. Köstlin, *Martin Luther: Sein Leben und seine Schriften* (Elberfeld, 1875), 2:506–7; on Calvin; see P. Henry, *Das Leben Johann Calvins des großen Reformators* (Hamburg, 1838), 2:417–18, and (Hamburg, 1835 [supplement]), 1:58–65.

229. BSRK XXXVII,14–21: "Confessio catholica de praecipuis fidei articulis, exhibita Sacratissimo et catholico Romanorum Impertori Ferdinando, et Filio suae Majestatis D. Regi Maximiliano, ab universo exercitu equitum et peditum S. R. M, a Nobilibus item et incolis totius vallis Agrinae, in nomine Sanctae Trinitatis ad foedus Dei custodiendum iuramento fidei copulatorum et decertantium pro vera fide et religione, in Christo ex scripturis sacris fundata. Anno 1562. Huic confessioni subscripserunt et Debrecien et locorum vicinorum Ecclesiae," ET: "Catholic confession of the most important articles of faith, presented to the most Holy and Catholic Ruler of the Romans, Ferdinand, and his son, His Majesty King Maximilian, from all the mounted cavalry and the infantry of His Royal Majesty, from the nobility and the citizens of the entire Eger Valley, in the name of the Holy Trinity, for the preservation of the covenant of God as sworn by the faith of the allies and those struggling for the decision for the true faith and true religion, founded on Sacred Scripture in

Christ. In the year 1562. The churches of Debrecen and the neighboring towns have signed this confession." [The "mounted cavalry and infantry" alludes to the medieval social division between those privileged classes that were permitted to ride horses in war and the commoners who had to fight on foot.—Trans.]

230. On the phrase used frequently by Barth, "beginning at the beginning," see the references in Chr. Dogm, 390–91, n. 14; further, Römerbrief 1, 163, 171; KD I/2, 971, ET: CD I/2, 868; KD III/4, 107, ET: CD III/4, 97, and passim.

231. BSRK 272,14: "Impletio legis Christus est."

232. See BSRK 272,16.

233. See BSRK 180,20–34, ET: Schaff 846.

233a. See BSRK 275: "liberos, volentes, obedientes [. . .], assentientes [. . .], sponte facientes bona. . . ."

234. BSRK 281,31; 282,9.

235. BSRK 282,9: "active per se agit."

236. BSRK 331,38–39: "tendunt ad unum scopum."

237. BSRK 354,14.

238. BSRK 353,44–45.

239. BSRK 289,2.

240. BSRK 289,6.

241. BRSK, 289,38: "vera ecclesia est coetus *visibilis* electorum," Barth's italics.

242. BSRK 290,10–11.

243. In 1563, the Transylvanian Synod in Torda recognized the Confession of the Hungarian Synod in Tarczal.

244. See BSRK XXXVII,39–46. Theodore Beza (1519–1605), French scholar, lawyer, poet, and then theologian, who ministered in Lausanne from 1549 to 1558, and then from 1558 on in Geneva, as rector of the academy there and close friend of Calvin, in whose spirit he cared for the relationships between Geneva and France, Germany, Holland, England, Hungary, and Transylvania; he became Calvin's successor in 1564. This confession is entitled, *Confession of the Christian Faith, and Also a Collection of the Papist Heresies (Confessio Christianae fidei, et eiusdem collatio cum Papisticis Haerisibus)* (1560).

245. BSRK XXXVIII,20–21.

246. BSRK 376,21–377,14.

247. BSRK 448,37–449,26.

248. BSRK 384,39–426,2.

249. BSRK 426,3–448,36.

250. See BSRK 386,9–10.

250a. BSRK 387,5: "id enim esset fidem substituere in locum Iesu Christi."

251. BSRK 387,44. See, e.g., Bernard of Clairvaux, *Sermones super cantica Canticorum*, Sermo LXI,1, in G. Winkler, ed., *Bernhard von Clairvaux: Sämtliche Werke lateinisch/deutsch* (Innsbruck, 1995), 6:310: "Quae cum venerit et perfecta fuerit, faciet spirituale coniugium; et erunt duo, non in carne una, sed in uno spiritu, dicente Apostolo: Qui adhaeret deo, unus spiritus est." ET: Bernard of Clairvaux, *On the Song of Songs*, vol. 3, trans. Kilian Walsh and Irene Edmonds (Kalamazoo, Mich.: Cistercian Publications, 1979), 140–41: "When she will have attained to it and become perfect, she will celebrate a spiritual marriage; and they shall be two, not in one flesh but in one spirit, as the Apostle says: He who is united to the Lord becomes one spirit with him."

252. See, e.g, BSRK 386,18; 387,25–29; 416,28.

253. See Th.C. 26, n. 27, ET: *Theology of Calvin* 22, n. 17.

254. See BSRK 388,10.
255. Art. 10–12, BSRK 388,3–391,21.
256. See BSRK 389,45: "ne bis in idem."
257. BSRK 390,46.
258. BSRK 391,41–392,3.
259. BSRK 392,13–36.
260. BSRK 392,44–48.
261. See BSRK 393,28.
262. BSRK 397,46–47: "non nascendo, sed renascendo, non ex naturae, sed ex regenerationis gratia."
263. BSRK 401–4.
264. BSRK 402,1: "in ipso mortis puncto," see BSRK 401,23–28.
265. See BSRK 402,21.
266. BSRK 402,41: "profundis gurgitibus [. . .] immersi."
267. See BSRK 403,27–28.
268. See BSRK 404,16.
269. The reference is to the fourth point in Article 19 of the confession (BSRK 400,32–501,17), esp. BSRK 401,6–9. The title of this article is "Quorsum nobis utilia sint bona opera apud Deum et apud homines" (BSRK 399,13–14), ET: "To What End Good Works Are Useful for Us in the View of God and Men."
270. BSRK 404,45–47: "omnino [. . .] necesse est, ut apud Deum deposita sit salus nostra, qui longe melius eam custodire posit quam nos ipsi." Barth's Latin citation is altered from the original in Müller, which reads "Omnino enim necesse est, ut penes eum deposita sit salus nostra . . . " apparently to emphasize that our salvation is deposited with God.—Trans.
271. BSRK 405,28.
272. BSRK 406,20.
273. BSRK 406,29.
274. BSRK 425,36.
275. BSRK 425,45–426,2; Barth translated the Latin into German for this citation.
276. BSRK 426–48.
277. BSRK 426,10–11: "coetus et multitudo hominum [. . .] selectorum."
278. BSRK 426,18.
279. BSRK 426,37–38: "cives . . . unius ejusdemque civitatis. . . ."
280. BSRK 434–44; on Calvin; see above, p. 102–104.
281. BSRK 444,15.
282. BSRK 444,32.
283. WA 40/I,170,23–182,18, ET: LW 26:92–100[6] and 359,15–373,17, ET: LW 26:226–36[6].
284. See, e.g., E. Troeltsch, *Die Soziallehren der christlichen Kirchen und Gruppen,* Gesammelte Schriften, vol. 1 (Tübingen, 1912), 622, ET: *The Social Teaching of the Christian Churches,* trans. Olive Wyon (Louisville, Ky.: Westminster/John Knox Press, 1992), 2:587: "Luther was always ultimately concerned with the individual's assurance of salvation [and blessedness]. . . . Calvin's view is different . . . [To him] the central point of religion is not the blessedness of the creature but the Glory of God."
285. WA.B. 3,604,36: "Spiritus enim non sic trepidat aut disputat," ET: *Luther's Correspondence,* trans. and ed. Preserved Smith and Charles M. Jacobs (Philadelphia: Lutheran Publication Society, 1918), 2:347: "For the Spirit is not so timid and does not argue as they do."

286. See Römerbrief 1, 293: "Joyfully I may return from the psychic depths in which horror dwells, from the inferno of Pietism where the demons do their work."

287. Anthony the Great (d. 356), the earliest known hermit, described by Athanasius in the 'Life of Antony' [Vita Antonii] as the perfect Christian, who resisted the many attacks of demons with the strength of his faith.

288. The German phrase translated "religiosity" is "Kirchen- und Kappellengeist," meaning the spirit found in churches and chapels, whereby "chapel" in this usage is the Swiss expression for the gatherings of the Pietistic societies.

289. J. W. von Goethe, *Egmont*, act 3, scene 2:

> Himmelhoch jauchzend,
> Zum Tode betrübt—
> Glücklich allein
> Ist die Seele, die liebt.

ET: *Goethe's Plays*, trans. C. E. Passage (New York: Frederick Ungar, 1980), 333:

> Sky high exulting
> To death burdened down;
> Happiness lives
> In the lover alone.

The German quotation is often used as a reference to mercurial or wildly fluctuating emotions.—Trans.

290. This consultation, convened by Polish king Vladislaw IV, took place from the end of August until the beginning of November, as an initiative of his secretary Nigrinus, who was first a Lutheran, then Reformed, then Catholic. His idea was that the consultation should serve to lead the Evangelicals back into the Roman church. This intention explains the tumultuous embitterment that emerged in the consultation where the three parties battled each other on all sides. Since the Lutheran side did not acknowledge G. Calixtus, who had traveled from Helmstedt to join them, as one of their own, he advised the Reformed side whose delegation consisted of twenty-four mostly Polish theologians but also two from Brandenburg-Prussia. This Reformed contingency responded to a Roman doctrinal presentation with the declaration under discussion here, while the Lutherans presented a revised version of the Augsburg Confession (Invariata) on September 20. The original title of the Reformed declaration was *Declaratio Doctrinae Ecclesiarum Reformatarum Catholicae de praecipius Fidei Controversiis* (Declaration of the Catholic Doctrines of the Reformed Churches with Primary Reference to the Controversies of Faith). See P. Tschackert, "Thorn, Religionsgespräch," in RE, 3d ed., 19, 745–51, ET: S/H 11:432–33.

291. See Tschackert, *Die Entstehung der lutherischen und reformierten Kirchenlehre* (see p. 230, n. 46), 408–9.

292. On what follows; see the stipulations in Trent, which were the basis of the Roman Catholic positions in Thorn (Tschackert, "Thorn Religionsgespräch," 748,18–19): "Justificatio . . . non est sola peccatorum remissio, sed et sanctificatio et renovatio interioris hominis per voluntariam susceptionem gratiae et donorum" (DS 1528), ET: Denzinger 251, par. 799: "Justification . . . is not merely remission of sins, but also the sanctification and renewal of the interior man through the voluntary reception of the grace and gifts." "Si quis dixerit, homines iustificari vel sola

imputatione iustitiae Christi, vel sola peccatorum remissione exclusa gratia et caritate, quae in cordibus eorum per Spiritum Sanctum diffundatur . . . atque illis inhaereat, aut etiam gratiam, qua iustificamur, esse tantum favorem Dei: anathema sit" (DS 1561), ET: Denzinger 259, par. 821: "If anyone shall say that men are justified either by the sole imputation of the justice of Christ, or by the sole remission of sins, to the exclusion of grace and charity, which is poured forth in their hearts by the Holy Spirit and remains in them, or even that the grace by which we are justified is only the favor of God, let him be anathema."

293. In Article 4, the second section deals with calling, the third with justification, and the fifth with perfection or fulfillment. Section 4 states: "Simulque Spiritu Caritatis in corda nostra effuso, ad sincerum Sanctimoniae et obedientiae novae Studium indies magis magisque renovat et sanctificat, seu iustos et sanctos facit" (Augusti 418), ET: "And at the same time, in that the Spirit of love is poured into our hearts, we are more and more renewed and sanctified, or made just and holy, for sincere holiness and for the living of new obedience." The text is also located in Niemeyer (as one of the Brandenburg confessions), 669–89.

294. "Falso item accusamur . . . Quasi omnem inhaerentem iustitiam fidelibus negemus, eosque sola externa iustitiae Christi imputatione, quae sit sine ulla interna renovatione, justificari statuamus" (Augusti 419–20), ET: "We are falsely accused . . . as though we deny all righteousness dwelling in believers, and that we assert that they were solely externally justified through the imputation of the righteousness of Christ, which were without any internal renewal."

295. " . . . cum tamen solis poenitentibus et viva fide in Christum credentibus, justitiam imputari, simulque per eandem fidem a Spiritu S. corda contrite vivificari, ad ardentem erga Christum caritatem, et novae obedientiae studium excitari . . . " (Augusti 420), ET: " . . . although righteousness is reckoned solely to those who repent and believe in Christ with vital faith, and simultaneously through that faith contrite hearts are made alive by the Holy Spirit and are moved to zealous love towards Christ and to the living of the new obedience."

296. "Id tantum addimus, perhanc inhaerentem Iustitiam propriam, quia in hac vita imperfecta est, neminem coram severo Dei Iudicio posse consistere, aut in ea confidere, ut a reatu mortis per eam iustificetur seu absolvatur, sed per et propter solam perfectissimam Christi Iustitiam ac Meritum viva fide apprehensum" (Augusti 420), ET: "We add this that through one's own inherent righteousness, which is imperfect in this life, no one can withstand before the severe Judge, nor trust in this righteousness that it might justify or forgive one for the guilt of death, but solely through and on account of the perfect righteousness of Christ and the apprehended merit of vital faith."

297. "Etsi enim sano sensu dici posit, fideles per caritatem aliasque virtutes infusas iustificari, i.e. justos sanctosque fieri, haec tamen justitia in hac vita imperfecta est . . ." (Augusti 422), ET: "It is nevertheless certainly possible and reasonable to say that believers are justified through infused charity and other virtues, that is, made just and holy even though this righteousness is imperfect in this life."

298. "[Falso item accusamur . . .] . . . Quasi fide sola, quae sit sine operibus, quaeque tantum credat sibi propter Christum remissa esse peccata, quamvis sine ulla resipiscentia in illis perseveret, hominem justificari fingamus" (Augusti 421), ET: "[We are falsely accused . . .] . . . as though we assumed that the human is justified solely through faith which is without works, and that he only believes that his sins are forgiven him because of Christ, although he persists in them without contrition."

299. "Solam autem justificari dicimus, non, quod sola sit, sed quod sola promissionem evangelii, adeoque ipsam justitiam Christi apprehendat, per et propter quam solam, gratis, sine ullo proprio merito, justificamur" (Augusti 421), ET: "We say, however, solely justified not because faith stands alone but because solely the promise of the Gospel and solely the righteousness of Christ is apprehended, we are justified through and on account of it solely, freely, without any merit of our own."

300. "[Falso item accusamur . . .] Quasi per hanc doctrinam studium bonorum operum tollamus, eorumve necessitatem negemus; cum tamen nec fidem justificantem, nec ipsam justificationem sine sanctificatione et bonorum operum studio in adultis ullo modo posse consistere, ex jam dictis manifestum sit. Quo sensu etiam ad salutem omnino necessaria esse agnoscimus, quamvis non, ut causas iustificationis aut salutis meritorias" (Augusti 421), ET: "[We are falsely accused . . .] As though we through this doctrine set aside the doing of good works and denied their necessity; even though it is clear from what has been said, that neither justifying faith nor justification itself can persist at all without sanctification and the doing of good works by the mature person. In this sense we acknowledge that they are certainly necessary for salvation although neither as the cause of justification nor as earned salvation."

301. See the previous citation.

302. Augusti 421–22.

303. "Quique nihilominus docent, neminem sine speciali revelatione certo scire posse, se gratiam Dei esse consecutum, tali certitudine, cui falsum subesse non possit, eoque semper omnes de gratia dubitare debere. At nos, etsi fatemur, etiam fideles et justificatos non temere et secure de gratia Dei debere praesumere, variis imo angoribus et dubitationibus saepe conflictari, tamen ex scriptures docemus, eos et posse et debere ad eam certitudinem in hac vita contendere, et divina gratia adjuvante pervenire, qua Spiritus S. testatur spiritui nostro, quod filii et haeredes Dei simus: cui testimonio non potest subesse falsum, etsi non omnes, qui spiritum Dei jactant, vere illud testimonium habent" (Augusti 423), ET: "And these teach, in spite of that, that one could know for certain without special revelation that he had gained God's grace, with such certainty that it were not possible for him to err, and that all must constantly be in doubt about grace. But we nevertheless teach from the Scriptures, even if we confess that the believers and justified also should not presume the grace of God so surely and confidently but on the contrary should often be distressed by trepidation and doubts, that they can and should strive for this certainty in this life, and that the divine grace comes to their help in that the Holy Spirit testifies to our spirit that we are children and relations of God: with this testimony one cannot fall into error even if all those who reject the Spirit of God really do not have that testimony."

304. DS 1540: "Nam, nisi ex speciali revelatione, sciri non potest, quos Deus sibi elegit," ET: Denzinger 255, par. 805: "For except by special revelation, it cannot be known whom God has chosen for himself." See n. 303.

305. See above, n. 303.

306. See DS 1533–34, 1563–66, ET: 802–3, 252–53, par. 823–26, 259.

307. See above, n. 303.

308. As a polemical response to Luther's *De captivitate Babylonica ecclesiae praeludium* (1520), there appeared in July 1522 Henry's *Assertio septem sacramentorum adversus Martinum Lutherum, aedita ab invictissimo Angliae et Franciae rege, et do. Hyberniae Henrico eius nominis octavo*; see WA 6,494–95. Pope Leo X conferred then

the title "Defender of the Faith" ["Defensor fidei"] upon Henry. Luther's response, *Contra Henricum Regem Angliae*, also appeared in 1522: WA 10/II, 180–222, and *Antwort deutsch auf König Heinrichs Buch*, WA 10/II, 223–62, ET: Hans J. Hillerbrand, *The Reformation in Its Own Words* (New York and Evanston: Harper & Row, 1964), 313. Under Henry VIII (1491–1547) the English or Anglican Church separated from Rome with the Supremacy Act of 1534.

309. See BSRK XLVII, 2–3,8–13. It was chiefly under the regency of Edward VI (1547–1553) that Archbishop Thomas Cranmer of Canterbury opened the English church to these "influences," increasingly those of the Zurich and Geneva Reformations. The Strassburg teacher P. Vermigli, born in Florence, came to Oxford in 1547, the Strassburg reformer M. Bucer came to Cambridge in 1549, and John Lasco (see above, n. 167) came in 1550 to London. During the Catholic reaction under the regency of Mary Tudor (1553–1558), Cranmer was executed and Vermigli (1553) and Lasco (1554) were expelled from England. Under the reign of Elizabeth I (1558–1603) the English state church, independent of Rome, really took shape and opened itself anew to Protestantism.

310. On Scotland's acceptance of the Westminster Confession, see BSRK XLVI,40–44. In 1635, the Anglican Articles were accepted in Ireland and replaced the Irish Articles of Religion of 1615 (BSRK XLIV,46–48, ET: Schaff 526–44). On the other hand, the Presbyterians who emigrated from Scotland to Ulster under Elizabeth I in 1608–1613 adopted the Westminster Confession (see W. Götz, "Irland," in RE, 3d ed., 9:422,50–54), which was easier to do since this confession is based upon the Irish Articles (see B. B. Warfield, "Westminster Synode," in RE, 3d ed., 21:182,24–30).

311. BSRK 505–22, ET: Schaff 486–516 [the ET does not contain the 1552 version to which Barth gives particular attention in what follows—Trans.].

312. The numbers in parentheses refer to the differing enumeration of the paragraphs in the versions of 1552 and 1562.

313. BSRK 507,32–33: *"Vetus Testamentum non est rejiciendum,"* ET: Schaff 491 [the Latin citation in the text appears only in the version of 1552; the 1562 title of the paragraph is "Of the Old Testament"—Trans.]; Barth's italics.

314. In the Scots Confession, see BSRK 250,44–251,18, ET: Schaff 442–43[V]; in Inst. II,x,1:428–49.

315. BSRK 508,6–9, ET: Schaff 492: "[Y]et notwithstanding, no Christian man whatsoever is free from the obedience of the Commandments which are called Moral."

316. BSRK 508,31–509,3, ET: Schaff 493–94 ("Of free will").

317. See Barth's emphasis of this thought in the *Berner Synodus*, above, pp. 87–89, which he sees as Bucer's influence (pp. 87, 89). On his influence in general; see Loofs 932. Bucer was active in Cambridge from 1549 until his death in 1551.

318. BSRK 511,40–41, ET: Schaff 498, footnote.

319. BSRK 512,6–9, ET: Schaff 499[XVIII].

320. BSRK 512,30–32, ET: Schaff 499[XIX].

321. Augsburg Confession, Art. VII (CA VII), BSLK 61,3–6: "Est autem ecclesia congregatio sanctorum, in qua evangelium pure docetur et recte administrantur sacramenta," ET: K/W 42–43(VII): "It is the assembly of all believers among whom the gospel is purely preached and the holy sacraments are administered according to the gospel."

322. BSRK 513,8: "divinorum librorum testis et conservatrix," ET: Schaff 500[XX].

323. BSRK 513,33–36: "potestas vocandi Ministros [. . .] publice concessa est," ET: Schaff 501[XXIII].

324. See BSRK XLIII,31–XLIV,15.

325. See BSRK XLIII,49–XLIV,7.

326. M. Bucer worked on the book of liturgies of the Church of England; see J. W. Baum, *Capito und Butzer: Straßburgs Reformatoren, Leben und ausgewählte Schriften der Väter und Begründer der reformierten Kirche*, Part 5 (Elberfeld, 1860), 562. [Barth refers here to the version of 1552, which is entitled "Book of Preaching and the Ceremonies of the Anglican Church" but is substantially changed in the 1562 version to the "Book of Consecration of Archbishops and Ordering of Priests and Deacons."—Trans.].

327. BSRK 519,33–35: "Rex Angliae est supremum caput in terris, post Christum, Ecclesiae Anglicanae et Hibernicae," ET: Schaff 512 [Barth is citing the Latin version of 1552; the Latin version of 1562 and its English translation of 1571 cited in Schaff refer, obviously, to "the Queen's majesty," and the American revision of 1801 speaks of "the civil magistrate.—Trans.].

328. BSRK 520,36–37, ET: Schaff 513.

328a. ET: Schaff 517–22.

328b. ET: Schaff 517. The American version uses "sponsors" rather than "Godfathers and Godmothers."—Trans.

329. See Loofs 932.

330. Barth's date on the margin of the manuscript refers to June 22, 1923. This was a Friday. If this were the correct date, then the lecture on Thursday would not have taken place. That is improbable. This would leave for the next lecture, which Barth certainly in error dated on June 15 (see below, n. 360), only Monday, June 25. But Barth did not lecture on Mondays in the summer semester of 1923. The lecture after the next one (see below, p. 141) is dated on June 26 and is apparently not in error, since that falls on the normal lecture day, Tuesday. The problems are resolved if one assumes that Barth made two errors in dating and one corrects the date of the lecture beginning at this point to be Thursday, June 21, in the normal lecture schedule of Tuesday, Thursday, and Friday.

331. BSRK 249–63, ET: Cochrane 166–84 (Schaff 437–79; since Schaff contains the Scottish dialect of the original version, we shall cite the modern English rendering in Cochrane which is generally also the version used in the Presbyterian *Book of Confessions*.—Trans.).

332. BSRK 263,6–9, ET: Cochrane 184 (Schaff 478–79); Barth translated the text into German for his lectures.

333. John Knox (1515?–1572), after joining the emerging Scottish Reformation a galley prisoner, from 1549 to 1554 clergyman at the English court, and then up to 1558 mostly in Geneva, became in May 1559 the head of the Scottish Reformation and was the major author of the Scottish Confession, which was written in four days. On August 7, 1560, against the objections of Mary Stuart, it was approved by the Scottish Parliament and ratified by the Reformed church in Scotland; see BSRK XXXVI,2–15.

334. See above, n. 314; the reference in BSRK 250,44–251,18, is to Article V, Cochrane 167–68, and to the Inst. I,ii,1:428.

335. BSRK 251,13: "sancta civitas," ET: Cochrane 168 (Schaff 443).

336. BSRK 253,18–19, ET: Cochrane 171 (Schaff 449). [Articles 7–8: Cochrane 168–69 (Schaff 444–46); Articles 9–11: Cochrane 169–71 (Schaff 446–50)—Trans.]

337. BSRK 253,25–28, ET: Cochrane 171 (Schaff 450). Barth translated the original into German.

338. See BSRK 253,31, ET: Cochrane 171 (Schaff 450).

339. See BSRK 253,47: "Ne minima quidem pars." This precise wording is not literally translated in either Cochrane or Schaff in their renderings of the Confession.—Trans.

340. BSRK 254,1–2: "Naturae nostrae sponte ne ad cogitandum quidem quicquam boni idonei," ET: Cochrane 172 (Schaff 450); [Barth's Latin varies slightly from the original, which reads " . . . boni sumus idonei"; it has no bearing on the ET.—Trans.].

341. BSRK 254,3: "ad gloriam et laudem nominis *sui*" (Barth's italics), ET: Cochrane 172 (Schaff 451) [Barth correctly cites the Latin original, "to the glory and praise of his name"; the English versions replace "of his name" with "undeserved grace," which appears to be a condensation of the final clause in the Latin text into the penultimate clause: " . . . ad gloriam et laudem nominis sui; quippe qui sua munera nobis gratis impartitur, non meritis vendit."—Trans.].

342. BSRK 254,6–7: "causa in nobis," ET: Cochrane 172 (Schaff 452). [The Latin "in nobis" ("in us") emphasized by Barth is not rendered in any version of the ET.—Trans.]

343. BSRK 255,21, ET: Cochrane 174 (Schaff 455).

344. BSRK 254,43: "autoritatem assumunt ex voluntate Dei nobis relevata," ET: Cochrane 173 (Schaff 454).

345. BSRK 256,7–9, ET: Cochrane 175 (Schaff 458).

346. BSRK 256,16: "non hominum *profanorum* vocatur communio, sed *sanctorum*," ET: Cochrane 175 (Schaff 458); Barth's italics.

347. BSRK 246,20, ET: Cochrane 175 (Schaff 458).

348. E.g., the *Westminster Confession* (Art. 4), BSRK 566,19–34(35), ET: Schaff 625–26; *Irish Articles* (Art. 31), BSRK 530,4–8, ET: Schaff 531–32; the *Anglican Articles* (Art. 18), BSRK 512,5–9, ET: Schaff 499. [BSRK contains the Westminster and Irish texts in English.—Trans.]

349. See BSRK 257,3, ET: Cochrane 176 (Schaff 460).

350. BSRK 257,20–26, ET: Cochrane 176–77 (Schaff 461–62); Barth's italics. [The ETs render the Latin "ecclesiastical discipline uprightly ministered," which does not have the force of the Latin as Barth emphasizes it.—Trans.]

351. BSRK 257,28: "ibi est ecclesia Christi," ET: Cochrane 177 (Schaff 462).

352. This is what motivated Barth to make this confession the basis of his twenty Gifford Lectures at the University of Aberdeen in the spring of 1937 and the spring of 1938; see *Gotteserkenntnis und Gottesdienst nach reformatorischer Lehre* (Zollikon, 1938), ET: *The Knowledge of God and the Service of God* (London: Hodder, 1938). He discovered in the process that "the Scots Confession, as I discovered both unhappily and happily upon my arrival, was as unknown and inaccessible up to 1937 in Scotland as was the Helvetic Confession in Switzerland up to a short time ago!" (*Gotteserkenntnis und Gottesdienst*, 5–6. [Unfortunately, Barth's foreword, from which this citation is taken, was not included in the ET.—Trans.]). On the replacement of the Scots Confession by the Westminster Confession, see above, n. 310.

353. BSRK XLIV,34–38. James Ussher (1580–1656), a highly regarded scholar of his age, wrote the Irish Articles for a synod in Dublin, after the Calvinist clergy of Ireland had refused to acknowledge the English Thirty-Nine Articles. Since the Irish Articles received only a mixed reception, he assisted, as archbishop of Armagh from 1624 on, in their replacement by the Thirty-Nine Articles. He participated for

a while in the assembly that wrote the Westminster Confession, which was strongly dependent upon the Irish Articles, until he rejected it because of its antiroyalism. See R. Buddiensieg, "Ussher, Jakob," in RE, 3d ed., 20:360–68.

354. See BSRK 528,35; 529,30, ET: Schaff 530, 531. Bullinger (and under his influence also Jud) did not proceed from a double covenant, as Barth describes; rather, he presupposes God's eternal covenant with Abraham, which Christ in the New Testament fulfills and confirms. See G. Schrenk, *Gottesreich und Bund* (see p. 263, n. 54), 40–44.

355. Johannes Cocceius (Koch) (1603–1669), professor in Bremen, Franeker, and Leiden, important representative of federal theology, with which Barth became acquainted from late 1922 to early 1923 in the book by G. Schrenk cited in n. 354. See also Bw.Th. II, 129, 129, and 186, ET: *Revolutionary Theology in the Making*, 120, 123. [The ET does not contain the third passage cited.—Trans.]. Barth's extensive debate with the federal theology of Cocceius is found in KD IV/1, 57–70, ET: CD IV/1, 54–66. See also KD II/2, 123, ET: CD II/2, 114–15.

356. BSRK 530,14–17, ET: Schaff 532[33].

357. See above, pp. 116–117

358. See Inst. III,xi,10: "Coniunctio igitur illa capitis et membrorum, habitatio Christi in cordibus nostris, mystica denique unio a nobis in summo gradu statuitur . . . ," ET: Inst. III,xi,10,1:737: "Therefore, that joining together of Head and members, that indwelling of Christ in our hearts—in short, that mystical union—are accorded by us the highest degree of importance." See CR 74 (=CO 46), 953, ET: John Calvin, *The Deity of Christ and Other Sermons*, trans. Leroy Nixon (Grand Rapids: Wm. B. Eerdmans, 1950), 195; and CR 79 (=CO 51), 492, 781, ET: John Calvin, *Sermons on the Epistle to the Ephesians*, trans. Arthur Golding (Carlisle, Pa.: Banner of Truth Trust, 1973), 291–92, 615.

359. BSRK 511,35, ET: Schaff 534[39].

360. The manuscript has the wrong date, "June 15, 1923," on the correction; see above, n. 330.

361. BSRK 542–612 [in English], see Schaff 600–673, BOC 6.001–6.193; 612–43, ET: BOC 7.111–7.306; 643–52; see Schaff 676–704, BOC 7.001–7.110.

362. In the context of the conflict between Parliament and the crown, the Presbyterian Reformation, supported by the Puritans, turned against the Episcopal Anglican church; the decisive event was the Westminster Assembly that met for over 1000 days between 1643 and 1652. The three results of this work mentioned here were approved by Parliament in 1647–1648. The confession was also approved by the Scottish General Assembly on August 27, 1647 (BSRK XLVI,40–42) and was first declared to be the "public confession of the church of England" by the "rump parliament" in 1660.

363. What precedes the doctrine of predestination in the confession are only chapter 1 ("Of the Holy Scripture," BSRK 542,12–547,8, see Schaff 606), and chapter 2 ("Of God and of the Holy Trinity," BSRK 547,9–548,43, see Schaff 606–8).

364. See E. Troeltsch, *Die Soziallehren* (see above, n. 284), 615, ET: *The Social Teaching*, 581. He speaks of the importance of the "idea of predestination, the famous central dogma of Calvinism."

365. The correct citation is Inst. III,xxi–xxiv,2:920–987.

366. See BSRK 547,14–20: "essentia et perfectione infinitus, Spiritus purissimus," "incomprehensibilis," "liberrimus, maxime absolutus"; see Schaff 606.

367. See BSRK 548,10–11: "fons omnis entitatis," see Schaff 607.

368. BSRK 548,20; see Schaff 607.

369. BSRK 549,10–11; see Schaff 608.

370. BSRK 551,9.19; see Schaff 609.

370a. BSRK 552,38–41: "de efficaci sua vocatione certiores facti, *ad aeternae suae electionis assurgere possint certitudinem*," see Schaff 610.

371. See BSRK 542,14; see Schaff 600. [Barth's notation "c.1" refers to chapter one of the Confession,—Trans.].

372. BSRK 553,31–33: "non . . . sine quadam violandi possibilitate," see Schaff 611.

373. See BSRK 554,23.28; see Schaff 612.

374. See BSRK 555,8–13; see Schaff 613.

375. See above all, S.th. I. q.105 a.5 et 6, ET: St. Thomas Aquinas, *Summa Theologiae* (London & New York: Blackfriars/Eyre & Spottiswood/McGraw-Hill: 1975), 14:75–83. On the terminology "first cause/second cause," see S.th. I q.14 a.13 ad 1, ET: 4:45–51; q.19 a.6 ad 3, ET: 5:25; q.19 a.8 i.c, ET: 5:35–39; and passim.

376. F. Schleiermacher, *Über die Religion: Reden an die Gebildeten unter ihren Verächtern*. Published in its original form by R. Otto (Göttingen, 1899), 22–74 (Second address, "On the Essence of Religion"), ET: *On Religion: Addresses to Its Cultured Critics*, trans. Terrence N. Rice (Richmond: John Knox Press, 1968), 26–101.

377. See above, p. 123.

378. BSRK 558,17–18: "Tanta est inter deum et craeturem distantia . . . "; see Schaff 616.

379. BSRK 558,24; see Schaff 616.

379a. The long parenthetical excursus on the problem of a "temporal history of salvation," with two parenthetical phrases within it, appears to end here; the German edition does not include the concluding parenthesis.—Trans.

380. BSRK 558,41; see Schaff 616.

381. BSRK 560,3; see Schaff 616.

382. BSRK 560,15–18: "*Non sunt ergo duo foedera* gratiae, re atque natura discrepantia; sed *unum idemque*, licet *non uno modo dispensatum*"; see Schaff 618; Barth's italics.

383. BSRK 564,34–35; see Schaff 623.

384. See BSRK 564,37; see Schaff 624.

385. See BSRK 5–65,7–8; see Schaff 624.

386. On Luther; see, e.g, *De servo arbitrio*, WA 18,767–71, ET: LW 33:263–70; on Calvin, see Inst. III,ii,1,10,1:542,554.

387. See above, pp. 92, 117–118.

388. See Chr. E. Luthardt, *Kompendium der Dogmatik*, 4th ed. (Leipzig, 1873), 205.

389. See above, p. 84.

390. *Aus Schleiermachers Leben: In Briefen* (Berlin, 1858), 1:309: "Herrnhuter höherer Ordnung."

391. See W. Herrmann, *Christlich-protestantische Dogmatik*, in P. Hinneberg, ed., *Die Kultur der Gegenwart*, Section 4, Part 1, Second Half, (Berlin/Leipzig, 1906), 593–95.

392. J. Chr. K. (von) Hoffmann (1810–1877, raised to the nobility), professor of theology in Rostock and Erlangen.

393. J. Chr. K. von Hofmann, *Der Schriftbeweis: ein theologischer Versuch*, First Half (Nördlingen, 1852), 10: "Theology is only a free science when it takes that which makes a Christian into a Christian, his independent relationship to God, and in scientific self-awareness and self-articulation makes a theologian into a theologian,

when I the Christian am the most appropriate content of my science as the theologian."

394. Chapter 10, BSRK 565–66; see Schaff 624–26.

395. BSRK 565,41–42: " . . . in hoc negotio se habet omnino passive," see Schaff 625.

396. BSRK 565,28; see Schaff 624.

397. BSRK 567,7; see Schaff 626.

398. BSRK 568,23; see Schaff 627.

399. See BSRK 569,12; see Schaff 628.

400. The German manuscript has "instead of from" and was corrected by the German editor.

401. Pencil notation on the margin of the manuscript, a summary of the lecture of June 25 with which Barth began the lecture on June 26: "*Westminster Confession* peculiarities: independent interest in the order of nature, in historical development, in the human subject in Christianity and thus in religious psychology. Chapters 10–20 calling, justification, 4. *Sanctification.*"

402. BSRK 570,33–34; see Schaff 629.

403. BSRK 570,31–38; see Schaff 629–30(III).

404. BSRK 570,21–22; see Schaff 629; Barth's italics.

405. BSRK 565–70; see Schaff 624–29.

406. BSRK 571,3; see Schaff 630; Barth's italics.

407. BSRK 571,7; see Schaff 630.

408. BSRK 571,37–38: "pro diversis ejus gradibus debilior [. . .] aut fortior," see Schaff 631.

409. See BSRK 572,2–3; see Schaff 631.

410. See BSRK 571,1; see Schaff 630.

411. See BSRK 572,11–12; see Schaff 631.

412. BSRK 575,5–8: *"habitus gratiae infusus,"* "actualis [. . .] influentia [. . .] Spiritus sancti"; see Schaff 634; Barth's italics. [The ET translates "infusus" with "received," which is probably why Barth uses the Latin to make his theological concern even more emphatically clear.—Trans.].

413. See above, pp. 124–5.

414. See HpB, 113, ET: H. Heppe, *Reformed Dogmatics: Set Out and Illustrated from the Sources*, ed. E. Bizer, trans. G. T. Thomson (London: George Allen & Unwin, 1950), 138–39.

415. See BSRK 577,7; see Schaff 636.

416. See BSRK 577,16; see Schaff 636.

417. BSRK 578,9–10: "quadantenus et quoad gradus nonnullos"; see Schaff 636. [Barth translates the Latin phrase into German to make his critique clear, and we have translated his German rather than quote from the English version; that version, "come to be deprived *of some measure* of their graces and comforts," weakens the emphasis of the Latin notably; see Schaff 636.—Trans.].

418. BSRK 579,26; see Schaff 638.

419. BSRK 579,30; see Schaff 638.

420. See BSRK 580,14; see Schaff 639.

421. BSRK 587,11–590,35; see Schaff 646–49.

422. BSRK 582,40–583,1; see Schaff 641. [Barth was apparently impressed by the Latin "vehementer" which is rather pallidly rendered as "great" in the English version.—Trans.].

423. BSRK 585,30–31: "Deus solus Dominus est conscientiae"; see Schaff 644.

424. BSRK 586,12–15; see Schaff 644; the German is Barth's rendering of the Latin original.

425. See BSRK 586,32; 587,15–16; see Schaff 645–46.

426. See BSRK 589,39–590,1; see Schaff 648.

427. See BSRK 589,39–590,1: "praeceptum morale positivum ac perpetuum"; see Schaff 648.

428. BSRK 590,15–17: "perpetuo ad finem mundi . . . Sabbatum Christianum," see Schaff 649.

429. See above, p. 101, at n. 128.

430. According to A. Lang, *Puritanismus und Pietismus: Studien zu ihrer Entwicklung von M. Butzer bis zum Methodismus* (Neukirchen, 1942), 25–26, this concern was actually introduced by Bucer into Puritan Presbyterianism.

431. See above, pp. 101–2.

432. See BSRK 598,16–17: "ordo ministrorum, oracula, instituta Dei"; see Schaff 658. [Where the Latin, which Barth cites, has "order of ministries" ("ordo ministrorum"), the English version has "ministries."—Trans.]

433. See BSRK 598,37–599,18; see Schaff 658–59 [5–6].

433a. Barth's reference to "society" is based on the Latin of the confession, whose term "societas" is rendered as "fellowship" in the ET; Barth's use of "Verein" (= "association"), for which there is no Latin basis, carries with it the sense of the distinctive role and social function of such voluntary associations in German and Swiss life.—Trans.

434. See BSRK 660,21; see Schaff 660.

435. BSRK 600,33–37; see Schaff 660; on the Anglican Articles, see BSRK 520,35–39, ET: Schaff 513[XXXVIII]; and above, n. 328.

436. BSRK 612–43; 643–652; ET: BOC 7.001–7.110, 7.111–7.306; see Schaff 676–704.

437. See BSRK 612,30–33, BOC 7.112.

438. The two parts of the catechism arise out of the statement, "The Scriptures principally teach, what man is to believe concerning God, and what duty God requires of man" ("Duo imprimis sunt quae Scripturae docent, quod homo de Deo credere debeat, quidque officii ab homine exigat") (BSRK 613,10–11, ET: BOC 7.115; see 624,10–12, ET: BOC 7.200/7.201; 643,17–18, ET: BOC 7.003; and also Schaff 676 [Q. 3]).

439. BSRK 619,44, ET: BOC 7.227.

440. Question 74, BSRK 621,20–26, ET: BOC 7.184.

441. Question 82, BSRK 622,35–39, ET: BOC 7.192.

442. Question 117, BSRK 629,12–21, ET: BOC 7.227.

443. This was the Roman Catholic view at that time.

444. CR 50 (=CO 22). The catechism was not incorporated until 1880, instead of in CR 33 (=CO 5) in 1866. See *Theology of Calvin* 271.

445. Explanations of this catechism since the sixteenth century are cited by M. Lauterburg in the article "Katechismus, Heidelberger oder Pfälzer," in RE, 3d ed., 10:165,17–29, ET: S/H 5:204–6.

446. See G. Finsler, *Kirchliche Statistik der reformierten Schweiz* (Zurich, 1854), 279, 352, 435, 681.

447. In 1816, the Hessian and Heidelberg Catechisms were repressed in the Reformed congregations of the district of Bovenden [in today's Lower Saxony —Trans.] and replaced with the Hannoverian Lutheran Provincial Catechism. There are also reports from the Reformed congregations in Stade from the middle of the nineteenth century that the Heidelberg Catechism had been almost completely

replaced by the Lutheran Provincial Catechism. See G. Nordholt, *Die Entstehung der "Evangelisch-Reformierten Kirche der Provinz Hannover,"* in *Die Evangelisch-reformierte Kirche in Nordwestdeutschland: Beiträge zu ihrer Geschichte und Gegenwart,* ed. E. Lomberg *et al.* (Weener, 1982), 96, 108. In the Reformed congregation of Ringstedt, Luther's Shorter Catechism was used instead of the Heidelberg Catechism until 1695 (see J. Göhler, *Herzogtum Bremen und Amt Bederkesa,* in Lomberg, *op. cit.,* 211). In the Palatinate, the Heidelberg Catechism was replaced with the Luther in 1579, as the result of a royal order (see E. Sehling, ed., *Die evangelischen Kirchenordnungen des XVI. Jahrhunderts* [Tübingen, 1969], 14:63).

3. The Controversy with Lutheranism

1. See, e.g., the account in E. Stähelin, *Johannes Calvin* (see p. 236, n. 127), 2:189–205.

2. The Cabinet Order of the Prussian king Friedrich Wilhelm III on September 27, 1817, established the Union of the Evangelical Churches, whose significance was explained in the Cabinet Order of February 2, 1834, with these words: "The Union neither intends nor means the dissolution of the confessions of faith heretofore. By entering into this Union, the spirit of moderation and mildness is expressed which no longer allows the differences of particular doctrinal points of the other confession to be a reason to refuse external ecclesial fellowship." Cited according to A. Hauck, "Union, kirchliche" in RE, 3d ed., 20:258,57–259,3, ET: S/H 12:79–81 (abridged ET). See J. Beckmann, "Ev. Kirche der Union (EKU)," in RGG, 3d ed., 6:1138; A. Adam, "Union im Protestantismus," in RGG, 3d ed., 6:1141–46.

3. See, e.g, F. Schleiermacher, *Der christliche Glaube nach den Grundsätzen der evangelischen Kirche im Zusammenhange dargestellt,* 3d ed. §24, supplement (Berlin, 1835), 1:138, ET: F. Schleiermacher, *The Christian Faith,* trans. H. R. Mackintosh and J. S. Stewart (Edinburgh: T. & T. Clark, 1928–1956), 107. Schleiermacher "starts from the assumption that the separation of the two lacked sufficient grounds, inasmuch as the differences in doctrine are in no sense traceable to a difference in the religious affections themselves, and the two do not diverge from each other, either in morals and moral theory or in constitution, in any way which at all corresponds to those differences of doctrines."

4. See Karl Barth, *Reformierte Lehre, ihr Wesen und ihre Aufgabe* (1923) [Lecture at the 19th General Assembly of the Reformed Federation, September 16–19, 1923], in V.u.kl.A. 1922–1925, 210–26.

5. The sources for the documents to be named here will be provided below when they are discussed in detail.

6. Manuscript: "toward which," changed by editor.

7. M. Goebel, *Die religiöse Eigenthümlichkeiten der lutherischen und reformierten Kirche: Versuch einer geschichtlichen Vergleichung,* (Bonn, 1837; 2d ed., Elberfeld, 1907), 84, characterizes the difference between Lutheran and Reformed distinctiveness in this fashion, "that the Lutherans comprehend Christianity as gospel and faith in Christ as that which brings salvation and blessings, whereas the Reformed [understand it] as the doctrine of Christ that one *must follow* to be saved, thus faith in Christ as God's commandment, which one must follow and obey."

8. For A. Schweizer, *Die christliche Glaubenslehre nach protestantischen Grundsätzen* (Leipzig, 1863), 1:8, the difference is to be seen chiefly in the fact "that we see Lutheran [Protestantism] structuring itself as primarily anti-Jewish and Reformed as anti-pagan."

9. M. Schneckenburger, *Vergleichende Darstellung des lutherischen und reformirten Lehrbegriffs*, ed. posthumously by E. Güder (Stuttgart, 1855), 280, sees the Reformed and Lutheran distinctiveness based on the fact "that the differences of the subjective emotional states are the formative principle for the divergent articulation of the objective doctrines, and as such a formative principle has unconsciously influenced both the modification of the traditional doctrinal material and also the exposition of Scripture, with the help of which the controversial doctrines solidified their positions against each other."

10. According to Troeltsch, *Die Soziallehren* [see lecture 3.2, n. 284], 605, ET: *Social Teaching*, 577, the difference between Calvinism and Lutheranism is essentially "in the active character of Calvinism, in its power for forming churches, in its international contacts, and its conscious impulse towards expansion, and, most of all, in its capacity to penetrate the political and economic movements of Western nations with its religious idea, a capacity which Lutheranism lacked from the very beginning."

11. According to Max Weber, *Die protestantische Ethik und der Geist des Kapitalismus*, 1904/05, in *Gesammelte Aufsätze zur Religionssoziologie*, 2d ed. (Tübingen, 1922; 6th ed., 1972), 1:17–206, ET: *The Protestant Ethic and the Spirit of Capitalism*, trans. T. Parsons (London: G. Allen & Unwin, 1930), the spirit of Calvinism expresses itself especially in the emergence of capitalism.

12. Joachim Westphal (1510/11–1574), pastor in Hamburg who defended Lutheran doctrine aggressively against Calvinist and Crypto-Calvinist influences.

13. J. Calvin, *Defensio sanae et orthodoxae doctrinae de sacramentis eorumque natura, vi fine, usu, et fructu* (1555), OS II, 259–87, ET: "Mutual Consent in Regard to the Sacraments" [Consensus Tigurinus], *Tracts and Treatises II*, 199–244; Calvin, *Secunda defensio piae et orthodoxae de sacramentis fidei adversus Ioachimi Westphali calumnias* (1556), CR 38 (=CO 9), 41–120, ET: "Second Defense of the Faith concerning the Sacraments in Answer to Joachim Westphal," *Tracts and Treatises II*, 245–345; *Ultima admonitio Ioannis Calvini ad Ioachimum Westphalium* (1557), CR 38 (=CO 9), 137–252, ET: "Last Admonition to Joachim Westphal," *Tracts and Treatises II*, 345–494.

14. W. Köhler, *Zwingli und Luther: Ihr Streit über das Abendmahl nach seinen politischen und religiösen Beziehungen*, vol. 1 (Leipzig, 1924); vol. 2 (Gütersloh, 1953) (=Quellen und Forschungen zur Reformationsgeschichte, vol. 6–7).

15. Zwingli assumed that illuminated pagans could be saved; see *Christianae fidei a Huldrico Zwinglio praedicate brevis et clare expositio* (1531), CR 91 (=Z 4), 65, ET: "A Short and Clear Exposition of the Christian Faith Preached by Huldreich Zwingli . . . ," in Hinke 2:271–72. See on this K. Barth, Th.C. 134–35, ET: *Theology of Calvin* 100–101; R. Pfister, *Die Seligkeit erwählter Heiden bei Zwingli: eine Untersuchung zu seiner Theologie* (Zurich, 1952).

16. See M. Luther, WA.DB, 6,10,33–34, ET: *Works of Martin Luther* (Philadelphia: Muhlenberg Press, 1932), 444.

17. BSRK 153,19–21; 155,19–24.

18. BSRK 778,18–780,4; 838,40–839,5.

19. BSRK 780,780,5–781,3.

20. BSRK 781,22–782,36.

21. BSRK 783,8–784,4.

22. BSRK 785,40–786,3.

23. BRSK, 729,37–730,12; 786,4–20.

24. BSRK 730,13–30; 786,21–787,22.

25. BSRK 788,19–36.

26. BSRK 790,44.

27. J. Arndt, *Vier Bücher vom wahren Christentum, das ist von heilsamer Buße, herz-licher Reue und Leid über die Sünde, und wahrem Glauben, auch heiligen Leben und Wandel der rechten wahren Christen nebst dessen Paradis-Gärtlein* (Berlin, 1847). The book first appeared in 1610 and has been reissued in countless editions and translated into many languages; later two more sections were added to it.

28. Johann Arndt (1555–1621). Because Arndt would not submit to the ordinance prohibiting exorcism and pictures in the church, issued by Duke Johann George von Anhalt, and thus resisted the Duke's tendency toward the Reformed movement, he had to give up his pastorate in Badeborn in 1590, after serving there since 1583.

29. See above, p. 285, n. 15.

30. BSRK 198,41–42: "Scimus enim Deum aliquot habuisse in mundo amicos, extra Israelis rempublicam," ET: Schaff 878: "For we know that God had some friends in the world that were not of the commonwealth of Israel."

31. See, e.g., Inst. II,vi,1: "Certe post lapsum primi hominis nulla ad salutem valuit Dei cognitio absque mediatore. . . . Quo foedior est eorum socordia, qui coelum pro-fanis et incredulis quibuslibet patefaciunt, absque eius gratia quem scriptura passim docet unicam esse ianuam qua in salutem ingredimur," ET: Inst. II,vi,1,1:341–42: "Surely, after the fall of the first man no knowledge of God apart from the Mediator has had power unto salvation. . . . Thus all the more vile is the stupidity of those persons who open heaven to all the impious and unbelieving without the grace of him whom Scripture commonly teaches to be the only door whereby we enter into salvation." The *Westminster Confession* also rejects this theological proposal; see BSRK 566,19–34, ET: Schaff 625. See also on this Chr. Dogm. 335–36.

32. See the "religious Apriori," a basic concept in the religious philosophy of E. Troeltsch; see chiefly his *Psychologie und Erkenntnistheorie in der Religionswissenschaft* (Tübingen, 1905), esp. 45ff.; also by him, *Zur Frage des religiösen Apriori,* in *Zur religiösen Lage, Religionsphilosophie und Ethik,* Gesammelte Schriften 3 (Tübingen, 1913), 754–68.

33. In his correspondence with Adolf von Harnack in the same year, 1932, John 6:44 forms Barth's 6th thesis; see K. Barth, *Theologische Fragen und Antworten* Gesam-melte Vorträge 3 (Zurich-Zollikon, 1957; 2d ed., Zurich, 1986), 11.

33a. The German terms "mittelbar" and "unmittelbar" translate as "mediate" and "immediate," where the German emphasis is upon the "medium," that which "mediates." Although this root idea is still present in the English terms, it is largely lost in current usage. To make Barth's point, we will translate the German terms with "mediated"/"mediatedness" and "unmediated/unmediatedness."—Trans.

34. See E. Troeltsch, *Moderne Geschichtsphilosophie,* in his *Zur religiösen Lage,* 679. In giving up the "establishment of an idealist view of life," the important thing is "to recognize the distinctiveness of the historical world over against nature" and to "relate [this] to an ideal system of values."

35. The "filioque" clause was first officially inserted into the so-called Nicaeno-Constantinopolitan Creed in 589 C.E. at the Council of Toledo, but it was only acknowledged in the Western churches. See DS 150, ET: Denzinger 35–36[86].

36. See above, pp. 80–81.

37. See Troeltsch, *Protestantisches Christentum* (see lecture 1, n. 128), 518–19. For Calvin's "religious sensibility," God is "not a love that saves all creatures but rather the free power of the will who can create a world full of suffering and sin as the demonstration of his power, and whose glory is then lauded by both the torments of the judged and damned and by the salvation of the elect." By contrast, "for

Luther the assurance of salvation is experienced and enjoyed in mood and feeling and God is primarily . . . love."

38. B. J. Gottschick, e.g., draws such a picture in *Die Heilsgewißheit des evangelischen Christen, im Anschluß an Luther dargestellt*, in Zeitschrift für Theologie und Kirche, vol. 13 (1903), 349–435.

39. See the Formula of Concord, Solid Declaration, XI, BSLK 1063–91, De aeterna praedestinatione et electione Dei, esp. 1064 and 1086, ET: K/W 640–56.

40. See above, pp. 98–99.

41. BSLK 284,44–45, ET: K/W 213[149]: "horrible terrors of the conscience."

42. See, e.g., A. Ritschl, *Geschichte des Pietismus* (Bonn, 1880), 1:76; Troeltsch, *Die Soziallehren* (see p. 273, n. 284), ET: *Social Teaching*, 2:592.

43. See Th.C. 131, n. 15, ET: *Theology of Calvin* 97, n. 12.

44. See G. Büchmann, *Geflügelte Worte: Der Zitatenschatz des deutschen Volkes*, 37th ed. (Frankfurt/Berlin, 1986), 302.

45. See A. Harnack, *Dogmengeschichte*, 8th ed. (Tübingen, 1991), 469, ET: *Outlines of the History of Dogma*, trans. E. K. Mitchell (New York: Funk & Wagnalls, 1893; reprint, Boston: Beacon Hill, 1957), 560: Speaking of Luther in the Communion controversies, "In that he however poured the new wine into the old wineskins, there arose a speculation regarding the ubiquity of the body of Christ which ranged over the loftiest heights of scholastic inconsistency."

46. See the conclusion of Barth's lecture of October 1922: *Das Wort Gottes als Aufgabe der Theologie*, in V.u.kl.A. 1922–1925, 175: "Can and should theology ever move beyond *prolegomena* to Christology? It could well be that with the prolegomena *everything* has been said."

47. Square brackets placed by Barth. [The following section summarizes the lecture to this point and thus repeats what has been said.—Trans.]

48. See M. Luther, e.g, *Disputatio Heidelbergae habita* (1518), in WA 1,362, ET: LW 31:52–53: " . . . God preached and God hidden"; in *De servo arbitrio* (1525), Luther distinguishes between 'God proclaimed and hidden' [Deus praedicatus et absconditus], WA 18,685, ET: LW 33:140.

49. See Loofs' reference on 761–62, that Luther had asserted "with growing decisiveness that the interest of a heart seeking the assurance of salvation in predestination would not be satisfied by reflections on the hidden will of God."

50. See the detailed typologization in Troeltsch, *Die Soziallehren*, 512–794, ET: Troeltsch, *Social Teaching*, 515–691.

51. This is perhaps an allusion to Luther's statement during the Marburg Colloquy on the Lord's Supper, October 1529, directed to Bucer and including Zwingli: "Ye have another spirit than we do," see Locher, *Die Zwinglische Reformation* (see lecture 1, n. 97), 325.

52. Next to this clause there is a double curving line on the margin of the manuscript, which was an indication of Barth's self-criticism of the thoughts expressed here.

53. For a survey of their documents regarding the Lord's Supper controversies, see Locher, *Die Zwinglische Reformation*, 310–18.

54. See the Formula of Concord, Solid Declaration, VII, BSLK 991,23–997,33, esp. 996,1–7: "Ex his manifestum est, quam inique virulentis sarcasmis Sacramentarii Domino nostro Iesu Christo et divo Paulo totique ecclesiae insultent, qui oralem et indignorum manducationem vocant duos pilos caudae equinae et commentum, cuius vel ipsum Satanam pudeat," ET: K/W 603–6[60–72], esp. 605[67]: "From such accounts it is clear how improperly and poisonously the sacramentarian enthusiasts

ridicule the Lord Christ, St. Paul, and the whole church by calling this oral partaking and the partaking of the unworthy 'two hairs of a horse's tail and an invention of which even Satan himself would be ashamed.'" [In K/W these passages are left in Latin in the main text and translated in the footnote.—Trans.].

55. See BSLK 1043,24–1044,3 and 1048,6–19; ET: K/W 631[78–79] and 633–34[92].

56. See below, n. 60.

57. BSRK 153–59. The document was written by H. Bullinger but published as the confession of the Zurich "servants of the churches."

58. The confession is the response to Luther's *Kurzes Bekenntnis vom heiligen Sakrament* (1544), WA 54,119–67, ET: "Short Confession concerning the Holy Sacrament," LW 38:281–319.

59. See BSLK 1019,26, ET: K/W 617[6]; BSRK 155,43–44.

60. BSRK 156,1–13: " . . . that the very body of Christ that was born of the virgin, then nailed to the cross and died thereon, then removed from it and lain in the grave, that this same and no other body . . . rose up from the dead and ascended into heaven, where he now sits at the right hand of God. And that this body of Christ, in essence and form, remained a true human body unchanged, although transfigured, namely that the humanity was not changed into the deity. . . . The characteristics of this true and even transfigured body . . . were not a Spirit, at one place only and not at one time everywhere."

61. See Troeltsch, *Protestantisches Christentum*, 572: "In Lutheranism . . . the proposition stands, 'the finite is capable of the infinite' [finitum capax infiniti]. Calvinism opposes this with its severe, abrupt, and pure voluntarism and spiritualism and constructs its imposing system out of it."

62. BSRK 154,10–13.

63. Zwingli, S II/2, 76: "Weer, weer, Luther weer, Marcion will dir in'n garten."

64. See BSRK 688,1, ET: Schaff 313. [The German note refers to the Scripture references appended in BSRK to each question in the Heidelberg Catechism; here, Heb. 11:1 is cited in support of Question 21, "What is true faith?"—Trans.].

65. Originally this was the priest's liturgical invitation at the prayer of thanksgiving before the Roman mass, to which the congregation responded, "We lift them to the Lord" ["Habemus ad Dominum"], according to *Das Volksmeßbuch für alle Tage des Jahres*, 4th ed., ed. U. Bomm (Einsiedeln/Köln, 1947), 13.

66. BSRK 158,23–24.

67. Barth perceives that the Swiss pastors are largely influenced by Ritschl and his school. See K. Barth, *Die kirchlichen Zustände in der Schweiz*, in V.u.kl.A 1922–1925, 35–36.

68. See BSRK 156,48.

69. BSRK 159,13–15.

70. BSRK 158,12.

71. BSRK 154,28.

72. BSRK 157,18–19.

73. (=CR 37); OS I, 433–36, ET: Reid, 168–69. See Th.C. 460–65, ET: *Theology of Calvin* 337–41. On the historical background of the eucharistic negotiations at that time, see E. Bizer, *Studien zur Geschichte des Abendmahlstreits* (see p. 262, n. 43).

74. OS I, 435: "ipsis . . . nos educari oportere," ET: Reid 168.

75. OS I, 435: "localem corporis sui praesentiam nobis abstulit," ET: Reid 168.

76. See OS I, 435: "peregrinantes in hac mortalitate," ET: Reid 168.

77. See OS I, 435: "non in eodem loco cum ipso includimur aut continemur," ET: Reid 168.

78. OS I, 435: "locorum spatiis," ET: Reid 168.

79. See OS I, 435: "vinculum participationis," ET: Reid 168.

80. See K. Barth, Th.C. 461–62, ET: *Theology of Calvin* 266.

81. See Seeberg 607–8, ET: "But when it is remembered that, in contrast with Zwingli's purely subjective commemorative view, Calvin maintains both a special 'presence of the living Christ' . . . and the religious influences exerted by it, quite in the spirit of Luther, the conclusion may, nevertheless, be reached . . . that in his religious conception of the sacrament Calvin stands nearer to Luther than to Zwingli," Seeberg/Hay, 2:414.

82. See CR 39 (=CO 11), 438. Calvin describes Zwingli's doctrine of the Lord's Supper as "profane" [meaning "unspiritual," "mundane" or "worldly"—Trans.]. See F. Blanke, *Calvin's Urteil über Zwingli*, in Zwingliana XI (1959): 66.

83. See Bizer, *Studien zur Geschichte des Abendmahlstreits*, 275–99.

84. See A. Drews, *Die Christusmythe*, 4th ed. (Jena, 1910), 234: "To trace the Christian doctrine of redemption to its true core" means "to place the idea of divine humanity in the center of one's religious world view."

85. See OS I, 435, ET: Reid 168.

86. See above, p. 170 at note 79.

87. See Inst. IV,xvii,36,2:1412–13; *La Forme des Prieres et Chantz ecclesiastiques* (1542), OS II,39–50, esp. 48,24–32, ET: "The Form of Church Prayers and Hymns . . . ," in Bard Thompson, *Liturgies of the Western Church* (Philadelphia: Fortress Press, 1980), 197–210, esp. 207.

88. See OS I,435: "communio, quam cum Christo *fideles* habent," ET: Reid 168. [Barth's italics stress the word "fideles" (= "believers") that Reid translates with "we."—Trans.]

88a. The ET appears to mistranslate Calvin's text and thus to miss its salient emphasis. The correct translation of the first two sentences, which are the theme of Barth's discussion here, should read: "We confess that the spiritual life which Christ bestows upon us does not *solely* rest on the fact that he vivifies us with his Spirit, but *even more* that the Spirit in its power makes us participants in his vivifying body, by which we are fed on eternal life." The italicized terms are omitted in the ET, but they constitute the Reformed "but" to which Barth alludes below.

89. OS I, 435: "Hanc autem carnis et sanguinis sui communionem Christus sub panis et vini symbolis in sacrosancta sua coena offert, et exhibit omnibus qui eam rite celebrant iuxta legitimum eius institutum," ET: Reid 168: "This communion of his own body and blood Christ offers in his blessed Supper under the symbols of bread and wine, presenting them to all who rightly celebrate it according to his own proper institution."

90. See below, pp. 173–79.

91. See note 89.

92. See Th.C. 357–63, ET: *Theology of Calvin* 265–69.

93. BSRK 159–63, ET: *Tracts and Treatises II*, 212–20.

94. See on this Stähelin, *Johannes Calvin* (see p. 236, n. 127), 2:112–24; Bizer, *Studien zur Geschichte des Abendmahlstreits*, 243–70.

95. When Bucer's letter of January 19, 1537, to Luther became known to the Swiss, in which he attempted to mediate between them and Wittenberg in the question of

the Lord's Supper, they felt that the wool had been pulled over their eyes, resulting in a strong Swiss resentment of Bucer; see Bizer, *Studien zur Geschichte des Abendmahlstreits*, 180–85, 201. See also Calvin's letter to Bucer of December 12, 1538, containing his reaction to the same matter, in R. Schwarz, ed., *Johannes Calvins Lebenswerk in seinen Briefen*, 2d ed. (Neukirchen, 1961) 58–64.

96. See on this and on what follows, C. H. Hundeshagen, *Konflikte des Zwinglianismus, Luthertum und Calvinismus in der Berner Landeskirche 1532–1588* (Bern, 1842).

97. On Viret and Farel, see p. 249, n. 30.

98. In particular, the young Zwingli strengthened the anti-French front because of his rejection of mercenary military service; see O. Farner, *Der Reformator Huldrych Zwingli, Sein Leben und Schaffen* (1917) (Zurich, 1949), 25.

99. See above, pp. 170–71.

100. See H. Bullinger, *Ioannis Calvini Propositiones de Sacramentis Annotationes breves* (1548), CR 35 (=CO 7), 694.

101. See J. Calvin, *Calvini Responsio ad Annotationes Bullingeri* (1549), CR 35 (=CO 7), 701–8.

102. See H. Bullinger, *Annotata ad Calvini Animadversiones* (1549), CR 35 (=CO 7), 714.

103. BSRK 163,3–8, ET: *Tracts and Treatises II*, 219[23].

104. See Stähelin, *Johannes Calvin*, 2:124.

105. *Confessio Gebennensis Ecclesiae Ministrorum de Sacramentis Bernensium Synodo oblata mense Martio 1549*, CR 35 (=CO 7), 717–22.

106. BSRK 162,38–39: "Christus, quatenus homo est," "mente et fidei intelligentia," ET: *Tracts and Treatises II*, 2:218–19[21].

107. BSRK 162,40: "perversa et impia superstitio," ET: *Tracts and Treatises II*, 219[21].

107a. BSRK 163,18: "supra coelus locus non est," ET: *Tracts and Treatises II*, 220[25].

108. See BSRK 163,18–19, ET: *Tracts and Treatises II*, 220[25].

109. See H. Zwingli, *Von der Taufe, von der Wiedertaufe und von der Kindertaufe* (1525), CR 91 (=Z 4), 218: "'Sacramentum' . . . is an exercise . . . in which whoever is marked by baptism wants to hear what God says to him, to learn his ordinances and live according to them. Whoever then in the remembrance or in the Lord's Supper thanks God together with the congregation, that one sets out to rejoice with all his heart at the death of Christ and to give thanks for it."

110. BSRK 160, 30–31: "notae . . . ac tesserae christianae professionis et societatis sive fraternitatis," ET: *Tracts and Treatises II*, 214[7].

111. BSRK 160,36: "quasi in rem," ET: *Tracts and Treatises II*, 2:214[7].

112. Calvin, Inst. IV,xiv,13: "Est autem hoc primum, ut fidei nostrae apud Deum serviant [scil. Sacramenta]: posterius, ut confessionem nostram apud homines testentur," ET: Inst. IV,xiv,13,2:1288–89: "Now, the first point is that the sacraments should serve our faith before God; after this, that they should attest our confession before men."

113. See Art. III of the Draft, CR 35 (=CO 7), 117: "Hic ergo sacramentorum finis est: primum ut Christo potiamur tanquam bonorum omnium fonte; deinde, ut beneficio mortis eius reconciliemur Deo, spiritu eius renovemur in vitae sanctitatem, iustitiam denique et salutem consequamur," ET: "For this is the goal of the sacraments: firstly, that we grasp Christ as the fountain of all good; then, that we are reconciled with God through the benefaction of his death, that we are renewed by his Spirit in the holiness of life, and finally that we attain to righteousness and salvation."

114. See BSRK 161,41: "ne minima portio salutis," ET: *Tracts and Treatises II*, 217[15].

115. See CR 35 (=CO 7), 723–24. Johannes Haller (1523–1575) worked in the spirit of H. Bullinger, whose assistant he was for a time, as a reconciliatory preacher in "the divided Bernese church, weakened by partisan struggles between the Zwinglian and Lutheran adherents and later between the Zwinglians and the Calvinists" (W. Hadorn, "Musculus, Wolfgang," in RE, 3d ed., 13:583,49–51). In this sense he welcomed the Consensus Tigurinus. See E. Bähler, "Johannes Haller," in *Berner Taschenbuch 1923* (Bern, 1923) 1–52.

116. BSRK 162,45–47: "Nam extra controversiam ponimus, figurate accipienda esse, ut esse panis et vinum dicantur id quod significant," ET: *Tracts and Treatises II*, 219[22]: "For we hold it out of controversy that they are to be taken figuratively— the bread and wine receiving the name of that which they signify."

116a. BSRK 163,26–27, ET: *Tracts and Treatises II*, 220[26].

117. OS I, 503–30: "Petit Traicté de la Saincte Cène," ET: *Tracts and Treatises II*, 164–98.

118. CR 77 (=CO 49), 471–96, ET: John Calvin, *The First Epistle of Paul the Apostle to the Corinthians*, trans. J. W. Fraser (Edinburgh and London: Oliver & Boyd, 1960), 226–57.

119. OS I, 435, ET: Reid 168–69.

120. See above, nn. 12–13.

121. Barth differs here from Stähelin, *Johannes Calvin* 2:189, who sees the cause of the "failure" of Calvin's "idea of unity" in the "resistance of a harsh Lutheranism." Stähelin cites for this A. Ebrard (190), H. Heppe (191), Merle d'Aubigné (195), G. Planck (212), L. Ranke (221), K. Fr. A. Kahnis (234).

122. See C. Pestalozzi, *Heinrich Bullinger* (see p. 235, n. 102, 392–97).

123. See, e.g., Loofs 892.

124. Augusti 254–55, 635–36. The negotiations between the theologians of the Lutheran and Reformed churches as well as the Moravian Brethren took place April 9–15, 1570, in Sendomir (Sandomierz an der Weichsel), at the urging of the Reformed nobility who were in the majority; the intent was to strengthen the Evangelical church of Poland over against the Roman church. It resulted in the declaration of Communion fellowship among the participating churches.

125. Augusti 256–63; CR 28,415–24. The citation refers to the chapter on "The Lord's Supper" ["De coena Domini"] in the "Confession of the Doctrines of the Saxon Churches" ["Confessio Doctrinae Saxonicarum Ecclesiarum"], written by Melanchthon as a submission to the second session of the Council of Trent, which opened on May 1, 1551.

126. Augusti 255: " . . . illa nuda et vacua esse asserimus, sed simul reipsa *credentibus* exhibere et praestare *fide*, quod significant. Denique ut expressius clariusque loquamur, convenimus, ut credamus et confiteamur, *substantialem praesentiam Christi*, non significari duntaxat, sed vere in coena vescentibus repraesentari, distribui, et exhiberi, symbolis adjectis ipsi rei, minime nudis, secundum Sacramentorum naturam," ET: " . . . we add that they are neither nude nor empty but that *in faith* they offer and give simultaneously in truth *to the believers* what they signify. Finally we say expressly and clearly that we agree that we believe and confess that the *substantial presence of Christ* is not only signified but truly represented, distributed, and offered to those who partake of this meal, in that symbols are added to the matter itself which are by no means naked, corresponding to the nature of the sacrament."

127. Augusti 258, CR 28,418: "... et extra usum institutum res ipsas non habere rationem sacramenti, sed in usu instituto in hac communione vere et substantialiter adesse Christum, et vere exhiberi sumentibus corpus et sanguinem Christi ... ," ET: "... and the instituted outward use does not of itself have the meaning of the Sacraments but rather in the instituted use Christ is truly and substantially present in this community, and the body and blood of Christ are truly offered to whose who participate."

128. Count Johann the Older of Nassau-Dillenburg and Siegen promoted the Reformed movement during his regency (1560–1606), and thus he accepted the Melanchthon adherents ("Crypto-Calvinists") who were driven out of Saxony. Among these was the member of the Wittenberg theological faculty, Chr. Pezel (1539–1604), who as the school inspector of Siegen wrote this confession, and then ministered as preacher in Herborn and Dillenburg. In 1580 he was called to Bremen, where as pastor of the Church of Our Lady and as professor of theology he led the transition of the Bremen church from Philippism to the Reformed side. Nassau-Dillenburg became definitively Reformed in 1581 when both the church order and the catechism of the Palatinate were officially adopted.

129. BSRK 722,35–37.

130. See BSRK 813,35–39 ("On the Holy Table of Our Lord," Staffort Book of 1599), 820,45–821,3 ("On the Holy Supper of Our Lord," Confession of the Kassel General Synod of 1607), 832,10–17 ("On the Holy Supper of Our Lord," Hessian Catechism of 1607), 839,11–17 (Confession of Sigismund of 1614).

131. BSRK 722,30; 723,41–48; 724,3.33–41; 725,7–14; 726,26–28; 727,38–41; 728,24–27, and passim.

132. BSRK LIII,27–36.

133. BSRK LIV,23–25. See above, n. 129. On Pezel, see J. Moltmann, *Christoph Pezel (1539–1604) und der Calvinismus in Bremen* (Hospitium Ecclesiae), Forschungen zur bremischen Kirchengeschichte 2 (Bremen, 1958).

134. BSRK 741,19–20: "... und was solchem Artickel anhengig ist"; Barth's italics.

135. BSRK 742,41–41.

136. BSRK 743,36.

137. See BSRK 746,14–17; the exposition is then in BSRK 746,18–748,29.

138. BSRK 746,9–11.

139. BSRK 748,27–28: "Quis infernos haec evomuit?"

140. The expression cannot be located in any of the literature that Barth otherwise used in this lecture. What is thematically meant can be seen, for example, in Aegidius Hunnius, *Libelli IIII, De persona Christi, eiusque ad dextram Dei sedentis divina majestate* (Wittenberg, 1607), 436: "Dextra Dei nusquam in universa Scriptura significat locum aliquem creatum in supremo coelo, quemadmodum nonnulli inter Calvinianos ausi fuereunt comminisci," ET: "The right hand of God is never described in the entire Scripture as some created place in the highest heavens, as not a few Calvinists are so audacious as to posit."

141. The Bremen Consensus documents such an interpretation of the statements about the ascension of Christ in the Formula of Concord (BSLK 1025,33–1026,13, ET: K/W 621[28–29]) by referring to a series of publications then in circulation (BSRK 749,16–20).

142. BSRK 749,14–16.

143. See BSRK 749,25.

144. BSRK 749,46–49.

145. BSRK 743,36.

146. See Loofs 811, n. 5.

147. See B. Spinoza, *Ethica* IV, praef., Spinoza Opera, im Auftrag der Heidelberger Akademie der Wissenschaften, ed. C. Gerhardt (Heidelberg, 1925), 2:206,212–13 (German: B. de Spinoza, *Die Ethik nach geometrischer Methode dargestellt*, ed. O. Baensch, (Phil. Bibl. 92 [Hamburg, 1955], 188), ET: *The Chief Works of Benedict de Spinoza*, trans. R. H. M. Elwes (New York: Dover Publications, 1951), 188, 193.

148. BSRK 749,48–49.

149. BSRK 766–68.

150. BSRK 930–35.

151. BSRK 766,45–46. [The admonition apparently implies that one need not speak unclearly with regard to the Communion elements, but one can say that the priest has the body and blood of Christ in his hands.—Trans.]

152. WA 30/III, 560,31–561,9.

153. BSRK 768–72.

154. See Small Catechism, BSLK 515,25–27, ET: K/W 358[21]; Large Catechism, BSLK 693,32–35, ET: K/W 458[14].

155. BSRK 769,33.

156. See BSRK 772,25.

157. Ebrard 196.

158. The Anhalt territories, united under Joachim Ernst in 1570, and ecclesiastically defined by the Phillipic *Repetitio Anhaltina* (1579) (Niemeyer, 612–14) was ruled jointly from 1586 on by his five sons, including Johann Georg I. As a result of the dispute about the Formula of Concord, they introduced Reformed doctrine in Anhalt in 1596.

159. Ebrard 75.

160. See M. Luther, WA 9,559,28–29; WA 18,164,25–27, ET: *What Luther Says*, ed. E. M. Plass (St. Louis: Concordia, 1959), 3:1161.

161. Ebrard 189; Barth's emendation.

162. See above, n. 65.

163. See BSLK 1013,25–1014,1; K/W 614[119]: The "sacramentarians" had reinterpreted "Christ must take possession of heaven" ["oportet Christum coelum accipere"] to read "Christ must be held by heaven or in heaven and circumscribed or enclosed there" ["oportet Christum coeli capi . . . Christum ita in coelum receptum, ut coelo . . . comprehendatur"].

164. See BSRK LIV–LV.; E. F. K. Müller, "Staffort Book," in RE, 3d ed., 744–45, ET: S/H 11:61.

165. BSRK 804–9.

166. BSRK 805,27.

167. BSRK 806,27.

168. See BSRK 806,41–42.

169. BSRK 807,47–49.

170. See above, p. 183, at note 137.

171. See ibid.

172. See BSRK 808,25–809,35.

173. See above, pp. 169f.

174. See, e.g, CR 89 (=Z 2), 141–44 (Exposition of the 18th Article of the "Conclusions of Ulrich Zwingli," July 14, 1523); CR 90 (=Z 3), 782–85, 790–92 ("De vera et falsa religione commentarius," March 1525); CR 93/I (=Z 6/I), 336–37 (Notizen und

Voten Zwinglis an die Berner Disputation, June 25, 1528); CR 93/II (=Z 6/II), 181–91 ("Über D. Martin Luthers Buch, Bekenntnis genannt [Grosses Bekenntnis vom Abentmahl], zwei Antworten v. Johannes Oekolampad u. Huldrych Zwingli," Zurich, August 1528).

175. See Locher, *Die Zwinglische Reformation* (see p. 234, n. 97), 489–91.

176. BSRK 808,48–50: "Nam caro Christi sola, quippe finita et finites viribus praedita, non potuisset gestare ac suffere infinitum onus irae Divinae, nisi a Verbo fuisset sustentata et adiuta ab infinita illa potentia," ET: "The flesh of Christ alone, because it was finite and endowed with finite powers, would not have been able to suffer the infinite burden of divine wrath, if it were not sustained by the Word and if it were not helped by that infinite power."

177. BSRK 809,19–20.

178. See BSRK 809,28.

179. BSRK 813–16.

180. BSRK 813,29–31.

181. BSRK 814:11–12: "Fidei vis est ut posit procul dissita cernere." The German is Barth's translation.

182. BSRK 815,25–26.

183. See BSLK 977,39–978,5, ET: K/W 596[16].

184. H. Heppe, *Kirchengeschichte beider Hessen* (see p. 233, n. 76), 2:2, nn. 1–2. Heppe quotes Vilmar in n. 2: "Vilmar emphasizes in discussing Landgrave Moritz's movement to the Reformed church, that 'it was the *Reformed Church* which, in the second half of the sixteenth century, through its martyrdom in France and the Netherlands, *gave the most marvelous testimony to its inner life which was granted the entire evangelical Church*, and thus had the most obvious advantage over the Lutheran church which had divided its forces in many doctrinal disputes, and thus it was sufficiently attractive to reach the one who sensed in himself the calling to be a witness.'"

185. A. F. C. Vilmar, *Geschichte des Confessionsstandes der evangelischen Kirchen in Hessen, besonders im Kurfürstentum* (Marburg, 1860), 193: "That this article [referring to Art. V (on the Lord's Supper) of the Confession of the Cassel General Synod, BSRK 820–21] contains a *clear* confession can certainly not be claimed. Rather, we constantly come across the Bucer-Melanchthonian form of expression, which covers over but does not resolve the contradictions, and which permits us to seek and to find Zwingli's doctrines among the expressions used as well as Luther's doctrines—a form of expression which wants to be Zwinglian and yet not appear to be."

186. See BSRK LV–LVI.

187. BSRK LV,41–45.

188. BSRK 818,41–819,26.

189. BSRK 820,5–821,44.

190. BSRK 820,30–32.

191. Vilmar, *Gerschichte des Confessionstandes*, 178: "For the *'breaking of the bread'* [*fractionem panis*] they baked heavy round iron cakes, to be broken into four thick pieces, made of a very coarse flour, that was not only difficult to break, but even harder to chew and to swallow, so that the people would be reminded that they were eating 'bread, bread, nothing but bread,' and would feel that they had eaten it when it was lying in their stomachs."

192. BSRK 820,33–36.

193. BSRK 820,46–821,5; Barth's italics.

194. BSRK 821,32–33.

195. That is, the Hessian Renitenz, the Lutheran free church in Hesse founded in 1873 by the followers of A. Vilmar in resistance to the Union; see Barth, KD I/2, 726, ET: CD I/2, 648; E. R. Grebe, *Die Geschichte der hessischen Renitenz* (Cassel, 1905); further, K. Barth, *Die protestantische Theologie im 19. Jahrhundert* (n. 242), 571, ET: Barth, *Protestant Theology in the Nineteenth Century* (Valley Forge: Judson Press, 1973), 627.

196. BSRK 819,11.

197. See H. Heppe, *Die Einführung der Verbesserungspunkte in Hessen von 1604–1610 und die Entstehung der hessischen Kirchenordnung von 1657* (Kassel, 1849), 81–95.

198. BSRK LVI,41–45. There are also some references (30–41) to the gradual spread of the Reformed movement into the County of Bentheim since 1562.

199. BSRK 834,16–17: "Spiritu Verbo et Sacramentis."

200. See Inst. II,ix,1,1:423–24; II,x,1.2.4.7,1:428–30, 1:431–32, 1:434; II,xi,10.13, 1:459–60,1:462–63; see also Chr. Dogm. 322–23.

201. E.g., *Loci communes* (1521), CR 21,196,7–18: "Ad eum modum fuerunt liberi etiam patres ante Christi incarnationem, quotquot spiritum Christi habuere. . . . Id est, cum non possent praestare legem patres, agnoverunt se quoque liberos esse per Christum, suntque fide in Christum iustificati, non operum, non iustitiarum suarum meritis," ET: Philip Melanchthon, *The Loci Communes*, trans. Charles L. Hill (Boston: Meador Publishing Co, 1944), 224: "To this degree even the fathers before the incarnation of Christ were free, as many as had the spirit of Christ. . . . That is, although the fathers could not satisfy the law, they knew that they too were free through Christ and were justified by faith in Christ, not by the merits of their own works of righteousness."

202. On the mood in the German Reformed churches of that time; see H. Vorländer, *Aufbruch und Krise: Ein Beitrag zur Geschichte der deutschen Reformierten vor dem Kirchenkampf*, Beiträge zur Geschichte und Lehre der Reformierten Kirche 37 (Neukirchen, 1974), 15,17.

203. See Bw.Th. II, 112–13, ET: *Revolutionary Theology in the Making: Barth-Thurneysen Correspondence*, trans. James Smart (Richmond: John Knox Press, 1964), 113–14; further, K. Koch, *Kohlbrüggianer in der Grafschaft Bentheim: Eine Studie zur reformierten Kirchengeschichte der Grafschaft Bentheim zwischen 1880 und 1950; Gleichzeitig ein Beitrag zur Geschichte des Kirchenkampfes*, in *Emsland/Bentheim: Beiträge zur Geschichte*, published by the Emsländischen Landschaft für die Landkreise Emsland und Grafschaft Bentheim e.V. (Sögel, 1996), 12:355–432.

204. Vorländer, *Aufbruch und Krise*, 16, quotes a voice in 1928 that speaks of "eight German Reformed faculties and academies that we have lost": Heidelberg, Herborn, Marburg, Duisburg, Burgsteinfurt, Lingen, Frankfurt/Oder.

205. For the historical background; see Krüger/Hermelink 232–33; G. Kawerau, "Sigismund, Johann, und die Einführung des reform. Bekenntnisses in der Mark Brandenburg," in RE, 3d ed., 18:331–38.

206. See K. Sudhoff (E. F. K. Müller), "Hospinian, Rudolf," in RE, 3d ed., 8:393.

207. BSRK LVII, 28.

208. BSRK LVII, 8–14.

209. Krüger/Hermelink 233.

210. BSRK LVII, 24–26.

211. This phrase, following the handbook of the legal scholar J. Stephani, *Institutiones juris canonici* (1599), was used as the formula for the result of the negotiation

of religious peace at Augsburg in 1555; see G. Pfeiffer, "Augsburger Religionsfriede," in TRE 4:644.

212. BSRK LVII,21; 842,47–843,13.

213. Krüger/Hermelink 294–95: "He was removed from office because he would not sign the declaration which obligated the clergy to follow the Elector's edicts in religious matters."

214. See above, p. 156 and p. 286, n. 28.

215. BSRK LVII, 34–35. Martin Füssel was superintendent in the Reformed city of Zerbst in Anhalt.

216. BSRK 837,3–48.

217. BSRK 837,36.

218. BSRK 837,44–45.

219. BSRK 839,6–841,19.

220. BSRK 839,30–31.

221. BSRK 839,42–48. M. Luther, *Festpostille: Am tag des heiligen warleichnams Christi, Euangelion Johannes: vj* (1522), in WA 17/II,439,38–440,2. See also K. Barth, *Ansatz und Absicht in Luthers Abendmahlslehre* (1923), in V.u.kl.A. 1922–1925, 262; there also are the sources for Zwingli's use of this Luther citation.

222. BSRK 841,7–18.

223. BSRK 837,49–839,5.

224. BSRK 841,20–842,29.

225. BSRK 842,4–10.

226. See Inst. III,xxi,1,2:922–23 (conclusion); III,xxiii,14,2:963–64.

227. Inst. III,xxi,7,2:931 (conclusion); III,xxiii,9,2:976 (conclusion).

228. See above, p. 154–55.

229. BSRK 842,30–843,13.

230. BSRK 843,1–9.

231. Johann Berg (1587–1658) was in 1615 professor at the Reformed theological faculty in Frankfurt/Oder, and from 1623 on was the unionist court preacher of the Elector. He participated in the Thorn Religious Conversation (1645) discussed above. Johann Crocius (1590–1659) was in 1612 the court preacher in Kassel, in 1616–1617 at the court of the Brandenburg Elector, and thereafter a professor and consistorial counselor in Marburg who was particularly concerned to reach agreement with the Lutherans. Matthias Hoë von Hoënegg (1580–1645) became known in 1613 for his polemic against the transfer of the Brandenburg Elector to the Reformed church, and was then the senior court preacher in Dresden. He republished the polemical book by the father of Polykarp Leyser of the same name (see n. 235) with the title, "Ob, wie und warum man lieber mit den Papisten Gemeinschaft haben solle denn mit den Calvinisten" ("Whether, how, and why one should preferably have fellowship with the papists than with the Calvinists") (see F. Dibelius, "Hoë von Hoënegg, in RE, 3d ed., 8:274,14–15. Barth follows the signature found in Augusti (410) for the spelling of the name Hoë von Hoënegg; in the church-historical literature the usual spelling is Höe von Höenegg.

232. Krüger/Hermelink 259. [The appellation "high priest" is probably a wordplay based on his name, which sounds in German like the first half of "Höhepriester" (= "high priest").—Trans.]

233. Krüger/Hermelink 259. This is the title of a polemical publication of 1621.

234. Krüger/Hermelink 259.

235. Polykarp Leyser II (1586–1633), theology professor in Wittenberg, from 1613 in Leipzig, where he was also superintendent.

236. Augusti 387.
237. Augusti 387.
238. Augusti 388.
239. Augusti 389.
240. See Augusti 390.
241. See Th.C. 421–25, ET: *Theology of Calvin* 310–13.
242. See Augusti 391.
243. What is meant is Zwingli's understanding of sin as "prästen" (CR 89 (=Z 2); 99.493,4–24, ET: "Divine and Human Righteousness," in Pipkin 1–42; 631,3–30); this could be understood as a weakening of human guilt, what G. W. Locher (*Huldrych Zwingli in neuer Sicht: Zehn Beiträge zur Theologie der Zürcher Reformation* [Zurich, 1969], 241) calls "the Lutheran misunderstanding" of this matter. [See also p. 262, n. 51.—Trans.]
244. See Augusti 391–92.
245. He is probably thinking of Bucer's accommodating approach to Luther's doctrine of the Lord's Supper in 1528; see Bizer, *Studien zur Geschichte des Abendmahlstreits* (see p. 262, n. 43), 25.
246. See WA.B. 5,331,47–51, ET: LW 49:302[10–14].
247. See Augusti 393–97. On the manuscript margin are pencil notations of the letters L and R, here reproduced in print. Barth wanted to designate in this way the Lutheran and Reformed elements in the common document.
248. See Augusti 397–98.
249. Augusti, 397.
250. Augusti 398–99.
251. What is meant is the ancient church doctrine that the deity of Christ is entirely in his humanity and at the same time outside (extra) of it; this was affirmed by the Reformed: Inst. II,xiii,4,1:481; Heidelberg Catechism, Question 48 (BSRK 695,12–15, ET: Schaff 322). See F. Loofs "Kenosis, in RE, 3d ed., 10:246–63. It was probably first formulated as an accusation by the Tübingen theologian T. Thumm and as such used by the Tübingen Lutherans in their dispute with the Giessen Lutherans: "illud ipsum Extra calvinisticum" (Loofs "Kenosis," 262,15).
252. See above, p. 198 at n. 233.
253. Augusti 400.
254. See Troeltsch, *Die Soziallehren* (see p. 273, n. 284), 512–794, esp. 605–15; Troeltsch, *Protestantisches Christentum* (see p. 236, 3.2, n. 128), 575–76: "The relationships of Geneva . . . condition the formation of Calvinism. And when Geneva later recedes, then in France, the Netherlands, England, and finally America the same advanced relationships continue even more strongly to shape it." See also 552.
255. Augusti 400.
256. Augusti 400.
257. Augusti 401–3.
258. See above, p. 199.
259. Augusti 401.
260. BSLK 248,15–18 (Latin version), ET: K/W 184, n. 269 (text appears only in the Latin version).
261. Augusti 401.
262. Augusti 402.
263. See, e.g, M. Luther, *Vom Abendmahl Christi. Bekenntnis* (1528), WA 26,442,33–35, ET: LW 37:300: "[H]e who eats this bread, eats Christ's body; he who crushes this

bread with his teeth or tongue, crushes with teeth or tongue the body of Christ"; and EA 55,75 (not in WA): The body of Christ is "bitten with the teeth."

264. See Augusti 403. See W. Köhler, *Das Marburger Religionsgespräch 1529: Versuch einer Rekonstruktion*, SVRG 148 (Leipzig, 1929), 19–20.

265. See Augusti 403–4.

266. See Augusti 404.

267. See Augusti 404–6.

268. See above, p. 197.

269. See Inst. III,xxi,2,2:923–24; III,xxi,4,2:925–26; III,xxiii,8,2:956–57; III,xxiii,12–13, 2:960ff.; III,xxiv,1,2:964–66; III,xxiv,5–6,2:970ff.

270. See Augusti 406–9.

271. On the Lutheran formula of the "foreseeing of faith" ("praevisa fide"), see K. Barth, KD II/2, 75–81, ET: CD, II/2, 70–76. It is described in the Colloquium (Augusti 407) with these words, "That God has elected those from eternity whom he saw that they would in time . . . believe in Christ."

272. Augusti 409.

273. See P. Tschackert, "Synkretistische Streitigkeiten," in RE, 3d ed., 19:252,55–253, 41; and C. E. Hering, *Geschichte der Kirchlichen Unionsversuche* (Leipzig, 1838), 2:157–62: September to May 1663 at the order of the Elector.

274. See Hering, *Geschichte der Kirchlichen Unionsversuche*, 421–83.

4. The Battle against Modern Christianity

1. Troeltsch, *Protestantisches Christentum* (see p. 236, n. 128), 253–458, esp. 254–69.

2. This is the view advocated, with some reservations, by, for example, A. Harnack, *Das Wesen des Christentums*, 3d ed. (Leipzig, 1900), 173–76, ET: *What Is Christianity?* trans. T. B. Saunders (New York: Harper & Brothers, 1957), 277–81.

3. In this entire section Barth recapitulates the thinking that he had developed more broadly in the Calvin lectures of 1922, Th.C. 15–92, ET: *Theology of Calvin* 13–68.

4. See Troeltsch, *Protestantisches Christentum*, 304–5.

5. Regarding this statement, which goes back to the Sophist Protagoras (ca. 481–411 B.C.), see H. Diels/W. Kranz, *Die Fragmente der Vorsokratiker*, 80 [Protagoras] B1, vol. 2, 16th ed. (Dublin/Zurich, 1972), 263.

6. On F. W. Foerster and his relation to Barth as well as Barth's controversy with him in the same summer of 1923, see V.u.kl.A. 1922–1925, 180–201.

7. Georg Calixt (1586–1656) advocated a reconciliation of the confessions on the basis of the "Consensus quinquesaecularis." See the two documents published in 1650: *Desiderium et studium concordiae ecclesiasticae* and *Iudicium de controversiis theologicis, quae inter Lutheranos et Reformatos agitantur, et de mutual partium fraternitate atquetolerantia propter consensum in fundamento.*

8. The Edict of Nantes, promulgated by Henri IV in 1598 but then abrogated in 1685 by Louis XIV, granted the Huguenots limited tolerance. [The freedom to practice their faith was not restored to the French Protestants officially until 1789. —Trans.]

9. Based on Psalm 35:20, the designation of a Pietistic movement.

10. In 1547, Calvin wrote his criticism of the Council of Trent taking place at the time: *Acta Synodi Tridentinae cum Antidoto*, CR 35 (=CO 8), 372–506, ET: "Acts of the Council of Trent, with the Antidote," in *Tracts and Treatises III*, 17–188.

11. On Karlstadt; see p. 258, n. 45. The Italian Lelio Sozini (1525–1562) found

refuge in Geneva in 1548 where he expressed doubts about Calvin's doctrine of predestination and moved on to Zurich. The Italian Georg Blandrata (1515–1590) emigrated to Poland and then to Geneva, where he opposed Trinitarian doctrine and became then the head of the Unitarians in Poland and Transylvania. Sebastian Castellio (1515–1563), originally from Savoy, lived in 1540 in Calvin's house in Strassburg; Calvin called him to be rector of the high school in Geneva in 1541, but they divided in 1543 over Calvin's predestination doctrine, and he went to Basel where he became professor of Greek literature in 1552; from there he opposed Calvin and his dealings with Servetus. Hieronymus Bolsec (d. 1584) was a French monk who converted to the Reformation but had to leave Geneva in 1552 because of his opposition to Calvin's doctrine of predestination; in France he became again Roman Catholic. Michael Servetus (ca. 1511–1553), Spanish doctor and anti-Trinitarian, took up contact with Oecolampadius and Calvin; in Vienne he was sentenced to die for his teachings. He then fled to Geneva, where he anticipated safe refuge because the Council at the time was made up of opponents to Calvin; the Council carried out the execution with the agreement of Calvin and many other Protestant leaders.

12. See Seeberg 667–83; see below, p. 211–12.

13. Johannes Bogerman (1576–1637), pastor in Leeuwarden, leader of the Synod of Dort.

14. See BSRK LXIII,44–47.

15. See p. 298, n. 1.

16. "Tell me thy company, and I'll tell thee what thou art," is a proverb that occurs in many civilized languages; it was incorporated by J. W. von Goethe in his "Sprüche in Prosa" [usually published today under the title "Maximen und Reflexionen"—Trans.]; see G. Büchmann, Geflügelte Worte, 2d ed. (Frankfurt am Main and Berlin, 1986), 257–58; the ET is from Cervantes, Don Quixote, Part 2, Book 3, chap. 23, as cited in John Bartlett, Familiar Quotations, (13th ed., Boston and Toronto: Little, Brown & Co, 1955), 108.

17. See p. 248, n. 21.

18. Krüger/Hermelink 262.

19. See above, pp. 70–71.

20. See 239, n. 206.

21. See J. Calvin, Contre la secte phantastique et furieuse des libertines qui se nomment spirituelz (1545, CR 35 (=CO 7), 149–248, ET: Treatises against the Anabaptists and against the Libertines, ed. and trans. Benjamin W. Farley (Grand Rapids: Baker Book House, 1982), 187–326.

22. See above, pp. 69f.

23. See Seeberg 668–71. [Very few of these figures are mentioned in the abridged ET of Seeberg's History of Doctrines.—Trans.]

24. See Seeberg 671–76.

25. See Seeberg 672.

26. See Seeberg 676; see in the ET, 2:421–22.

27. Franz Gomarus (1563–1641), also spelled Gomar in English. See Seeberg 676.

28. Krüger/Hermelink 362: "bona conscientia paradisus."

29. See Seeberg 677, ET: Seeberg 2:421.

30. See Krüger/Hermelink 217.

31. See Krüger/Hermelink 263.

32. See Krüger/Hermelink 263.

33. (1583–1645); see Krüger/Hermelink 263.

34. See Krüger/Hermelink 267.

35. Franciscus Gomarus (1563–1641), born in Flanders, grew up in the Palatinate, and in 1587 became pastor of the Reformed congregation in Frankfurt and 1594 theology professor in Leiden. Gisbert Voetius (1589–1676), preacher in Heusden in 1617, from 1634 on was professor of theology and Oriental languages in Utrecht. Georg Cruciger (1575–1637), son of a banished Wittenberg Crypto-Calvinist, during the Reformed phase of the theology faculty in Marburg (1605–1624) was a theological teacher there. Heinrich Alting (1583–1644) from Emden, in 1613 was theological professor in Heidelberg, and in 1627 in Groningen. Abraham Scultetus (1566–1624), from Silesia, at first Philippist Lutheran, was in Heidelberg from 1590 on, where he became a theological professor in 1618, and from 1622 on a preacher in Emden. Johann Jakob Breitinger (1575–1645) from Zurich, studied theology at German and Dutch universities and from 1613 on was the influential president of the Church of Zurich. Markus Rütimyer (1580–1647) was an academic and preacher in Bern. Giovanni Diodati (1576–1649) from Lucca, fled for the sake of his faith to Geneva, where he became a significant preacher and theology professor.

36. See Krüger/Hermelink 264.

37. See Krüger/Hermelink 264.

38. See the two richly illustrated booklets *Les Jubilés de Genève en 1909*, which were in Barth's possession. The jubilee was celebrated from July 2 to 7, 1909. In September 1909, Barth began to serve as vicar of the German Reformed congregation in Geneva. See K. Barth, *Reformation*, in V.u.kl.A. 1909–1914, 1–5; Th.C. 251,390, ET: *Theology of Calvin* 187–88, 287.

39. BSRK 843–61, ET: Bray 453–78; the Latin text is in Schaff 550–80. [The Bray edition is based on Schaff and incorporates the parts that were translated into English (581–97).—Trans.]

40. BSRK 846,37–45, ET: Bray 453–54 [1]; 850,40–47, ET: Bray 454 [2]; 854,31–45, ET: Bray 454 [3–4]; 859,31–46, ET: Bray 454 [5].

41. BSRK LIX–LXIII.

42. BSRK 846–48, ET: Bray 460–63; 850–51, ET: Bray 464–66; 854–56, ET: Bray 470–72; 859–61, ET: Bray 474–76.

43. BSRK LIX,27–LX,35.

44. BSRK 846,22–848,38, ET: Bray 460–63.

45. BSRK 847,25, ET: Bray 461 [4].

46. BSRK 843,16–846,21, ET: Bray 457–60 (Of Divine Predestination); also in Schaff 581–85.

47. BSRK 844,16–17, ET: Bray 458 [07.], also in Schaff 582[VII].

48. See BSRK 844,17–18, ET: Bray 458 [076.], also in Schaff 582[VII].

49. BSRK 845,27, ET: Bray 459 [14.], also in Schaff 584[XIV].

50. See BSRK 845,40–41, ET: Bray 460 [15.], also in Schaff 585[XV].

51. See BSRK 846,13, ET: Bray 460 [18.], also in Schaff 585[XVIII].

52. See Troeltsch, *Protestantisches Christentum*, 349: "At the same time the customary thinking of Calvinism is generally systematic and universal, in that, based on the large context of the concept of God, its basic religious position leads one to think of everything proceeding from God and returning to God. This gives all Calvinist thinking a tendency toward the vast and comprehensive, uniform and systematic, whereas in Lutheranism both thought and action appear somewhat truncated through constant return to the spiritual miracle of justification."

53. See Th.C. 69–76, ET: *Theology of Calvin* 52–57.
54. See BSRK 845,33–34, ET: Bray 459[15.], also in Schaff 584[XV].
55. BSRK 845,40–41, ET: Bray 460[15.], also in Schaff 584[XV].
56. See above, pp. 143–45.
57. Exposition of Romans 9–11 in Römerbrief 2, 314–409, ET: Romans 330–423.
58. BSRK LX,36–LXI,10.
59. BSRK LXI,5: "actu et vere in Christum credant."
60. BSRK 850–51, ET: Bray 464–66.
61. See BSRK 850,37–38, ET: Bray 465[04.]. The Unitarian Fausto Sozzini (1539–1604) rejected a justification based upon an alien righteousness and held it to be founded on obedience to the command of Christ and on trust in the promise of eternal life. See O. Zöckler, "Socin und Socinianismus," RE, 3d ed., 18, 487,27–47.
62. See BSRK 851,1–3, ET: Bray 465[05.]. [Barth's Latin in the first phrase cited reverses the terms in the Dort text; it should read 'gratia foederis'; the inversion does not seriously change the meaning.—Trans.]
63. BSRK 848,40–849,47, ET: Bray 463–64, also in Schaff 586–87.
64. See Anselm of Canterbury, *Cur Deus Homo*, esp. Book 2, chap. 6–7, in *S. Anselmi Cantuariensis archiepiscopi opera omnia*, vol. 2, ed. F. S. Schmitt (Rome, 1940), 101 s., ET: *Anselm of Canterbury: The Major Works*, ed. Brian Davies and G. R. Evans, (Oxford & New York: Oxford University Press, 1998), 260–356, esp. Book 2, chap. 6–7, 319–21.
65. BSRK 685,15–687,6, ET: Schaff 311–13 [Questions 11–18]. [The German editors have broadened Barth's reference to include the last question and answer of Part 1.—Trans.]
66. See WA 30/I, 133,7, ET: *Dr. Martin Luther's Large Catechism*, ed. R. Malmin, trans. John N. Lenker (Minneapolis: Augsburg Publishing House, 1935), 44; BSLK 560,21–22, ET: K/W 386[3].
67. See S. Kierkegaard, *Die Krankheit zum Tode: Eine christlich-psychologische Entwicklung zur Erbauung und Erweckung von Anti-Climacus*, in *Gesammelte Werke*, vol. 8, ed. H. Gottsched and Chr. Schrempf (Jena, 1911), 46,62,104, ET: *The Sickness unto Death: A Christian Psychological Explanation for Upbuilding and Awakening*, ed. and trans. H. V. and E. H. Hong (Princeton: Princeton University Press, 1980), 49, 67, 110; idem, *Der Begriff Angst: Eine simple psychologisch-wegweisende Untersuchung in Richtung auf das dogmatische Problem der Erbsünde von Vigilius Haufniensis*, in *Gesammelte Werke*, vol. 5 (Jena, 1923), 156–63, ET: *The Concept of Dread*, trans. W. Lowrie (Princeton: Princeton University Press, 1946), 139–45.
68. Augustine; see Loofs 385; see Inst. III,xxiii,3,2:950–51.
69. See above p. 274, n. 288.
70. BSRK LXI,11–LXII,35.
71. BSRK LXI,14.
72. See BSRK LXI,23–24: "gratia praeveniens, excitans, prosequens et cooperans."
73. See BSRK LXI,39.
74. BSRK LXI,16.
75. J. W. von Goethe, *Faust II*, lines 11934–41:
Gerrettet ist das edle Glied
Der Geisterwelt vom Bösen:
"Wer immer strebend sich bemüht,
Den können wir erlösen."

Und hat an ihm die Liebe gar
Von oben teilgenommen,
Begegnet ihm die selige Schar
Mit herzlichem Willkommen.

The cited passage experiences a range of translations in English, some of which do not communicate Barth's point. The version used here is *Goethe's Faust*, trans. Barker Fairley (Toronto and Buffalo: University of Toronto Press, 1970), 201.

76. See BSRK LXI,31–33.

76a. The German editors do not explain these brackets.—Trans.

77. BSRK LXI,42.

78. BSRK LXII,5.

79. See BSRK LXII,16,20–21.

80. See BSRK LXII,27: "non posse non peccare respectu Decreti divini."

81. BSRK 854,26–856,44, ET: Bray 470–72.

82. See BSRK 855,32–35, ET: Bray 470[05.].

83. BSRK 855,38, ET: Bray 470[05.].

84. See BSRK 855,49, ET: Bray 471[06.].

85. See BSRK 856,10, ET: Bray 471 [07.].

86. BSRK 851,27–854,25, ET: Bray 466–69 (Of the Corruption of Man, His Conversion to God and the Manner Thereof); also in Schaff 587–92.

87. BSRK 851–31, ET: Bray 466[01.], also in Schaff 587[I].

88. BSRK 851,32, ET: Bray 466[01.], also in Schaff 587[I].

89. See BSRK 851,33–36: "coecitas, tenebrae, vanitas, perversitas, . . . malitia, rebellio, durities, . . . impuritas," ET: Bray 466[01], also in Schaff 588[I].

90. See BSRK 851,37–38: "procreavit corruptus corruptos," ET: Bray 466[02.], also in Schaff 588[II].

91. BSRK 851,40: "per . . . propagationem," ET: Bray 466[02.], also in Schaff 588[II].

92. BSRK 852,1–2: "*lumen . . . naturae,*" ET: Bray 466[04.], also in Schaff 588[IV].

93. See BSRK 852,6: "in naturalibus und civilibus," ET: Bray 466[04.], also in Schaff 588[IV].

94. BSRK 853,7, ET: Bray 468[11.], also in Schaff 590[XI].

95. See BSRK 853,9, ET: Bray 468[11.], also in Schaff 590[XI].

96. BSRK 853,18–19: "supernaturalis, potentissima simul et suavissima, mirabilis, arcana, et ineffabilis operatio," ET: Bray 468[12.], also in Schaff 590[XII].

97. BSRK 853,22: "certo, infallibiliter et efficaciter," ET: Bray 468[12.], also in Schaff 590[XII].

98. See BSRK 853,23–24: "agit a Deo acta," ET: Bray 468[12.], also in Schaff 590[XII]; ET emended to capture Barth's point—Trans.

99. See BSRK 853,34: "credere, . . . credere *velle,*" ET: Bray 468[14.], also in Schaff 591[XIV]; Barth's italics.

100. BSRK 854,2–3: "spiritualiter vivificat, sanat, corrigit, flectit," Bray 469[16.], also in Schaff 591[XVI].

101. BSRK LXII,36–LXIII,38.

102. See BSRK 859, n. 1, ET: Bray 454[5.].

103. See BSRK LXIII,37.

104. BSRK 859,1–861,9, ET: Bray 474–76.

105. BSRK 859,8, ET: Bray 475[01.].

106. BSRK 859,29, ET: Bray 475[03.].

107. See above, pp. 125–26.

108. See BSRK 860,41: "fides iustificans et salvificans," ET: Bray 476[07.].

109. BSRK 856,46–858,46, ET: Bray 472–74 (Of the Perseverance of the Saints); also in Schaff 592–95.

110. See BSRK 857,26, ET: Bray 473[5.]; also in Schaff 593[V].

111. See BSRK 857,45–46: "Quoad *ipsos*," "respectu autem *Dei*," ET: Bray 473[8.]; also in Schaff 594[VIII].

112. See BSRK 858,15, ET: Bray 474[11.]; also in Schaff 594 [XI].

113. BSRK 858,37–46, ET: Bray 474[15.]; also in Schaff 595[XV]; Barth translated the Latin into German for his lecture—Trans.

114. See BSRK LXIII,6–23.

115. The words "over against the created person" are underlined in pencil in the manuscript; on the margin there is a wavy line and a question mark next to them.

116. See BSRK 855,46–50 (in the rejection of the Remonstrants), ET: Bray 471[06.]: "[The synod rejects the errors of those who teach that] . . . in the true conversion of a man it is not possible for new qualities, habits or gifts to be imparted to him by God against his will, and even the faith by which we are first converted and by which we are called believers, is not a quality or gift imparted by God. It is only an act of man, nor can it be called a gift except with respect to the power it conveys to come to faith."

117. See above, p. 222 at n. 111.

118. See above, p. 220 at n. 84.

119. See n. 116.

120. See above, p. 239, n. 207.

121. Barth is alluding here to an old Swiss proverb: "Dei providentia et hominum confusione Helvetia regitur": "Switzerland is ruled by the providence of God and confusion of humans." See V.u.kl.A. 1922–1925, 18, n. 12.

INDEX OF LUTHERAN CONFESSIONS

INDEX OF REFORMED CONFESSIONS

INDEX OF SCRIPTURE REFERENCES

INDEX OF NAMES

INDEX OF TERMS